Stagflation,
Savings, and the State

A World Bank Research Publication

Stagflation, Savings, and the State

Perspectives on the Global Economy

Edited by
Deepak Lal and Martin Wolf

Published for The World Bank
Oxford University Press

Oxford University Press

NEW YORK   OXFORD   LONDON   GLASGOW
TORONTO   MELBOURNE   WELLINGTON   HONG KONG
TOKYO   KUALA LUMPUR   SINGAPORE   JAKARTA
DELHI   BOMBAY   CALCUTTA   MADRAS   KARACHI
NAIROBI   DAR ES SALAAM   CAPE TOWN

Manufactured in the United States of America
First printing February 1986

Library of Congress Cataloging in Publication Data

Main entry under title:

Stagflation, savings, and the state.

  (A World Bank research publication)
  "Published for the World Bank."
  Includes bibliographical references and index.
    1. Unemployment—Effect of inflation on—Addresses,
essays, lectures. 2. Debts, External—Developing
Countries—Addresses, essays, lectures. 3. Developing
countries—Economic conditions—Addresses, essays,
lectures. I. Lal, Deepak. II. Wolf, Martin.
III. International Bank for Reconstruction and
Development. IV. Series.
HG229.S74   1986   330.9172′4   85-31981
ISBN 0-19-520496-4

Foreword

THIS BOOK contains the background papers prepared for the World Bank's *World Development Report 1984* and distilled into the section of that report entitled "Recovery or Relapse in the World Economy?" As this title suggests, the report sought to put in historical and analytical perspective the most recent recession in industrial countries, which unlike its predecessor was transmitted to developing countries. The report examined the causes of the stagflation that had plagued the industrial world in the 1970s, and its effects on developing countries, by asking whether the steady and sustained global growth of the 1950s and 1960s could be resumed.

In answering this question, the report marked an extension in the scope of the Bank's annual analysis of the global economy. With the increasing integration of the world economy through trade and capital flows, the determinants and effects of the *domestic* policies of industrial economies were found to be increasingly relevant to the economic prospects of developing countries. By contrast, in the past the primary focus of the Bank's global analysis had been on the *international* economic policies of industrial countries, which impinge on the economic environment worldwide, as well as on the domestic policies that determine growth in the developing countries. While continuing to emphasize the importance of domestic policies in the developing countries, the 1984 report argued that the apparent problems of the global economy since the oil shock of 1973—sporadic growth, incipient inflationary pressures, rising protectionism, and burdensome international debt—are partly the result of a secular deterioration in the economic performance of industrial countries. The causes of this deterioration are similar to those that past *World Development Reports* have emphasized in explaining the relatively poor performance of many (but by no means all) developing countries. These are the rigidities in the workings of the price mechanism, which have been induced by public policy in many industrial and developing economies, and the macroeconomic imbalances reflected in the management of the public finances, which have increasingly led to a global problem of undesirable fiscal deficits. The second of these causes of global disorder is new; with the increasing integration of the world capital market in the

1970s, the actions of national public sectors can affect the global market for savings and investment and the terms on which they are mediated.

Because these underlying problems of the global economy have by no means been satisfactorily resolved, the subject of this volume—the crisis of public policy in both industrial and developing countries, which the editors believe to be continuing—remains of considerable current relevance. A proper understanding of the processes at work and of their long-term consequences is important in changing the perceptions on which policies are based, and the papers in this book should therefore help to inform discussions of these continuing problems of the global economy.

Many of the papers in the book summarize the historical record and the theoretical debates on the economic performance and policies of industrial and developing countries; they should be of considerable general interest. Others are based on original research done at the World Bank and should interest the research community worldwide. Their integration into this volume reflects the two functions that research performs in the Bank, providing both an intermediate input into the Bank's own operations as a policy adviser and an important final output. Although these background papers are being published for the Bank, the views expressed and the methods explored should not necessarily be considered to represent the Bank's views or policies. Rather, they are offered as a modest contribution to the great discussion on the best means of promoting worldwide economic development.

ANNE O. KRUEGER
Vice President, Economics and Research
The World Bank

Contents

Contributors

AQUILES ALMANSI is an assistant professor of economics at the University of Michigan.

ALAN GELB is an economist in the Productivity Division of the Development Research Department at the World Bank.

GOTTFRIED HABERLER is a professor emeritus at Harvard University and a resident scholar at the American Enterprise Institute in Washington, D.C.

LEONARDO HAKIM is a senior economist at the Institute of International Finance in Washington, D.C.

CARLOS HURTADO is a professor at the Instituto Tecnologico Automimo de Mejico.

DEEPAK LAL is a professor of political economy at the University of London and the research administrator, economics and research, at the World Bank.

ROBERT Z. LAWRENCE is a senior fellow at the Brookings Institution in Washington, D.C.

CONSTANTINO LLUCH is chief of the Labor Markets Division, Development Research Department at the World Bank.

ANGUS MADDISON is a professor of economics at the University of Groningen.

PRADEEP K. MITRA is a senior economist in the Resource Mobilization and Public Management Division of the Country Policy Department at the World Bank.

LARRY A. SJAASTAD is a professor of economics at the University of Chicago and the Graduate Institute of International Studies in Geneva.

SWEDER VAN WIJNBERGEN is a senior economist in the Trade and Adjustment Policy Division of the Country Policy Department at the World Bank and a research fellow at the Center for Economic Policy Research in London.

CHRISTINE WALLICH is a senior economist in the Financial Policy and Analysis Department at the World Bank.

MARTIN WOLF is the director of studies at the Trade Policy Research Center in London.

Stagflation,
Savings, and the State

Introduction

Deepak Lal and Martin Wolf

IN JUNE 1984, as this introduction is being written, the world economy seems to be recovering from the deepest global recession in fifty years. Will the recovery be sustained? Can there be a renewed period of relatively stable and steady growth such as characterized the first two postwar decades, which are already wistfully being called a Golden Age? How can the world economy be made to recover its élan?

Part I of *World Development Report 1984* attempted to answer these questions by considering the underlying causes of the stagflationary crisis that has beset the industrial countries since the first oil shock and was transmitted in the late 1970s to the developing countries. The latter weathered the first emanation of this crisis fairly well after the 1973 oil price shock. Many middle-income oil importers were able to cope by means of countercyclical borrowing on international financial markets awash with newfound liquidity based on the financial surpluses of the oil producers. This commercial borrowing represented the reopening of international financial markets to developing countries after their defaults in the 1930s. This borrowing, however, has come to haunt many of the developing countries, as well as the international financial system, in the form of a global "debt crisis."

The present book contains a set of background papers prepared for Part I of *World Development Report 1984*. Chapter 8, by Lal and Wolf, more fully states the arguments advanced in the Report. The rest of the background papers analytically and empirically validate these arguments. Each paper is relatively self-contained, although in content the chapters inevitably overlap somewhat.

The Overall Perspective

The 1960s were marked by confident predictions that technocratic economic advances had banished the business cycle. The 1970s have forcefully demonstrated that these predictions just reflected economists' hubris. The novel feature of the cycles in the late 1960s and 1970s has been the persistence of inflation even during downturns and even with the progressive worsening of President Carter's "misery" index—the postulated tradeoff between the rates of unemployment and inflation during each cycle. Furthermore, there has been a decline in productivity and net savings in industrial countries, a marked slowing of world trade, and a boom-bust cycle in commercial bank lending to developing countries.

The most recent recession in industrial countries—which was very deep partly because of concerted attempts to control inflation—seems to have dampened the stagflationary pattern. Nevertheless, fears are being expressed that the world economy may as a result be falling into another great depression. Chapter 1 in this book, by Maddison, attempts to determine whether this is the case. The following chapters seek to identify the causes of the secular deterioration in economic performance in industrial countries and the modes of transmission of the resulting stagflation to developing countries through the two major global channels of trade and capital flows.

If we assume that business cycles will persist, the important questions for public policy in any country are: (a) whether there are feasible methods for smoothing the cycle and (b) what sort of economic environment should be established to allow economic agents to cope most efficiently with the volatile world economy in the sense of promoting the trend growth of productivity and output.

Answers to the first question are at present the subject of fierce theoretical controversy. Chapter 2, by Haberler, assesses the various theoretical debates on macroeconomic policy. The macroeconomic policies adopted can have important effects on an economy's microeconomic flexibility and will therefore help condition answers to the second set of public policy questions. The trend growth rates of output and real incomes of economies are in large measure determined by the efficiency of their resource use and the incentives provided by their domestic economic environment for productivity and thrift.

The link between inappropriate macroeconomic policies and the microeconomic rigidities and distortions which were their inevitable by-product is a major theme of chapter 8, by Lal and Wolf. It argues that the continuing crisis in the world economy has two deep-seated causes, of which the stagflation and rising protectionism in industrial countries, as well as the debt crisis, are dramatic symptoms. These causes are: (a) the microeconomic rigidities that were steadily built into many economies—both developed and developing—partly as a result of inappropriate public policies, and (b) the management of the public finances, which has become a global problem with the continuance of problematic fiscal deficits in many developing countries and the likely emergence of structural budget deficits in the United States, and possibly in some other industrial countries, in the future.

The role of protectionism and inappropriate public interventions that lead to rigidities in wages and prices has often been discussed in the context of the economic performance of both developed and developing countries. The role of public finances is a more novel and controversial topic, as it has only recently become apparent that, with the integration of international financial markets in the 1970s, there is now a global market for savings and investment. The actions of national public sectors in economies that bulk large in the world economy can affect the international uses of world savings and the terms on which they are intermediated. In this global framework the public sectors of both developed and developing countries are increasingly competing with each other and with private agents for the available global savings. The problems of stagflation and Third World debt and the reactions to them can be seen, then, to be due in part to an emerging phenomenon: the "crowding out" of global savings by the public sectors in both developed and developing countries. Most of the chapters in the present volume are concerned with providing the empirical or analytical basis for this view.

The Historical Perspective

Chapter 1, by Maddison, sets the 1980–83 recession in historical perspective, comparing its effects with those of the Great Depression on some major developing countries (accounting for 70 percent of the population of the developing world). He shows that even though the two periods were marked by some similar phenomena—recession, a fall in world trade, the growing problem of debt, and a reverse flow of capital from developing to developed countries—their magnitude in recent years was far removed from that seen in the 1930s.

Stagflation and Public Finance in Industrial Countries

Chapter 2, by Haberler, and appendix 1, by Hakim and Wallich, are more directly concerned with the links between stagflation and public finance in developed countries. Haberler presents a survey of alternative theoretical perspectives on the problem of stagflation. He distinguishes between (a) the Keynesian view, which was dominant in the first two postwar decades and still continues to be influential; (b) a general monetarist position, of which the so-called new macroeconomics based on rational expectations is a variant; and (c) a traditional conservative, or classical, position. The Keynesian position neglects inflationary expectations, being based on the notion of a Phillips curve that postulates a more or less permanent tradeoff between unemployment and inflation. It emphasizes the importance of fiscal policy and the ability of governments to fine-tune the economy by skillful demand management. It deals with inflation by some form of incomes policy. This framework of thought is particularly unsuited, Haberler argues, to dealing with the problems of stagflation, being essentially "depression economics," or addressed to a time when wages and prices could be assumed to be constant. In an inflationary environment, incomes policies have not proved to be workable as a method for curbing wage inflation.

The monetarist and rational expectations theorists, by contrast, emphasize the role of monetary policy, downgrade fiscal policy, reject fine tuning, incomes policy, and price controls, and emphasize the role of expectations. They reject the Phillips curve on the grounds that an extended period of inflation at a significant rate would ignite inflationary expectations, lead market participants to take anticipatory action, and undo the stimulatory effects of an inflationary macroeconomic policy on unemployment. The rational expectations view takes this approach to an extreme and argues that macroeconomic policies cannot affect the "real" economy even in the short run, as rational private agents will determine the consequences of any predictable government policy and will take anticipatory action. Only by acting in a surprising and unpredictable way can governments affect the real economy in the short run and even then not for long. Although this view seems extreme, argues Haberler, a variant identified by Fellner, called the "credibility approach," does have some merit. Fellner maintained that, if the government's policies—for instance, on disinflation—are credible, they can condition inflationary expectations and can thus mitigate the pain of disinflation. The monetarist position on fiscal policy is that loose fiscal policy and large deficits need not cause inflation if monetary policy is tight. Depending on the size of the deficits, however, interest rates could rise, which (a) could accelerate the velocity of circulation and lead to inflation even without an increase in money supply, and (b) could cause productive private investments to be crowded out by public expenditures at the cost of slowing down long-run growth—hence the monetarist theorists' preference for combining monetary with fiscal restraint.

The traditional, or classical, view, Haberler argues, agrees with the monetarist and rational expectations theories regarding the Phillips curve and regarding the role of monetary and fiscal policy and expectations, but stresses the importance of institutional rigidities—in particular, wage and price rigidities, which are assumed away in the monetarist world of instantaneously or rapidly clearing markets. Haberler then cites the empirical evidence extending from the 1930s—when the New Deal period saw the first example of stagflation—to the present. This evidence supports the classical view as providing the best explanation for the stagflation of the 1970s and 1980s. Haberler also outlines the various explanations provided for the productivity slowdown of the 1970s. Again, he finds that the basic causes are the increasing rigidities owing to inappropriate microeconomic interventions and the uncertainty caused by inappropriate fiscal and monetary policies in the working of the price mechanism, rather than any fundamental underlying change in the technological bases of productivity growth. His survey of international money and exchange rates in the postwar period leads him to favor the existing floating-rate system and to counter various misconceptions about its workings as well as about the presumed current (1984) overvaluation of the dollar.

The policy prescriptions that follow from Haberler's discussion are a tight monetary and fiscal policy and the removal of rigidities in the working of the price mechanism, particularly in the labor markets of industrial countries and especially those in Europe. This approach requires both the promotion of free trade and the removal of various policy-induced distortions that have hardened the economic arteries of industrial economies.

Appendix 1, by Hakim and Wallich, statistically summarizes on the basis of work done by the secretariat of the Organisation for Economic Co-operation and Development (OECD), the role and implications of the public sector's net expenditure policies in industrial countries. It documents the components of public expenditure and revenue that have led to the emergence of large *actual* (nominal) budget deficits in many industrial countries and asks to what extent they are structural in nature. Hakim and Wallich find that the growth of social expenditure on health and pensions is the major source of the dramatic growth of public expenditure in the OECD area in the 1960s and early 1970s. The increase was due largely to gains in the coverage and level of the health and pension benefits, with demographic factors (particularly the aging of the population) playing a smaller role. By the end of the 1970s, however, benefit growth had slowed, as had coverage. After the turn of the century, demographic pressures could again make it hard for some countries to contain the growth of expenditures on health and pensions. At the same time, Hakim and Wallich show that it will be increasingly difficult to raise revenues in OECD countries, particularly by means of fiscal drag if tax systems continue to be indexed. Although the resulting budget deficits in the 1970s and 1980s had a controversially high cyclical element in OECD estimates, there is a danger that structural deficits will emerge if the future growth of social expenditures is not contained, especially toward the end of the century.

The appendix next summarizes the evidence on the decline in savings in the OECD area from about 1965. Though some of this decline is associated with the cyclical downturn, the major cause of the decline in savings is the increasing dissavings in the government sector (budget deficits), which have not been matched by corresponding increases in household or corporate savings. It is not clear, however, to what extent the decline in savings can be extrapolated into the future. If government budget deficits are reduced, inflation rates fall, and real interest rates remain positive, OECD savings may be expected to stabilize.

It should be noted that there are certain omissions in the discussion of OECD savings, deficits, and inflation in this volume. The most important concerns the interaction of unindexed tax systems with variable inflation in altering the net returns to savers and borrowers on different physical and financial assets; the general effects of this interaction receive some discussion, however, in chapter 7. The second is the effect of inflation on the public finances themselves and the corresponding interpretation of the unadjusted budget deficits, as well as those of estimated deficits derived from various adjustments that are now increasingly being made by researchers. Some adjustment may need to be made to the nominal budget deficit; the analyst could have any of three different reasons for finding it of economic interest.

For Keynesians, the relative size of the budget deficit is a measure of the net *fiscal stance* of the government, which needs to be judged by the conjunctural state of aggregate demand. If, as Haberler argues, this Keynesian framework is not very useful in formulating fiscal or monetary policies for these stagflationary times, adjustments to the nominal budget to judge the fiscal stance would not be very relevant.

A second reason for looking at the budget deficit is to assess its impact on the *public sector's net worth*. A deficit, which implies an increase in the real public debt, will mean that the public sector's net worth (the difference between public assets and liabilities) will decline, a tendency that may be of concern in some contexts but not when we are trying to find a way out of stagflation.

The third and for our purpose most relevant aspect of the budget deficit is its implications for *financial policy* and the effects of the changing government demand for private domestic savings: an increase in government borrowing, if it occurs, has implications for interest rates, the money supply, and the division of financial flows between the private and public sectors. Acceptable inflation-adjusted national accounts suitable for assessing the financial implications of deficits would be valuable but were not available for the OECD countries as a whole.

The Transmission Mechanisms

Chapters 3 and 4, by Lawrence and Mitra, deal with the transmission mechanisms of shocks to developing countries that emanate from the policies and economic performance of industrial countries and are transmitted through the trade and financial flows linking developed and developing countries.

Lawrence is concerned with delineating the causes and nature of the current Third World debt crisis. He questions the popular view that this crisis is fundamentally a matter of liquidity, or solvency. The notion of insolvency is not applicable to nations, he argues, as they are likely to be *unwilling* to service their debts well before they are technically insolvent—in the sense that the present discounted value of the nation's assets is less than its liabilities. The resulting default decision will depend upon the costs and benefits of default rather than upon the country's net worth. The situation is, on the surface, clearly a liquidity crisis. Lawrence argues, however, that it is fundamentally due to an underestimation of the *systemic* risk associated with the conjunction of a number of events considered to have a low probability of occurring in the global economy between 1979 and 1983—the dramatic rise and fall in oil prices, unprecedentedly high and volatile real interest rates, large fluctuations in real exchange rates, the deepest global recession in fifty years, the largest slump in world trade in the postwar period, and the sharp decline in the global inflation rate. If these events had not conjoined to destabilize the world economy, studies suggest, developing countries could have sustained and serviced their debt levels in the 1980s.

Lawrence documents the various types of objective risks, particularly systemic risk (the possibility of a major series of synchronous losses for the lenders), that were underestimated. The error was not unreasonable, however, inasmuch as (a) developing countries seemed to have weathered the 1974–75 recession well, maintaining and improving their export performance, which suggested that they might have been uncoupled from the global business cycle, and (b) the handling of the Herstatt and Franklin National bank failures suggested that the financial system could contain and absorb individual shocks. In addition, the subjective evaluation of the risks of lending to developing countries was affected because of the expected response of policymakers. The praise that the international banks received for recycling the financial surplus of the Organization of Petroleum Exporting Countries (OPEC) after the 1973 oil shock, and an assumption that they would be bailed out in the event of a default affecting the health of the global banking system, may have lowered their subjective estimates of the risk involved. Lawrence discusses various ways in which the systemic risk might be reduced, essentially through diversification. He notes that much of the debt was incurred to finance various public goods having no measurable returns and for which it is not possible to issue securities contingent upon income. He also argues that, given the relative success of cooperative solutions in the form of debt rescheduling that involves the banks, debtors, and international organizations, the past system based on bank rather than bond lending may have been relatively more stable, as banks are less concerned with transitory financing problems.

Chapter 4, by Mitra, charts the trade links between developed and developing countries and in particular examines the question of efficient adjustment to external shocks. Mitra estimates the effects and responses to the external shocks suffered during the 1970s by developing countries in an open economy macroeconomic model for each of thirty-three countries over the 1963–81 period, assuming a structural break after 1973. The actual outcomes in dealing with exogenous shocks in the 1974–81 period for these countries are then compared with hypothetical outcomes that presuppose responses based on the countries' 1963–73 experience. The external shocks considered are (a) terms-of-trade effects, (b) the effects of global recession, and (c) net interest rate effects. The sum of those external shock effects during 1974–81 ranged from an unfavorable annual average of 7 percent to 9 percent of GNP to a favorable 10 percent. Of the thirty-three countries considered, twenty-four suffered adverse external shocks.

Mitra then estimates the responses to the unfavorable shocks in terms of four modes of adjustment (and therefore of combinations): (a) trade adjustment, (b) domestic resource mobilization, (c) a slowing down of investment, and (d) additional external financing.

Developing Countries in Crisis

Chapter 5, by Gelb, and chapter 6, by Sjaastad and others, chart the nature of the economic crisis for two major sets of developing countries, namely the oil producers and the major Latin American debtors. Both chapters delineate the ways in which, for different reasons, the crisis essentially involves the public finances in these countries. It was brought about by unexpected shortfalls in public revenue (the case of the oil exporters) and unexpected increases in expenditure on servicing the public external debt (the case of the Latin American debtors), which were in turn caused by the recession and its unexpectedly high level of interest rates as well as declining primary product prices.

Gelb shows how the rise in oil revenues led to an unparalleled growth in the size and role of the public sector in virtually all oil-exporting countries. The windfall gains were channeled into industry—often large-scale and capital-intensive industry—and into expanded programs of transfer payments and subsidies. The momentum of this vast increase in public expenditure proved difficult to control when oil revenues fell after 1981. The resulting need to curtail public expenditure led to a rapid deceleration in the non-oil part of these economies, to surplus domestic capacity, and to slack labor markets. The contraction was accentuated in some countries by private capital outflows. The real exchange rate appreciation that had accompanied the earlier oil-based boom had led to disincentives to expansion of non-oil exports and had encouraged dependence on imported intermediate and capital goods. When external circumstances worsened, it proved difficult to compress the previously expanded public expenditures—giving rise to fiscal deficits—or to reverse the relative price changes that were no longer appropriate. Many of the large-scale investments, for instance in steel, soured as the expectations of future global demand on which they were based worsened with the global recession. Microeconomic rigidities and unsustainable public finances were thus the fundamental causes of the economic distress of these countries in the global recession.

Chapter 6 charts the paths to crisis and adjustment of five major indebted Latin American countries: Argentina, Brazil, Chile, Mexico, and Venezuela. The authors argue that the origins of Latin America's debt crisis precede the inability of the Mexican government to service its debt in August 1982. The implicated factors include a rapid and enormous growth of external debt with a shortening of its maturity structure and a sudden and large rise in dollar interest rates, accompanied by worldwide dollar deflation. As a result, the buildup of debt since 1973—in anticipation of oil price rises to finance ambitious public sector investments—and the change in the external environment in the early 1980s led to increases in debt service rates (interest plus amortization) that more than offset the earlier inflation-induced decline of the real value of their debt in the mid-1970s. The dollar prices of exports for many countries fell at the same time. The debt-service-to-debt ratio worsened (even though the level of debt in 1982 was not high by historical standards) without an accompanying improvement in the ability of the countries to generate the requisite fiscal and trade surpluses to pay for debt service.

This adverse outcome, however, in turn reflected more deep-seated problems of overambitious public investment programs, which led to uncontrolled and growing fiscal deficits, financed most often by levying the inflation tax, and to trade policies with a bias against exports and against domestic savings. Low-cost foreign loans, obtainable when OPEC financial surpluses were being recycled after the first oil shock, helped to finance the actual and incipient fiscal deficits during the 1970s. As foreign loans slowed down, many of these countries resorted to the inflation tax once again.

In coping with the crisis, governments have tried to cut back their fiscal deficits and have taken measures to restrict imports and to generate the fiscal and trade surpluses required to service their debt. The compression of imports has been an inefficient form of adjustment, as it has caused a fall in industrial output and employment, whereas exports have increased only slightly. Even if more efficient adjustment policies were followed under present capital market conditions, however, with nominal interest rates in excess of 10 percent and amortization rates in excess of 20 percent, the fiscal and trade adjustments that would be required are daunting. The normalization of world capital markets is therefore of importance if (given improved domestic policies) these countries are to find feasible ways of servicing their debts.

The Global Balance

Chapter 7, by Lal and van Wijnbergen, and appendix 2, by Lluch, are concerned with the global balance between the demand for and supply of savings. Lluch's appendix puts together data on incremental capital-output ratios and savings rates for developing countries and considers how different regions have shifted from being net exporters or importers of capital in the postwar decades. For developing countries the major points that emerge are (a) the marked and sustained increase in domestic savings in the last three decades except in sub-Saharan Africa, where the upward trend was reversed in the 1970s, and (b) the extremely high variance and volatility of incremental capital-output ratios across countries and over time in the same country. For developed countries the data in appendix 1 show a declining trend in domestic savings and a change in the capital-exporting status of its major economy, that of the United States.

Chapter 7 emphasizes how with the increased global financial integration there is a direct link between the actions and reactions of the public sectors in both developed and developing countries. In both sets there is pressure for public expenditure increases. In developed countries the aging of the population will add to pressure for increased spending on health and social security. In developing countries the growth of population intensifies pressure for increases in public expenditure on human and physical infrastructure. The financing of this public expenditure through taxation is posing problems in both sets of countries, and as a result incipient or actual fiscal deficits are being financed either through the inflation tax or through borrowing. The latter, in the increasingly integrated world economy, puts upward pressure on world real interest rates and suggests the possibility of a global crowding out of expenditures—private worldwide and public in developing countries—by the incipient structural deficits of developed countries. Lal and van Wijnbergen calibrate a three-region formal model of these global interactions with data for the 1970s. It seems to explain satisfactorily the terms-of-trade and real interest movements that have been observed in the last decade. The current debt crisis is seen as following essentially from a global fiscal crisis. The possibility then emerges that, unless "old age–related" public expenditures in developed countries can be contained, they will increasingly crowd out at the margin the infrastructural developmental expenditures in developing countries that are required to raise the living standards of the latter's poor, young, and growing labor forces.

Chapter 1

Developing Countries in the 1930s: Possible Lessons for the 1980s

Angus Maddison

LITERATURE on the world economic crisis of the 1930s is extensive and includes several respectable general surveys of the situation in the advanced countries (notably Arndt 1972; Haberler 1976; Hodson 1938; Kindleberger 1973; and Lewis 1949). Controversy is, of course, still lively about the causes of such a deep depression in the epicenter countries (Brunner 1981; Friedman and Schwartz 1963; and Temin 1976 on the United States; Balderston 1977; Falkus 1975; and Temin 1971 in Germany), and none of the studies just mentioned has exploited the potential for comparative cross-country analysis that quantitative economic historians have made possible by reconstituting many of the basic modern cyclical indicators—GDP and its components, trade volumes, terms of trade, and payments flows.

For the developing countries, the situation is much less favorable for sophisticated analysis. None of the older surveys that I have just cited gives adequate treatment to the situation in the Third World, and helpful recent attempts to fill the gap (Rothermund 1982; Thorp 1984) are constrained in cross-country analysis by lack of comparable data. The most ambitious cross-country study to use a standardized quantitative framework is that by Birnberg and Resnick (1975), which is only incidentally concerned with the 1930s. Regional cross-country analysis has gone furthest in Latin America (Diaz Alejandro 1981, 1982), thanks in part to efforts to produce comparable quantitative data (ECLA 1976, 1978; Wilkie and Haber 1982).

Although the data situation for the developing world is improving as research progresses, the basic weakness is the paucity and poor quality of the national accounts for prewar years. This chapter is therefore confined to the nine countries for which the basic data were either available or derivable. Fortunately these countries include almost 70 percent of the population of the developing world and may therefore be considered

For a more detailed analysis of the issues discussed in this chapter, see Maddison (1985).

"representative," although they do not include any African countries. Even for this group, the available national account aggregates are based on GDP by industry of origin rather than by type of expenditure. Although inferential clues are available, it is difficult to provide hard or comparable evidence on movements in demand components except exports and imports.[1]

It is also difficult to reach firm conclusions about the efficacy of policy, because fiscal, monetary, and balance-of-payments series that in principle can be reconstituted in comparable form are, for the present, often only sketchily available. Fortunately a growing number of scholarly country monographs, particularly from the Yale Growth Center, provide some basis for assessment.

The Aggregate Dimensions of the Depression

The world depression of 1929–32 was much bigger and more general than any earlier or later peacetime shock. Between 1929 and 1932, the aggregate GDP of the advanced countries fell 17.1 percent and world trade volume by 26.8 percent. In 1974–75, by contrast, the corresponding falls were only 0.6 percent and 5 percent, respectively. The 1981–82 recession in advanced countries was on the same order as that which occurred in 1974–75.

The epicenters of depression were the United States and Germany, where the primary recession was exacerbated by a collapse of financial institutions. In the epicenter countries (and their immediate neighbors, that is, the United States, Canada, Germany, and Austria) the average peak-to-trough GDP decline was 24.6 percent (see table 1-1). The recession in the other advanced countries averaged only 7.5 percent. Because of the huge size of the United States, the weighted average decline was 17.1 percent as compared with a nonweighted average of 11.7 percent.

In the nine developing countries in our sample, the average peak-to-trough GDP decline was 12.2 percent within the 1929–34 period, with an average of 15.8 in Latin America and 4.9 percent in Asia. The weighted average peak-to-trough decline for the Third World was very small, at 3.6 percent, because of the huge weight of China, and because the fluctuations in the Chinese economy differed in timing from those elsewhere.

There were major changes in terms of trade in the 1929–32 period, which meant that the fall in real *income* in the Third World was invariably worse than the fall in GDP. For my sample of nine developing countries, the average impact of the 1929–32 worsening in terms of trade was a 4.5 percent fall in real income to be added to the fall in GDP.

Table 1-1. *Amplitude of Recessions and GDP Growth Experience,*
1929–38

Country	Maximum peak-trough percentage fall in GDP (annual data)	Annual average compound growth rate, 1929–38
Advanced countries		
Australia	−8.2	1.9
Austria	−22.5	−0.3
Belgium	−7.9	0.0
Canada	−30.1	−0.2
Denmark	−2.9	2.2
Finland	−6.5	3.8
France	−11.0	−0.4
Germany	−16.1	3.8
Italy	−6.1	1.4
Japan	−7.2	4.7
Netherlands	−9.1	0.3
Norway	−8.3	3.1
Sweden	−9.2	2.3
Switzerland	−8.0	0.6
United Kingdom	−5.0	1.9
United States	−29.5	−0.7
Unweighted average	−11.7	1.5
Weighted average	−17.1	1.0
Developing countries		
Argentina	−13.8	1.3
Brazil	−7.3	4.6
Chile	−26.5	1.0
China	−8.7	0.6
Colombia	−2.4	3.5
India	−1.8	0.2
Indonesia	−4.1	1.5
Mexico	−19.0	1.7
Peru	−25.8	2.5
Unweighted average	−12.2	1.9
Weighted average	−3.6	0.8

Sources: Advanced countries from Maddison (1982); developing countries from statistical sources in References.

Depression-Induced Changes in the World Economic Order

The recession was very deep and general because normal international transmission mechanisms were reinforced by the collapse of the liberal world economic order. This collapse had three (highly interrelated but analytically distinguishable) components.

The international monetary system disintegrated. The surplus countries with big gold reserves (France and the United States) did not take conjunctural policy action to help nations in deficit. No country acted as lender of last resort, as the United Kingdom had done before 1913. No international institutions were available to provide liquidity as they do today. The demise of the gold standard was a messy and prolonged three-stage affair, involving sterling in 1931, the dollar in 1933, and the gold bloc (France and the Netherlands) in 1936. The breakdown itself was not a major tragedy. The economic damage was caused by the unnecessary deflation involved in adherence to the classical rules for debtors. A general decision to float all major currencies at an early stage would have been less deflationary.

The second complication resulted from the quarrels of the big countries over war debts and reparations. In 1929 the total stock of private capital invested abroad was about $50 billion.[2] In addition there were government war debts to the United States, the United Kingdom, and France that amounted to $20 billion and reparations due from Germany that had originally been fixed at $31.5 billion in 1921 and were twice scaled down, in 1924 and 1929. After a one-year moratorium in 1931, these government-to-government claims became permanently delinquent in 1932.

Acrimony among the major Western powers precluded mutual help with liquidity problems, and quarrels over intergovernment debt prepared the way for massive default on private obligations and cessation of equilibrating international capital flows. In the 1930s the major capital exporters of the advanced world became capital importers. The trade problems of deficit countries, particularly in the Third World, were compounded by lack of credit.

The third element of the international order that disintegrated was the liberal trade system. It is true that in 1929 tariffs were somewhat higher than they had been in 1913, but they were the only important trade restriction and were generally applied on a nondiscriminating basis. The United States gave an unfortunate lead to protectionism with the Hawley-Smoot tariff of 1930 without having the excuse of the balance-of-payments problems that drove other countries to such action. In 1930–32, the situation with regard to trade restrictions changed completely. Virtually all countries raised tariffs. New discriminatory trading blocs were created, and tariffs were reinforced by quantitative restrictions and exchange controls that were also applied in a discriminatory way. The most important of the new arrangements was the system of imperial preference devised in Ottawa in 1932 and supported by the sterling area payments system. Hitherto the British had not had tariff preferences in their colonies. The French had had colonial tariff preferences since the 1890s, and in 1931 these were reinforced and a new system of compensation funds and quotas was established to help Indochinese rice, tea, and corn as well as African coffee. In 1934–35 these tariff preferences were renewed and strengthened in the Imperial Economic Conference held in Paris. As a result France concentrated even more of its trade on the franc area. Japan, Germany, and Italy also built up new autarkic colonial and semicolonial trading blocs. Preferential systems favored some developing countries and damaged others, mainly in Latin America.

The Export Shock for Developing Countries

In 1929 developing countries were generally rather open economies. The exporting interests were strong politically in Latin America, where relatively high tariffs existed as much for revenue as for protection, and most African and Asian countries were colonies with low tariffs. Most of the latter were on the gold standard, and their initial response to payments difficulties was to play by the rules of the game and deflate. Their implicit long-term growth strategies involved growth diffusion via the liberal world order, without much governmental intervention. African and Asian countries were therefore rather vulnerable to external shock, and all the evidence suggests that the recessionary forces originated in the developed world. In China there was a very bad harvest in 1934 and war in 1937, but such autonomous cyclical causality was rare.

Table 1-2 shows the relative size of the trade shock for my sample of developing countries and for the advanced countries on a peak-to-trough basis. Because the timing of the trough varied between 1931 and 1933, the peak-to-trough export volatility of table 1-2 is bigger than that for 1929–32 shown in table 1-9, but the same basic characteristics stand out. The fall in volume of commodity exports in both developing and advanced countries averaged somewhat more than a third, but in developing countries this drop was compounded by worsening terms of trade, which meant that the purchasing power of commodity exports over imports fell by more than half, as compared with just under a third in the developed world. The big European countries (France, Germany, the United King-

Table 1-2. *Fluctuations in Export Volume, Export Purchasing Power,
and Import Volume, 1929–38*

Country	Export volume	Purchasing power of exports	Import volume
Developing countries			
Argentina	−35.8	−41.9	−53.2
Brazil	−31.1	−45.6	−63.8
Chile	−71.2	−84.5	−83.0
China	−48.6	−64.8	−50.5
Colombia	−12.5	−36.6	−63.1
India	−30.6	−39.2	−30.3
Indonesia	−15.2	−40.4	−47.5
Mexico	−41.5	−64.8	−61.1
Peru	−29.7	−57.1	−63.3
Average	−35.1	−52.8	−57.3
Advanced countries			
Australia	−6.0	−20.5	−48.0[a]
Austria	−45.5	−40.7	−45.4
Belgium	−31.4	−28.9	−20.0
Canada	−32.0	−41.2	−55.5
Denmark	−20.9	−21.3	−25.8
Finland	−15.7	−23.9	−46.7
France	−46.9	−34.8	−28.0
Germany	−50.1	−36.7	−36.2
Italy	−67.9	−72.0	−53.1
Japan	−8.4	−17.7	−21.9
Netherlands	−33.4	−27.9	−24.8
Norway	−12.0	−12.7	−21.7
Sweden	−37.0	−40.6	−23.5
Switzerland	−50.0	−41.5	−21.7
United Kingdom	−37.6	−25.3	−13.0
United States	−48.5	−38.3	−39.6
Average	−34.0	−32.8	−32.8

Note: Fluctuations are given as maximum percentage peak-to-trough fall in annual data.
a. 1929–31 period only.
Sources: Latin American countries from ECLA (1976); China from Hsiao Liang-lin
(1974:275); India from Birnberg and Resnick (1975); Indonesia from League of Nations,
Review of World Trade, 1938; advanced countries from Maddison (1962,1982), and sources
cited in appendix F of Maddison (1982).

dom) and the United States all saw major improvements in their terms of trade.

Because of the fall in capacity to import in the Third World, which was magnified by perverse capital flows, the payments problems of developing countries were very severe, and their import volume was cut on an average peak-to-trough basis by 57 percent. Thus the deflationary impact of these direct export losses and payments constraints was much bigger in developing countries than in advanced countries.

The biggest loss of purchasing power occurred in Chile, where the spontaneous repercussions of exogenous recessionary forces from the outside world were compounded by specific U.S. protectionist action on copper imports, which led U.S. companies operating in both Chile and the United States to favor their U.S. products. Chile was also the Latin American country that clung most closely to deflationary gold standard rules in defending its exchange rate. (See Birnberg and Resnick 1975 on the impact of U.S. protection and Hirschman 1963 on Chilean monetary policy.)

Colombia was the country most lightly affected by the recession in trade; its coffee export prices were sheltered because of Brazilian stock-piling policy, whereas its exports of coffee were not restricted, as were those of Brazil. Colombia also took internal policy measures to promote import substitution, hence its import volume fell a good deal more than its export purchasing power. (See Thorp 1984 for Colombian policy in the depression.) The size of the recessionary impact depended upon the luck of the commodity lottery rather than upon degree of export diversification. China with its rather diversified exports suffered a bigger export decline than Brazil, which was much more highly specialized (see table 1-3).

The traditional geographic distribution of exports (see table 1-4) also had relatively little effect on the degree of export decline of a particular country in the first stages of recession. Price falls for particular commodities were felt worldwide, and in relatively free markets, export destinations could be varied. In most cases, the initial fall in exports in 1929–32 was dominated by spontaneous repercussions of the deep decline in activity in the advanced countries and did not derive from protectionism, but the Hawley-Smoot tariff increases in the United States in 1930 sparked a great wave of tariff restrictions and quantitative export and exchange controls in 1931.

These restrictions had their major effect on the recovery process rather than on the depth of the recession. The recovery of imports in advanced countries after 1932 was much smaller than it would otherwise have been,

Table 1-3. *Percentage Composition of Commodity Exports in 1929*

Country	Exports
Argentina	wheat 29.2, maize 17.6, frozen, chilled, and tinned meat 12.8, linseed oil 12.6
Brazil	coffee 71.0
Chile	nitrates 42.1, copper 40.4
China	vegetable oils and seeds 28.4, raw silk 16.3, hides and skins 4.5, tea 4.1, coal 3.0
Colombia	coffee 60.6, petroleum 21.3
India	jute and jute products 25.5, cotton 20.9, rice 10.1, oilseeds 8.5, tea 8.4
Indonesia	sugar 21.6, rubber 16.0, petroleum 12.4, copra 6.7, tea 6.0, tobacco 5.8, coffee 4.8
Mexico	silver 20.6, other minerals 47.0
Peru	oil 29.7, copper 22.4, wool 21.1, sugar 11.5, lead 5.2

Source: Statistisches Reichsamt (1936).

Table 1-4. *Geographic Distribution of Exports in 1929*
(percentage of total)

Country	France	Germany	Japan	United States	United Kingdom
Argentina	7.1	10.0	0.0	32.2	9.8
Brazil	11.1	8.8	0.0	6.5	42.2
Chile	6.1	8.6	0.0	13.3	25.4
China	5.5	2.2	25.2	7.3	13.6
Colombia	0.5	2.1	0.0	4.7	75.2
India	5.4	8.6	10.4	21.4	11.7
Indonesia	0.0	2.6	3.3	8.9	11.4
Mexico	3.9	7.6	0.0	10.3	60.7
Peru	1.3	6.1	0.0	18.3	33.3

Source: Statistisches Reichsamt (1936).

and the recovery process was highly import substitutive in the developing world. Specific studies of the impact of trade restrictions are rather scarce, but it has been rather conclusively demonstrated that, in the Chilean case, exports would have been a good deal higher without U.S. trade restrictions (see Birnberg and Resnick 1975).

Similarly, U.S. sugar quotas favored U.S. Philippine and Puerto Rican producers at Cuba's expense. In general, Latin American countries were more exposed to the adverse impact of protection in the 1930s than were European colonies, which usually enjoyed some degree of discriminatory protection from their metropole. Germany did offer some discriminatory

Table 1-5. *Impact of Trade Discrimination: Percentage Share of "Empire Trade"*

	Imports		Exports	
Country	1929	1938	1929	1938
United Kingdom with Commonwealth and colonies	30.2	41.9	44.4	49.9
France with colonies	12.0	27.1	18.8	27.5
Japan with Formosa, Korea, and Manchuria	13.9	39.0	19.3	46.6
Germany with SE Europe and Latin America	16.7	27.6	12.8	24.7
Netherlands with colonies	5.5	8.8	9.4	10.7

Source: League of Nations, *Review of World Trade, 1938.*

market access privileges to Latin America in return for some reciprocity. The United States, with some exceptions just noted, held to the most-favored-nation principle. Table 1-5 shows the impact of discriminatory blocs on trade patterns.

Service Payments

The information is poorer for service transactions than for commodity trade. Mexico, because of its proximity to the United States, was probably worst affected by the loss of tourist earnings. All developing countries enjoyed lower freights on shipping, supplied generally by the advanced countries; the fall in shipping freights does not seem to have been as steep as the fall in commodity prices.

Payments for profit remittances on direct foreign investment fell sharply because this income was cyclically very sensitive. In Latin America and Eastern Europe, such remittances were usually blocked or were limited by exchange control from 1931–32 onward, but even in colonies such as India and Indonesia, where such movements were not controlled, they fell substantially. With respect to payments of interest on bonded debt, the situation was much worse, because the fall in price levels made such payments very onerous at a time when there was little access to new funds of this character.

The nature of the payments problem and the kinds of possible accommodation are illustrated in table 1-6 for the Indian case. There was a

Table 1-6. *Items in India's Balance of Payments, 1929–38*
(millions of rupees)

Year	Merchandise exports	Exports of precious metals	Service receipts	Merchandise imports	Imports of precious metals	Service payments	Balance on non-commercial transactions	Net foreign investment and borrowing
1929–30	3,613.4	15.7	54.3	2,694.4	277.7	936.7	35.8	45.6
1930–31	2,578.5	24.3	40.9	1,892.6	269.1	790.5	−93.8	403.6
1931–32	1,819.0	629.1	29.5	1,403.5	74.1	706.0	−166.2	−69.1
1932–33	1,538.6	679.2	29.7	1,459.1	31.2	744.2	−178.8	45.2
1933–34	1,713.4	591.9	26.5	1,295.7	20.8	737.2	−368.0	112.7
1934–35	1,757.3	577.3	30.1	1,486.4	52.2	760.1	−227.3	4.9
1935–36	1,860.3	418.8	30.8	1,520.2	56.6	786.9	138.0	−51.7
1936–37	2,262.5	300.0	30.3	1,405.4	156.8	836.6	−106.0	−174.1
1937–38	2,254.7	183.2	37.2	1,775.2	40.2	870.6	−58.1	−37.1
1938–39	2,032.3	147.0	32.3	1,532.2	22.4	804.1	−89.6	−64.5
Average, 1930–38	1,979.6	394.5	31.9	1,530.0	80.4	781.8	−127.8	18.9

Note: Figures are given for fiscal years beginning April 1.
Source: Banerji (1963:27, 90, 137, and 195).

sharp 57 percent fall in export values from 1929 to 1932, and thereafter exports did not regain their 1929 value; on average, export values for 1930–38 were only 55 percent of export values for 1929. To meet this payments constraint, India also cut imports back sharply; for 1930–38 they averaged only 57 percent of their level in 1929.

For developing countries during the period, service earnings were typically negligible, and service payments were considerable—equivalent to 35 percent of 1929 commodity imports. It was much more difficult to cut these miscellaneous service burdens than it was to cut imports, and 1930–38 service payments averaged 83 percent of those for 1929. Foreign borrowing for the period 1930–38 averaged only 41 percent of the 1929 level. A major balancing item was the reversal of the precious metals flow. India was a traditional importer of precious metals for indigenous savings hoards. In 1929 the net inflow was 262 million rupees. In 1930–38, however, the average annual outflow was 314 million rupees. Finally, we should note the drain stemming from noncommercial flows, which largely resulted from India's colonial status. These flows were substantial and negative in 1930–38.

Perverse Capital Flows and Their Impact

A feature of the 1930s situation that worsened the recessionary impact of the fall in export earnings was the reversal of the 1920s capital flow. This reversal is less well documented for developing countries than for developed countries because the annual prewar League of Nations figures for the balance of payments are rather weak. The overall situation of developed countries is rather clear from table 1-7, however; in the 1920s their net capital exports were more than $700 million a year, but in 1930–38 they had an average annual inflow of capital of about $540 million. The countries most affected by this reversal of capital flows were mostly in Latin America, where the bulk of the Third World's capital receipts had concentrated in the 1920s and where the debt was greatest (see table 1-8). When this capital dried up, it made the balance-of-payments adjustment process more difficult, initially forcing deflationary policies to be more restrictive, or tariffs, quantitative restrictions, and exchange controls to be stricter. Except for Argentina, all the Latin American countries defaulted (but did not repudiate) their official debt obligations in the 1930s. In Asian countries that were colonies, debt default was not permitted, and official monetary and budgetary policy in India and Indonesia was tighter than in Latin America or in China, where debt default did occur.

Table 1-7. *Net Foreign Investment Flows from and to Advanced Countries, 1924–38*
(millions of U.S. dollars)

Country	1924–29	1930–38
Australia	182	7
Canada	−32	−14
Denmark	2	−7
Finland	6	−21
France	−365	10
Germany	661	−77[a]
Japan	54	−49[b]
Netherlands	−72	14
New Zealand	31	1
Norway	17	−3
Sweden	−36	−12
Switzerland	−68	42
United Kingdom	−341	99
United States	−762	552
Total	−723	542

Note: Figures represent average annual flow in the years specified. A minus sign denotes flow from a country.
a. 1930–35.
b. 1930–36.
Source: United Nations (1948).

Table 1-8. *Per Capita Net Foreign Capital Liabilities in 1938*
(U.S. dollars)

Country	Amount
Latin America	
Argentina	230
Brazil	51
Chile	258
Colombia	38
Mexico	93
Peru	48
Arithmetic average	120
Asia	
China	3
India	11
Indonesia	35
Arithmetic average	16

Sources: Lewis (1984) and Gurtoo (1961).

The transfer burden for bonded debt was probably most severe in Indonesia. There was (see Creutzberg 1975–86, vol. 2:82–83, vol. 5:70) a rise from 1.7 percent of income (net domestic product) in 1929 to 5.4 percent in 1934. A good deal of the rising burden stemmed from falling price levels, but some was due to debt redemption.

Year	Percentage of Indonesian net domestic product
1929	1.7
1930	1.9
1931	2.6
1932	4.6
1933	5.1
1934	5.4
1935	3.7
1936	3.5
1937	2.6
1938	2.7

In the 1930s, there was a very large capital outflow from both China and India in the form of precious metals, mainly gold from India and silver from China, amounting to $1 billion in each case.

In general, the penalties incurred for debt default were rather small in the 1930s. The precedent had been set by the major powers in connection with war debts and reparations, and there was widespread domestic acceptance in those countries of the need to write down farm and mortgage debt, so the principle of temporary default (as distinct from repudiation) was hard to refuse, and the number of defaulters was too large for sanctions to be workable.[3] Of the $5.3 billion Latin American securities outstanding in 1938, $3 billion were in default, as compared with $340 million in 1913 and about $1.4 billion in 1929.[4] The proportion of defaulted East European, Greek, and Yugoslav bonds seems to have been even higher. China and Turkey were also defaulters. Debt default was a very important item in alleviating the balance-of-payments problems of some countries. The saving in foreign remittances of interest was about $50 million annually for Brazil and $25 million for Mexico. In addition these countries economized on amortization.[5] Much of the default was ultimately accepted by the creditors (mainly the United Kingdom and the United States) in wartime and postwar debt settlements. In the 1930s there was no real restoration of private international capital flows. There was, however, a considerable growth in government-guaranteed export credits tied to the goods of the creditor country. There was a big extension of such credits from Germany, the United Kingdom, and the U.S. Ex-

Table 1-9. Contribution of Change in Export Volume and Terms of Trade to Change in Real Income, 1929–32

Country	1929 ratio of commodity exports to GDP[a]	Percentage change in volume of commodity exports, 1929–32	Percentage change in purchasing power of commodity exports, 1929–32	Impact of fall in commodity export volume, 1929–32[b]	Impact of change in commodity terms of trade, 1929–32[b]	Percentage change in GDP, 1929–32	Percentage change in real income, 1929–32	Direct real income effect of 1929–32 change in purchasing power of commodity exports[b]	Real income effect of other conjunctural policy differences
Argentina	26.7	−12.6	−34.7	−3.4	−5.9	−13.8	−18.9	−9.3	−9.6
Brazil	15.4	−19.2	−45.6	−3.0	−4.1	−4.9	−8.8	−7.1	−1.7
Chile	30.0	−71.2	−84.5	−21.4	−4.0	−26.5	−29.4	−25.4	−4.0
China	(4.0)	−41.1	−57.8	−1.6	−0.7	(5.5)	4.8	−2.3	7.1
Colombia	(21.0)	−2.0	−28.2	−0.4	−5.5	4.0	−1.7	−5.9	4.2
India	7.8	−30.6	−39.2	−2.4	−0.7	−1.7	−2.4	−3.1	0.7
Indonesia	29.0	−6.5	−34.5	−1.9	−8.1	0.6	−7.5	−10.0	2.5
Mexico	12.4	−41.5	−64.8	−5.1	−2.9	−19.0	−21.3	−8.0	−13.3
Peru	(30.0)	−29.7	−57.1	−8.9	−8.2	−25.8	−31.9	−17.1	−14.8
Average	19.1	−28.3	−49.6	−5.3	−4.5	−9.1	−13.0	−9.8	−3.2

Note: Figures in parentheses are estimates.
a. At 1929 prices.
b. As percentage of 1929 GDP.
Source: Table 1-12 sources and tables 1-14–1-16.

port-Import Bank. Generally these credits were issued for a maximum term of five years.

The Income Effect of the Export Shocks

Table 1-9 shows the direct first-round impact of the export collapse on real income in 1929–32, weighting the impact by the ratio of exports to GDP. The decline in volume accounted for an average GDP fall of 5.3 percent for the sample, and worsening terms of trade meant an additional income loss equivalent to 4.5 percent of GDP. The total income loss was the GDP change multiplied by the terms-of-trade change, making a total average decline of 13 percent.

The total income loss due to trade (that is, the change in export purchasing power) amounted to 9.8 percent of GDP for the sample. The last column of table 1-9 shows the residual GDP change in these years that is not "explained" by falling commodity exports. These residual, apparently endogenous items of conjuncture and policy accounted on average for an income fall of only 3.2 points, so for the group as a whole the direct export shocks "explain" the bulk of the recession. This situation contrasts with that in the developed world, where endogenous deflationary elements were bigger than those attributable to the export shocks.

The "residual" effects in the developing countries should not in fact be interpreted as endogenous, because the export shocks and the sudden drying up of previous foreign capital flows produced further indirect deflationary effects, either spontaneously or as a result of government attempts to balance budgets and to curb payments deficits by expenditure cuts and tax increases.

In view of the general lack of comparable quantitative information, it is not easy to assess the significance of the residuals on a country-by-country basis. In India and China, where international trade was a relatively small part of the economy, the secondary deflationary effects of the export shock would probably be more limited than in countries more exposed to trade. It is also clear that countries with relatively high income levels, such as Argentina and Chile, had higher levels of expenditure on cyclically compressible items of demand—with respect to both investment and consumption—than did countries such as China and India, which had very large subsistence sectors. In the Latin American countries, investment levels were affected not only as a secondary effect of the export shock and its payments repercussions but also more directly by the reversal of the significant capital inflows of the 1920s and by the close geographic, institutional, and psychological links with the extremely depressed U.S. markets.

The impact of the export shock also depended on the nature of the export economy. In Chile, for example, the export sector was a geographic enclave with rather small employment, and a good part of the depressive impact was absorbed within the enclave by the profit remittances of foreign companies. The secondary recessionary effects of the export shock would therefore tend to be smaller than in Argentina, where a larger part of the labor force was employed in production and in processing a given value of product.

The residuals also provide some guide as to the efficacy of policy in withstanding the impact of recession. It would appear that Colombia and Brazil were most successful in this area and Peru, Mexico, and Argentina the least successful in Latin America. In Asia, by contrast, none of the three countries had negative residuals, and the situation was distinctly better than in Latin America.

The Recovery Phase, 1932–37

In discussions of the 1930s, it is too readily assumed that the whole decade was one of depression, but table 1-10 shows that there was a vigorous recovery process under way from 1932 to 1937 in Latin America. In Asia the recovery process was much more modest. The recovery process was interrupted in 1938 by the sharp U.S. recession of that year, which did not affect other advanced countries but had an adverse effect

Table 1-10. *Annual Average Change in GDP in Three Cyclical Phases*
(compound rates)

Country	1929–32	1932–37	1937–38
Argentina	−4.8	5.2	1.2
Brazil	−1.7	8.4	5.1
Chile	−9.8	8.3	0.0
China	1.8	0.5	−2.5
Colombia	1.3	4.2	6.6
India	−0.6	1.0	−0.3
Indonesia	0.2	3.3	−3.2
Mexico	−6.8	7.2	1.8
Peru	−9.5	11.5	−2.5
Average	−3.3	5.5	0.7

Source: Table 1-12.

on several developing countries because of its effect on primary commodity prices.

In 1932–37 the volume of commodity exports increased in all countries except China, although in Argentina, Chile, and India commodity exports did not recover their 1929 levels. The only cases with very significant terms-of-trade improvement were Argentina and Chile, and only in Argentina were 1937 terms of trade better than in 1929. As a result, trade expansion contributed only 6.6 percentage points of the average 34 percentage point increase in real income. The bulk of the recovery process was therefore explained by endogenous nontrade forces.

The cyclical contrast between 1929–32 and 1932–37 was sharpest in Latin America. There the residual (nonexport shock) components in recession accounted for an average decline of 2.3 percent a year in real income in the three years 1929–32, and in the recovery phase, these endogenous expansionary elements were vigorous everywhere. The contrast was least marked in Colombia, which was most successful in dealing with recession in 1929–32 and therefore had less scope for sharp recovery in 1932–37.

In Asia the situation was quite different. In the first place the recession phase involved no endogenous declines, but the recovery phase was so weak that it was indistinguishable from the recession phase. We could therefore claim that the 1930s were a decade of stagnation in Asia. The difference between the Latin American and Asian situations from 1932 onward is in fact traceable to policy differences. In Latin America most countries followed sharper policies of import substitution than in Asia because they were politically freer to impose trade and exchange controls and they were also freer politically to follow unorthodox budget and fiscal policies that achieved a fuller use of domestic resources and involved some degree of inflation. In addition they were free to follow policies of debt default. In contrasting Latin American and Asian policy, we must more or less exclude the Chinese case because of both the impact of war (the seizure of Manchuria in 1931, the Japanese invasion of 1937, and the continual civil wars of the 1930s) and the special currency experience, which helped put China's cyclical experience on a different time schedule.

The Impact of Policy in Developing Countries

Although there is a distinct family resemblance in policy between the different Latin American countries in the recovery period from 1932 onward, policies differed in the first phase of recession.

Argentina abandoned the gold standard at an early stage in 1929. This action softened the deflationary impact of the fall in export earnings, helped to discourage imports, and meant that internal prices fell less, thus mitigating the secondary deflation caused in many countries by distressed debtors forced into liquidation. These policies were later followed by exchange controls and tariff increases. The recession created a loss of income and political power for the old oligarchy, which had favored free trade. The regime that took over in the 1930s was more willing to raise tariffs and to follow policies of import-substituting industrialization. In the case of Brazil, which did not leave the gold standard until 1930, the populist leader Vargas gave the state a major role in promoting import substitution through government enterprise. The new inward orientation of policy helped little with immediate cyclical problems but was of major long-term significance in reducing the trade ratio in these countries.

Argentina's export dependence was twice as big as that of Brazil; Argentina was a more developed country, with higher ratios of the more volatile domestic GDP components, such as investment and consumer durables. For this reason and others, the recession was deeper in Argentina. Furthermore, Argentina had strong bilateral trade ties with the United Kingdom, and the possibility of U.K. trade retaliation (articulated in the negotiations for the Roca-Runciman treaty of 1933) led Argentina to honor its debt commitments, whereas Brazil was delinquent to a very significant extent and thereby eased its payments constraints.

Brazilian domestic policy offset the exogenous shock to a significant degree because it happened to enter the recession with a well-established price support apparatus for stockpiling coffee. Unfortunately, lack of adequate planting restrictions or taxes on coffee production meant that Brazil continued to produce huge stocks of coffee that were eventually destroyed. Some of the apparent GDP buoyancy thus did not represent real income, though activity was maintained and the impact of recession was diffused away from the coffee sector. Cumulatively coffee's stock destruction over the period 1931–38 was equal to a loss of 17.7 percent of 1929 GDP. The major beneficiaries of Brazilian coffee policy were other producers, who enjoyed the price support benefit without the stockpiling costs. The most important of these producers were Colombia and Indonesia, which exported 3.8 million and 1.4 million bags respectively in 1934–38, as compared with Brazil's 14.6 million.

In Chile, the impact of the depression via trade was extremely severe. Exports fell in volume by 70 percent from 1929 to 1932, and the terms of trade deteriorated nearly 40 percent. The purchasing power of imports fell more than 80 percent, and the substantial inflow of capital that had characterized the 1920s dried up. In the Chilean case the export loss was very severe partly because exports were heavily concentrated on minerals, the category of goods for which demand fell most, but also because

Chile was adversely affected by U.S. action in 1932 in imposing a specific tariff of four cents a pound on copper imports. The tariff was equivalent to a 70 percent ad valorem duty. It has been estimated (Birnberg and Resnick 1975:234–35) that Chile's exports in 1932 would have been twice as high had it not been for these U.S. export restrictions, which caused U.S. copper interests to reallocate production from their Chilean mines to their U.S. mines. Because Chile had an export dependence of about 30 percent of GDP in 1929, the fall in exports had a very large effect on GDP. This effect was exacerbated by the Chilean policy of defending the exchange rate by deflation until March 1932. The new central bank created on the advice of Kemmerer in 1925 pushed up the discount rate to 9 percent in a period of falling prices. Policy changed with the massive inflation of the brief socialist government in 1932, which paved the way for recovery (Hirschman 1963:179–83), and exchange controls forced profits to be reinvested domestically when they reemerged.

In Mexico, the situation in 1929 was different from that elsewhere in Latin America in two contradictory respects. On the one hand, for political reasons there was a bigger endogenous policy element in Mexican experience. The revolution and civil wars of 1910–20 had led to partial debt default, which meant a low capital inflow in the 1920s. The partial default also reduced oil exploration by foreign companies, which instead built up Venezuelan production, cutting into Mexican export markets. The Calles and Calles-dominated presidencies in the 1920s and 1930s followed conservative fiscal and monetary policy, both to pay off debt and to manage Mexico's rather complicated bimetallic currency. On the other hand, Mexico, being a closer neighbor of the United States with its epicenter economy, had a bigger across-the-board dependency relationship than several other Latin American countries. Its trade dependency on the United States was high; it depended more on tourism and migrant remittances; its border areas were closely integrated with the U.S. economy; American enterprise and management were relatively important; and banking and credit links were strong.

The first policy response of Mexico to the depression was as deflationary as that in Chile. Montes de Oca, the minister of finance, followed a tight money policy and raised taxes to balance the budget.

This policy changed sharply in 1932 when Pani became minister of finance, switched to a more expansionary budget and fiscal policy and to exchange depreciation, and tolerated more inflation. He also demonetized silver, switched to a paper currency, and sold some of the Mexican silver stocks in 1934–35, during the period when the U.S. government was supporting silver prices.

From 1934 to 1940, under the Cardenas government, policy became more nationalist than it was elsewhere in Latin America, with greater use

Table 1-11. *Price Movements, 1929–38*
(1929 = 100)

Year	Argentina	Brazil[a]	Chile	China	Colombia	India[a]	Indonesia[a]	Mexico[a]	Peru
1929	100.0	100.0	100.0	100.0	100.0	100.0	100.0	100.0	100.0
1930	101.0	98.5	98.9	112.4	79.2	80.7	96.5	102.4	95.8
1931	87.0	95.1	98.2	122.8	64.0	71.9	73.1	89.6	89.6
1932	78.0	95.1	104.4	114.8	53.6	68.7	57.8	80.0	85.6
1933	88.0	95.1	129.6	105.5	55.2	65.0	47.6	84.8	83.4
1934	78.0	101.9	129.7	97.2	76.8	66.4	45.4	87.2	85.2
1935	82.7	107.8	132.4	97.1	80.0	66.9	45.8	88.8	86.1
1936	89.7	123.3	143.6	108.9	84.8	67.1	44.4	96.8	90.4
1937	92.1	133.0	161.7	125.7	86.4	68.9	48.6	119.2	96.5
1938	91.5	138.3	—	221.2	97.3	69.3	49.5	125.6	—

Note: Dashes indicate that figures are not available.

a. Brazil, India, Indonesia, and Mexico indexes are national income, or GDP, deflators.

Sources: Brazil from Contador and Haddad (1975); India from Sivasubramonian (1965); Indonesia from Polak (1979); Mexico from Solis (1984:92). For other countries, the figures are generally cost-of-living indexes. Argentina and Colombia from Diaz Alejandro (1981:16). China from Feuerwerker (1977); 1929–36 is the average of the implicit Tientsin and Shanghai wholesale indexes for consumer goods given on pp. 46–47, and 1937 is from the Shanghai index, linked to the 1937–39 index of retail prices in the main cities of unoccupied China. Chile and Peru from League of Nations, *Statistical Yearbook* (cost-of-living indexes for Santiago and Lima).

of indigenous developmental and financial institutions to promote development and outright nationalization of mineral resources. The nationalization included de facto expropriation of foreign oil interests in 1938, which provoked sharper sanctions against Mexico than the more diplomatic defaults farther south. This action also meant that oil exploration in Mexico was delayed for several decades.

In India and Indonesia, two big Asian countries that were still European colonies, the policy was very different in style from that in Latin America and paralleled action in the respective metropoles. India entered the recession with tight monetary and fiscal policy to defend the rupee's parity with sterling and to defend sterling itself. From 1925 onward it was generally held that sterling was overvalued, and Indian nationalist economists argued that the rupee was overvalued relative to sterling (the rupee stood at a higher parity when India readopted the gold standard in 1927 than it had in 1913). In 1931 when sterling was allowed to float against other currencies, the rupee was pegged at the same rate relative to sterling. Virtually all Indian opinion (including that in the viceroy's executive council) opposed this policy, but Whitehall insisted. To back up the exchange rate and balance the budget, the government cut civil service salaries, reduced the military establishment, and by 1932 had cut capital expenditure on railways and civil works to a quarter of their 1929 level. The 1931 supplementary budget levied a 25 percent surcharge on income tax, excise taxes, and import duties. In the course of the 1930s, the government built up exchange reserves. It was able to do so because of the huge dishoarding of precious metals in the 1930s. Between September 1931 and March 1939, the outflow was more than a billion dollars.

Tariff autonomy had been regained in the 1920s, and between 1930 and 1933 tariffs on non-British textiles were raised from 15 percent to 75 percent. Quotas were imposed on imports of Japanese piece goods, and the 1932 Ottawa agreements established imperial preference. Increased protection gave a boost to Indian manufacturing and to some import substitution in agriculture, for example in the case of sugar. The impact of the recession on Indian output was relatively mild for reasons that I have mentioned. The main impact of restrictive policy was to keep growth lower than it could have been in the 1930s had the Latin American options of easier monetary and fiscal policy and debt default been followed.

One of the most interesting differences between the Indian (and Indonesian) situation and that in Latin America was the depth of fall in prices. The domestic price level fell 35 percent in India from 1929 to 1933, without much recovery before the war (see table 1-11). In Indonesia, the price fall was even bigger, but only in Colombia did the price fall exceed that in India in the recession phase, and Colombian prices recovered substantially from 1932 onward. It is difficult to interpret the real impact of falling prices, because the intercountry variation in price experience bore no obvious relation to the depth of the recession, and it is difficult to judge the extent to which decisionmaking was affected by price changes and very high real interest rates. The price declines did not have as damaging an institutional impact in the Third World as they did on U.S. financial institutions, but they created many bankruptcy situations for debtors and windfall gains for moneylenders and landlords who were able to collect fixed money rents. They also raised the incidence of tax burdens. It would appear that the price decline had an important distributional impact whose effects have not been very satisfactorily diagnosed. Governments made various attempts to mitigate the burden on debtors, and also to help credit institutions threatened by bad debt, but analysis of the macroeconomic impact of such policy is sadly lacking.[6]

In Indonesia, fiscal and monetary policy followed a deflationary style similar to that in India, with cuts in civil service salaries and in capital expenditure, increases in taxation, and fulfillment of foreign debt service commitments, with net redemptions in the 1930s. The major difference was that the Netherlands guilder (the Indonesian currency unit) retained an unchanged gold parity until 1936, with the result that Indonesian prices had to fall further than prices in India to remain competitive on international markets. In response to foreign tariff increases and quotas, the Netherlands abandoned its traditional free trade policy, raised Indonesian tariffs, imposed quotas on Japanese imports, and discriminated in favor of bilateral trade. The Netherlands also entered into restrictive commodity arrangements for sugar and rubber that it had previously eschewed.

The creditor/debtor problem was probably worse in Indonesia than in India and led to liquidity problems for various kinds of banks catering to the indigenous population. The income cycle was worse for Indonesia than for India, because Indonesia had a much bigger traded sector. Indonesia, however, also had a bigger concentration of cyclically volatile income in the hands of expatriate and Chinese traders, so that the impact on the indigenous population was smaller than on the economy as a whole. The rather detailed Indonesian national accounts estimates by Polak (1979) for 1921–39 unfortunately relate to real income rather than to GDP. Our estimates for the latter are rather crude and partial, but the GDP volatility was much less than the real income movement. In Indonesia, the plantation labor of coolies was proportionately much more important than in India, and these coolies suffered very big pay cuts and unemployment in the recession, for which some of them compensated in part by producing subsistance crops on small plots.

Lessons from the 1930s

Recent economic events in the Third World have been very different from those of the 1930s. There has not been a deep fall in output in the advanced countries, and the volume of their imports from non-oil Third World country exporters has been very well sustained. The terms-of-trade dichotomy was not between Third World primary producers and the advanced countries exporting manufactures but between oil producers and non-oil producers. The Third World had long cast aside deflationary gold standard economics as a technique for dealing with external shock and was equipped with a monetary-fiscal and exchange control armory that permitted more growth-oriented tradeoffs. Balance-of-payments accommodation to external shock was greatly facilitated after 1973 by the massive availability of credit, whereas the 1930s problem had been greatly complicated by lack of credit. The sharp decline in the pace of world inflation, the rise in U.S. interest rates after 1979, and the Mexican moratorium of August 1982, however, sparked off a debt crisis and checked the compensatory flow of capital. As a result, most of Latin America plunged into a recession in 1983.

It is difficult to draw "lessons" from the experience of the 1930s for application to the 1980s because of the big difference between the two periods and also because the more obvious lessons of the 1930s, of the type that Arndt drew in 1944, have already been embodied in the new liberal international economic order, which has thus far proved rather robust. Another big difficulty is that the really substantial cyclical problems of the Third World arose rather recently (from 1982 onward), so that it is perhaps premature to push the conclusions too far. The "lessons" already learned have been several.

1. Articulate cooperation and consultation between the major advanced countries to avoid beggar-your-neighbor trade and payments measures. Developing countries have thus not faced the catastrophic trade volume collapse of the 1930s, and their terms of trade have not fared worse than those of developed countries.

2. Built-in stabilizers and more sensible discretionary action prevented developed countries from inducing a recession anywhere nearly as serious as that in 1929–32, but the advanced countries made a major mistake by pursuing a macropolicy (fiscal and monetary) that was too deflationary, with an increasing proportion of the labor force unemployed and other

Table 1-12. 1929 GDP Levels at 1929 U.S. Relative Prices and Movement of Gross Domestic Product (1929 = 100)

Year	Argentina	Brazil	Chile	China	Colombia	India	Indonesia	Mexico	Peru	Total
1929 level (millions of dollars)	5,190	2,842	1,759	40,729	798	23,741	5,470	1,339	491	82,359
1929	100.0	100.0	100.0	(100.0)	100.0	100.0	100.0	100.0	100.0	100.0
1930	95.9	95.6	95.9	(101.2)	99.1	100.0	100.4	93.2	88.8	99.9
1931	89.2	92.7	76.9	102.3	97.6	98.2	96.3	96.6	78.2	98.7
1932	86.2	95.1	73.5	105.5	104.0	99.6	100.6	81.0	74.2	100.6
1933	90.3	107.3	83.5	105.5	109.9	102.1	101.6	89.7	100.0	102.6
1934	97.4	116.9	94.7	96.3	107.6	100.7	102.5	95.6	116.9	98.9
1935	101.7	122.4	98.4	104.1	119.6	101.4	103.6	100.5	120.1	103.8
1936	103.0	137.1	101.6	110.7	126.0	106.4	112.5	110.9	125.4	110.1
1937	111.3	142.3	109.4	(108.0)	127.9	106.4	118.1	114.7	128.1	110.1
1938	112.6	149.6	109.4	(105.3)	136.3	101.8	114.3	116.8	124.9	107.6

Note: Figures in parentheses are estimates.

Sources: Argentina: ECLA (1978). Brazil: Zerkowski and de Gusmao Veloso (1982). Chile: ECLA (1978). China: 1931–36 from Yeh (1979); 1929–31 extrapolated from 1914/8–1933 growth rate in Perkins (1975:117); GDP assumed to drop 2.5 percent in both 1937 and 1938 because of the impact of the Sino-Japanese war. Colombia: ECLA (1978). India: Maddison (1971). Indonesia: derived from J. J. Polak in Creutzberg (1975–86, vol. 5:84); combination of food crop production and export crops. This crude indication should correspond more closely with the GDP movement than Polak's national income figures (p. 70), which are strongly affected by changing terms of trade. Mexico: ECLA (1978). Peru: Boloña Behr (1981).

forms of underutilized growth potential. The reason was partly that the advanced countries exaggerated their payments problems with OPEC and partly that they were too ambitious in their aspirations to mitigate inflation. The result was a rather weak recovery phase after the 1974–75 recession and also after the 1981–82 recession.

3. In the United States the recent recovery has been much more satisfactory than in Europe but has involved a policy mix that keeps the dollar and interest rates too high, greatly complicating debt problems.

4. During 1973–82, developing countries weathered external shocks rather well. Their macropolicy posture was generally much more expansionary than that of developed countries, because of a willingness to trade off growth against higher inflation rates and to live with substantial payments deficits. The latter was possible to a much greater degree than in the 1930s, because of the willingness of the advanced countries both to provide the financing capital flow and to tolerate a dichotomous international order such that developing countries can keep trade and payments restrictions while advanced countries remain relatively free of them. The debt crisis of 1982–83, however, demonstrated that Latin American countries had underestimated the risks involved and the potential costs of overborrowing.

5. Because credit was available on such liberal terms, important parts of the developing world based too much of their expansion on borrowing and not enough on export competitiveness. They would have done better to have grown somewhat more slowly and to have borrowed less. As in the 1930s, we see a contrast between Latin America and Asia. This time the colonial context has disappeared, and Asian countries have been better able to follow policies in their own interest. They seem, on the whole, to have judged their interests better than Latin America because they relied more on export competitiveness and less on borrowing to finance their expansion. Stabilization exercises (for example, in Korea), have acted more quickly and have been more successful than in Latin America.

Statistical Appendix

Economic data for Argentina, Brazil, Chile, China, Colombia, India, Indonesia, Mexico, and Peru in the period 1929–39 are presented in Tables 1-12 to 1-18.

Table 1-13. *Relative Size of Economies in 1929*

Country	Population (thousands)	GDP at 1929 U.S. relative prices ($ million)	GDP per capita 1929 U.S. relative prices	Exports ($ million)	Exports per capita ($)
Argentina	11,592	5,190	448	908	78
Brazil	32,894	2,842	87	462	14
Chile	4,333	1,759	406	283	65
China	490,382	40,729	83	650	1.3
Colombia	6,927	798	115	124	18
India	333,100	23,741	71	1,177	3.5
Indonesia	59,830	5,470	91	582	10
Mexico	16,337	1,339	82	285	17
Peru	5,860	491	84	117	20
Total	961,255	82,359	—	4,588	—
Other developing countries	437,000	—	—	3,611	—
World	2,100,000	—	—	33,024	—

Note: Dashes indicate that figures are not available.

Sources: 1950 GDP levels in 1965 dollars adjusted for differences in purchasing power by the production method (except Chile and Indonesia) from Maddison (1983a); Chile from Maddison (1970); Indonesia (same method used) from Maddison (1983b). The 1950 estimates are backcast to 1929 with the GDP indicators, giving GDP in 1929 at 1965 U.S. prices. To convert to 1929 prices I adjusted all series by the ratio of U.S. 1929 GDP in 1929 prices to U.S. GDP in 1929 at 1965 prices (from U.S. Department of Commerce 1977).

Table 1-14. *Export Volume*
(1929 = 100)

Country	1930	1931	1932	1933	1934	1935	1936	1937	1938
Argentina	69.3	95.3	87.4	81.9	85.8	90.6	81.9	95.6	61.4
Brazil	109.6	117.3	80.8	100.0	111.5	128.9	142.3	128.8	155.8
Chile	65.0	60.0	28.8	41.3	66.3	67.5	67.5	95.0	88.8
China	87.7	91.3	58.9	54.1	51.4	54.9	54.4	n.a.	n.a.
Colombia	109.8	96.1	98.0	98.0	103.9	113.7	127.5	125.5	131.4
India	89.4	76.4	69.4	79.8	81.3	81.9	99.4	95.5	n.a.
Indonesia	96.8	84.8	93.5	88.1	89.7	90.6	100.1	112.5	n.a.
Mexico	81.1	82.1	58.5	62.3	84.9	86.8	95.3	112.3	50.0
Peru	91.9	81.1	70.3	86.5	102.7	108.1	113.5	129.7	105.4

n.a. = not available.
Source: Statistical sources listed in references.

Table 1-15. *Terms of Trade*
(1929 = 100)

Country	1930	1931	1932	1933	1934	1935	1936	1937	1938
Argentina	95.9	71.4	74.5	70.4	85.7	85.7	105.1	120.4	110.2
Brazil	61.6	53.6	67.5	60.3	62.9	55.0	54.3	58.3	43.0
Chile	95.7	67.0	55.1	60.0	57.3	61.6	70.3	76.8	54.1
China	90.9	77.2	71.7	65.0	68.4	73.9	85.1	n.a.	n.a.
Colombia	73.6	83.6	72.9	63.6	81.4	64.3	64.3	67.1	60.0
India	92.4	85.3	87.6	87.1	88.7	94.6	94.1	87.1	n.a.
Indonesia	76.4	72.7	70.0	67.6	69.0	69.9	71.3	67.8	58.1
Mexico	77.5	59.8	59.8	61.8	66.7	77.5	64.7	61.8	132.4
Peru	72.4	58.6	61.8	59.2	69.7	71.7	69.7	62.5	63.8

n.a. = not available.
Source: Statistical sources listed in references.

Table 1-16. *Purchasing Power of Exports*
(1929 = 100)

Country	1930	1931	1932	1933	1934	1935	1936	1937	1938
Argentina	66.9	68.5	65.3	58.1	74.2	78.2	86.3	115.3	67.7
Brazil	67.1	62.0	54.4	59.5	69.6	70.9	77.2	74.7	67.1
Chile	62.2	40.5	15.5	25.0	37.8	41.9	47.3	73.0	48.0
China	79.7	70.5	42.2	35.2	35.2	40.6	46.3	n.a.	n.a.
Colombia	81.7	80.3	71.8	63.4	84.5	73.2	83.1	84.5	78.9
India	82.6	65.2	60.8	69.5	72.1	77.5	93.5	83.2	n.a.
Indonesia	74.0	61.6	65.5	59.6	61.9	63.3	71.4	76.3	n.a.
Mexico	63.0	49.1	35.2	38.9	56.5	67.6	62.0	69.4	66.7
Peru	66.1	48.2	42.9	51.8	71.4	78.6	80.4	82.1	67.9

n.a. = not available.
Source: Statistical sources listed in references.

Table 1-17. *Volume of Imports*
(1929 = 100)

Country	1930	1931	1932	1933	1934	1935	1936	1937	1938
Argentina	87.8	61.5	46.8	51.3	56.4	58.3	61.5	80.8	76.3
Brazil	59.4	39.1	36.2	50.7	55.1	62.3	63.8	78.3	72.5
Chile	92.0	48.0	17.0	19.0	25.0	38.0	43.0	48.0	44.0
China	93.7	92.8	72.8	62.3	54.4	53.4	49.5	n.a.	n.a.
Colombia	52.3	44.6	36.9	50.8	63.1	69.2	78.5	90.8	84.6
India	81.1	69.7	80.6	69.8	80.1	84.5	76.8	n.a.	n.a.
Indonesia	85.2	72.3	57.9	57.3	53.7	52.5	53.0	69.0	70.7
Mexico	74.1	48.1	38.9	44.4	55.6	57.4	66.7	85.2	70.4
Peru	73.3	50.0	36.7	40.0	70.0	80.0	83.3	90.0	90.0

n.a. = not available.
Source: Statistical sources listed in references.

Table 1-18. *Exchange Rates*
(U.S. cents per unit of national currency)

Year	Argentina	Brazil	Chile	China	Colombia	India	Indonesia	Korea	Mexico
1929	95.13	11.81	12.06	41.90	96.55	36.20	40.16	46.10	48.18
1930	83.51	10.71	12.08	29.92	96.49	36.07	40.23	49.39	47.13
1931	66.74	7.03	12.07	22.44	96.57	33.70	40.23	48.85	47.65
1932	58.44	7.12	7.91	21.74	95.28	26.35	40.39	28.11	31.85
1933	n.a.	7.96	7.68	28.60	81.70	31.82	51.72	25.65	28.11
1934	33.58	8.43	10.15	34.09	61.78	37.88	67.38	29.72	27.74
1935	32.66	8.30	5.08	36.57	56.01	36.96	67.71	28.71	27.78
1936	33.14	5.88[a]	5.12	29.75	57.08	37.52	64.48	29.02	27.76
1937	32.96	6.20[a]	5.17	29.61	56.73	37.33	55.04	28.79	27.75
1938	32.60	5.84	5.17	21.36	55.95	36.59	55.01	28.45	22.12
1939	30.85	5.13[a]	5.17	11.88	57.06	33.28	53.33	25.96	19.30

n.a. = not available.
a. Free rate.
Source: Federal Reserve System, *Banking and Monetary Statistics.*

Notes

1. In any case, even the GDP aggregates for these countries cannot be regarded as definitive. There are competing estimates for Brazil (Haddad 1978 versus Zerkowski and Veloso 1982), India (see Maddison 1984), and Mexico (Solis 1973 versus ECLA 1978). We had to make crude estimates for Indonesian GDP, as the Polak series refer to income rather than product. For China for 1929–38 we used trend estimates, as annual data were not available.

2. "Billion" means "thousand million."

3. A detailed description of the processes of debt "readjustment" is provided in Young (1971). China actually went into default in the 1920s when civil disturbance reduced the earmarked revenues below service obligations. Thereafter China played a prolonged cat-and-mouse game with creditors that involved writing down and rollovers of debt, sweetened by occasional repayments. In the Chinese case a substantial part of debt also involved government claims arising from indemnities following the Sino-Japanese war and the Boxer Rebellion.

4. See C. Lewis (1948:42), and Royal Institute of International Affairs (1937:303).

5. The average annual amortization and interest receipts of the United States and the United Kingdom combined fell more than $800 million from 1925–28 to 1932–34. See Royal Institute of International Affairs (1937:283).

6. It is alleged by J. C. Scott (1976) that the increased burden of debt service and taxation caused by falling prices led to widespread falls in peasant living standards and to peasant rebellions in Asia (evidence is supplied mainly for Burma and French Indochina). A recent review of Southeast Asian evidence on prewar peasant living standards puts the Scott thesis in doubt; see Ian Brown (1983).

References

Advanced Countries

GENERAL ANALYSIS

Arndt, H. W. 1972. *The economic lessons of the 1930s*. London: Cass. Originally published 1944.

Haberler, G. 1976. *The world economy, money, and the Great Depression, 1919–1939*. Washington, D.C.: American Enterprise Institute.

Hodson, H. V. 1938. *Slump and recovery, 1929–1937*. London: Oxford University Press.

Kindleberger, C. P. 1973. *The world in depression, 1929–1939*. London: Allen Lane.

Lewis, W. A. 1949. *Economic survey, 1919–1939*. London: Allen and Unwin.

Maddison, A. 1962. Growth and fluctuation in the world economy, 1870–1960. *Banca Nazionale del Lavoro quarterly review*, June.

———. 1985. *Two Crises: Latin America and Asia, 1929–38 and 1973–83*. Paris: Organisation for Economic Co-operation and Development (OECD) Development Center.

GERMANY

Balderston, T. 1977. The German business cycle in the 1920s: A comment. *Economic history review*.

Falkus, M. E. 1975. The German business cycle in the 1920s. *Economic history review*.

Temin, P. 1971. The beginning of the depression in Germany. *Economic history review*.

UNITED STATES

Brunner, K., ed. 1981. *The Great Depression revisited*. Boston: M. Nijhoff.

Friedman, M., and A. J. Schwartz. 1963. *A monetary history of the United States, 1867–1960*. Princeton, N.J.: Princeton University Press.

Temin, P. 1976. *Did monetary forces cause the Great Depression?* New York: Norton.

Developing Countries

GENERAL ANALYSIS

Birnberg, T. B., and S. A. Resnick. 1975. *Colonial development: An econometric study*. New Haven, Conn.: Yale University Press.

Brown, Ian. 1983. Rural distress in South East Asia during the world depression of the 1930s. Manila; processed.

Diaz Alejandro, C. F. 1981. Stories of the 1930s for the 1980s. New York: National Bureau of Economic Research; processed.

———. 1982. Latin America in depression, 1929–39. In M. Gersovitz and others. *The theory and experience of development*. London: Allen and Unwin.

Rothermund, D., ed. 1982. *Die Peripherie in der Weltwirtschaftskrise*. Schöningh: Paderborn.

Scott, J. C. 1976. *The moral economy of the peasant*. New Haven: Yale University Press.

Thorp, R., ed. 1984. *Latin America in the 1930s: The role of the periphery in world crisis*. London: Macmillan.

ARGENTINA

Diaz Alejandro, C. F. 1970. *Essays on the economic history of the Argentine Republic*. New Haven: Yale University Press.

BRAZIL

Contador, C. R., and C. L. Haddad. 1975. Produto real, moeda, e preços: A experiencia brasileira no periodo 1861–1970. *Revista brasileira de estatistica*, July–September.

Fishlow, A. 1972. Origins and consequences of import substitution in Brazil. In L. di Marco, ed. *International economics and development: Essays in honor of Raúl Prebisch*. New York: Academic Press.

Haddad, C. L. S. 1978. *Crescimento do produto real no Brasil, 1900–1947*. Rio de Janeiro: Vargas Foundation.

Instituto Brasileiro de Geografia e Estatistica (IBGE). 1960. *O Brasil en números*. In *Anuario estatistico do Brasil, 1960*. Rio de Janeiro: IBGE.

Zerkowski, R. M., and M. A. de Gusmao Veloso. 1982. Seis decadas de economia brasileira atraves do PIB. *Revista brasileira de economia*, July–September.

CHILE

Hirschman, A. O. 1963. *Journeys toward progress*. New York: Twentieth Century Fund.

CHINA

Feuerwerker, A. 1977. *Economic trends in the Republic of China, 1912–1949*. Ann Arbor: University of Michigan, Center for Chinese Studies.

Hsiao Liang-lin. 1974. *China's foreign trade statistics, 1864–1949*. Cambridge, Mass.: Harvard University Press.

Perkins, D. H., ed. 1975. *China's modern economy in historical perspective*. Stanford: Stanford University Press.

Young, A. N. 1971. *China's nation building effort, 1927–1937*. Stanford: Stanford University Press.

U.S. Congress. Joint Economic Committee. 1982. *China under the four modernizations*.

INDIA

Banerji, A. K. 1963. *India's balance of payments*. Bombay: Asia Publishing.

Gurtoo, D. N. 1961. *India's balance of payments (1920–1960)*. Delhi: Chand.

Maddison, A. 1971. *Class structure and economic growth: India and Pakistan since the Moghuls*. London: Allen and Unwin.

———. 1984. What did Heston do? Paper prepared for the Cambridge Conference on the Economic History of India. Cambridge, April.

Sivasubramonian, S. 1965. National income of India, 1900–01 to 1946–47. Delhi: Delhi School of Economics; processed.

INDONESIA

Creutzberg, P., ed. 1975–86. *The changing economy in Indonesia*. 10 vols. The Hague: Martinus Nijhoff.

Polak, J. J. 1979. The national income of the Netherlands Indies, 1921–1939. In P. Creutzberg, ed. *National income*. The Hague: Martinus Nijhoff. Originally published New York, 1943.

MEXICO

Solis, L. 1984. *La realidad economica mexicana*. Mexico City: Siglo Veintiuno.

PERU

Boloña Behr, C. A. 1981. Tariff policies in Peru, 1880–1980. Ph.D. dissertation, Oxford University.

Other

Lewis, C. 1948. *The United States and foreign investment problems*. Washington, D.C.: Brookings Institution.

Royal Institute of International Affairs. 1937. *The problem of international investment*. London: Oxford University Press.

Statistical Sources for Tables 1-12 to 1-18

Federal Reserve System. Monthly issues, various years. *Banking and monetary statistics*. Washington, D.C.

League of Nations, Various years. *Statistical yearbook, World production and prices, Review of world trade, Balances of payments, Money and banking, Public finance*. Geneva: League of Nations.

Maddison, A. 1982. *Phases of capitalist development*. Oxford: Oxford University Press.

———. 1983a. A comparison of levels of GDP per capita in developed and developing countries, 1700–1980. *Journal of economic history*, March.

———. 1983b. Estimates of Indonesian population, GDP, export volume, and real product levels since 1820. Groningen: University of Groningen; processed.

Mitchell, B. R. 1982. *International historical statistics: Africa and Asia*. London: Macmillan.

Statistisches Reichsamt. 1936. *Statistisches Handbuch der Weltwirtschaft*. Berlin: Statistisches Reichsamt.

United Nations. 1948. *International capital movements during the inter-war period*. Lake Success: United Nations.

———. Economic Commission for Latin America (ECLA). 1976. *America Latina: Relacion de precios del intercambio: Cuadernos estadisticos de la CEPAL*. Santiago: United Nations.

———. 1978. *Series historicas del crecimiento de America Latina: Cuadernos estadisticos de la CEPAL*. Santiago: United Nations.

U.S. Department of Commerce. 1977. *National income and product accounts of the United States, 1929–1974*. Washington, D.C.

Wilkie, J. W., and S. Haber, eds. 1982. *Statistical Abstract of Latin America*. Los Angeles: University of California, Latin American Center.

Woytinsky, W. S., and E. S. Woytinsky. 1955. *World commerce and governments*. New York: Twentieth Century Fund.

Chapter 2

The Slowdown of the World Economy and the Problem of Stagflation

Gottfried Haberler

THERE IS NOW general agreement that the first quarter century after World War II was a period of almost unprecedented growth and prosperity for the advanced industrial countries as well as for the less developed countries as a group. In sharp contrast with the twenty years after World War I, the interwar period, 1919–39, was marked by the severe depression of 1920–21 and the Great Depression of the 1930s.

The post–World War II period has seen recessions but no depression, if by "depression" we mean a decline in economic activity on the order of magnitude of the depressions of the interwar period and earlier. The climate of optimism or even euphoria that characterized the 1950s and 1960s, however, has given way to pessimism and gloom since the early 1970s. There is again talk of depression and crisis. Two related developments account for the changed outlook. First, the recent recessions, 1973–75 and 1980–82, have been more severe in the United States than the earlier ones and have been marked by the unsettling experience of stagflation, with prices rising even in periods of falling output and employment. Second, there has been a distinct slowdown of productivity growth in all advanced countries since about 1972.

The talk about crisis and depression, however, and the widespread fear that the dismal experience of the 1930s is about to repeat itself seem to me greatly exaggerated. An extreme example of totally unwarranted pessimism is provided by Raúl Prebisch (1984:175). He refers to the recent recessions and slowdowns in productivity growth as "the second great crisis of capitalism." The first great crisis was the Great Depression of the 1930s. It certainly was a crisis, but as we shall see presently, it was due to avoidable policy mistakes. It is a fatal misinterpretation to call it a crisis of capitalism.

This paper was written in winter 1983–84. It was possible to add, mainly in footnotes, references to later events and to new source materials, but there was no comprehensive updating of the text.

I will now try to put recent developments and the present malaise in historical perspective.

During World War II and the immediate postwar period it was not generally realized that the world economy was on the verge of an extended vigorous expansion. On the contrary, it was widely believed that the dismal pattern of the interwar period would repeat itself. In fact, most Keynesian economists thought that deflation and unemployment, not inflation, would be the order of the day, and in each of the early recessions many experts saw the beginning of the postwar depression.[1]

The actual fate of the world economy during the twenty-five or even thirty years after World War II has been authoritatively described by Simon Kuznets: "Even in this recent twenty-five year period of greater strain and danger, the growth in peace-time product per capita in the United States was still at a high rate; and in the rest of the world, developed *and less developed* (but excepting the few countries and periods marked by internal conflicts and political breakdown), material returns have grown, per capita, at a rate higher than ever observed in the past (Kuznets 1977:14, emphasis added; also see Kuznets 1971 and 1976).

In "Aspects of Post–World War II Growth in Less Developed Countries," Kuznets remarked: "For the LDCs as a group, the United Nations has estimated annual growth rates of total and per capita GDP (gross domestic product at constant factor prices) from 1950 to 1972. The growth rates of per capita product . . . for the twenty-two years was 2.61 percent per year. . . . Such growth rates are quite high in the long-term historical perspective of both the LDCs and the current DCs." These high growth rates are largely a recent phenomenon. "While the historical data for LDCs rarely provide a firm basis for judging their long-term growth," it can be established indirectly that in earlier periods the growth rates must have been lower. Applying the recent growth rates to earlier periods "would have meant impossibly low levels of per capita product and consumption at the beginning of the preceding quarter of a century." Kuznets further observes that, for the current developed countries for which we have long-term growth rates, "the observed rates (for well over half a century of their modern growth) are generally well below those cited for the LDCs" (1976:40–41). (From 1960 to 1972 the average growth rate of per capita GNP of some sixty-seven developing countries with more than 1 million population each, and omitting major oil exporters, was 2.6 per year [Kuznets 1976:42].)

Kuznets is, of course, fully aware of the danger of using broad aggregate measures of growth for the developing countries as a group, given their great diversity. He discusses and carefully evaluates possible biases in the procedures. Still, after everything has been said and done, he confirms the basic soundness of his findings and expresses his bewilderment that, despite the "impressively high" growth rates "in the per capita product of LDCs over almost a quarter of a century," the general sentiment in the developing countries is one of dissatisfaction and gloom that "seems to ignore the growth achievements." He conjectures, and gives ample reasons for the speculation, that "a rise in expectations has produced a negative reaction to economic attainments which otherwise might have elicited litanies of praise for economic miracles" (1976:41 and passim).

Kuznets's findings were confirmed in an important paper by Kravis and Lipsey (1984) based on statistical data that became available after Kuznets wrote. The authors concluded that "the three decades 1950–80 were unique in economic history in two important respects. First the industrial countries, which had enjoyed rapid economic growth in previous eras, experienced unprecedented rates of expansion. What is even more remarkable is the diffusion of growth to, and rapid growth of, almost the entire world . . . including a large fraction of the people of the developing world." There are, of course, some exceptions, including a number of countries "concentrated in Africa between the Mahgreb and South Africa and in the Indian subcontinent" (1984:134–35).

When the widely expected depression again and again failed to materialize, pessimism about the future gave way to optimism and euphoria. Keynesians claimed credit for the good showing. I cite a typical example. In 1967 Sir Austin Robinson wrote: "In the year 1947–1948 we began to use in peacetime the principles that Maynard Keynes had worked out for war finance. We began to plan the use of national resources. If we are looking to the credit side I think we can honestly say that the world today is a different place from what it was in the 1930s in very large measure as a result of the economic thinking that began in this Faculty in Cambridge in those exciting years of the 1930s" (1967:43). Similar claims were made by American Keynesians. It was widely assumed that the business cycle had been all but eliminated by skillful demand management and fine tuning of the economy.

The Keynesians proved to be mistaken. The business cycle is still with us, although it has indeed become much milder. No decline in economic activity even approaching the depression of the 1930s has occurred since 1945. The absence of such a decline is a great achievement, despite the recent slowdown and the threat of inflation and stagflation.

In my opinion, monetarists and liberals—liberals in the classical nineteenth-century sense—have a better claim to credit for the improved performance than the Keynesians. For there can be no doubt that the avoidance of deep depressions during the postwar period is mainly due to the fact that there has been no serious deflation in the sense of a decline either in the supply of money or in nominal GNP. This general statement follows from what I regard as an established conclusion that all major cyclical downswings—depressions as distinguished from recessions, in modern terminology—have been strongly intensified, if not caused, by monetary contractions.[2]

The monetary factor was especially pronounced in the case of the Great Depression of the 1930s. The exceptional severity of the Great Depression in the United States was due to the fact that the U.S. monetary authorities, by acts of commission and omission, let the money supply shrink by 30 percent. (Similar mistakes have been made in other countries, for example in Germany.) This explanation is, of course, in line with the monetarist theory but also with the views of Joseph A. Schumpeter, whose theory of the business cycle was decidely non-monetarist. Schumpeter emphasized that the Great Depression was not a regular cyclical downswing but was due to special "adventitious" circumstances. He wrote: "I do not see how it could be denied that it was the—avoidable—three bank epidemics [bank failures] that . . . spread paralysis through all sectors of the business organism, turned retreat into rout and thus were the most important reasons . . . for the prevailing distress and unemployment" (1951:214). What would have been a recession, perhaps a relatively severe one, was thus turned into a catastrophic depression.

The monetarist-liberal interpretation of post–World War II events is strongly supported by the German "economic miracle," which started with the currency reform of 1948 and the simultaneous abrupt dismantling of all wartime controls by Ludwig Erhard. Restoration of sound money and continuing monetary discipline was essential for the spectacular growth of the German economy, which in turn had a galvanizing effect on Western Europe. The prospects of the German reform were completely misjudged by leading American and British Keynesians (Haberler 1980; Hutchison 1979, esp. p. 435 ff.).[3]

The first quarter century after World War II was by general agreement a period of almost unprecedented growth and prosperity for the whole Western world, including the developing countries. The last ten years have been marred by rising inflation in the modern vicious form of stagflation, by more severe recessions, and by a slowdown or even stagnation of productivity growth. In no country, however, has there been a decline in economic activity approaching the depression of the 1930s or earlier ones. Furthermore, the U.S. economy has staged an unexpectedly vigorous cyclical recovery that started in December 1982. It is still going strong and is stimulating the world economy. Inflation has sharply declined, but it is too early to say, as many experts (especially Keynesians) are inclined to do, that inflation has been licked and is no longer anything to worry about.

My next five sections deal with different aspects of the problems of inflation, stagflation, and disinflation in the last ten years. I shall first discuss the nature and cost of rising inflation, stagflation, and disinflation. In the following three sections I shall present three alternative explanations, the "Keynesian" position, the "monetarist–rational expectations" position, and the "traditional conservative," or "classical," position. I shall subsequently discuss the elusive problem of the productivity slowdown in industrial countries since the early 1970s and the evolution of the international monetary system in the post–World War II period. Finally I shall describe the policy implications of my analysis.

The Cost of Stagflation and Disinflation

We have seen that two distinct but related unsettling developments account for the change from optimism and euphoria of the 1950s and 1960s to pessimism and gloom in the 1970s and 1980s—the slowdown of productivity growth, on the one hand, and, on the other hand, the relative severity and inflationary character of the 1973–75 and 1981–82 recessions. I shall address the second development first.

The proximate cause of the severe recessions of 1973–75 and 1981–82 in the United States and the other industrial countries is not hard to find. Inflationary pressures had increased everywhere since about the middle 1960s and reached a high point in 1974, a recession year. Suffice it to say that, in the United States, inflation, measured by the consumer price index, topped 12 percent. Even in Switzerland it climbed to the unheard-of level of 10 percent. Thus the industrial countries were forced to step on the monetary brake. In the United States the inflation rate was reduced to a little below 5 percent by the end of 1975, and Switzerland abruptly deflated to practically zero inflation; output contracted sharply, but unemployment rose only slightly because of the buffer of foreign workers.

In the United States, inflationary pressures again increased after 1976 when the Carter administration switched from fighting inflation to stimulating the economy. In the late 1970s inflation reached again the two-digit level. It once again became necessary to take restrictive monetary measures, hence the famous "dollar rescue operation" of October 1979 after Paul Volcker had been appointed chairman of the Federal Reserve Board.

We can say, then, that the proximate cause of the recession was the policy of disinflation, which in turn was forced on the authorities by the high rate of inflation, notwithstanding the fact that in the United States in the early as well the late 1970s the pronounced weakness of the dollar in the foreign exchange markets was the greatest worry of the monetary authorities and induced them to take restrictive measures. The weakness of the dollar, however, was the consequence of the fact that the high rate of inflation in the United States greatly exceeded that in a number of industrial countries, primarily Japan, West Germany, and Switzerland. Let me recall that the weakness of the dollar led to its devaluation in 1971, especially vis-à-vis the Japanese yen, the German mark, and the Swiss franc, and later in early 1973 to the breakdown of the Bretton Woods regime of stable but adjustable exchange rates and the adoption of managed floating of all major currencies. The recessions, that is, were due to the fact that high rates of inflation forced countries to adopt restrictive monetary policies. It is practically impossible to wind down inflation without creating transitional unemployment—without, in other words, creating a recession.

Two questions arise. What were the reasons for the high rate of inflation? Why did prices continue to rise even during the recession, as they had not done in earlier recessions and depressions? In other words, why stagflation? It should be mentioned that in the 1930s an early case of stagflation, or cost-push inflation, as it was called at that time, was caused in the United States by the policies of the New Deal. Milton Friedman described the episode:

> The only example I know of in United States history when such a cost-push was important even temporarily for any substantial part of the economy was from 1933 to 1937, when the NIRA [National Industrial Recovery Act], AAA [Agricultural Adjustment Administration], Wagner Labor Act, and associated growth of union strength unquestionably led to increasing market power of both industry and labor and thereby produced upward pressure on a wide range of wages and prices. This cost-push did not account for the concomitant rapid growth in nominal income at the average rate of 14 percent a year from 1933 to 1937. That reflected rather a rise in the quantity of money at the rate of 11 percent. . . . The cost-push does explain why so large a part of the growth in nominal income was absorbed by prices. Despite unprecedented levels of unemployed resources, wholesale prices rose nearly 50 percent from 1933 to 1937, and the cost of living rose by 13 percent. Similarly, the wage cost-push helps to explain why unemployment was still so high in 1937, when monetary restriction was followed by another severe contraction. [1966:22]

The alarming rise in prices forced the Federal Reserve System to step on the monetary brake. The result was a short but very sharp depression.

In thirteen months unemployment rose from 10 percent to 20 percent, real GNP dropped by 13.2 percent, and industrial production fell by 32.4 percent.

An exogenous factor is often regarded as a major cause of inflation in the 1970s and 1980s—the two oil shocks, the quadrupling of crude oil prices by OPEC in 1973 and the doubling of oil prices in 1979.[4] These were indeed highly inflationary and disruptive events, but the direct impact of the oil price rise on inflation in the United States and other industrial countries has been greatly exaggerated. The first oil shock was preceded by a highly inflationary commodity boom, which in turn was superimposed on an inflationary groundswell that started in the middle 1960s (see IMF 1981).

It can be argued, however, that the oil price had a significant indirect effect on inflation, through the manner in which the economy reacted to it. Let us assume, for example, that money wages and other incomes (or even real wages through widespread formal or informal indexation) are rigid downward, and let us also reflect that the oil price rise constitutes a sharp deterioration in the terms of trade, which implies a reduction in the standard of living. The consequence of the rise will be unemployment and inflation. I shall have more to say on this point later.

The Keynesian Position on Inflation and Stagflation

As we have seen, a sharp distinction must be made between Keynesian economics and the economics of Keynes himself. Keynes was concerned about inflation all his life except during the Great Depression of the 1930s when he wrote *The General Theory*. In 1937, a year later, however, he again became concerned about inflation. What he would have said about stagflation—the vicious combination of high or even rising unemployment and inflation—is a matter for speculation; he died before the problem became acute in the post–World War II period.

Until very late in the game (see below), the views of Keynes's followers were characterized by emphasis on fiscal policy, by optimism that the economy can be fine-tuned by skillful demand management, and by unconcern about the rising danger of inflation as well as by neglect of inflationary expectations. This attitude of course sharply contrasts with monetarism and its offshoot, the modern theory of rational expectations, as I shall presently explain.

The Keynesian unconcern about inflation and the neglect of inflationary expectations is highlighted by the theory of the Phillips curve, which postulates a more or less permanent tradeoff between unemployment and inflation; lower levels of unemployment can be obtained by accepting higher rates of inflation. This theory for years played a leading or even dominating role in the Keynesian discussions of inflation. I cite two examples of prominent Keynesians.

In 1960 Paul A. Samuelson and Robert M. Solow wrote the celebrated article "Analytical Aspects of Anti-Inflation Policy." It presented a modified Phillips curve for the United States, which the authors described as "the menu of choice[s] between different degrees of unemployment and price stability (1960:192). See figure 2-1. The authors mentioned

Figure 2-1. *Modified Phillips Curve for the United States*

Average annual price rise (percent)

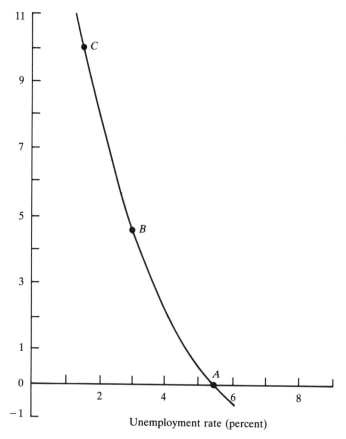

Unemployment rate (percent)

Note: This shows the menu of choices between different degrees of unemployment and price stability, as roughly estimated from the last twenty-five years of U.S. data.
Source: Samuelson and Solow (1960:192).

specifically two "obtainable" choices: price stability with 5.5 percent unemployment and 3 percent unemployment with 4.5 percent inflation a year, marked as (A) and (B) on the graph.

Now, the point I wish to make is that the authors do not say whether they regard other points on the curve as "obtainable" choices, for example, the point that I mark (C), 1.10 percent unemployment with 10 percent inflation. As we see matters now, this point would not be "obtainable." With 10 percent inflation, the short-run Phillips curve would not stay put. Inflationary expectations leading to anticipatory action by market participants would shift the curve upward. Although the authors envisage shifts of the curve due to structural changes in the economy, they do not mention that inflationary expectations would shift the curve. It is true that there is a fleeting reference to inflationary expectations, but it comes earlier in the paper and is not made in connection with the Phillips curve. The authors say that inflationary expectations would be caused by "a period of high demand and rising prices." Inflationary expectations would "bias the future in favor of further inflation." The importance of the matter is immediately played down, however: "Unlike some other economists, we do not draw the firm conclusion that unless a firm stop is put, the rate of price increase must accelerate. We leave it as an open question: It may be that creeping inflation leads only to creeping inflation" (Samuelson and Solow 1960:185). Can we define "creeping"? Surely 10 percent inflation cannot be described as a creep. Inflation would accelerate, or if it is stopped the result would be recession.

I think it is fair to say that the paper by Samuelson and Solow illustrates my point that Keynesian economics until recently was characterized by unconcern about the dangers of inflation and neglect of inflationary expectations. The paper, as I have noted, was written in 1960. The inflationary excesses of the last ten to fifteen years have sensitized inflationary expectations of market participants and have alerted economists to the dangers of inflation. The change in outlook has reached its climax in the theory of rational expectations, as I shall show.

I now turn to my second example of the Keynesian blind spot concerning inflation. As late as 1972, shortly before inflation in the United States and other industrial countries soared into the two-digit range, James Tobin extolled the virtues of inflation in adjusting "blindly, impartially and nonpolitically the inconsistent claims of different pressure groups on the national product" (1972:13). He later gracefully admitted that he had "been overoptimistic about the trade-off [between unemployment and inflation] and too skeptical of accelerationist warnings" (1973:622). Keynesian economics was ill equipped to deal with the problem of stagflation because it was essentially depression economics; wages and prices were assumed to be constant. It seems fair to say that this was accepted by Keynes's followers and his critics as the central message of *The General Theory*.[5]

My point is illustrated by the following true story from Nazi Germany. When Hitler came to power, there was an influential Keynesian economist in the economics ministry named Wilhelm Lautenbach, who had advocated deficit spending for some time. In fact, there had been deficit spending even before Hitler, but under Hitler the deficit became much larger, though there was still great fear of inflation. Hitler called Lautenbach, who was not a Nazi, into his office and asked: "Isn't this a little dangerous, what we are doing? Are we not risking a serious inflation?" Lautenbach answered: "Mein Führer, you are a very powerful man, but there is one thing you cannot do: you cannot make inflation with 30 percent unemployment!" What Hitler supposedly could not do—produce inflation in the midst of heavy unemployment—the New Deal accomplished in the United States.

In the late 1960s and 1970s the dangers of inflation, despite substantial unemployment, could no longer be ignored. The first reaction of Keynesians was to recommend "income policies" to support macro policy. I shall return to the problem of incomes policy in the section on policy implications below.

More important, there has been a gradual shift of Keynesian economics away from depression equilibrium with stable wages and prices of the *General Theory* to a neoclassical position. We might also describe this shift by saying that the Keynesians have been catching up with the master, who in 1937 already realized that the economic climate had changed.

A good example of that shift is Paul A. Samuelson. In his sparkling contribution to the Keynes Centenary Conference in Cambridge in 1983 he stated that in the present world neither the "depression Keynesian model" of the *General Theory* nor "the market-clearing new classical theory model" works well anymore. He concludes: "If I had to choose between these two extreme archetypes, a ridiculous Hobson's choice, I fear that the one to jettison would have to be the Ur-Keynesian model"; and "people learn faster these days and the easy Keynesian victories are long behind us" (Samuelson 1983:212).

I myself have expressed the same idea by saying that today the world is closer to the classical position than to the Keynesian one.

Monetarism and Rational Expectations

Monetarism and its offshoot the theory of rational expectations are characterized by reliance on monetary policy, the downgrading of fiscal policy, the rejection of fine-tuning, incomes policies, and controls, and emphasis on the role of expectations. The two schools are liberal in the classical nineteenth-century sense and are direct descendants of the quantity theory of money.

Broadly speaking, the quantity theory of money is undoubtedly correct, namely in the sense that there has never been a significant inflation, with prices rising by, say, 4 percent or more per annum, for perhaps two, three, or more years without a significant increase in the quantity of money. Furthermore, a reduction of monetary growth is a necessary condition for reducing or eliminating inflation.

Such statements are empirical. Exceptions are thinkable. If output fell sharply because of a natural catastrophe, a string of crop failures, or a war, for example, the price level would rise even with a constant quantity of money. War inflations have in fact been aggravated by a drop in output, but there can be no doubt that most wartime price rises were always due to inflationary methods of financing the war. The oil price rise imposed by OPEC is often mentioned as a nonmonetary cause of inflation. We have seen, however, that the direct impact of the oil shocks on the price level has been greatly exaggerated.

There is furthermore the problem of a change in the velocity of circulation of money. A sharp increase in velocity would spell inflation, and a decrease would spell deflation—even with a constant quantity of money. Does that statement not invalidate the quantity theory as formulated above? The answer is no for the following reason: it is true that the velocity does change over time. There are slow structural changes, and velocity has a cyclical pattern; it tends to rise in business cycle upswings and to decline in downswings. These changes are not large enough to invalidate the quantity theory as formulated above.

Large changes that would invalidate the quantity theory, *if they were autonomous*, are clearly the consequence of inflation or deflation caused by changes in the quantity of money. The point is well illustrated in the case of high inflation. During the well-documented case of the German hyperinflation in 1922–23, for example, the velocity of circulation of money rose to fantastic heights, far outstripping the rise in the (nominal) quantity of money and in the price level. This inflation, however, was clearly the consequence of printing money.[6]

Policy conclusions are straightforward. To curb inflation, monetary growth must be reduced. It is impossible to stabilize a significant level of inflation, say, 6 percent per annum or more. Monetarists and rational expectations theorists reject the idea of a permanent tradeoff between inflation and unemployment as enshrined in the Phillips curve. An extended period of significant inflation cannot mark an equilibrium position, because inflationary expectations would quickly develop and market participants would take anticipatory measures. Interest rates would rise, labor unions would press for higher wages, and wholesale commodity prices would rise—all of which would rob inflationary policies of their stimulating power, and unemployment would rise again. If an attempt was made to prevent a rise in unemployment by expansionary measures, the consequence would be accelerated inflation.

Rational expectations theorists have pushed that argument to an extreme. They say that macroeconomic policies of expansion or contraction have no effect whatsoever, not even in the short run, on the "real" economy, on output and employment. Such policies merely affect the price level and nominal interest rates. The reasoning behind this surprising conclusion is that market participants, "agents," by and large act rationally. They determine what the likely consequence of government policy will be, and they take anticipatory action.

Limitations of space preclude my discussing the rational expectations theory, which has been developed, criticized, and defended in scores of papers, in greater detail. Suffice it to say that the "hard-line version" of the theory, to wit that macropolicies have no effect on the real economy, is widely regarded, also by monetarists, as an exaggeration that cannot be reconciled with the facts. There is widespread agreement, however, that the longer inflation lasts, even in the intermittent, stop-and-go form, the more firmly entrenched inflationary expectations become, and the harder it is to stop the inflation. This reasoning leads to the conclusion that it is impossible to stabilize a significant rate of inflation. The goal of the policy must be to bring down inflation by monetary restraint to a very low level, say, 2–4 percent.

At this point I must mention the so-called credibility approach, which was developed by William Fellner in several important papers (1976, 1979a, 1980). Fellner was a sympathetic critic of the rational expectations theory. His theory tries to capture what he called "the valid core" of the rational expectations theory, namely that rational market participants are trying to determine what the government policy is likely to be. If the authorities make their policy of disinflation "credible," if they persuade the public that they will stick to it and will not give up, as they did so often in the past when unemployment rose a little bit, they will "condition" inflationary expectations. Labor unions and other pressure groups will be put on notice that they will price themselves out of the market if they push up wages and prices. As a result there will be a good chance that wage and price demands will moderate and thus the pains of disinflation will be reduced, although it is too optimistic to assume that disinflation will become entirely painless.[7]

Two important questions arise: what is the role, if any, of fiscal policy in the monetarist scheme of things, and is there any room at all for incomes policy in some sense of that ambiguous term? The importance of fiscal policy is highlighted by the current debates about the large budget deficits of the United States and other countries. Naturally the large current and projected deficits of the United States, whose economy looms so large in the world, have become the prime subject of the debate. Before discussing the question that interests us most at this point—whether the deficit threatens to abort the current expansion and to reignite inflation—let me say a few words on the international aspects of the problem.

The U.S. deficits have become a matter of great concern and anxiety abroad. U.S. fiscal policy has been strongly criticized by international officials and foreign governments: the budget deficits have raised U.S. interest rates, which attracts foreign capital, pushes up the dollar in the foreign exchange markets, and creates huge U.S. trade deficits. Foreign countries are thus forced to finance U.S. trade and budget deficits, are put under inflationary pressure, and are compelled to raise interest rates.

There certainly is much truth in the criticism, but it has been somewhat defused by the vigorous recovery of the U.S. economy that has developed and is still going strong despite the drag of the large trade deficits and the appreciation of the dollar. It can, indeed, be argued that the trade deficit and the appreciation of the dollar have prolonged the expansion by slowing its pace to a more sustainable speed and by keeping inflation at a lower level. Moreover, the U.S. recovery is making a major contribution to the recovery of the world economy from the recession.

I now come to the question of the role of fiscal policy and budget deficits in a closed economy as exemplified by the United States at the present time. There is widespread fear, which is probably shared by a great majority of professional economists of different schools, that the large budget deficits will reignite inflation and will jeopardize the recovery.[8]

How do fiscal policy in general and budget deficits in particular fit into the monetarist picture of the world? In every major inflation, government deficits have been blamed as a prime source of the trouble. Austerity programs prescribed by the International Monetary Fund (IMF) for troubled countries that ask the Fund for help invariably include provisions for fiscal discipline. The reason is that troubled countries put the monetary authorities under irresistible pressure to "finance" the deficit by printing money. Monetarists would, however, insist that if the central bank stands firm and does not increase the money supply, even large budget deficits will not cause inflation.

The statement is true, but monetarists would agree that it is not the end of the story. Large deficits push up interest rates, causing a doubly or triply adverse effect on the economy: higher interest rates could speed up the velocity of circulation of money and so could lead to inflation even without an increase in the money supply; more important, high interest rates could abort the cyclical recovery, and productive private investments would be crowded out by government profligacy, slowing long-run growth.

We see, then, that loose fiscal policy and large budget deficits need not cause inflation if monetary policy is sufficiently tight. Depending on the magnitude of the deficits, however, the adverse side effects of loose fiscal policy can be very serious. For this reason monetarists often insist that monetary restraint brings best results when it is supported by fiscal restraint.

Finally, I should say a few words on the Keynesian reaction to this picture. Let us recall that in the 1930s, during the Great Depression, when Keynes wrote his *General Theory*, the economic situation was entirely different from that which we see today: there was mass unemployment, prices were falling, expectations were deflationary, and the general mood was one of despair and gloom. In that climate Keynes was quite right to call for deficit spending and monetary expansion; present-day monetarists should agree. If my memory serves me right, I heard Milton Friedman himself on television say so. We may recall that Frank Knight, Jacob Viner, and Henry Simons, the teachers of the present-day monetarists in Chicago, recommended deficit spending and monetary expansion.[9]

To be sure, if monetary expansion had been applied in time, it would have stopped deflation in its tracks, and after the deflationary spiral had gathered momentum, vigorous monetary expansion through open market operations would eventually have pulled the economy out of the slump. The cure would have taken some time, however, and in the process a large pool of liquidity would have been created that would have caused inflationary troubles after the economy had turned upward again. It was therefore better to inject money directly into the income stream by deficit spending.

The 1930s were the heroic age of Keynesianism. Today the situation is quite different; unemployment is low compared with its level in the 1930s, below 10 percent as against 25 percent.[10] There is inflation, and expectations are inflationary. Keynes himself recognized, as we have seen, the change in climate already in 1937, one year after he wrote *The General Theory*, but some Keynesians still live in the heroic age. James Tobin (1983) repeatedly speaks of the "Volcker and Thatcher depression" (not recession), which suggests that the last cyclical decline was on the order of magnitude of the depression of the 1930s or earlier ones.

The development of the British economy under the Thatcher government was completely misjudged by the Keynesians, as *The Economist* observed: "When the government raised taxes and cut public borrowing in the 1981 budget, 364 academic economists" issued a manifesto predicting dire consequences. "Shortly thereafter recovery began," and the economy is still growing at a healthy pace, despite the fact that the government has continued to shrink public sector borrowing (*Economist* 1984:13).[11]

The Traditional Conservative, or Classical, Position

What I call the traditional conservative, or classical, view concurs with the basic tenets of the monetarist–rational expectations theory concerning the role of monetary policy, fiscal policy, and expectations, including the rejection of a permanent tradeoff between unemployment and inflation as outlined above.[12] The traditional conservative view stresses, however, the importance of growing wage and price rigidity caused by labor unions and other pressure groups, aided and abetted by government policies—institutional rigidities—which are downplayed by the monetarist and rational expectations school. Members of the school (monetarists for short) usually use models that assume perfect competition—in other words, instantaneously or at least rapidly clearing markets. For many problems, especially those concerning long-run adjustment, these models give an acceptable approximation. A satisfactory solution of the problems of unemployment and stagflation is not possible, however, if we presuppose perfectly competitive markets. In fact, persistent unemployment and extended periods of stagflation are inconsistent with perfect competition. Unemployed workers would compete for jobs; thus wages would decline relative to prices, and full employment would be restored.

An instructive contrast in policy that strikingly illustrates the importance of wage control is provided by the New Deal in the United States and Nazi Germany. Roosevelt and Hitler came to power at about the same time fifty-two years ago. Each man found his country in deep depression and immediately undertook expansionary measures.[13] Economic recovery in the United States, although long and pronounced, was (as we have seen) marred by rising prices, which led to the interruption of the upswing, long before full employment had been reached, by the very vicious though brief depression of 1937–38. The German recovery, on the

other hand, proceeded without interruption, and Germany reached substantially full employment within two or three years. Even more important, the price level in Germany remained remarkably stable for several
years.

It would be tempting to attribute the rapidity of the German recovery
as compared with the U.S. recovery to massive expenditures on arma-
ment. Heavy public spending there was indeed, but massive rearmament
came only later. Possibly German public spending was comparatively
larger than the American, but this difference would not explain the
different price performances. The basic difference between the American and German recovery policies lies elsewhere: the New Deal combined spending with deliberate price and wage boosting. As a consequence, an exceptionally large part of the rising nominal GNP in the
United States took the form of higher prices rather than larger output and
employment. Full employment was reached only after the outbreak of
the war in Europe when defense spending soared—a dismal failure
indeed. In Germany, by contrast, money wage rates remained fairly
stable, although average annual earnings of labor rose rapidly in monetary and real terms, along with rising output and employment, because
unemployment disappeared and the work week lengthened.

We might object that price controls and rationing make real wage
figures under the Nazi regime meaningless. True, there were wage and
price controls right from the beginning of the Nazi dictatorship; and
later—say from 1936 on, when the rearmament boom came into full
stride—scarcities, unavailabilities, and the deterioration in quality of
certain commodities made the official cost-of-living index increasingly
unreliable. Fortunately we have the careful study by Bry and Boschan
(1960). Bry makes adjustments in the cost-of-living index to take the
controls into account. His figures show that, from about 1937 on, the
official index understates the true rise in the cost of living. For the earlier
years (1933–37), however, the corrections are minimal. There can, then,
be no doubt about the great economic success of the Hitler regime. It is
no exaggeration to speak of a German economic miracle.[14]

The present situation in all industrial countries is that the rise of
powerful labor unions and other pressure groups, aided and abetted by
government policies—minimum-wage laws, generous unemployment
benefits, welfare payments—have made wages and many prices rigid
downward. Before I go into detail, I must say a few words about the
concept of unemployment and full employment.

For two reasons full employment clearly does not mean that unemployment is zero or near zero. First, the measured unemployment always
contains some spurious "voluntary" unemployment, that is, workers who

do not care to work at the ruling wage for the type of work that they are qualified to do (although they may work at a higher wage) but who are somehow counted as unemployed and who receive unemployment benefits. Voluntary unemployment has plainly become an important factor since the advent of generous unemployment benefits and welfare payments.

Second, there is "frictional" unemployment, or workers "between jobs," in Keynes's felicitous phrase. Workers who have lost their jobs or wish to change their employment usually take their time to find a suitable new position. Again, generous support for unemployeds plainly leads to an increase in frictional unemployment because workers can afford to take more time to look for a new job.

The same reasoning applies to the so-called structural unemployment, which can be described as fricitional unemployment writ large—dislocation and layoffs caused by large structural changes in the economy, for example when horses are replaced by tractors or when cheap imports take the place of comparatively expensive home production. (I shall have more to say about structural unemployment below.)

The difference between frictional and structural unemployment is one of degree, and the magnitude of voluntary, frictional, and structural unemployment can only be guessed. Our guesses take the form of statements that at present in the United States 6 percent unemployment would be compatible with full employment.

Measured unemployment minus voluntary, frictional, and structural unemployment is what Keynes called "involuntary unemployment."[15] The concept and Keynes's definition of it have given rise to much controversy. The commonsense definition is this: a man is involuntarily unemployed if he is not working but is seeking work and is willing to work at the ruling wage and working condition for the type of work for which he is qualified.[16] Such a definition guides the compilers of unemployment statistics, who must be on their guard to keep voluntary unemployment out of their figures.

The main causes of unemployment are fairly clear. Wages have always been sticky. They were sticky even before labor unions became as powerful as they are now and before the modern welfare state with generous unemployment benefits and welfare payments came into existence in the Great Depression of the 1930s. Labor markets have never been, and in the nature of the case cannot be, perfectly competitive auction markets. For this reason there was much unemployment in earlier depressions, even before unions reached their present level of power, even when the modern welfare state did not exist. There can be no doubt, however, that the stickiness of wages has greatly increased since the Great Depression.

I shall first mention two striking examples of this trend. In the United States and some other industrial countries, legal minimum-wage laws have caused heavy unemployment among teenagers, as much as 40 percent among blacks. Second, in the U.S. steel and automobile industries, although unions have made some concessions, wages are still more than 50 percent higher than the average in U.S. manufacturing industries, despite the fact that unemployment in these two industries is very high because of foreign competition.

The growing rigidity of wages and the resulting unresponsiveness of wages and of prices to the decline in economic activity during recessions have been widely discussed in the literature. I cite two papers that I found especially important, Cagan (1975) and Sachs (1980; this paper has extensive references to the literature). See also Price (1982) and Sachs's reply (Sachs 1982). Phillip Cagan concludes that "wholesale prices show a smaller decline in the recessions after 1948–49 than formerly" and that "there has clearly been a gradual decline in price response to recessions over the postwar period, except mainly for raw materials prices" (1975:54–55). Sachs uses two methods to demonstrate the decreasing responsiveness of inflation to changes in aggregate demand, with special emphasis on wage behavior. The first approach follows Cagan's method and leads to the same conclusion for a longer period. A striking finding is that "for mild contractions, downward price flexibility seems to have ended with the pre–World War II period. For moderate and severe contractions, similarly, the response of wages and prices has fallen significantly since 1950" (1980:81).

The second approach is described as an econometric Phillips curve estimation. The result that the short-run Phillips curve has become steeper strongly supports the hypothesis of decreasing responsiveness of wages to declines in economic activity. The causes of this development are fairly obvious. The spread of unionization and the increased strength of labor unions, which is largely traceable to the New Deal legislation of the 1930s, is surely basic. Union wages are notoriously stickier than nonunion wages; their even greater stickiness on the upside of the cycle is far more than counterbalanced by the rapid lengthening of union contracts providing hefty wage increases for each year. The overlapping and leapfrogging of union wage contracts in the United States have greatly exacerbated the wage inflation caused by unions (see Taylor 1982 and the specialized literature that he quotes). In other industrial and industrializing countries, too, the power of labor unions has sharply increased, and so have wage push and what J. R. Hicks calls "real wage resistance." Naturally the pattern and force of this development vary from country to country, depending on the structure of the economy, the history of the labor movement, and labor's alliance in many countries with political, mainly socialist, parties.

Without going into too great detail, I should mention that in most European countries a much larger percentage of the labor force is unionized than in the United States and that in some countries—Austria and Sweden, for example—central organizations represent labor as a whole and allow it to speak with one voice. Whether strong centralized organizations representing most or all of labor increase or decrease the dangers of inflationary wage push, compared with the U.S. decentralized system of essentially independent unions, is difficult to say. On the one hand centralized organizations increase the power of unions and their political clout. On the other hand, however, such organizations eliminate leapfrogging, and the leaders of an all-embracing organization of labor may perhaps be assumed to be more responsible, more aware of the general good of the population as a whole, than the bosses of independent unions.

International comparisons could throw some light on these questions. I must confine myself, however, to two remarks. International comparisons are complicated by the fact that union power depends also on the structure of the economy. It is well known, for example, that unions are more moderate in small countries, where competition from world markets is strong because foreign trade plays a much greater role than in large countries. Second, Japan is a special case that merits close attention. Wages of workers are much more flexible in Japan than in Europe and the United States because Japanese workers receive a large part of their earnings in the form of a bonus that varies in size with the level of profits. In recessions, when profits are low, wages and the cost of labor thus automatically decline. For this reason and others, unemployment is lower in Japan, and the Japanese economy rebounds more quickly from recessions than do the economies of most other industrial countries.

A few remarks should be made about recent developments in the United States as compared with the situation in Europe. In the last U.S. recession, which came to an end in November 1982, wages became more responsive to unemployment and slack than was expected. Partly for this reason, inflationary pressures until now have remained comparatively mild during the vigorous cyclical recovery that started in December 1982 and is still going strong. It is very doubtful, however, that there has been a basic change. The dilemma of stagflation has not disappeared, and inflation will probably accelerate as the expansion continues.

The contrast between the United States and Europe, however, is remarkable. The European economic picture is much less bright: the recovery from the recession started later and is slower than in the United States, unemployment is higher, and there is more inflation in most

European countries than in the United States. What accounts for this difference? The basic structural reasons have been very well described by Stephen Marris, the former chief economic adviser of the Organisation of Economic Co-operation and Development (OECD; Marris 1984). I quote some salient facts as presented by Marris:

> European economies are in important respects less flexible than the American economy. . . . European workers are generally better protected against economic misfortune than their American counterparts. Collective agreements and government regulations give them more job security. But this makes it more difficult and expensive for European employers to lay off workers when demand weakens. And, they are more reluctant to take on new workers when demand picks up, preferring instead to work overtime. Provisions for unemployment are also more generous in Europe. Laid-off workers have more time to look around for a new job. But, by the same token, this slows down the movement of labor from declining to expanding industries.
>
> Labor mobility is also inhibited in Europe by the greater rigidity of the *relative* wage structure between industries, occupations, and regions. It is more difficult for employers in expanding industries to bid up wages to attract labor, or for laid-off workers in declining industries to bid down wages to get their jobs back. . . .
>
> The main culprit is the downward rigidity of real wages, coupled with the high taxes. . . . Europeans have been reluctant to swallow the rapid rise in taxation needed to finance the very rapid rise in public expenditure. Between 1960 and 1983 the ratio of general government expenditure to gross national product (GNP) in the European Community rose from 32 percent to 52 percent. . . .
>
> In America the overall burden of taxation is lower, and real incomes seem to have adjusted more flexibly to the shocks of the 1970s. 20 million new jobs have been created in America since 1973. . . . Against this, there was a net *loss* of around 2.5 million jobs in the European Community over the same period. Compared with Europeans, Americans coming into the labor force have been more willing to accept whatever level of real wages was necessary to induce employers to hire them; in other words, to "price themselves" into jobs. [Marris 1984:14–15.]

To Marris's list of European handicaps I would add the following: the U.S. economy enjoys the tremendous advantage of a large free trade area and of private competitive enterprise in the fields of transportation, communications, and electric power. The European Common Market is supposed to have established free trade among the members of the

European Community (EC). There still exist many impediments to the free movement of commodities, however. Customs formalities and inspection at the borders are still in place. Even more important, European countries are burdened in various degrees by the existence of national public monopolies in the areas of transportation, communications, and electric power. These public monopolies suffer to a varying extent from bureaucratic inefficiencies and are impervious to international competition. In addition, numerous nationalized industries suffer from the same handicaps. As we shall see presently, monopolies, private or public, also greatly strengthen the power of labor unions, making wages rigid and adding to the wage push.

Another inflationary factor in all industrial countries, and one that derives its importance partly from the existence of powerful unions, is the rise of Keynesianism and the resulting emphasis on antidepression and antirecession policy. Keynesianism has had a double inflationary effect: it has reduced the price decline in the downswing of the business cycle and has stiffened the resistance of workers and their unions to wage cuts because they assume that unemployment caused by large wage boosts will not last long—in other words, that government policy will bail them out if they cause unemployment by excessive wage demands.

It is now widely recognized that wage rigidity, real wage resistance, and real wage push are the most serious impediments for regaining price stability at high levels of employment and higher growth rates. In recent years more and more economists have come to the conclusion that a decisive and lasting recovery from the world recession requires a reduction of the level of real wages and a substantial increase in profits to stimulate investment and growth. This solution implies a moderate decline in the share of wages in GNP; "wages," of course, include salaries.

Statements about the adverse effect of wage rigidity and real wage resistance apply also to other incomes or prices that have been made rigid by government action ranging from farm supports to social benefits of various kinds. I cite a few examples of the trend in thinking about wages. Two years ago, a group of prominent German economists, including several of monetarist persuasion, issued a statement urging a temporary wage freeze to let productivity growth catch up with the wage level and to permit a little inflation to bring down real wages. The plea was not heeded; wages continued to rise, and unemployment has reached the two-digit level. Herbert Giersch, an author with monetarist leanings, has argued in several important articles (1982, 1983) that all industrial countries suffer from excessively high real wages and too low profits. He thinks it will take several years to bring the necessary adjustment in the income distribution.

The theme has been taken up by *The Economist* (London) in two important articles (1982*a*, 1982*b*). *The Economist* asks for a substantial cut in *money* wages to bring about an increase in profits for the purpose of stimulating investment, growth, and employment. Predictably, this call has shocked many of *The Economist*'s Keynesian readers.[17]

The main argument against cutting money wages as a recovery measure is that it reduces total spending by reducing money income of labor and thus is a deflationary factor that intensifies the recession. This argument is fallacious, however, and rests on a misunderstanding of the aim of a wage cut. The purpose is not to reduce effective demand (nominal GNP); if such a reduction is necessary, it should be done by monetary-fiscal measures. The purpose of cutting money wages is to boost profits and stimulate investment, employment, and growth by making labor more competitive with robots and other machines—in other words, with capital. If hourly wage rates are cut by 10 percent, the wage bill and spending power of labor will not necessarily be reduced. If the elasticity of demand for labor is greater than unity (as it almost certainly is in the medium run), employment will rise by more than 10 percent, and so will the wage bill and spending. True, if employment rises by less than 10 percent, labor incomes will decline, but total incomes and spending will not necessarily decline as well. A shift to profits will stimulate investment, employment, and growth. This tendency could be assisted by monetary expansion, for the reduction of unit labor cost would reduce the inflationary danger of easier money.

These three statements of the problem share the assumption that, if a moderate cut in the wage level is achieved, and macroeconomic levers are set right, market forces will, in due course, bring about the necessary restructuring of the economy to achieve substantially full employment. *The Economist* (1982*a*) voices that assumption very clearly. It argues that entrepreneurs would find hundreds of ways of substituting labor for capital if labor costs were reduced, just as entrepreneurs found ways to substitute capital for labor when wages went up.

The Economist's optimistic conclusion will be challenged by structuralists. In the 1930s it was widely believed that part of the unemployment problem was that labor-saving inventions had reduced the demand for labor or that the "structure of production" had been distorted in some other way. In other words, it was argued that a large part of unemployment was "technological" and "structural," requiring large-scale reallocation of factors of production, a time-consuming, painful process. There can be no doubt that subsequent developments were entirely at variance with the structuralist theory. Experience showed that as soon as deflation was stopped, the huge structural distortions that had been diagnosed by theorists during the depression shriveled as quickly as they had surfaced earlier. Monetary contraction, sometimes called "secondary deflation," proved to be a much more important cause of high unemployment than structural distortions, which may have triggered the deflationary spiral. In other words, the great bulk of unemployment was "Keynesian," or monetarist, if you like, not structural, or "Hayekian."

Extreme structuralist views can be heard again today. It has been said that robots and other "smart" machines have put human labor in the position that horses were in when tractors came into wide use. This analogy is, however, very misleading. Tractors replaced not only horsepower but also manpower. Unlike horses, however, human labor could be shifted to producing tractors.

I do not deny that technological progress may possibly require reallocations of factors of production that may cause some structural unemployment until the transfer and retraining of labor have been carried out. As we have seen, a modest decline of the share of labor in the national product is probably required at the present time. It is most unlikely, however, that a large reduction of the marginal productivity of labor, an intolerable drop in real wages, and a massive decline of the share of labor (and salaries) would occur, as the analogy with the horses suggests. As far as we can tell, the share of labor in the national product has remained remarkably stable over the long pull—apart from cyclical fluctuations—despite the tremendous technological changes, including mechanization and automation, that have occurred since the industrial revolution in England.

Nowadays we hear gloomy forecasts of the disaster that will befall us unless radical reforms are undertaken that involve massive redistribution of income to spread work. I believe that these forecasts will prove to have been totally unfounded and will share the fate of earlier, similarly gloomy prophecies regularly made in periods of depression, beginning with those underlying the Luddite movement in the early nineteenth century and extending to the most famous one, Karl Marx's theory regarding the increasing misery of the working classes—prophecies that were completely disproved and discredited by subsequent developments.

The Slowdown of Productivity and GNP Growth since 1970

We have seen that two developments account for the change in outlook from optimism and euphoria in the 1950s and 1960s to pessimism and gloom in the 1970s and 1980s, first, the severity and inflationary character of the last two recessions and, second, the slowdown of productivity growth in all industrial countries since 1970.

It was suggested that the comparative severity of the recent recession can be attributed to the fact that all industrial countries were forced, after an extended period of inflationary abuse, to curb inflation by monetary restraint. It is simply impossible to stop an entrenched inflation without creating considerable transitional unemployment. The slowdown of productivity growth is a much more elusive problem and indeed an exceedingly complex one. Many different explanations have been offered, and a combination of factors is doubtless responsible.[18]

There are two connections between the two developments. The rising tide of world inflation, which started in the middle 1960s and led to the inflationary recessions of the 1970s and 1980s, was probably a major cause of the slowdown of productivity growth, which in turn reinforced inflation. Persistent inflation, especially the vicious form of stagflation, does not offer a healthy climate for the investment by innovating entrepreneurs on which long-run productivity growth depends. Second, the "adjustment," or "supply-oriented," policies that have been recommended by many experts to ease the pains of disinflation—that is, measures designed to bring the economy closer to the competitive ideal by attacking and eliminating monopolistic restrictions in labor and commodity markets—are surely also required to speed up long-run productivity growth.

In the extensive literature on the slowdown of the world economy, many other causal factors have been mentioned. A favorite among policymakers is the two oil shocks of 1973 and 1979, for which policymakers cannot be held responsible. The oil price rise is supposed to have been largely responsible for inflation as well as for the slowdown. We have seen above, however, that the importance of the oil shock for inflation has been greatly exaggerated. True, the oil price rise was a burden on the importing countries, but it was not a very heavy one. For the United States, for example, the quadrupling of the oil price in 1973 caused an increase in the annual oil import bill of about $20 billion, or 1.2 percent of GNP. (For other countries that depend more heavily on imports the burden was, of course, greater, but for no country was it crushing.) It follows that a once-for-all reduction of real incomes by 1.2 percent would have eliminated the problem. In an ideal, fully competitive economy, a once-for-all decline in money wages (incomes) would solve the problem at a stable price level. Alternatively, if we assume wage rigidity, a once-for-all increase in the price level by 1.2 percentage points, not a matter of great importance in a period of two-digit inflation, would solve the problem.

Only indirectly, via perverse reactions of the economy and of economic policy, is it possible to make the oil price rise responsible for continuing inflation, for example, if there is widespread formal or de facto indexation of wages and other incomes. In other words, if labor unions and other pressure groups resist the reduction of their real income by pressing for money wage increases, there is bound to be trouble. If the monetary authorities stand firm, the consequence will be unemployment; if they try to prevent unemployment by expansionary ("Keynesian") policy, an inflationary spiral will be started.

The oil price rise, or more broadly the rise in energy prices triggered by the Organization of Petroleum Exporting Countries (OPEC) is also widely regarded as one of the factors that have slowed down productivity growth. I believe that the argument put forward with respect to inflation also applies to productivity growth: only indirectly via adverse economic and economic policy reactions can the rise in energy prices cause a slowdown of productivity growth. If the economy adjusts promptly to the oil levy imposed by OPEC, that is to say, if real incomes are reduced by 1.2 percent, it is difficult to see why productivity growth should not resume, starting from the lower level. The proponents of the theory cite microeconomic reaction as the cause of the slowdown of productivity growth, to wit, a shift from "energy intensive methods." There have been such shifts, of course; large, fuel-inefficient automobiles have been replaced by small, fuel-efficient ones, and producers everywhere have found hundreds of ways to conserve energy. True, these shifts usually require investments. But I cannot see why the adjustment of economic agents to changes in relative prices, in a way that minimizes the impact of the OPEC oil levy on overall output and basic needs, should lead to a slowdown of productivity growth. Unfavorable indirect adverse effects on productivity growth through real wage resistance leading to unemployment and inflation, however, are possible and even likely.

I believe the same analysis applies to several other factors that are usually mentioned as causes for the slowdown, for example: "Governmental controls have required the diversion of a growing share of the labor and capital employed by business to pollution abatement and to the protection of employee safety and health. Also, rising crime has forced business to divert resources to crime prevention, and thefts of merchandize have directly reduced measured output" (Denison 1979:75). The impact of these changes on output is negative, but if the economy adjusts promptly to the increased costs of regulatory compliance and crime prevention by accepting the unavoidable reduction of wages and other incomes, there is no reason why productivity and output growth should not resume from the lower level. Again, it is possible that the adjustment may be delayed and dragged out by real wage resistance, causing extensive periods of unemployment and/or inflation. Clearly a string of independent adverse effects could produce a period of stagnant output. It is generally assumed, however, that there is more to the productivity slow-down than a series of exogenous shocks.

Observers have offered several reasons for a permanent or at least long-lasting slowdown in productivity growth. To begin with, a decline in the number of new inventions and discoveries has been postulated; in other words, it has been suggested that technical progress has slowed down. The evidence cited is a decrease in the quantity of new patents granted by the patent offices of the United States and other countries. As Martin N. Baily (1983) notes, however, this evidence is far from convincing. Moreover, in the 1930s, we may recall, the theory of secular stagnation was based partly on the assumption that technological progress had sharply slowed. Subsequent developments have emphatically disproved that theory.

Much more plausible is the theory that the rate of savings and investment has been sharply reduced by government policies. The main culprit is tax disincentives for savings and investments. Specifically, high marginal tax rates blunt the incentives both to save and to invest. Inflation exacerbates the disincentive effects of the income tax by pushing taxpayers into higher tax brackets. Indexation of the income tax would stop the process. Suffice it to say, quoting John Kendrick's excellent discussion, that "the U.S. tax system is biased against capital formation—more so than is true of most other industrial countries, which have significantly higher ratios than the United States of gross saving and investment in GNP" (Kendrick 1979:53). The tax reform of 1980 should go a long way to correct the bias. There is a danger, however, that the fruits of the tax reform will be squandered by the huge budget deficits that have been allowed to develop.

Another reason for a protracted slowdown of productivity growth is said to be an erosion of "work effort." Generous welfare payments, unemployment benefits, and other social welfare measures make it difficult for employers to enforce work disciplne, the argument goes; the threat of losing a job is no longer a strong spur to hard work. There is surely some truth in this statement, but it is hard to evaluate. The fact that labor unions have been weakened in the recent recession and that the wage push has abated much more than was expected would seem to weaken the force of the argument.

In this connection Mancur Olson's well-known theory (Olson 1982) of the arteriosclerotic and arthritic afflictions of "aging" societies should be mentioned. The rise of what Olson calls "distributional coalitions" (vested interests and pressure groups) tends to make modern economies more and more rigid and inflexible. The process of rigidification can be halted, however, and is often reversed by defeat in war or by revolutions that dissolve groups of vested interests. The two German economic miracles, one under Hitler (which I mentioned above) and the spectacular expansion after World War II, are striking examples.

It is extremely difficult to determine the comparative strength of the various forces and tendencies, to describe how they interact, and to say what the chances are that the slowdown will soon reverse itself (see Kendrick 1984; Kendrick gives reasons for assuming that the productivity growth in the United States will accelerate). Fortunately it is possible to indicate with confidence which policies would speed up productivity growth *without precisely evaluating the force of the different possible causes of the slowdown*. The supply-oriented adjustment policies outlined earlier would certainly be conducive to stimulating growth. Attacks on monopolies and restrictive practices in labor and commodity markets, the elimination of barriers to external and internal trade, and the deregulation of industry would go a long way toward stimulating growth. It is vitally important to avoid large budget deficits in order to bring down interest rates and to make capital available for productive private investment, including outlays on research and development. If taxes must be raised to reduce deficits, then consumption taxes should be raised rather than income taxes, for high marginal tax rates that impede savings and investment are poison for productivity growth. Most obviously.

The International Monetary System in the Postwar Period

World trade has grown by leaps and bounds since World War II, with only small declines in recession years.[19] This situation sharply contrasts with trends in the 1930s. The main reason, of course, is that there was no depression in the postwar period. In addition, the international monetary system of the postwar era was an enormous improvement over that of the interwar period. The restoration of the gold standard after World War I was badly mismanaged; for example, the British pound was overvalued and the French franc undervalued. The misalignment of exchange rates put a heavy strain on the world economy. Under the gold standard there existed no mechanism for orderly changes in exchange rates.

The rigidity of exchange rates under the gold standard had catastrophic consequences when the depression struck in 1929. The slow-motion depreciation of all currencies in terms of gold—the British pound in 1931, the dollar in 1933–34, the gold bloc currencies in 1936, and so forth—was a sadistic procedure, like cutting a dog's tail piecemeal instead of all at once. The consequence was a protectionist explosion and the imposition of tight exchange control in many countries. Thus world trade shrank by about 30 percent in real terms and 50 percent nominally, the difference reflecting the sharp decline in the price level.

The Bretton Woods regime of "stable but adjustable exchange rates" was a great improvement. It served the world well for twenty-five years by providing an orderly method of changing exchange rates, but it came under increasing stress when world inflation soared after 1965. Stable but adjustable exchange rates cannot function under highly inflationary conditions because it is impossible for sovereign countries to agree on a common inflation rate of, say, 8 percent or more, which would be necessary to operate a fixed-rate system in an inflationary environment.

Since the final breakdown of Bretton Woods in 1973, the international monetary system, or nonsystem, as some experts like to call it, has been one of widespread managed floating. All major currencies and many others float, but some thirty-six currencies are pegged to the dollar, with others pegged to the French franc or to some other currency, and the eight members of the European Monetary System maintain a precarious stability in their exchange rates.

Floating has again come under criticism. Floating has, it is said, exacerbated, if not caused, world inflation and has led to excessive volatility of exchange rates and misalignments of exchange rates, the alleged overvaluation of the dollar in recent years being the prime example. Few critics recommend a return to Bretton Woods or to the gold standard. More often recommended is more vigorous intervention by central banks in the foreign exchange markets, international cooperation to set "target zones" for exchange rates, and international coordination of macropolicies.

To say flatly that floating was responsible for world inflation confuses cause with effect. Inflation forced floating on reluctant policymakers. In particular, the rising inflation in the United States after 1965 sounded the death knell for Bretton Woods, because the three strong currency countries, Japan, West Germany, and Switzerland, and some other countries, after costly efforts to prop up the dollar by massive interventions in the foreign exchange market, recognized that they would have to accept an intolerable inflation if they continued to keep their exchange rate with the dollar stable. Thus in 1973 all major currencies began to float. Floating was legalized by the second amendment to the IMF Articles of Agreement 19.

It has been argued that floating ratchets up prices worldwide. Whenever there is a change in exchange rates, prices rise in the countries whose currencies have depreciated but fail to decline in the appreciating countries. This theory overlooks the fact that the prices of imports automatically decline in the appreciating countries. The theory is also inconsistent with the facts that in the 1970s floating shielded the strong currency countries from U.S. inflation and that the strong dollar in the 1980s has been a potent antiinflationary factor in the United States.

Let us consider the alleged malfunctioning of floating, starting with the alleged overvaluation of the dollar. The rise of the dollar since 1980 has indeed been dramatic. From January 1981 to January 1985 the dollar has risen about 53 percent in trade weighted terms, 26 percent against the yen, 58 percent against the German mark, and 46 percent against the Swiss franc.

This appreciation is said to have had most serious effects on the U.S. economy as well as on the economies of other countries. Quoting American sources *The Economist* writes: "American business has been priced out of markets both at home and abroad by the strong dollar; its costs are about 28 percent less competitive than they were in 1979. As a result, America's real gross national product was reduced by about 2¼ percent between 1980 and early 1983 compared with what would have happened without an overvalued dollar, and more than one million jobs were lost (1983:9).

This analysis is seriously flawed. True, the strong dollar and the large trade deficits have been depressive factors, but they are also potent antiinflationary factors, an aspect that the argument fails to take into account. If the dollar had not gone up, for example because investors had lacked confidence in the U.S. economic policy, inflation would have been much worse. If we assume, as we must, that inflation had to be brought down, the Federal Reserve Board would have had to tighten money. Thus the recession would have been about the same, although the impact on industries producing traded and nontraded goods would have been a little different. Alternatively, if the Federal Reserve Board had intervened massively in the foreign exchange market to prevent the dollar from rising, a measure that some critics of floating urged, it would have undercut the antiinflation policy, a consequence that would obviously not have been acceptable.[20]

The unexpectedly vigorous recovery of the U.S. economy since December 1983, despite large trade deficits and the strong dollar, has undermined the theory that the strong dollar produces a dismal effect. Although the speed of the expansion has been slowed down by the strong dollar to a more sustainable level, the length of the upswing has been increased, thus creating more jobs.

It is true that the strong dollar has inflationary effects on other countries and forces them to tighten money and to raise interest rates. The dollar has remained strong longer than anybody expected. In fact, it has gone higher and higher, despite repeated attempts by central banks to hold it down by substantial interventions in the foreign exchange market. Since Stephen Marris (1983) raised the specter of an impending "collapse" of the dollar in his article "Crisis Ahead for the Dollar," however, a chorus of voices has been heard predicting that the dollar will plunge from its present height, with disastrous consequences for the United States and the rest of the world. The argument has become familiar by now. The United States cannot go on indefinitely running large current account deficits and importing capital. Sooner or later "the nerves of foreign investors will crack," and there will be a stampede out of the dollar.

To speak of an impending collapse of the dollar seems a bit melodramatic. I agree, however, that sooner or later the dollar will decline and that a sharp reversal cannot be excluded if the huge budget deficits continue. I submit, however, that if the retreat became a rout, it is inconceivable that the IMF and central banks would stand idly by and let the dollar plunge. They would organize a dollar rescue operation, as they did in 1978. The markets probably understand this point, although the doomsayers of the dollar do not. There is, therefore, a good chance that there will be no collapse of the dollar—in other words, that there will be a soft landing rather than a crash landing.

This is not, however, the end of the story. Suppose that huge budget deficits continue, that capital imports and the trade deficit shrink, and that the dollar declines in a more or less orderly fashion. In such a case U.S. interest rates would go up and government borrowing would crowd out private investment. The consequence would be either a recession if the Federal Reserve Board stands firm or, if the monetary policy is lax, inflation followed later by a more serious recession.

It is, therefore, of the utmost importance for the budget deficits to be reduced gradually. If they were, more savings would be available for productive private investment, offsetting the decline of capital inflow from abroad. Thus a smooth transition is conceivable. In practice, of course, things may not work out so smoothly even if the macroeconomic levers, budget deficits, and monetary policy are set correctly. We cannot assume that fine tuning will be completely successful. After all, the business cycle is still alive.

I would argue, however, that a mild recession is not a calamity. There is, I believe, fairly general agreement that various interrelated developments account for the strong dollar. The vigorous cyclical recovery of the U.S. economy and the huge budget deficits have pushed up interest rates, which pull in capital from abroad, thus financing the large trade and

current account deficits. The pull is strengthened by the apparent economic and political stability of the United States, in contrast with the
economic sluggishness in Europe and with unsettled political conditions
in other parts of the world, which have made the United States again a
safe haven for foreign investors (also see Haberler 1985a and 1985b).[21]

Whatever the precise relationship between these factors and their
relative strength, one thing is certain. Under fixed exchanges, foreign
countries would have been put under intense deflationary pressure; much
more foreign capital would have been attracted than under floating rates
(because there would be no exchange risk). Thus foreign countries would
have suffered large losses of international reserves, forcing them to
tighten money and raise interest rates.

For many countries, especially for developing countries, the large U.S.
trade deficit, the strong dollar, and the vigorous recovery of the U.S.
economy from the recession have been a great boon. The U.S. economy
has been a powerful locomotive, pulling the world economy out of the
recession.

I conclude that the system of floating exchange rates has worked quite
well, but I do agree with the critics of floating that the ideal international
monetary system would use fixed exchange rates—provided that all
participating countries maintained monetary discipline and that wage and
price flexibility was such as to prevent any country from enduring excessive unemployment because of the balance of payments. These conditions were roughly fulfilled during the heyday of the gold standard, but
they are surely not being met in the present-day world. There are exceptions to the rule. Small countries that peg their currency to that of a
dominant trade partner must, and in fact do, adjust their macropolicies to
that of the country to whose currency they peg. I would argue, however,
that the EMS is no exception. Its members have not been able to coordinate their policies sufficiently to prevent frequent misalignment of exchange rates, which causes destabilizing capital flows, and some members
of the groups (especially France) have been forced to maintain tight
exchange control.

The question remains as to whether the performance of the floating
system can be improved by skillful intervention in the foreign exchange
market, by "official forecasts," or by "target zones" for exchange rates
and similar devices (see Williamson 1983 for a good discussion of such
devices that reaches different conclusions). I must confine myself to
saying that I am skeptical because I do not believe, as the proponents of
such devices assume, that the authorities are in a position to identify
equilibrium exchange rates. My skepticism is fortified by the widespread

misconceptions regarding the working of the floating system that I have detailed above.

Policy Implications

We have seen that the global recession, the severest in the post–World War II period, from which the world economy is emerging at the present time, came about because the major industrial countries, led by the United States, were forced to step on the monetary brake after many years of inflationary abuse. It is simply impossible to wind down an entrenched inflation without creating transitional unemployment—in other words, without a more or less serious recession.

The recession in the United States and in the world has been widely misinterpreted, by economists as well as by noneconomists, as something much more serious than a reaction to disinflation. Grandiose schemes of coordinated global reflation to "save the world economy" have been proposed by well-known statesmen and economists, not to mention the shrill voices demanding a "new economic order" and massive "resource transfers" from North to South. The vigorous recovery of the U.S. economy (despite the "overvalued" dollar and the large U.S. trade deficit) and the emergence of the world economy from the recession that seems to have been sparked by the U.S. recovery contradict all the pessimistic forecasts.

We have also seen that monetarists are undoubtedly right when they say that inflation, including stagflation, is a monetary phenomenon in the sense that it cannot be stopped without monetary restraints—a reduction of monetary growth. Monetary restraint is not only a necessary condition to bring down inflation but also a sufficient condition in the sense that sufficient monetary restraint can bring down inflation, irrespective of union strength, cost-raising policies of the government, and the size of the government budget deficit.

Despite large budget deficits it is possible to stop inflation by tight money. If the deficits exceed a certain limit, however, the side effects make it politically harder and economically costlier, if not impossible, to stop inflation. Large deficits drive up interest rates and crowd out productive private investment. The political pressure on the central bank to bring down interest rates by expansionary measures is bound to increase sharply. Moreover, the rate of growth of real GNP will decline if and when productive private investment is reduced. As a consequence, a larger reduction in monetary growth will be required to achieve price stability.

The policy conclusion is straightforward: for best results monetary policy should be supplemented and assisted by an appropriately tight fiscal policy, as monetarists themselves have often recommended.

How about incomes policy? We have seen that Keynesians and some non-Keynesians often recommend that demand management should be supplemented by incomes policy to prevent labor monopolies (unions) and business monopolies from driving up wages and prices. The trouble is that "incomes policy" means different things to different people. It is often interpreted as denoting more or less comprehensive wage and price controls. In that form incomes policy must be rejected. Wage and price controls are too crude; they deal only with symptoms, distort the economy, and have never worked. This negative judgment also applies to TIP, which substitutes tax incentives and deterrents for absolute controls. TIP would be an administrative nightmare; for that reason it has never been tried. Similarly, wage and price freezes have been tried but never with success.

It should be admitted, however, that proponents of incomes policy have a point when they say that the policy of disinflation will have a better chance of succeeding if excessive wage increases can be prevented. I myself have distinguished between Incomes Policy I, and Incomes Policy II. The former I define as more or less comprehensive wage and price controls (including TIP and wage and price freezes); the latter is a bundle of measures designed to move the economy closer to the competitive ideal.

Before indicating the kind of measures that would bring about this situation, let me mention that the general approach sails under different flags. In Europe, for example, it is often called "supply-oriented economic policy." This policy is largely the same as my Incomes Policy II, a bundle of measures designed to make the economy more flexible and efficient by breaking down impediments to competition in commodity and labor markets that would result in increasing supplies all around. Obviously the composition of the bundle of measures must be assumed to change over time and to vary from country to country, depending on the structural problems confronting each country. Supply-oriented policy is a much broader concept than, and must be distinguished from, supply-side economics, which flourishes in the United States but is hardly known in Europe.[22]

Still another label for the same approach is "adjustment policies," a bundle of measures designed to speed up the economy's adjustment to changing conditions. Adjustment policies have been the theme of two important reports, one by the General Agreement on Tariffs and Trade (GATT 1978) and the other by OECD (1983b).

Adjustment policies and supply-oriented policies (or supply-side economics, for that matter) should not be regarded as alternatives or antitheses to "demand-side economics" (demand management). The two are complements, not substitutes. Demand management, furthermore, should not be equated with Keynesianism. It is, after all, the task of monetary policy to keep aggregate demand on an even keel so as to avoid inflationary or deflationary spirals. (This statement is independent of the precise rule, monetarist or not, that monetary policy follows to achieve its goal.)

I shall now cite concrete measures of adjustment or supply-oriented policies. This is, of course, a vast area. I can discuss here only some basic facts and principles. To bring the economy closer to the competitive ideal, we must attack all forms of monopolies and restrictions of trade. It is convenient to consider business or industrial monopolies (including oligopolies and cartels), labor monopolies (labor unions), and the government separately.

Business and labor monopolies have rather different rules of conduct. Both sets of rules, however, restrict supply, keep prices and wages higher than they would be under competition, and slow down productivity growth. In my opinion, labor unions in the present-day world are much more powerful, present a greater danger for price stability and full employment, and are much more difficult to deal with than business monopolies.

Compared with labor unions, private business or industrial monopolies are little of a problem except in the area of public utilities. The most effective antimonopoly policy, which is at the same time easy to carry out from the economic and administrative point of view (although it is not easy politically), is free trade. We have seen enormous growth in world trade, especially in manufactures in the last forty years, great advances in the technology of transportation, communication, and information, and the emergence of new industries in scores of developed and developing countries. Because of this growth, few, if any, monopolies could survive in a free trade world outside the area of public utilities, where prices are under public control anyway.

Free trade policy must, of course, be defined broadly. It would include not only the phasing out of tariffs, import quotas, and exchange control but also the elimination of administrative protectionism, the so-called voluntary restrictions imposed on foreign exporters (often called "orderly marketing agreements," or omas), the takeover of noncompetitive firms by the government, and their operation with great losses at the expense of the taxpayer. A policy along these lines would not require any new government bureaus or larger bureaucracies. On the contrary, it would reduce government activities, shrink the public sector, and lighten the tax burden.

I now come to the problems of the labor market. To begin with, the liberalization of internal and international trade would go a long way to curb the monopoly power of labor unions. Unions know or quickly find out that striking against world markets is risky. For this reason labor unions in small countries where the international sector is a large fraction of the economy are usually much more reasonable and moderate than labor unions in large countries where the international sector is small. This point is strikingly illustrated by two recent developments, although they did not occur in the international arena: the deregulation in the United States of the trucking and airline industries. Until recently the two industries were tightly regulated by two huge federal bureaucracies. The dismantling of the controls is equivalent to the introduction of internal free trade.

Deregulation—free trade—changed the structure of the two industries dramatically. New, largely nonunionized firms (regional airlines) with lower cost and dynamic management sprang up, providing better and much cheaper service to the public. In both cases the power of the unions was sharply reduced. The wage rates and wage costs of the new airlines are much lower than those of the old ones. It is not surprising that the unions are strongly opposed to deregulation. The unions of the airline pilots went so far as to threaten a general strike to force the government to restore tight regulations in order to protect the exorbitant salaries that they had been able to obtain under the earlier system. It is interesting to ask what would have happened if the competition for the established airlines had come from abroad rather than from domestic sources. Surely the resistance to deregulation would have been much stronger.[23]

Finally I mention a few specific measures that would promote efficiency of the labor market, would reduce the monopoly power of labor unions, would increase the overall productivity of labor, and would thus lead to a rise in real wages. Consider minimum-wage laws, for example. They exist in many countries, including France and the United States. Legal minimum wages serve no useful purpose. On the contrary, it has been shown conclusively that in the United States the legal minimum wage is largely responsible for the shockingly high unemployment (as much as 40 percent) among teenagers, especially blacks. The minimum wage deprives young people of the on-the-job training that is so important to their future careers. Minimum-wage laws should be abolished (see Hashimoto 1981 and Rottenberg 1981).

In the United States the Davis-Bacon Act and similar laws obligate the government to buy only from firms that pay highest union wages. Given the large size of the public sector and the huge volume of government purchases—ranging from paper and pencils to trucks and turbines—these laws add considerably to the monopoly power of unions and to the size of the government budget. Such laws, too, should be abrogated (see Gould and Bittlingmayer 1980).

Now that I have discussed private monopolies of business and labor and what to do about them, I must say a few words about the role of the government. Actually, the government itself is the worst offender. The list of its misdeeds is very long indeed. To begin with, public policy is largely responsible for the power of private monopolies. We have seen that, without protection from imports, few, if any, private monopolies, oligopolies, or cartels would exist outside the public utility area. In fact, in most countries public utilities, postal services, railroads, and telephone and telegraph services are government monopolies. Prices in this area are notoriously rigid, and in many countries these public enterprises operate inefficiently and add substantially to the deficit of the government budget, crowding out productive private investment. We should further mention the enormous burdens of the welfare state and the overregulation of industries that contributes to the tax burden, blunting incentives to work, save, and invest.

When producers are too numerous to organize themselves to cut production and raise prices, the government steps in and does for them what unions do for their members. Farm price support is the most important example although not the only one. In the United States and even more so in the European Community (Common Market), farm price supports have become a heavy burden on the government budget and a source of inflation.

There are thus infinite opportunities for adjustment policies and supply-oriented policies to improve the performance of the economy, to make it more efficient and competitive and to speed up the rate of productivity and GNP growth.

Summary

There should be general agreement that inflation, including stagflation, cannot be curbed without monetary restraint, or a reduction of monetary growth; that inflation must be stopped; that there is no permanent tradeoff between unemployment and inflation; and that the longer inflation lasts, the more inflationary expectations become entrenched, the stronger the tendency of inflation to accelerate, and the harder it becomes to stop inflation. It is true that sufficiently tight money can stop inflation irrespective of large budget deficits and regardless of wage and price pressures exerted by powerful trade unions and other pressure groups.

Monetarists should agree, however, that adverse side effects of large deficits, wage rigidity and wage pressure from powerful labor unions, and similar pressures exerted by other special interest groups will cause much unemployment that will make disinflation politically very difficult, if not impossible. Therefore, monetary tightness should be assisted by fiscal discipline and by what have become known as adjustment, or supply-oriented, policies—that is, measures designed to bring the economy closer to the competitive ideal by attacking all kinds of monopolies and restrictions of trade.

The most effective and administratively easiest antimonopoly policy is external and internal free trade. In a free trade world, there would be hardly any monopolies outside the public utility area. Free trade in commodities would also be a powerful restraint on union power. This point has been strikingly demonstrated by the deregulation of the airline and trucking industries in the United States. The deregulatory policy, which is equivalent to internal free trade in these industries, has dramatically weakened the monopoly of the unions in these industries and has sharply reduced labor cost.

Notes

1. As various writers have explained many times, a distinction must be made between Keynesian economics and the economics of Keynes himself. When he wrote *The General Theory* during the Great Depression, Keynes was concerned, it is true, with deflation, and he recommended deficit spending. Early in 1937, less than a year later, however, he argued in three famous articles published in *The Times* that it was time to switch from fighting deflation to curbing inflation, although at that time unemployment was still above 10 percent and inflation was low by post–World War II standards. Most of Keynes's followers, however, continued to preach expansionary policies.

2. The terminology—"depression" signifying severe cyclical declines and "recession" mild ones—is of modern origin. The words "depression" and "recession" were of course used in the older literature but in a different sense. The distinction between severe and mild cyclical downswings, however, was made in the earlier literature, for example by A. H. Hansen ("major" and "minor cycles") and by Milton Friedman ("mild" and "deep" depression cycles). The difference between depression and recession is one of degree, but it is a fact that most cyclical downswings can unequivocally be classified, with perhaps one or two borderline cases.

3. A distinction must again be made between Keynes and the Keynesians. It is true that Keynes had a nationalistic-protectionist-interventionistic period. During the war, however, when he worked on plans for postwar reconstruction, he returned to his early liberal beliefs. In a famous, posthumously published paper (Keynes 1946), he castigated the views of his

radical followers as "modernist stuff gone wrong and turned silly and sour" (1946:186) and urged that "the classical medicine" be allowed to do its work.

4. It has been argued that the oil price rise in the 1970s should not be regarded as "completely exogenous," that it resulted partly from surging demand on the world oil market generated by rapid economic growth in the industrial countries and, in the later 1970s, in major developing countries as well (letter from Peter B. Clark to Gottfried Haberler). This reasoning is surely true, but it does not affect my argument in the text.

5. Again, we must distinguish between Keynesian economics and the economics of Keynes, but I think it is fair to say that in *The General Theory* wages and prices are assumed to be constant to the point of full employment, although Keynes hints at some qualifications. The assumption is clearly stated and repeated in the first part of *The General Theory*. It should be stressed, however, that in later chapters, especially in chapter 19, "Changes in Money Wages," important qualifications are made to what Samuelson called the "Ur-Keynesian model" (see Samuelson 1983:212).

6. In the German case the stock of money in real terms (especially if it is measured by the foreign exchange rate) *fell* to a small fraction of its normal level. This fact was misinterpreted by influential German economists at that time, who argued that it invalidated the quantity theory of money, according to which the increase in the money supply causes the price rise and the depreciation of the currency. For details see Haberler (1936:57–60).

7. There is evidence that in the current U.S. expansion there has indeed been a moderation of wage demands as described by Fellner. See Cagan and Fellner (1984).

8. There is also a mixed group of dissenters: orthodox supply-siders and orthodox Keynesians. James Tobin (1983) recently hailed the large deficits as the proper "Keynesian" measure (adopted, of course, for the wrong reason) that lifted the economy out of the "depression." He would probably agree, however, that there may be too much of a good thing.

9. Milton Friedman writes: "There is clearly great similarity between the views expressed by Simons and by Keynes—as to the causes of the Great Depression, the impotence of monetary policy, and the need to rely extensively on fiscal policy. Both men placed great emphasis on the state of business expectations and assigned a critical role to the desire for liquidity [on the] 'absolute' liquidity preference under conditions of deep depression. . . . It was this that meant that changes in the quantity of money produced by the monetary authorities would simply be reflected in opposite movements in velocity and have no effect on income or employment" (1966:7). See also Stein (1969, 1983) and Davis (1971).

10. Actually, the figures greatly understate the difference, because present-day unemployment is quite different from that in the 1930s. It contains much frictional and voluntary unemployment, which I shall discuss.

11. It has been argued that, if the figures of public sector borrowing quoted by *The Economist* are replaced by cyclically adjusted figures (OECD 1983a:34), the fiscal restraint appears to have declined sharply in 1982 and to have given way to a mild stimulus in 1983. Actually, the fiscal restraint did not decrease in 1982, but there was indeed a mild fiscal stimulus in 1983. Thus it is still true that the policy of the Thatcher government was and is decidely "unKeynesian" and that the prediction of the 364 economists about the dire consequences of the Thatcher policy have turned out to be quite wrong.

12. I call this view traditional because it reflects, I believe, the outlook of the founders of the Chicago School. My favorite quotation comes from Frank H. Knight: "In a free market these differential changes would be temporary, but even then they might be serious, and with important markets so unfair as they actually are—and wages and prices as sticky . . . —the result takes on the proportion of a social disaster" (Knight 1946:224). Knight wrote with the deflation of the 1930s in mind, but his comments apply also to the

disinflation of our times, and surely the stickiness of wages and prices has greatly increased since he wrote.

13. It is true that the German economy had a head start, for it had turned the corner in August 1932, six months before Hitler came to power. That fact does not, however, vitiate the comparison with the New Deal, because in the first six or seven months the German recovery was slow, and we cannot date the trough of the U.S. depression to 1933 with precision; the depression has been described as "double bottomed," the first bottom having occurred in 1932.

14. On Hitler's economic miracle, see Haffner (1979), described by the reviewer in *The Economist* as "a brief, incisive, adequate account of the monster which leaves no more, worth saying, to be said" (*Economist* 1979:133). Another German miracle is the phenomenal rise of the German economy, starting in 1948, from the ashes of the Hitler regime.

15. Keynes expressly excluded frictional unemployment from his concept of involuntary unemployment (1936:15–16). He does not mention structural unemployment, but it seems to me that it is in the spirit of the Keynesian theory to treat frictional unemployment and structural unemployment in the same way.

16. Keynes's much-quoted definition is: "Men are involuntarily unemployed if in the event of a small rise in the price of wage-goods relative to the money wage, both the aggregate supply of labour willing to work for the current money wage and the aggregate demand for it at that wage would be greater than the existing volume of employment" (1936). This statement is, to my mind, unnecessarily complicated. I am encouraged by the fact that Richard Kahn, Keynes's closest collaborator and disciple, reached the same conclusion (Kahn 1975).

17. For samples of the dissenting letters, see *The Economist* for December 18, 1982. *The Economist* rightly argues that Keynes, if he were alive, would support its position and not that of its Keynesian critics. It is one thing to say, as Keynes did in the 1930s, that a deflationary spiral should be stopped by expansionary measures rather than by wage reduction; it is an entirely different thing to insist in a period of persistent, severe stagflation that the level of money wage rates must not be touched. As I mentioned earlier, one year after the publication of his *General Theory*, Keynes urged a shift in policy to fight inflation. We must distinguish between Keynesian economics and the economics of Keynes.

18. The literature on the subject is enormous. There are the few standard works by Edward Denison and John Kendrick. For reference see Kendrick (1979) and Denison (1979). See also the brief but very illuminating introduction by William Fellner, "The Declining Growth of American Productivity: An Introductory Note," and Mark Perlman, "One Man's Baedeker to Productivity Growth Discussions," both in Fellner (1979b); and Baily (1983).

19. Since this chapter was written in 1983 and 1984 an in-depth analysis of the international monetary system by Morris Goldstein has appeared. See Goldstein (1984) and *IMF Survey* (1985).

20. Furthermore, we cannot counter the above-stated argument by saying that *sterilized* interventions would eliminate the danger of inflation, for there is general agreement that sterilized interventions are ineffective.

21. This situation could change overnight. The imposition of an import surcharge combined with an "interest equalization tax" to restrain capital import, for example, would do the trick. The attraction of the surcharge is that it would deal with the trade and budget deficits at the same time and would be administratively easy to apply provided it was applied across the board. There are two hitches, however. There will surely be exceptions. Canada and some Latin American countries will be exempted. As a consequence, imports from these countries into the United States will soar, but so will imports into these countries from

Japan, Europe, and elsewhere. The result will be a distortion of trade and a reduction in the effectiveness of the surcharge. The other hitch is that retaliation to a surcharge, especially from the European Common Market, will be swift. The interest equalization tax, a tax on interest payments to foreign investors, too, would have distorting and evasive reactions. Such a tax is discriminatory in two ways: it discriminates between interest income on financial assets on the one hand and income on other types of investment on the other hand, such as income from real estate, speculative capital gains, and the like. There would thus be a strong inducement for foreign investors to switch from financial assets to other kinds of investment. The other area of discrimination is between foreign investors and American investors abroad. Foreign investors would be discouraged from exporting capital to the United States. American investors abroad, however, would be encouraged to repatriate some of their money to take advantage of the interest differential caused by the interest equalization tax. Nobody can forecast with certainty the comparative magnitude of these conflicting reactions, and the psychological effect of the whole operation, import surcharge, and interest equalization tax may be very powerful and disturbing, especially because it would highlight the unwillingness to solve the problem of the budget deficits.

22. Let me make my position clear. Supply-siders have a valid point when they say that high taxes, especially high marginal tax rates, have become a drag on incentives to work, to save, and to invest. It is dangerously overoptimistic to assume, however, as supply-siders do, that tax reductions all by themselves will turn the economy around almost overnight and that the resulting increase in output will take care of even large budget deficits. Supply-oriented policy will include, as one element among many others, removal of tax impediments to work, save, and invest.

23. The large size of the U.S. market, which makes possible competition in industries that are subject to increasing returns to scale, is a great national asset. Few other countries enjoy that advantage.

References

Baily, Martin Neil. 1983. *Will productivity growth recover?* Discussion papers in economics. Washington, D.C.: Brookings Institution.

Bry, Gerhard, with Charlotte Boschan. 1960. *Wages in Germany, 1931–1945.* Princeton, N.J.: National Bureau of Economic Research, Princeton University Press.

Cagan, Phillip. 1975. Changes in the recession behavior of wholesale prices in the 1920's and post–World War II. In *Explorations in economic research.* Occasional papers, vol. 2, no. 1. Cambridge, Mass.: National Bureau of Economic Research.

Cagan, Phillip, and William Fellner. 1984. The cost of disinflation, credibility, and the deceleration of wages, 1982–1983. In William Fellner, ed. *Contemporary economic problems, 1983–1984.* Washington, D.C.: American Enterprise Institute.

Davis, J. Ronnie. 1971. *The new economics and the old economists.* Ames, Iowa: Iowa State University Press.

Denison, Edward. 1979. Where has productivity gone? In William Fellner, ed. *Contemporary economic problems, 1979.* Washington, D.C.: American Enterprise Institute.

Economist. 1979. Review of "The Meaning of Hitler" by Sebastian Haffner. *Economist* (October 20):133.

———. 1982*a.* Work on a pay cut. *Economist.* November 27:11–12.

———. 1982*b*. Wage cuts. *Economist* (December 18):14–15.

———. 1983. The overblown dollar. *Economist* (December 17):9.

———. 1984. UnKeynesian Britain. *Economist* (February 4).

Fellner, William. 1976. *Towards a reconstruction of macroeconomics: Problems of theory and policy.* Washington, D.C.: American Enterprise Institute.

———. 1979*a*. The credibility effect and rational expectations: Implications of the Gramlich study. *Brookings papers on economic activity* 1:167–78.

———, ed. 1979*b*. *Contemporary economic problems, 1979.* Washington, D.C.: American Enterprise Institute.

———. 1980. The valid core of rationality hypotheses in the theory of expectations. *Journal of money, credit, and banking*, pt. 2(November).

Friedman, Milton. 1966. What price guideposts? In George P. Schultz and Robert Z. Aliber, eds. *Guidelines, informal controls, and the market place: Policy choices in a full employment economy.* Chicago: University of Chicago Press.

General Agreement on Tariffs and Trade (GATT). 1978. *Adjustment, trade, and growth in developed and developing countries.* Geneva: GATT.

Giersch, Herbert. 1982. Prospects for the world economy. *Skandinaviska Enskilda Banken quarterly review*: 104–10.

———. 1983. Arbeit, Lohn, und Productivität. *Weltwirtschaftliches Archiv* 119(no. 1): 1–18.

Goldstein, Morris. 1984. The exchange rate system: Lessons of the past and options for the future. Occasional paper 30. Washington, D.C.: International Monetary Fund, Research Department.

Gould, John P., and George Bittlingmayer. 1980. *The economics of the Davis-Bacon Act: An analysis of prevailing wage laws.* Washington, D.C.: American Enterprise Institute.

Haberler, G. 1936. *The theory of international trade.* London and New York: Stonier and Benham. Reprint, New York: Augustus M. Kelly, 1968.

———. 1980. The Great Depression of the 1930s—Can it happen again? In *The business cycle and public policy, 1920–80*, a compendium of papers submitted to the Joint Economic Committee, 97th U.S. Congress, 2d session. Also available Washington, D.C.: American Enterprise Institute Reprint 118, January 1981.

———. 1984. "The international monetary system in the world recession." In *Essays in contemporary economic problems—Disinflation, 1983–1984*, William Fellner, ed., Washington, D.C.: American Enterprise Institute.

———. 1985*a*. "International issues raised by criticisms of the U.S. budget deficits." In *Contemporary economic problems, 1985*, Phillip Cagan, ed., Washington, D.C.: American Enterprise Institute.

———. 1985*b*. *The problem of stagflation: Reflections on the microfoundation of macroeconomic theory and policy.* Washington, D.C.: American Enterprise Institute. Also to appear in *Political business cycles and the political economy of stagflation*, Thomas D. Willett, ed., San Francisco: The Pacific Institute for Public Policy.

———. Forthcoming. "Liberal and illiberal development policy. 'Free trade like honesty is still the best policy.'" in *Pioneers in development*, vol. 2, Gerald M. Meier, ed., Washington, D.C.: The World Bank.

Haffner, Sebastian. 1979. *The meaning of Hitler.* New York: Macmillan.

Hashimoto, Masanori. 1981. *Minimum wages and on-the-job training.* Washington, D.C.: American Enterprise Institute.

Hutchison, T. W. 1979. Notes on the effects of economic ideas on policy: The example of the German social market economy. In *Currency and economic reform: West Germany after World War II: A symposium. Zeitschrift für die gesamte Staatswissenschaft* 135(September):435ff.

IMF Survey. 1985. New fund study sees floating rate system as a qualified success. February 18, p. 49.

International Monetary Fund (IMF). 1981. *International financial statistics.* Supplement on price statistics, supp. ser. 2. Washington, D.C.: IMF.

Kahn, Richard. 1975. Unemployment as seen by the Keynesians. In G. D. N. Worswick, ed. *The concept and measurement of involuntary unemployment.* London: Allen and Unwin.

Kendrick, John. 1979. Productivity trends and the recent slowdown: Historical perspective, causal factors, and policy options. In William Fellner, ed. *Contemporary economic problems, 1979.* Washington, D.C.: American Enterprise Institute.

———. 1984. Long-term economic projection: Stronger U.S. growth ahead. Presidential address before the Southern Economic Association. Reprinted in *Southern economic journal* (April).

Keynes, J. M. 1936. *The general theory of employment, interest, and money.* London: Macmillan.

———. 1946. The balance of payments in the United States. *Economic journal* 56.

Knight, Frank H. 1946. The business cycle, interest, and money. In Frank H. Knight, ed. *On the history and methods of economics.* Chicago: University of Chicago Press.

Kravis, Irving B., and Robert E. Lipsey. 1984. The diffusion of economic growth in the world economy, 1950–1980. In John Kendrick, ed. *International Comparisons of Productivity and Causes of the Slowdown.* Cambridge, Mass.: Ballinger.

Kuznets, Simon. 1971. *Economic growth of nations.* Cambridge, Mass.: Harvard University Press.

———. 1976. Aspects of post–World War II growth in less-developed countries. In A. M. Tang, E. M. Westfield, and James E. Worley, eds. *Evolution, welfare, and time in economics: Essays in honor of Nicholas Georgescu-Roegen.* Lexington, Mass.: Lexington Books.

———. 1977. Two centuries of economic growth: Reflections on U.S. experience. Richard T. Ely lecture. *American economic review* 67, no. 1(February):1–14.

Marris, Stephen. 1983. Crisis ahead for the dollar. *Fortune.* December 26.

———. 1984. Why Europe's recovery is lagging behind, with an unconventional view of what should be done about it. *Europe* (March–April).

Olson, Mancur. 1982. *The rise and decline of nations: Economic growth, stagflation, and social rigidities.* New Haven: Yale University Press.

Organisation for Economic Co-operation and Development (OECD). 1983a. *Economic outlook* (December):34.

———. 1983b. *Positive adjustment policies: Managing structural change.* Paris: OECD.

Prebisch, Raúl. 1984. *Pioneers in development.* New York: Oxford University Press for the World Bank.

Price, James E. 1982. The changing cyclical behavior of wages and prices, 1890–1976: Comment. *American economic review* 72(December).

Robinson, E. A. G. 1967. *Economic planning in the United Kingdom.* Cambridge: Cambridge University Press.

Rottenberg, Simon, ed. 1981. *The economics of legal minimum wages*. Washington, D.C.: American Enterprise Institute.

Sachs, Jeffrey. 1980. The changing cyclical behavior of wages and prices: 1890–1976. *American economic review* 70(March):78–90.

————. 1982. The changing cyclical behavior of wages and prices, 1890–1976: Reply. *American economic review* 72(December):1191–93.

Samuelson, Paul A. 1983. In David Worswick and James Trevithick, eds. *Keynes in the modern world*. Cambridge: Cambridge University Press.

Samuelson, Paul A., and Robert M. Solow. 1960. Analytical aspects of anti-inflation policy. *American economic review* 50(May):192.

Schumpeter, Joseph A. 1951. The decade of the twenties. In Richard V. Clemence, ed. *Essays of Joseph A. Schumpeter*. Cambridge, Mass.: Addison-Wesley.

Stein, Herbert. 1969. *The fiscal revolution in America*. Chicago: University of Chicago Press.

————. 1983. Early memories of a Keynes I never met. *AEI economist* (June).

Taylor, John A. 1982. *Union wage settlements during a disinflation*. Working paper 985. Cambridge, Mass.: National Bureau of Economic Research.

Tobin, James. 1972. Inflation and unemployment. *American economic review* 62(March):13.

————. 1973. Comment of an academic scribbler. *Journal of monetary economics* 4:622.

————. 1983. Keynes' policies in theory and practice. *Challenge* (November-December).

Williamson, John. 1983. *The exchange rate system*. Washington, D.C.: Institute for International Economics.

Chapter 3

Systemic Risk and Developing Country Debt

Robert Z. Lawrence

MUCH OF THE CURRENT DEBATE about the debt facing developing countries focuses on liquidity or solvency problems. For some purposes this debate is useful. If the present problems indicate simply insufficient finance, rescheduling and postponing of payments may be necessary. If, on the other hand, these problems are so large that a return to sustainable external financing would have to be postponed almost indefinitely, some of the special proposals for debt relief may merit consideration. By concentrating research on distinguishing between solvency and liquidity, however, we may miss some important considerations.

The notion of solvency is misleading when applied to a nation. Technically a firm is insolvent when the present discounted value of its earnings is less than its liabilities. Nations, however, are likely to default prior to reaching this point. The nation is a unit of consumption as well as production and will be unable and unwilling to service its debts before it is insolvent. For a nation, the relevant question, therefore, is when to default. The default decision is a function of the costs and benefits of default rather than of the difference between future income and liabilities.

If the current crisis is associated with major defaults or losses for lenders, it will have a substantial impact on future borrowing. Simulations indicate, however, that with appropriate adjustment by the developing countries and a return to a 3 percent growth path in the developed countries, the developing countries can restore their debt measures (for example, debt-export ratios) to their 1980 levels (see Cline 1983). The simulations imply a lack of liquidity in the world economy. With world growth, the characterization suggests, international lending can return to its former arrangement. These optimistic conclusions need qualification, however. Even if the current crisis reflects deficiencies only in debt-servicing capabilities rather than in ultimate net worth, its impact will not be transitory. If the debt indicators are restored to their 1980 levels, global financial market behavior is likely to undergo substantial structural change. Viewed ex post facto, the international system has severely underestimated the effects of systemic risk.

Between 1979 and 1983, the global economy experienced an extraordinary degree of turbulence. In only three years there was a dramatic rise and fall in oil prices, unprecedented levels and volatility in real interest rates, enormous fluctuations in real exchange rates, the largest slump in world trade of the postwar era, and a global recession, all leading to great financial instability. Without these destabilizing influences, studies suggest, developing countries could have sustained and serviced their 1980 debt levels (see, for example, Morgan Guaranty Trust 1983:6).

With hindsight we may be surprised to note how vulnerable borrowers, lenders, and the international financial system were to the shocks that occurred in the 1980s. The urgency of borrowing changed the terms of typical lending arrangements. Much of the borrowing by developing countries took the form of credits financed by bank loans, with an increasing amount of borrowing denominated in dollars. Short-term debt became more common; even the long-term debt was typically negotiated at floating interest rates.

Banks and developing countries appear to have neglected various types of risk. Developing countries ignored the risk of maturity mismatch, funding large long-term projects by short-term loans. They ignored the risks of income fluctuation by borrowing at fixed terms. They overlooked the impact of recessions on their ability to sustain payments, allowing the proportion of equity financing to decline significantly. They neglected the risks of exchange rate fluctuations, and in particular dollar appreciation, by borrowing in U.S. dollars. Thus, as calculated by the Federal Reserve Bank of New York, if developing countries had followed the practice of denominating their borrowing in proportion to their exports to developed countries, their burdens would have been approximately $30 billion lower (Solomon 1983:3). They ignored the risks of refinancing by increasing the share of short-term debt that had to be renegotiated frequently. They assured the risk of import price fluctuations by committing their governments to maintaining the domestic prices of tradable goods such as food. In addition they overlooked the risk of interest rate fluctuations by funding at variable interest rates tied to the London interbank offered rate (LIBOR).

The banks, which were the major creditors, took some steps to ensure against certain types of risks. They sought to avoid interest rate fluctuations by linking both deposits and loans to LIBOR. The dramatic growth of the interbank market illustrates their concern about maturity mismatch, currency exposures, and so forth. In addition, ignoring the fallacy of composition, they individually sought to maintain their flexibility by financing with short-term loans. (This development might have lowered perceived risks individually but actually raised risks for the system.)

Nonetheless, banks neglected the risk associated with possible default by major debtors among the developing countries. Banks were willing to expose amounts equal to 40 percent of their capital to individual developing country borrowers. They also ignored the dangers of creditor servicing difficulties and the costs of immobilizing substantial portions of their balance sheets by participating in syndicated credits in nonmarketable instruments. Confidence in the creditworthiness of developing countries was not confined to a few banks. Capital markets in general gave borrowing by developing countries low risk ratings. Banks are highly leveraged institutions with capital in major U.S. banks that is typically equal to about 5 percent of total assets. If these banks were threatened by international default, their stock values would surely respond. There was no significant evidence, however, that they were initially penalized by the market for their developing country debt. Foreign branches in developing countries participated freely in U.S. and European interbank markets without incurring risk premiums. Spreads on developing countries' borrowing as compared with developed countries' borrowing declined gently from about sixty-three basis points in 1976 to fifty-one basis points in 1979 (Sachs 1981:244). Apparently banking authorities viewed the rapid growth of this lending as fairly benign; they took little action to curtail it. They failed to consider the damage that a major default might have upon domestic banking systems.

Viewed ex post facto, to disregard the implications of risk may seem negligent. Indeed many discussions of developing country borrowing assume so. Yet ex ante lenders may not have overlooked relevant market information. A risk-averse market equates the marginal benefits of risk reduction with its marginal cost. The benefit of risk aversion is in turn related to (a) the probability of risk—objective risk, (b) the perceived cost of that risk—subjective risk, and (c) the degree of risk aversion. Consider briefly the factors involved in evaluating sovereign nation risk and the possibilities for reducing it.

Objective Risk

The particular features of lending to sovereign nations change the nature and degree of risk involved and make evaluation more complex. Domestic lending to a private company allows creditors claims on the assets of the company. Creditors can also enter into legal contracts, for example covenants, which restrict the capacity of the borrower to undertake other commitments. In contrast, the assets of sovereign borrowers are located in their own territories and cannot be liquidated. Furthermore, legal sanctions against sovereign borrowers are difficult to exercise. To be sure, banks may attempt to seize the foreign assets of a defaulting nation; however, the borrower may take considerable precautions to reduce such costs. International loans are subject to greater uncertainty than domestic loans. Loans to private institutions in developing countries involve the intrinsic risks of the project, the risks associated with international legal complications, and risks associated with profit repatriation.

Yet other considerations suggest that sovereign lending may be less risky than private lending. Private liabilities may be restricted by bankruptcy in the case of individuals and by limited liability provisions in corporate charters. Nations exist in perpetuity, however. Repudiation of debt may be particularly difficult if the nation (especially its present government) wishes one day to return to the international capital market. As in the case of the private market, default against bondholders may not forestall access to bonds for all times (Sachs 1982). Default against the relatively few banks in international lending, however, may deny the borrowing country access for longer periods of time. Behind a company's debts stand its limited assets, but behind the debts of a sovereign nation stands its taxing ability. For most nations, furthermore, international debt is below national income, not to mention national wealth. Thus outright debt repudiation is extremely rare. Countries in trouble will reschedule and will perhaps obtain relief from private and official creditors.

The international lending norms since World War II are very different from those for earlier periods. The recent norms are marked by cooperative solutions that rarely entail default or forgiveness of principal. Instead lenders more typically extend maturity and renegotiate interest rates and fees. Official involvement through loan guarantees and so forth has led to renegotiation of government-to-government loans in the Paris Club. Private renegotiations have involved debtor countries and banks acting in a coordinated fashion with a committee. The International Monetary Fund (IMF) also plays a coordinating role. Thus the system has reduced the danger of outright default. Noting that market spreads have contained little provision for risk, Guttentag and Herring (1985) suggest that banks expect these loans to be virtually risk free because write-offs can be delayed indefinitely. As my discussion indicates, the risk directly associated with loans to a particular borrowing country receives most of the attention. Yet considerations overlook some important factors about market risk. What matters in the market provision for risk is systemic risk.

The evidence of relatively low market provision for risk that I adduced above need not indicate market failure. Even if assets have highly variable returns, risk will command a low price, provided that asset returns are independent. Financial theory suggests that loan interest rates will reflect, not the total variance of an asset, but rather the covariance between the returns from that asset and from the rest of the portfolio (see Sharpe 1964). If an asset's return is independent of the rest of the portfolio, it is possible to diversify away from the risks associated with holding that asset.[1]

The concern of individual banks for their own risk is quite understandable. To minimize the risk of a portfolio composed of assets with independent returns, their shares should be inversely proportional to their variance. From the viewpoint of the market, however, the borrower's own risk is not important. Since no single asset has a significant share in the market portfolio, the dominant determinant of the price of risk will be the covariance of an asset's returns with those from the rest of the portfolio. Assets that have returns inversely correlated with the portfolio will have risk discounts; those whose returns show a positive correlation (positive betas) will require risk premiums. *The loans to individual developing countries reflect risk only to the degree that they add to the nondiversifiable component of total market holdings of wealth of all kinds.* In addition, in an empirical investigation of the risks of international bank lending, Laurie Goodman concluded, "Country-specific risks appear to loom large relative to the common problems faced by non-OPEC [Organization of Petroleum Exporting Countries] LDCs" (see Goodman 1982:261).[2] Thus the key issue from a systemic viewpoint was the probability of a major series of synchronous losses. This probability depends on: (a) the possibilities of major global disturbances and (b) the likelihood that such disturbances would induce losses synchronous with those in the rest of the market.

By a number of indicators, global shocks in 1981 and 1982 lay outside the range of relevant historical experience and were therefore beyond the range of outcomes that could reasonably be anticipated.[3] Judged by postwar norms, real interest rates, the decline of world trade, the volatility of real exchange rate fluctuations, the downward movement in global average inflation rate, and so forth were extraordinary.

In view of the experience in the 1974–75 recession, the dangers that a global recession would spread to the developing countries were increasingly discounted in 1981–82. Indeed the ability of the developing countries as a group to weather the 1974–75 recession indicated the resilience of the system.

Developing countries were able to sustain their growth and to avoid the stagnation that was occurring in developed countries. This trend suggested that capital markets could decouple the business cycles of developed and developing countries. Borrowing by developing countries had been successfully used to finance investment rather than consumption, which led to an effective export performance, indicating a capacity to service existing debts (Sachs 1981). Lending had proven profitable to lenders, with debt renegotiation clearly the exception rather than the rule.[4] Some countries had experienced difficulties (for example, Peru, Mexico, Turkey, Zaire, Sudan), but these were isolated instances and actually strengthened the view that contagion could be avoided. Overall, bankers frequently noted, loan loss experience with developing countries was superior to experience with domestic loans. Similarly, the limited impact of bank failures, for example of Herstatt and Franklin National, had also strengthened the view that the system could contain and absorb individual shocks. Increasing the share of these countries in portfolios thus seemed to be a way of reducing rather than increasing risk.

Subjective Risk

Even if risk is objectively high, lenders' perceptions of the costs of risk may be affected by anticipation of government assistance in the event of major shocks or by inaccurate or incomplete information. From a policy viewpoint, a key issue is the degree to which costs of risk were underestimated in 1980–82 because of the responses that were expected from policymakers. Did banks believe that major defaults were unthinkable precisely because so much of the major banking system was involved? To what extent did they seek simply to match their competitors who securely believed that in the event of default, a lender of last resort and other public facilities would prevent major losses to shareholders? Banks play a major public role as a means of payment. Deposit insurance in the United States is one of the special privileges such institutions enjoy. In other nations, banks are government owned. Banks have serviced the international system by recycling the OPEC surplus cash and have deservedly been praised by the policymakers. Did they perceive themselves acting in more than a private capacity, so that they were, in their eyes, due public aid in the face of trouble? Moreover, the use of official guarantees and of IMF money in cases of difficulty both indicated that public money would be available to support borrowers in the event of major difficulties.

Yet bankers' expectations of policymakers should not be exaggerated. Bankers witnessed several reschedulings in which governments did not bail them out. Rescheduling avoided default, but the banks incurred the costs of involuntary lending and in some cases reductions in revenue. Did individual banks and other actors have too little information? Some actors undoubtedly made loans simply by following the herd. It seems clear that regional banks with little knowledge of the nations moved to lend in syndicated credits to countries and to foreign branches in the interbank market. Herd behavior, however, is not unknown in stock and bond markets. For markets to be efficient, complete information need not be available to all actors. As long as major actors can influence decisions at the margin, markets are efficient. There were undoubtedly lacunae in bank information, particularly about aggregate country borrowing in the short run; it is difficult to make the case that positions built over a number of years were due solely to ignorance of the true state of affairs.

Risk Aversion

In public finance literature it is argued that a nation has superior risk-pooling abilities and therefore should ignore risk (Arrow and Lind 1970:364–78). Thus the riskless rate is the appropriate discount rate for social projects. The behavior of the developing countries did not appear to indicate much risk aversion. Their willingness to shoulder interest rate fluctuation and exchange rate risk, to borrow short term, and to use debt financing all support this conclusion. On the other hand, even if risk reduction is desired, it may be seen as too costly.

The very nature of country borrowing leads to the use of debt rather than equity. Nations often undertake projects to provide public goods; it is difficult and perhaps impossible to measure the benefits of these services precisely. Improvements in public health, education, transportation, population control, and regulation should all raise national income. To undertake such investments, however, the government must appropriate the returns indirectly by taxes instead of through service charges. Returns to these investments are implicit and hard to measure, and thus securities contingent upon income are unlikely to exist. Indeed there have been numerous proposals (for example, Kubarych 1982:245) for financing instruments that link returns to developing country export earnings or income growth, but the difficulty of measuring these accurately (particularly when the country would have an incentive to understate them) is a major obstacle.

Second, there are costs associated with institutional underdevelopment. Private entrepreneurs could theoretically undertake many public investments, but entrepreneurial ability is often scarce in a developing country. If foreign entrepreneurs were used, then direct foreign investment in domestic equity would reduce the riskiness of investments. Institutional deficiencies, however, inhibit the development of large equity markets that allow portfolio investments to reduce risk by dissociating ownership and control. Furthermore, political difficulties inhibit direct foreign investment because domestic corporations fear foreign control. Thus information and transactions costs have been a major impediment to risk reduction. Given the relatively low risk aversion exhibited by developing countries, they were unwilling to pay these costs.

Experience during the Crisis: A Cause for Reappraisal?

Experience during the past few years has confounded observers who argued that the system was too vulnerable to sustain major shocks. The pattern of cooperative solutions to debt problems that was set during the postwar period has been followed and extended. Instead of major defaults, solutions have entailed adjustment programs for the countries as well as rescheduling and increased (forced) lending by the banks and official institutions.

These events and outcomes of the recent past, however, suggest that a reappraisal might be made of the risks and costs of international lending. Instead of avoiding the global business cycle, developing countries suffered the most damage. International lending, once a means of decoupling developing countries from the international business cycle, has become a source of pressure to magnify the cycle. Refinancing difficulties have driven countries to the International Monetary Fund for assistance. In return for loan rescheduling, developing countries have been forced to implement stringent adjustment programs. National authorities and policymakers in developing countries have spent considerable time dealing with foreign creditors. Ultimately this activity has severely constrained their ability to pursue domestic policies. Even relatively creditworthy countries in Latin America, such as Colombia, have experienced financing difficulties as a result of systemic contagion.

In the developed world, banks have had a difficult time. The stock market has been penalized. In the first quarter of 1982 the average price-earnings ratio of the four largest U.S. banks was about 70 percent of the market average; by the third quarter of 1983 it was 42 percent of the market average. Major portions of bank portfolios have been frozen. Overnight deposits in Mexican banks became long-term deposits. Previous commitments have required additional lending. Many bank executives who operated the programs have lost their jobs. Holders of developing country bonds have experienced substantial capital losses.

The central banking authorities have been forced to monitor and at times to become actively involved in the crisis. As a result, international lending arrangements operate under tightened regulations and increased capital requirements as well as various other constraints, such as greater provisions in the event of loan loss.

Future Innovations

A system dependent on bank finance is highly vulnerable to default crisis but is probably less vulnerable to transitory refinancing crisis. Banks are easier to coordinate than bondholders. Banks have long-term relationships with borrowers. The relative success in the debt-restructuring experience suggests that the system may actually have been more stable than one with other institutional forms. The burden of debts that lenders currently shoulder, however, will make them wary. Furthermore, even if developing countries return to their previous levels of borrowing (that is, to previous debt-income ratios and debt-export ratios), they may not be of comparative creditworthiness, given the level of real interest rates. For the next few years, objective risks, subjective perceptions of those risks, and risk aversion are all likely to be high. I have argued in this chapter that what is important for the market is the likelihood of systemic loss. The recent short-run liquidity crisis has made this loss seem a possibility.

Bank lending is likely to grow more sensitive to interest rate fluctuations and recessions, thereby increasing the possibility that business cycle risks are transmitted internationally. Thus for the foreseeable future, the betas (systemic risk premiums) on developing country borrowing will be positive rather than close to zero or even negative. We can no longer assume that individual banks are able to protect themselves from imminent crisis by holding short-term debt.

The events of the recent past have also clarified subjective perceptions of policy response to crisis. Authorities have resisted efforts to bail out the banks. The authorities' responses to a crisis of this sort will now more easily be anticipated. Banks cannot reasonably expect to adjust their portfolios quickly in the face of future crisis. They will recognize the possibility of participating in future rescue packages by raising their exposure as dictated by the IMF and by work-out committees. The thought that the present crisis might recur will haunt financial markets for at least the next decade. Psychological studies suggest that individuals give relatively higher weight to recent experience (Guttentag and Herring 1984). Thus actors throughout the system will be more willing to pay for risk reduction. Lending patterns will therefore change to reflect this preference. Let us consider some of the forms these patterns could take.

New types of instruments and contracts could evolve. Payment terms could be based on contingencies rather than on fixed rates, perhaps involving equity or instruments that tie payments to major commodity prices and interest rates—for example, an instrument that automatically reschedules with fixed interest payments but variable maturity. Direct foreign investment could grow. In addition, the more developed of the developing countries could raise portfolio capital via equity market investment.

Banks could move away from syndicated credits kept on their books toward more marketable instruments. They might continue to originate loans but seek greater flexibility in the disposition of loans. Hedging vehicles, such as futures markets for currencies, commodities, and interest rates, could be used more frequently. Interest rate swaps that allow less creditworthy borrowers access to fixed interest rate financing via arbitrage between the fixed and variable interest rate markets are another possibility.

What implications would such an evolution have for policymakers? The movement toward greater market risk diversification would make the overall system more resilient. Even the default of a major borrower such as Brazil could easily be handled by a portfolio fund with, say, Citibank's liabilities and assets, whereas Citibank as a leveraged bank could find that half its capital had been wiped out. The move toward more contingency-based payments forms would provide a greater buffer, thus reducing the danger of rescheduling. Improved hedging by developing country borrowers could likewise mitigate the potential adjustment costs from major global shocks, making the system better able to endure such shocks. On the other hand, movement too far in the direction of market-based instruments and away from banks and official lending might lead to another set of instabilities, so that coordinated and cooperative solutions would become less likely. Observers who criticize banks for their herdlike behavior often overlook the fact that markets may be even more prone to violent swings in mood and behavior.

Many policy measures should be instituted to deal with the emerging environment. First, policy should encourage officials in the developed countries to remove the regulations that prohibit major investment institutions from holding developing country loans, for example, pension funds. Second, countries such as Germany and Japan have at times had ambivalent attitudes toward the use of their domestic markets for international lending. Policy should encourage these countries to remove impediments to such lending, thereby diversifying the currency of developing country borrowing. Third, policy should encourage countries to build up the long-term and aid components of lending to developing countries, since market forces may tend toward short-term debt, which such countries have difficulty in servicing.

The international organizations will also require changes. Since private international capital is less likely to provide the liquidity necessary to sustain programs in developing countries during recessions in developed countries, greater liquidity is required in the IMF. Programs to shoulder income fluctuation risks, such as the Compensatory Financing Facility, should be expanded. Countries with, for example, major exports of commodities traded on futures markets should be encouraged to use these to hedge against price fluctuations. The IMF could provide greater access to unconditional lending at market interest rates during recessions as a form of countercyclical stabilization policy. The Fund and the World Bank also need to monitor country risk exposure, planning not simply for one scenario of steady growth but also for potential recession and other major shocks. Continuous review of national risk exposure should be instituted. The World Bank should also be wary of contributing to the global cycle. The share of bank-funded projects provided by domestic finance could be tied to a global cyclical indicator.

The World Bank and the IMF also need to provide increased expertise and to improve information. Banks enjoy economies of scale in information processing. A more open and market-based system requires more information. In addition, programs to provide insurance for direct foreign investment could be expanded. The World Bank might consider emulating the Federal Home Loan Bank, which bundled mortgages for sale to private investors by bundling loans in developing country projects.

Developing countries need to improve risk management. An important component entails maturity matching of projects and finance. A second is avoiding commitments to unrealistic market prices and exchange rates that entail large subsidies and thus borrowing requirements in response to disturbances. Direct foreign investment has unfortunate political implications for many observers. The development of equity markets that allow for a dissociation of ownership and control needs to be encouraged. To create such markets, expertise as well as legal and regulatory infrastructures must be developed.

The above-described view of greater systemic risk also suggests the dangers inherent in certain proposals to deal with the current debt crisis. The current rescheduling arrangements have unfortunately failed to deal with the interest rate risk faced by developing countries. Rescheduled debts have taken the form of fixed maturity and variable interest rates. A rise in global rates would leave these programs exposed. A superior method would have been to allow for fixed payment but variable amortization schedules. Many of the proposals for long-term solutions require developed countries, the IMF, or the World Bank to provide guarantees that allow the banks to reduce their developing country debt holdings. These solutions, however, would remove from the banking system the systemic risk currently concentrated there and would concentrate it elsewhere. It would be more desirable to diversify such risks by the use of nonguaranteed instruments that are widely held.

Notes

1. Recall that the variance of a portfolio of independent assets is equal to the sum of the variances of the assets each multiplied by the *square* of their weights in the portfolio. Thus if two assets each have independent returns and a given variance V, a portfolio with equal shares of each will have a variance of $0.5V$; if four assets each have independent returns and a variance V, the portfolio with equal shares of each will have a variance of $0.25V$. In other words, the investor's own risk can be reduced by holding a diversified portfolio.

2. Goodman (1982) found that for most countries the bulk of the risk was diversifiable.

3. Indeed Guttentag and Herring (1984) suggest that the recent experience leads to increased uncertainty rather than to risk because these were not regular events with a corresponding probability.

4. In fact it can be argued, using Mynsky's theory of financial crisis, that the very success of developing country adjustment earlier and the existence of high rates of return from long-term investment would induce a system with insufficient liquidity to deal with sudden disturbances.

References

Arrow, Kenneth, and Robert Lind. 1970. Uncertainty and the evaluation of public investment decisions. *American economic review* 60(June):364–78.

Cline, William. 1983. *International debt and the stability of the world economy*. Washington, D.C.: Institute for International Economics.

Goodman, Laurie. 1982. Risk and international bank lending. In Paul Wachtel, ed. *Crisis in the economic and financial structure*. Lexington, Mass.: Lexington Books.

Guttentag, Jack M., and Richard J. Herring. 1984. Credit rationing and financial disorder. *Journal of finance* 39(December):1359–82.

———. 1985. *The current crises in international banking*. Washington, D.C.: Brookings Institution.

Kubarych, Roger. 1982. Discussion of Jeffrey D. Sachs, "LDC debt in the 1980's: Risk and reform." In Paul Wachtel, ed. *Crisis in the economic and financial structure*. Lexington, Mass.: Lexington Books.

Morgan Guaranty Trust. 1983. Global debt: Assessment and prescriptions. In *World financial markets*, pp. 1–14. New York: Morgan Guaranty Trust Company of New York.

Sachs, Jeffrey D. 1981. The current account and macroeconomic adjustment in the 1970's. *Brookings papers on economic activity* 1:201–82.

———. 1982. LDC debt in the 1980's: Risk and reform. In Paul Wachtel, ed. *Crises in the economic and financial structure*. Lexington, Mass.: Lexington Books.

Sharpe, William. 1964. Capital asset prices: A theory of market equilibrium under conditions of risk. *Journal of finance* 19(3):425–42.

Solomon, Anthony M. 1983. Toward a more resilient international financial system. *Federal Reserve Bank of New York quarterly review* 8(3):3.

Chapter 4

A Description of Adjustment to External Shocks: Country Groups

Pradeep K. Mitra

THE 1970s will be remembered as a decade that witnessed serious convulsions in the world economy.

- Petroleum prices quadrupled in 1973–74, fell by a sixth between 1974 and 1978, and then increased by 80 percent in real terms during 1979–80.
- The industrial market economies went into a recession in 1974–75 and thereafter recovered strongly before plunging into another recession in 1979–80, from which a slow recovery is under way. Stagflation was born in the countries of the Organisation for Economic Co-operation and Development (OECD), with successive peaks of economic activity occurring at ever higher levels of unemployment.
- The end of the decade saw an interest rate shock following the use of restrictive monetary policies to combat inflation in the leading industrial countries. In addition, in the early 1980s, the real prices of major primary products exported by developing countries—adjusted for rising prices of imported manufactures—fell to their lowest levels since World War II.

Some perspective on the magnitude of these convulsions may be obtained from the following statistics. World trade in fuels increased from $29 billion in 1970 to $535 billion in 1980.[1] Paying for the 1970s' fuel price increases was equivalent to finding the money to buy all the exports of another United States or Federal Republic of Germany. The current account deficits of the oil-importing developing countries as a proportion of GNP doubled from about 2.5 percent in 1973 to 5 percent in 1980. Debt-servicing payments of all developing countries, deflated by their export unit values, rose nearly threefold between 1972 and 1979; interest

The work reported in this paper has been undertaken in the context of World Bank research project no. 672-74, "Adjustment in Oil-Importing Countries." The author is deeply indebted to Hector Sierra for exceptional research assistance.

rates, deflated by export prices, rose from − 10 percent in 1979 to 20 percent in 1981.

This chapter is a first report on work on developing economies' adjustment to external shocks in the 1970s and early 1980s. It articulates a framework to impose analytical order on descriptions of shock and adjustment; to construct comparators that can place individual performance in perspective; and to locate empirical regularities among growth performance, external shocks, modes of adjustment, and, when data permit, policy variables.

The paper also develops the analytical framework with a number of examples. The analytical framework is used in the third section to classify thirty-three developing economies into five groups, according to certain features of their adjustment, which are then reviewed. The review provides a convenient backdrop against which individual country adjustment may be viewed, a task to which two companion papers (Mitra 1985a and 1985b) are devoted. The conclusion, in a fourth section, is followed by appendix A, which lists data sources. Appendix B classifies thirty-three economies into five broad groups.

Methodology

The following methodology underlies the comparative analysis. (A more formal account of the model and decomposition method appears in Mitra 1984, 1985a, and 1985b.) An open economy macroeconomic model is estimated for each country over the 1963–81 period, with an assumed structural break after 1973. The output of the model during the 1974–81 period is then compared with the output for the same period as if the 1963–73 parameters had prevailed and under certain assumptions about the course of variables exogenous to the model. I refer to the hypothetical development as the "counterfactual." The changes in the principal macroeconomic aggregates between the two scenarios are then decomposed into price and quantity changes.

External Shocks

External shocks comprise (a) international price effects, (b) recession-induced effects, and (c) net interest rate effects. International price effects measure the balance-of-payments impact of changes in an economy's terms of trade relative to the counterfactual and are the sum of the export price effect and the import price effect. The export price effect measures the net impact of a fall in the purchasing power of exports over manufactures exported by the OECD countries relative to the counterfactual. The import price effect measures the net impact of a rise in the purchasing cost of imports in terms of manufactures exported by the OECD countries relative to the counterfactual.

Both export and import price effects may each be subdivided into two components. First, the relative increase (decrease) in import (export) prices exerts an unfavorable impact on the balance of payments—the direct effect. Second, the price effect impoverishes the economy and, with unchanged policies, restrains imports, thereby exerting a favorable impact on the balance of payments—the indirect effect. It can be shown that, if the economy's savings propensity is positive, the direct effect dominates the indirect effect, so that a relative increase (decrease) in import (export) prices always exerts a damaging effect on the balance of payments.

When measured against a 1971–73 base as a percentage of GNP, international price effects averaged on an annual basis over the 1974–81 period ranged from an extremely unfavorable 7.5 percent in Chile and 5.9 percent in Uruguay through a somewhat less unfavorable 3.5 percent in Malawi, 2.9 percent in the Philippines, and 2.6 percent in Taiwan to a moderately favorable 3.5 percent in Malaysia and 3.7 percent in Tunisia to an extremely favorable 9.8 percent in Nigeria and 14.2 percent in Indonesia. Although import price effects were unfavorable in all cases, the magnitude of export price effects was extremely unfavorable in Chile and Uruguay on the one hand and very favorable in Nigeria and Indonesia on the other.

Recession-induced effects on the balance of payments are twofold. The export volume effect (a direct effect) is the shortfall in an economy's exports as a result of a slowdown in the rate of growth of GNP in principal trading partners. From this effect must be subtracted the import-saving effect (or indirect effect), that is, the restraint in the growth of imports, with unchanged policies, due to the slowdown in income growth induced by the export volume shortfall.

Recession-induced effects were generally positive, ranging as a percentage of GNP from 0.1 percent in Spain and Uruguay through 1.4 percent in the Republic of Korea and 1.9 percent in Taiwan to 3.7 percent in Indonesia.

Net interest rate effects are twofold. The payments effect measures the impact on the balance of payments of an increase in *real* interest rates (in terms of manufactures exported by OECD countries) payable on a country's debt relative to the counterfactual. From this figure must be subtracted the receipts effect, that is, the impact on the balance of payments

of an increase in *real* interest rates (in terms of manufactures exported by
OECD countries) earned by a country's interest-bearing assets relative to
the counterfactual.

Net interest rate effects, when measured vis-à-vis real interest rates
prevailing in 1971–73, ranged as a percentage of GNP from −0.6 percent
in Mali and −0.2 percent in Kenya to 2 percent in Korea and 2.5 percent
in Bolivia. Payments effects were particularly important in Bolivia,
Korea, and Singapore; the payments effect on short-term debt was
important in Singapore and, to a lesser extent, in Portugal.

Modes of Adjustment

Economies unfavorably affected by external shocks had four basic
ways (and combinations thereof) of responding to external shocks:
(a) trade adjustment, (b) domestic resource mobilization, (c) investment
slowdown, and (d) additional external financing. To avoid unnecessary
repetition the reader is asked to remember that, as with shocks, all modes
of adjustment are measured as deviations from the counterfactual. The
examples provided below have been drawn from a list of the economies
that suffered rather than benefited from external shocks during the
1974–81 period.

Trade adjustment is the sum of export expansion and import substitution. Export expansion is the increase in the responsiveness of exports to
changes in GNP growth in principal trading partners. It has a twofold
effect. The direct effect measures the favorable impact on the balance of
payments of boosting exports. From this figure must be subtracted the
indirect effect, that is, the boost in import growth due to the expansion in
income growth induced by the direct effect. Of the thirty-three economies to which the analysis underlying this chapter has been applied, those
in which export expansion played a prominent role include Singapore,
Korea, the Philippines, Chile, and Thailand as well as Taiwan.

Import substitution is the reduction in the responsiveness of the economy's import demand to income. The direct effect measures the balance-of-payments impact of restraining imports. From this figure must be
subtracted the indirect effect, that is, the boost in import growth due to
the expansion in income growth induced by the direct effect. Examples of
adjustment through significant import substitution are Brazil, Yugoslavia, and Malawi.

Both export expansion and import substitution improve the trade
balance and boost GNP growth.

Domestic resource mobilization measures the import-restraining effect

of a slowdown in income growth induced by improved savings performance as defined below. It may be broken down into its private and public
components. "Private resource mobilization" is the reduction in the
responsiveness of private consumption to income. This was important in
Honduras, Morocco, Singapore, Yugoslavia, Jamaica, and Korea. "Public resource mobilization" has two parts, "public consumption restraint,"
or the reduction in the responsiveness of public consumption to income,
and "tax intensification," or the increase in the responsiveness to income
of indirect taxes less subsidies. This term therefore ignores any changes in
the direct tax effort, an omission that may be justified on grounds of their
relative unimportance in developing economies. El Salvador, Singapore,
and Honduras favored this mode of adjustment.

Investment slowdown measures the import-restraining effect of a slowdown in income growth brought about through a reduction in the ratio of
investment to income relative to the period 1971–73.[2] This was a dominant mode of adjustment in Jamaica, Singapore, Mali, and Kenya.

Net additional external financing measures changes in gross additional
external financing (defined as capital flows, reserves, and transfers and
services net of interest payments, deflated by a price index of manufactures exported by OECD countries) less changes in net interest payments
resulting from changes in real net debt relative to the counterfactual.[3]
This measure played an important role in a large number of countries, for
example, Mexico, El Salvador, Honduras, Morocco, Mali, Portugal,
Spain, Guatemala, Turkey, the Philippines, Uruguay, and Kenya.

Patterns of Adjustment

An analysis of the experience of thirty-four developing economies over
the period 1974–81 reveals that twenty-five of them suffered adverse
external shocks. Their responses to these shocks varied considerably, a
feature that is worth bearing in mind in the following discussion. To
impose a measure of analytical order on the richness and diversity of
experience, however, it is convenient to divide the economies into five
groups, according to the sign of external shocks and the degree of reliance
on different modes of adjustment.[4] Group 1 (Chile, Costa Rica, Philippines, Singapore, Korea, and Taiwan) adjusted principally through *export expansion and public resource mobilization*. Group 2 (Argentina,
Brazil, Guatemala, Honduras, India, Kenya, Malawi, Mali, Thailand,
Turkey, and Uruguay) relied on *either export expansion or public resource mobilization*, whereas Group 3 (Jamaica, Portugal, and Yugoslavia) was characterized by *import substitution and negative public resource*

mobilization. Group 4 (El Salvador, Mexico, Morocco, and Spain) resorted to financing without domestic adjustment. Finally, Group 5 (Benin, Bolivia, Colombia, Indonesia, Ivory Coast, Malaysia, Niger, Nigeria, and Tunisia) experienced favorable external shocks. The (un-weighted) average shock adjustment figures for the 1974–81 period are shown for the five groups in table 4-1.

Export expansion and public resource mobilization. The average shock was highest for Group 1 at 3.98 percent of GNP. International price effects accounted for roughly 60 percent of total shocks, with the recession-induced and net interest rate effects contributing equally to the remain-der. All economies of the group resorted heavily to export expansion, which exceeded external shocks by more than one-third and to public resource mobilization, of which the principal component was tax inten-sification. Together, export expansion and public resource mobilization accounted for 154 percent of external shocks. Import substitution was significantly negative everywhere except in Costa Rica, especially during the later years of the period. Whereas Chile, the Philippines, and Taiwan relied on substantial additional external financing and stepped up their ratio of investment to GNP, Korea sustained an investment boom with comparatively limited recourse to additional external resources. In con-trast, Singapore adopted a somewhat contractionary package, with a cut in the share of investment and real repayment of borrowed funds; Costa Rica had a similar adjustment profile as well. The ratio of external financing to external shocks was higher in 1974–81 than in 1974–78 but was nevertheless quite modest for this group in relation to the others.

Export expansion or public resource mobilization. International price effects accounted for roughly 80 percent of external shocks for Group 2. This group occupies a position between Groups 1 and 3 in terms of adjustment characteristics. Three broad patterns of adjustment may be distinguished. First, Argentina, Guatemala, India, Mali, and Uruguay resorted to export expansion while exhibiting negative import substitu-tion and negative public resource mobilization, which was significantly worse in the years 1979–81 than in 1974–78. Second, and in quite a contrast, Honduras and Kenya adjusted through a combination of import substitution and public resource mobilization, with export expansion turning negative. Third, the remaining countries—Brazil, Malawi, Thai-land, and Turkey—relied on a combination of export expansion and import substitution, with negative public resource mobilization aggravat-ing the balance-of-payments impact of disturbances from the inter-national environment. For the group as a whole, negative public resource mobilization added 40 percent to external shocks. There was significant additional external financing, especially in countries such as Honduras,

Table 4-1. *Balance-of-Payments Effects of External Shocks and Modes of Adjustment, 1974–78 and 1974–81 Averages*
(percentage of local currency GNP)

Effect	Group 1		Group 2		Group 3		Group 4		Group 5	
	1974–78	1974–81	1974–78	1974–81	1974–78	1974–81	1974–78	1974–81	1974–78	1974–81
					External shocks					
1. International price effects										
a. Export price effect										
i. Direct effect	−1.97	−2.87	−0.63	−0.45	−3.86	−3.24	−3.16	−2.31	−7.59	−9.26
ii. Indirect effect	−2.38	−3.05	−0.37	−0.37	−2.87	−2.34	−1.75	−1.06	−2.93	−3.57
Difference (= i − ii)	0.41	0.18	−0.27	−0.08	−0.99	−0.89	−1.41	−1.25	−4.66	−5.69
b. Import price effect										
i. Direct effect	6.08	8.06	3.16	3.71	4.55	4.98	2.03	1.28	2.03	2.41
ii. Indirect effect	4.81	5.80	1.44	1.72	3.20	3.47	1.03	0.53	0.90	1.24
Difference (= i − ii)	1.27	2.25	1.72	2.00	1.34	1.51	1.00	0.75	1.13	1.17
Sum (= 1a + 1b)	1.68	2.43	1.45	1.91	0.35	0.61	−0.41	−0.50	−3.53	−4.52
2. Recession-induced effect										
a. Export volume effect	1.97	2.04	0.60	0.69	1.18	1.30	1.22	1.46	0.73	1.27
b. Import saving effect	1.27	1.28	0.30	0.39	0.84	0.91	0.65	0.81	0.08	0.33
Difference (= 2a − 2b)	0.70	0.76	0.30	0.30	0.34	0.39	0.57	0.66	0.65	0.93
3. Net interest rate effect										
a. Payments effect										
i. Medium and long term	0.11	0.68	−0.09	0.18	0.05	0.72	0.06	0.45	0.10	0.75
ii. Short term	−0.01	0.87	−0.01	0.16	0.00	0.40	−0.03	0.22	−0.01	0.15
Sum (= i + ii)	0.10	1.54	−0.10	0.34	0.04	1.12	0.03	0.68	0.09	0.90
b. Receipts effect	0.01	0.76	−0.01	0.09	−0.10	−0.15	0.00	0.06	0.00	0.28
Difference (= 3a − 3b)	0.10	0.78	−0.09	0.25	0.14	1.27	0.04	0.62	0.09	0.63
Total shock (= 1 + 2 + 3)	2.48	3.98	1.66	2.47	0.83	2.27	0.20	0.77	−2.79	−2.96

(Table continues on the following page.)

109

Table 4-1. (continued)

Effect	Group 1 1974–78	Group 1 1974–81	Group 2 1974–78	Group 2 1974–81	Group 3 1974–78	Group 3 1974–81	Group 4 1974–78	Group 4 1974–81	Group 5 1974–78	Group 5 1974–81
				Modes of adjustment						
1. Trade adjustment										
a. Export expansion										
i. Direct effect	12.79	17.05	0.75	1.66	−7.60	−7.31	0.63	−0.02	−0.02	0.25
ii. Import augmenting effect	9.09	11.60	0.18	0.55	−5.41	−5.23	0.32	−0.13	−0.91	−0.58
Difference (= i − ii)	3.70	5.45	0.57	1.11	−2.19	−2.08	0.31	0.15	0.89	0.83
b. Import substitution										
i. Direct effect	0.97	−4.20	0.87	0.85	4.68	4.43	−3.32	−3.28	−3.88	−5.04
ii. Indirect effect	1.45	−2.59	0.36	0.38	3.38	3.13	−1.55	−1.28	−0.17	−0.36
Difference (= i − ii)	−0.48	−1.61	0.50	0.48	1.31	1.30	−1.77	−2.00	−3.71	−4.68
Sum (= 1a + 1b)	3.22	3.84	1.07	1.59	−0.88	−0.78	−1.46	−1.86	−2.82	−3.85
2. Resource mobilization										
a. Private	1.08	0.54	−0.61	−0.44	−1.53	−0.96	0.72	0.65	0.98	1.27
b. Public										
i. Public consump. restraint	−0.09	0.19	−0.69	−0.88	−2.93	−4.04	−0.61	−0.87	0.25	0.16
ii. Tax intensification	0.49	0.49	−0.10	−0.12	0.28	0.39	−0.25	−0.24	−0.86	−1.14
Sum (= i + ii)	0.40	0.68	−0.79	−1.00	−2.65	−3.64	−0.86	−1.11	−0.61	−0.98
Sum (= 2a + 2b)	1.48	1.22	−1.39	−1.44	−4.18	−4.61	−0.14	−0.46	−0.37	0.29
3. Investment slowdown	−1.13	−1.91	−0.46	−0.69	2.48	2.78	−1.60	−0.84	−1.31	−1.74
4. Net additional ext. financing	−1.09	0.83	2.45	3.01	3.41	4.88	3.39	3.93	0.97	2.34
Total (= 1 + 2 + 3 + 4)	2.48	3.98	1.66	2.47	0.83	2.27	0.20	0.77	−2.79	−2.96

Note: Definitions of Groups 1–5 are in Appendix B.
Source: See text and Appendixes A.

Mali, Guatemala, Turkey, Kenya, and Thailand, with this mode of adjustment exceeding external shocks by more than 20 percent for the group as a whole. There was some increase in the share of investment in GNP in all countries except Mali, Kenya, and Malawi.

Import substitution and negative public resource mobilization. Although the shocks experienced by Group 3 were less unfavorable than those affecting Groups 1 and 2, their composition was rather different. International price effects accounted for less than 30 percent of external shocks, whereas net interest rate effects exceeded 55 percent of shocks, largely because of their relative importance in Jamaica. The adverse balance-of-payments impact of negative public resource mobilization was more than one and one-half times as large as that of external shocks in this group, with the effect being extremely strong in Jamaica. Import substitution played a dominant role in all of the countries in Group 3; export expansion was significantly negative. External financing was much more important than in Groups 1 and 2 but much less so in the later years of the period. The average, however, conceals marked intercountry differences: although it played a prominent role in Portugal, it was much less important in Jamaica and was virtually negligible in Yugoslavia.

Financing without adjustment. External shocks averaged 0.77 percent of GNP for Group 4. Recession-induced and net interest rate effects accounted for one and two-thirds times this figure, principally because of their overwhelming importance relative to external shocks in El Salvador and Mexico. Table 4-1 clearly indicates the virtual lack of domestic adjustment across the board. Export expansion was negative except in Mexico (because of petroleum) and especially in Morocco and El Salvador. A major import and investment boom was under way in Morocco and, in relation to external shocks, in El Salvador. Public resource mobilization was positive in El Salvador but was more than offset by worsening performance in the other countries, especially Morocco and Spain. Additional net external financing was extremely important in all countries and was more than five times as important as external shocks for the group as a whole.

Favorably affected countries. The countries of Group 5 experienced favorable shocks usually because they had been exporters of petroleum or of other primary commodities, so that the boom in prices in the mid-1970s allowed them to benefit over the period as a whole. International price effects alone exceeded total shocks by more than one-half in absolute terms. Export price effects, as a proportion of shocks, were extremely favorable in the nonfuel primary producers (the Ivory Coast, Bolivia, Tunisia, and Malaysia), followed by petroleum exporters (Nigeria and Indonesia), which were in turn succeeded by Colombia.[5] Import price effects, though significant in the Ivory Coast, were distinctly less important. Differences in the relative price movements of primary commodities during the 1970s accounted for variations in the pattern and timing of adjustment among members of the group. On average, however, adjustment to favorable shocks took the form of an import boom that intensified in 1979–81 as compared with 1974–78, a stepping up of the share of investment in GNP, a slackening of public resource mobilization efforts, and substantial additional external financing at the end of the period under review. With respect to particular countries, there was an import boom in Bolivia, Colombia, Malaysia, and Tunisia and, to a somewhat lesser extent, in Indonesia and Nigeria. It was accompanied by an investment boom, which was particularly marked in the Ivory Coast and Benin. There was a slackening of public resource mobilization efforts in the Ivory Coast and less of one in Malaysia and Tunisia. Net real additional financing was important in Tunisia, Colombia, and Bolivia, was negligible in Indonesia and Nigeria, and was negative in Malaysia and the Ivory Coast.

Conclusions

The framework developed in this chapter serves to impose a measure of analytical order on the richness and diversity of individual experience. It has been applied to thirty-three economies, and the results have been aggregated to describe the broad contours of group adjustment, both as an end in itself and with a view to placing individual performance in perspective. It is against this background that the experience of individual countries is discussed in two companion papers (Mitra 1985a and 1985b).

Appendix A. Data

Data on national accounts, price deflators, and exchange rates are taken from the World Bank's *World Tables*. The index of international inflation is the unit value index of manufactured exports f.o.b. from developed countries and is taken from various issues of the *United Nations Monthly Bulletin of Statistics*. Export and import trade weights are taken from the International Monetary Fund's *Direction of Trade Statistics*.

The calculations distinguish public and publicly guaranteed medium- and long-term debt from short-term debt. The latter has a maturity of less than one year. Outstanding medium- and long-term disbursed debt belongs to different vintages and carries different interest rates. Data on interest payments therefore reflect such terms and conditions. In the absence of a detailed breakdown, the nominal interest rate on medium- and long-term debt has been calculated as

$$\frac{\text{interest payments}}{\text{outstanding and disbursed debt}}.$$

Both numerator and denominator are taken from the World Bank's *Debtor Reporting System*, which, however, reports only public and publicly guaranteed medium- and long-term debt.

It is assumed that the rate payable on short-term debt as well as that earned by the country's interest-bearing assets, equals the London interbank offered rate (LIBOR). This rate has been understood to correspond to six months' maturity (source: Salomon Brothers until 1978 and the *International Financial Statistics* [IFS] of the International Monetary Fund thereafter). Short-term debt data is derived from the Bank for International Settlements' *Maturity Distribution of International Bank Lending*. Interest-bearing assets are defined as follows: Total Reserves minus Gold (line 1 l.d. in the IFS) *less* Use of Fund Credit (line 2 e.s. in the IFS), expressed in dollars. Gold has not been included as part of reserves.

Appendix B. Composition of Groups

Group 1: Chile, Costa Rica, Philippines, Republic of Korea, Taiwan, Singapore.
Group 2: Argentina, Brazil, Guatemala, Honduras, India, Kenya, Malawi, Mali, Thailand, Turkey, Uruguay.
Group 3: Jamaica, Portugal, Yugoslavia.
Group 4: El Salvador, Mexico, Morocco, Spain.
Group 5: Benin, Bolivia, Colombia, Indonesia, Ivory Coast, Malaysia, Niger, Nigeria, Tunisia.

Notes

1. "Billion" means "thousand million."
2. This measure could be broken down, data permitting, into its private and public investment components.
3. See equation (A.26) in Annex 1 of Mitra 1984 or Mitra 1985*a* for an algebraic statement.

4. The members of each group are listed for easy reference in appendix 2.

5. Export price effects were extremely favorable in Niger as well, but here external shocks were positive in 1974–78, with the terms of trade improving sufficiently thereafter to yield negative shocks for the period 1974–81 as a whole.

References

Mitra, Pradeep. 1983. World Bank research on adjustment to external shocks. *World Bank research news* 4:3 (Fall/Winter).

———. 1984. A description of adjustment to external shocks: Country groups. Development Research Department discussion paper 85. Washington, D.C.: World Bank.

———. 1985a. Adjustment to external shocks in selected semi-industrial countries. In G. Szego, ed. *Studies in banking and finance*. Amsterdam: North Holland. Forthcoming.

———. 1985b. Adjustment to external shocks in selected less developed countries. Washington, D.C.: World Bank, Country Policy Department. Processed.

World Bank. 1981. *World development report 1981*. New York: Oxford University Press, chap. 6.

Chapter 5

The Oil Syndrome: Adjustment to Windfall Gains in Oil-Exporting Countries

Alan Gelb

DEVELOPING COUNTRIES with only a limited range of exports—typically primary products—have greater fluctuations in their terms of trade than more diversified advanced economies. Mineral exports tend to be among the most volatile, and because highly specialized exporting countries tend to have high ratios of exports and imports to GDP, mineral exporters are prone to exceptionally large fluctuations in national income. Because a high proportion of natural rent on rich mineral deposits usually accrues to producer governments, the conduct of fiscal policy is often central in determining the use of resources from favorable but temporary movements in terms of trade and their ultimate benefit to producing economies.[1]

The external shocks experienced by oil producers during the past decade have been exceptional even by the standards of monoexporters. World oil prices quadrupled in 1973–74, then decreased slightly in nominal dollar terms in 1975–78. They then redoubled in 1979–80, peaking at about thirty-five dollars per barrel. As the world economy moved into recession, and conservation measures in the major consuming countries began to affect the demand for energy (particularly petroleum-based energy), prices fell by six to eight dollars per barrel. New sources of supply, notably the North Sea, came on stream. Output increased rapidly in Mexico, and energy sales from the Soviet Union to Europe rose. These developments placed additional stress on traditional exporters, who saw their sales contract in 1980–83, in some cases to little over half of their peak levels.

A small group of producers—the capital surplus exporters such as Saudi Arabia and Kuwait—have exceptionally large oil reserves, with low recovery costs, small populations, and underdeveloped non-oil economies. With very limited absorptive capacity, such countries face, in the first instance, a portfolio-choice problem: whether to store their major asset in the ground or to deplete reserves more rapidly and accumulate assets abroad.[2] The capital surplus exporters are not considered in this chapter, which focuses on a sample of countries—Algeria, Ecuador, Indonesia, Nigeria, Trinidad and Tobago, and Venezuela—with smaller reserves and projected oil incomes insufficient to defray the costs of development for more than perhaps two decades, a short period in historical perspective. The main questions addressed concern (a) the magnitude of the windfalls from oil over the past decade, (b) how they have been used, and (c) the impact on non-oil producer economies. Has oil laid a basis for self-sustaining growth at a higher rate than would otherwise have been possible? Or have the difficulties of economic management through fluctuating income severely reduced the benefits of oil windfalls and resulted in increased oil dependence of producing countries?

Dimensions of the Oil Windfall

Gains from higher oil prices can be measured in a number of ways. My approach is to estimate the increase in domestic income resulting from an enlarged oil sector in current-value terms relative to the non-oil economy. So that the data remain comparable, such computations are better performed with the economy partitioned into mining and nonmining segments rather than into oil and non-oil segments, a change that has only a minor effect on the results. Figure 5-1 indicates the (unweighted) average time profile for 1973–81 of the windfall for the above-mentioned six countries expressed in each year relative to their nonmining economies.[3] In 1974 the average windfall peaked at 33 percent of nonmining income, but by 1978 this figure had contracted to 15 percent. The time and country average, for 1974–78, was 22 percent.

The second oil price increase raised the windfall to 27 percent of nonmining output in 1980 and maintained it at 23 percent of nonmining GDP for 1979–81. The main factor reducing the impact of the second oil price rise was the reduced size of oil sectors in constant prices relative to the rest of producer economies. For the period 1979–81, constant-price mining sectors were on average 8.5 percent smaller relative to the nonmining economies than they had been in 1970–72. The second oil price shock thus impacted on a relatively smaller oil sector than had the first. Slumping prices and contracting sales for 1982–83 in combination appear to have halved the windfall gain.

Figure 5-1. *The Oil Windfall and Its Use, 1970–72 to 1981*

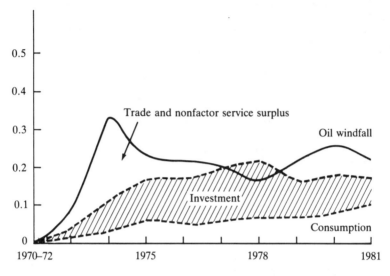

Percentage of nonmining GDP

Note: Unweighted average for Algeria, Ecuador, Indonesia, Nigeria, Trinidad and Tobago, and Venezuela.
Source: World Bank data.

Use of the Windfall: The Fiscal Response

With little direct linkage between the oil sector and the rest of a developing economy, and upward adjustment of tax and royalty rates to reduce the share of rent accruing to the oil multinationals, the above-mentioned fluctuations were mainly reflected in fiscal revenues, as shown in table 5-1. For the six countries mentioned above, central government revenues jumped from 20 percent of nonmining GDP to 37 percent with the first oil price increase.[4] The implication is that on average about four-fifths of the windfall as previously measured accrued to producer governments. Iran, for which data after 1977 are limited, experienced a particularly large windfall, 36.7 percent of non-oil GDP for 1974–77, which was reflected in fiscal revenues. Although there were significant differences in non-oil fiscal performance between countries, almost all the increase in the ratios of fiscal revenues to nonmining income is attribut-

Table 5-1. *Central Government Revenues as a Percentage*
of Nonmining GDP

Country	1970–72	1974–78	1979–81
Algeria	32.6	59.9	57.4
Ecuador	14.2	12.9	14.2
Indonesia	15.6	23.1	30.9
Iran	31.7	71.1[a]	—
Nigeria	12.3	27.7	—
Trinidad and Tobago	19.9	55.9	57.2
Venezuela	25.2	42.1	36.3
Mean: six countries			
(excluding Iran)	19.9	36.9	—
Mean: five countries			
(excluding Nigeria)	21.4	38.8	39.2

Note: Dashes indicate years for which data were judged unreliable or estimates that were
not compatible with series for earlier years.
a. 1974–77.
Sources: IMF 1983; World Bank data; and national authorities.

able to increased taxes and royalties on oil, except in Algeria, where
non-oil taxes were unusually high and buoyant.

Levels of development and income per head vary significantly between
the above-mentioned producers. So do the economic role of government
and the weight of the public sector in the economy. All countries had
extensive and growing public involvement in the hydrocarbon industry
during the 1970s, with virtually total nationalization in Algeria and
Venezuela. At the one extreme, however, central government and public
enterprises are estimated to account for about 90 percent of domestic
Algerian investment, whereas at the other, the role of the Ecuadorian
public sector beyond the traditional functions of administration, defense,
and the provision of physical and human infrastructure has been quite
limited. These differences reflect both the varying ideological tendencies
of successive governments and historical accident. The extensive involvement in agriculture of Algeria's socialist government, for example, and
(conservative) Indonesia's considerable public sector holdings in timber
and plantation crops both stemmed from the departure at independence
of colonial proprietors, French and Dutch, respectively. Nevertheless, all
of the oil exporters saw unparalleled growth in the size of the public
sector after 1973, and most experienced a considerable extension of its
role, toward direct participation in industrial production. Although most
governments expanded their activities in virtually all directions, there
were considerable differences of emphasis between countries. Algeria

and Trinidad and Tobago placed high priority on natural gas, the former for sale in primary form and the latter through gas-based industrialization. Venezuela emphasized the development of metals industries, and Nigeria the expansion of road networks and school (and later university) enrollment. Ecuador's public programs were directed largely toward promoting private industry, wnereas Indonesia pursued a strategy relatively balanced between physical infrastructure, education, agricultural promotion, and capital-intensive industrial ventures.[5]

For 1970–72, current account deficits in the six countries had averaged 5.1 percent of nonmining GDP. In these years, deficits were especially high in Trinidad and Tobago (14.5 percent) and Ecuador (7.1 percent) because of large investment expenditures to finance oil extraction and because of spending in anticipation of higher revenue flows. As indicated in figure 5-1, during 1974–78 about one-quarter of the windfall was saved abroad through reductions in trade (and current) deficits and one-quarter was consumed. Slightly more than half of the increase in consumption relative to nonmining value added was public, slightly less than half private. The remainder was used for domestic investment. Although non-oil private investment boomed in certain countries, notably Venezuela in 1976–78, increased investment outlays were overwhelmingly those of the public sector. The pattern for 1979–81 was similar except that private consumption increased its share of the windfall at the expense of domestic investment, which accounted for only one-third of the second windfall.

Central government investment expenditures and net lending thus expanded particularly rapidly. On average they grew more than twice as fast as the respective non-oil economies after the first oil price increase, but their growth slowed after 1978. Recurrent expenditures also increased but less rapidly. Wage and salary expenditures of central government grew, on average, at about 110 percent of the rate of increase in non-oil incomes. An exception to the pattern of moderate growth in central government current expenditure was the category of subsidies and transfers, which I shall discuss further below.

Some Consequences of Increased Domestic Expenditures

As would be predicted from a standard Salter-Swan model (see, for example, Bruno 1975; Corden and Neary 1982; and Gelb 1981), the rapid increase in domestic absorption of goods and services was reflected in a tendency for real exchange rates to appreciate. The degree of real appreciation is shown in table 5-2. Relative to their average levels in 1970–72,

Table 5-2. *Real Exchange Rate Movements, 1974–83*

	Trade-weighted real exchange rate[a]			Nonmining output deflator relative to MUV of imports of developing countries		
Country	1974–78	1979–81	1982–83	1974–78	1979–81	1982–83
Algeria	90.8	103.3	121.7	88.3	92.1	—
Ecuador	106.4	112.7	120.0	91.8	101.0	—
Indonesia	133.8	129.5	140.2	115.6	103.2	—
Iran	100.4	119.2	151.1	—	—	—
Nigeria	131.0	170.0	209.1	98.9	108.0	—
Trinidad and Tobago	101.4	107.7	138.8	88.0	104.2	—
Venezuela	97.6	103.2	124.7	81.6	93.4	—
Mean[b]	110.2	121.1	139.1	94.0	100.3	—
Memo: United States	92.3	93.4	105.2	82.1[c]	82.9[c]	98.2[c]

Note: MUV = manufacturers' unit value. Base = 1970–72. Dashes indicate that data are not available.

   a. Averages.
   b. Excluding Iran.
   c. Wholesale price index relative to MUV deflator.

Sources: International Monetary Fund, *International Financial Statistics*; World Bank data; and United Nations, *Monthly Bulletin of Statistics*.

trade-weighted real exchange rates (here defined as the ratio of the domestic price level of the oil exporter to those of its trading partners, converted at average market exchange rates) were 10 percent higher in 1974–78, 21 percent higher in 1979–81, and almost 40 percent higher in 1982–83.[6] It should, however, be noted that during the 1970s the unit value of manufactures imported by developing countries (manufactures' unit value, or MUV, index) rose markedly relative to the price levels of most countries largely because of the oil and other primary intermediate price shocks. This relative price shift limited the tendency for consumption and investment prices to decrease relative to the cost of domestically produced non-oil goods, as would be normal with real currency appreciation. Purchasers in producing countries were thus cushioned from increased import price shocks by their own real exchange appreciation.

As noted above, in addition to expanding their traditional functions, governments typically channeled windfall gains into industry, especially petrochemicals and heavy metals. They also invested heavily in physical infrastructure, notably to develop their transport and communications systems. Public projects tended to be large and complex and were frequently highly capital intensive. In fact, among a sample of the top nineteen developing countries with investments in projects exceeding $100 million each, all but five were found to be oil exporters (Murphy 1983). The dimensions of the part of the investment programs of the above-mentioned set of countries that consisted of such large projects may be seen from table 5-3, which is mostly based on a sample of some 1,600 large projects in the developing countries for the period 1970–79. Iran, which ranked an overall second after Saudi Arabia, included in its investment program 108 projects averaging more than $1 billion dollars each. The total capital cost was equivalent to more than one and one-half times its 1977 GNP, or ten times its 1977 oil windfall as previously computed. Venezuela's investment program, which in contrast to Iran's was largely directed toward metals (notably steel and aluminum), represented five times its 1980 oil windfall, or half its 1980 GNP. The large projects identified in table 5-3 represent, on average, very roughly four and one-half years' average oil revenue for 1974–81. Indonesia and Nigeria, the poorest producers, were somewhat less inclined to mortgage oil for large projects, but their investments of this type were still considerable.

In addition to such large investment commitments, most countries created or expanded programs of subsidies and transfer payments directed toward holding down the rate of inflation and supporting loss-making firms. Between 1970–72 and 1974–78, fiscal subsidies and transfers expanded, on average, twice as rapidly as nonmining GDP. Between 1974–78 and 1980–81 they rose about 1.6 times as rapidly. In addition, producer governments were reluctant to raise domestic oil prices, choosing to pass part of the windfall on to domestic consumers in the form of lower prices. In a number of cases, these were set at roughly the cost of production, so that government derived no revenue from the part of oil output that was consumed at home. Several producers, notably Ecuador and Indonesia, raised domestic prices of oil derivatives in the early 1980s, but they still typically remained below world levels, and as domestic consumption grew more rapidly than non-oil economies, the implicit fiscal burden on the state increased.[7] Energy subsidies in 1980 were estimated to be equivalent to almost 10 percent of household income in Ecuador, while fiscal subsidies rose sharply in Trinidad and Tobago, to about 7 percent of GDP or 11 percent of nonmining GDP by 1981. These subsidies were directed primarily to keeping down prices of consumer goods but were also extended to support unprofitable industries.

Such estimates do not include the subsidies implicit in loans made to loss-making (and frequently public) firms, nominally for investment, and in guarantees permitting them access to commercial sources of finance. It is difficult to estimate such subsidies (since many such firms would prob-

Table 5-3. *Macroprojects in Oil-Exporting Countries*

Country	Number of projects included	Cost (US$ billions)	Average cost (US$ millions)	Cost/ 1980 GNP	Cost/ 1980 oil windfall	Rank among developing countries	Project sector (percentage)			
							Hydrocarbons	Metals	Other industry	Infrastructure
Iran	108	119.6	1,107	1.57[a]	10.2[a]	2	30	7	9	54
Algeria	69	38.7	561	1.07	4.2	5	36	7	33	23
Venezuela	27	27.4	1,015	0.51	5.4	10	33	41	7	19
Mexico	59	26.0	441	0.18	5.1	2	46	17	12	25
Nigeria	19	14.4	758	0.17	0.9	15	26	11	16	47
Indonesia	44	14.4	327	0.23	1.1	16	41	18	16	25
Trinidad and Tobago[b]	7	6.9	983	1.35	4.5	—[c]	61	29	0[d]	0[d]

Note: Data are for projects in which costs exceeded US$100 million.

a. 1977 GNP and oil windfall.

b. Gas-based industrial projects only. Includes Tenneco-Midcon liquefied natural gas project proposed for 1988.

c. No data.

d. Zero by definition, because gas-based industrial projects alone have been included.

Sources: Murphy (1983), table 2.5; Auty (1984).

ably have been unable to borrow from commercial sources at any price without support), but they appear to have been considerable and to have been accorded to some extremely unprofitable firms. By 1983, for example, it was estimated that the production costs of Caroni Sugar in Trinidad were five times those of efficient world-scale producers, despite the fact that some of the latter, notably in Australia, had unit labor costs several times higher.

In addition to supporting firms, some oil-producing governments stimulated employment directly through public works programs. The INPRES (Instruksi Presiden) programs in Indonesia and the Special Works programs in Trinidad and Tobago employed some 2.5 percent of the two countries' respective labor forces. The impact of such programs depends on their administration and on the extent to which labor is a major constraint to production, particularly in agriculture. While the impact of INPRES appears to have been beneficial in labor-surplus Java, the Trinidad programs (which offered pay at least twice as high as the rate prevailing in agriculture) contributed to the acceleration of a rapid movement off the land that led to a drop in agricultural output. Per capita food production and agricultural production as a whole were both reduced by about 20 percent in the period 1969–71 to 1982, during which time population expanded by only 16 percent. The main loser was sugar, which saw its output fall by 62 percent.

The larger public projects had a greater tendency to overrun initial estimates both in terms of cost and time, as shown in table 5-4. One-third of the largest projects in the sample on which the table is based experi-

Table 5-4. *Cost and Time Overruns in Macroprojects*

Item	Project size (US$ millions)			
	100–249	*250–499*	*500–999*	*1,000+*
Percentage of total projects with cost escalations, completion delays, or postponements/suspensions	21	28	38	47
Average cost escalation (percent)	30	70	106	109
Percentage of total projects				
with cost escalation	10	18	28	34
with completion delay	11	14	16	16
with postponement/suspension	7	10	13	20

Source: Reprinted by permission of Westview Press from *Macroproject Development in the Third World: An Analysis of Transnational Partnerships* by Kathleen J. Murphy. Copyright © 1982 Westview Press, Boulder, Colorado.

enced cost overruns that averaged 109 percent. Overruns on the smaller projects were less frequent and more modest at 30 percent. Delays of between one and two years plagued half the troubled projects; a further 25 percent experienced delays of three to four years. These estimates greatly understate the true extent of cost and time overruns, because many projects were not completed by 1980; many are still under construction, and a number may never reach completion.

The tendency to overrun initial estimates and the poor operating performance of many plants once installed reflect a variety of factors, none specific to oil-exporting countries, but all accentuated by the scope and pace of their investment growth.[8] First, projects were, in many cases, inadequately prepared and assessed. In no country does there appear to have been systematic assessment of relative costs and benefits across a spectrum of potential projects. Second, larger projects tended to be more complex, both technologically and in terms of the organization necessary to integrate the project with its necessary infrastructure. Some involved state-of-the-art technology, which, in certain cases, was installed without the involvement of an experienced expatriate operating company. With little detailed knowledge of the industry or plant in question, public financing agencies were also sometimes slow to detect and correct emerging problems in construction, startup, and operation. Third, about half of the purchasing power of oil relative to domestic construction costs was eroded by increases in the latter for 1973–78. Increased construction costs were a major factor in real appreciation of the exchange rate. As noted above, international inflation in traded manufactured goods was also high. Finally, certain industrial investments of the oil producers were severely affected by the global recession in the 1980s, as described below.

The momentum of accelerated public investment (some of which implied large future recurrent obligations) and growing subsidies proved hard to curb when oil revenues fell, as they did in 1978 and after 1981. Central government deficits averaged 4.1 percent of nonmining GDP in 1978, and excluding Trinidad and Tobago, where expenditures accelerated more slowly, current account deficits averaged 11.8 percent of nonmining GDP. A number of exporters moved to slow domestic absorption of goods and services. Indonesia devalued by 50 percent in November 1978, seeking to restore the domestic purchasing power of oil revenues and to promote non-oil exports.

These contractionary moves were interrupted by the second oil price increase, which resulted in a current balance surplus of $11.8 billion in 1980 for the six countries (excluding Iran). As current-dollar commodity exports contracted by 21.6 percent during 1980–82 and imports rose by 22.3 percent, this surplus shifted to a current deficit of $19.6 billion by

1982. Of the current account deterioration between 1980 and 1982, 58 percent may be attributed to decreases in merchandise export revenues and 36.8 percent to increased imports of goods.

These swings in the exporters' current accounts often mirrored developments in their respective public sectors. Ecuador's public sector, for example, ran surpluses of about 2 percent of GDP in 1973–74, but these turned into deficits of 5 percent of GDP in 1977–78. With the second oil price increase, the deficit declined, but with contracting revenues and mushrooming subsidies and interest payments it rose to about 8 percent of GDP in 1982.

Economic management through the fluctuation in oil prices was rendered more difficult by the fact that access to international capital tended to vary with the level of oil prices, which affected future price and revenue expectations rather directly. Algeria was able to boost the expenditure impact of increased oil revenues by 50 percent during 1974–78 through borrowing abroad, largely to finance a transition from an oil to a natural gas–based hydrocarbon sector. Mexico augmented its comparatively small oil windfall (3.5 percent of nonmining GDP in 1979–81) by two-thirds by financing a growing deficit on goods and nonfactor services. In addition, Venezuela and Mexico were able to cushion the impact of growing private capital outflows by large public borrowings until the outlook in world oil markets deteriorated.

The impact of expanded investment on growth has been, at first sight, disappointing, as shown in table 5-5. Excluding Iran, where data are limited, only Ecuador proved able to accelerate the growth rate of its nonmining economy for 1972–81 significantly relative to performance for 1967–72. On average, non-oil economies (excluding Iran) were 4.1 percent smaller in 1979–81 than they would have been had they maintained their 1967–72 growth trajectories.

On closer examination, the growth record is less adverse than appears from historical trends. Algeria, Indonesia, and Nigeria had all previously been in recovery phases, two from internal disturbances and one from a protracted war of independence, while Ecuador and Trinidad had been stimulated by oil development and the prospect of growing export revenues. The non-oil growth performance of the sample had therefore been exceptional in 1967–72 at 7.3 percent, some 1.5 percent higher than the average growth of GDP in middle-income developing countries. Although the higher growth initially stimulated by spending from the first oil price increase was not sustained, the non-oil economies still grew 0.9 percent more rapidly than they had through the favorable period of the 1960s. Much of this growth was, however, demand led rather than supply generated in the sense that non-oil growth responded to increased

Table 5-5. *Growth Trends in the Oil Exporters, 1967–81*
(percent)

| | Nonmining GDP | | Domestic investment | | Goods and nonfactor service | | | |
| | | | | | Exports | | Imports | |
Country	1967–72	1972–81	1967–72	1972–81	1967–72	1972–81	1967–72	1972–81
Algeria	9.5	8.6	16.7	10.8	5.7	–1.0	11.6	10.8
Ecuador	4.7	7.6	3.2	10.2	15.9	6.0	6.0	9.7
Indonesia	8.5	8.2	24.3	13.0	15.7	4.3	16.7	19.1
Iran[a]	10.1	13.3	10.2	21.1	12.9	–0.3	17.7	23.7
Nigeria	9.2	5.3	—[b]	8.7	—[b]	–4.2	—[b]	15.3
Trinidad and Tobago	5.3	5.4	6.1	9.3	2.5	–6.5	6.6	8.4
Venezuela	6.5	5.1	11.9	3.5	–1.3	–8.7	7.7	12.8
Unweighted mean (excluding Iran)	7.3	6.7	12.4	9.3	7.7	–1.7	9.7	12.7
Memo: middle-income oil importers	5.8[c]	5.1[c]	8.2	5.6	6.7	4.0	7.4	1.5

a. 1967–72 and 1972–77.
b. Deflated data unreliable before 1970.
c. 1960–70 and 1970–82 GDP.
Source: World Bank data.

absorption after 1974 but slowed after 1978 despite the expectation that the large investment undertaken in 1975–78 would begin to contribute to output growth.

Although growth was only moderate, it was often poorly balanced. Construction had been the leading growth sector over the 1970s, followed by services and protected import-competing industry, with agriculture and non-oil export industry lagging in most cases. Only Ecuador, Indonesia, and Venezuela managed to raise domestic food and agricultural supply per head during the 1970s, the latter from an extremely small base (in 1970–72 Venezuelan agriculture represented only 8 percent of non-mining GDP). Despite a policy objective common to all governments, that of reducing dependence on oil, the volume of non-oil exports contracted in all countries except in Ecuador (which saw a considerable shift toward processed products and manufactures) and in Indonesia, which maintained a fairly strong non-oil export performance across a wide range of traditional and nontraditional commodities. Overall export volumes contracted, on average, by 1.7 percent annually in the period 1972–81.

After 1981: The End of the Oil Boom?

The downturn in world oil markets after 1981 revealed the fragility of the development patterns of the oil exporters. Shifts in the allocation of resources toward the nontraded sectors that had cumulated over the 1970s could not be rapidly reversed, and reluctance to devalue (plus competitive devaluations of trading partners) caused real exchange rates to remain at an appreciated level in 1982–83, as shown in table 5-2. The massive infrastructural and educational investments that had been undertaken since 1974, whatever their implications for future productivity, did not represent an autonomous source of income to replace oil incomes. More seriously, the global outlook changed for a number of sectors—notably steel, aluminum, and natural gas—which had figured prominently in the investment programs. In 1980, for example, the Organisation for Economic Co-operation and Development (OECD) was forecasting a doubling of global steel demand to 1,400 million tons by the year 2000. More recent forecasts project a 20 percent rise to only 900 million tons. The difference has serious implications, particularly for countries with domestic markets too small to absorb full-capacity output of large capital-intensive plants that had gone forward without foreign partners to assure marketing outlets. Such countries would need to be competitive with the globally most efficient (or most highly subsidized) exporters to overcome trade and transport margins and a preference for domestic supply in major markets. In the case of steel, a producer such as the Iron and Steel Company of Trinidad and Tobago (ISCOTT) was required to undercut U.S. minimills by 15 percent, although its production costs were some 50 percent higher than their estimated level of $270/tonne in 1982.

As the pressure of demand slackened, the transient boom of the mid-1970s was followed by deceleration in non-oil growth, by surplus capacity, and by slackening labor markets. A further factor decelerating demand was the tendency for private capital to flow abroad, particularly in oil-exporting countries with open capital markets, such as Venezuela and Indonesia. In 1978–81 the total cumulative current balance deficits of the six countries, at $5.6 billion, accounted for only 31 percent of the deterioration in their net foreign assets, where "net foreign assets" is defined as the change in external debt less that in currency reserves. Venezuela may have experienced an outflow equivalent to almost 10 percent of GDP in 1982, impelled by a stagnant economy, interest rate ceilings, and reluctance to adjust the exchange rate in line with perceived trends in world oil prices. In 1979–82 its non-oil economy virtually stagnated despite massive investments and considerable increases in the labor force, which should have assured growth of some 4 percent per annum even in the absence of any productivity improvements.

Conclusions

Oil-exporting countries entered the mid-1970s with high expectations that access to seemingly unlimited quantities of foreign exchange would accelerate development and would lead to the creation of a modern, productive, self-sustaining non-oil economy. Toward this end, they allocated the bulk of their increased oil income to domestic investments, which were mainly large scale and were overwhelmingly carried out by the public sector. Multiplier effects of investment expenditures, cost overruns, subsidy growth, and the recurrent spending needs of much past investment all resulted in a tendency to overshoot available revenues when the latter fell. The result has been a pronounced "stop-go" rhythm that has made economic management difficult.

It is not yet possible to assess the impact on producer economies, because many domestic investments, notably in transportation and education, would be expected to have long gestation lags. Overall, however, the yield on much domestic investment has probably fallen well short of that which could have been obtained abroad, and its supply-side growth impact has been moderate. With hindsight, the oil exporters would probably have enjoyed a larger benefit from their windfalls had they saved a higher proportion abroad and limited domestic investments through applying market criteria more rigorously. This conclusion abstracts, of course, from the impact of such a strategy on the global recycling problem.

Notes

1. Government may also absorb fluctuations in nonmineral export revenues.

2. Although the Hotelling rule predicts that unit natural resource rents should rise at the rate of interest, the medium-run fluctuations about any such long-run relationship have major fiscal consequences. An extra 250,000 barrels/day sold through 1981, with the proceeds invested in U.S. government treasury bills, would, by February 1984, have yielded approximately $4 billion ("billion" means "thousand million") against an estimated value of $2.6 billion for the same volume of oil valued at February prices. The capital surplus countries are discussed in Hablutzel (1981).

3. The windfall is expressed as the difference between the ratio of mining sector value added to value added in the nonmining economy and the value of this ratio in the base period 1970–72. Consumption and investment effects are similarly expressed. For details, see Gelb (1984).

4. The decrease for Ecuador is explained by (a) the fact that some oil revenues accrue to special funds outside government as defined here and (b) the fact that certain non-oil taxes eased after 1974.

5. These choices and the reasons behind them are discussed more extensively in Gelb (1984).

6. Algeria, the most notable exception to the pattern of real exchange appreciation, is analyzed in Conway and Gelb (1984).

7. Petroleum subsidies conceded by producer governments are usually implicit rather than fiscal, because revenues forgone through selling oil for domestic use at levels below world prices are not included in fiscal accounts.

8. As witness the $8 billion cost of the trans-Alaskan oil pipeline versus its $900 million original budget, cost overruns can be large in developed countries also. Their peculiar significance for the oil exporters is due to the weight of large projects relative to the size of their economies.

References

Auty, R. 1984. The deployment of oil rents in a small parliamentary democracy: The case of Trinidad and Tobago. Washington, D.C.: World Bank; processed.

Bruno, M. 1975. The two sector open economy and the real exchange rate. Jerusalem: Hebrew University of Jerusalem, Falk Institute.

Conway, P. J., and A. H. Gelb. 1984. Oil rents in a controlled economy: A case study of Algeria. Development Research Department discussion paper. Washington, D.C.: World Bank.

Corden, W. M., and J. P. Neary. 1982. Booming sector and de-industrialization in a small open economy. *Economic journal* 11:2(February):119–41.

Garcia Araujo, M. 1982. The impact of petrodollars on the economy and the public sector of Venezuela. Paper delivered at the tenth national meeting of the Latin American Studies Association, Washington, D.C., March 4.

Gelb, A. H. 1981. Capital importing oil exporters: Adjustment issues and policy choices. World Bank staff working paper 475. Washington, D.C.: World Bank.

————. 1984. Adjustment to windfall gains: A comparative analysis of capital-importing oil exporters. Developmental Research Department discussion paper. Washington, D.C.: World Bank.

Hablutzel, R. 1981. Development prospects of the capital surplus oil exporting countries. World Bank staff working paper 483. Washington, D.C.: World Bank.

International Monetary Fund (IMF). 1983. *Government financial statistics*. Washington, D.C.: IMF.

Morgan, D. R. 1979. Fiscal policies in oil importing countries. *International Monetary Fund Staff Papers 26*.

Murphy, K. 1983. *Macroprojects in developing countries*. Boulder: Westview Press.

Nankani, G. 1979. Development problems of mineral exporting countries. Staff working paper 354. Washington, D.C.: World Bank.

Chapter 6

The Debt Crisis in Latin America

Larry A. Sjaastad,
Aquiles Almansi, and
Carlos Hurtado

THIS CHAPTER discusses the various aspects of the current external debt problem in five Latin American countries: Argentina, Brazil, Chile, Mexico, and Venezuela. These countries were chosen because they account for a very large portion of total Latin American external debt and because they have all experienced severe payments difficulties since 1982. Other countries could have been included. Costa Rica, for example, was the first Latin American country to experience an external debt crisis in recent times, but Costa Rica has a very small external debt (at least in a comparative sense), and its problems do not conform to the global debt syndrome. Similarly, Panama could have been included on the ground that its debt is one of the largest in the world relative to its GDP. The cases that we have considered, however, permit us to cover a great deal of the problem and involve countries with highly different characteristics and histories.

What Triggered the Crisis?

The debt crisis was sprung on the world in August 1982, when the Mexican government became unable to continue debt service, and quickly spread to a number of other Latin American countries. We shall argue, however, that the crisis formed much earlier, with the coincidence of a number of quite independent phenomena: the rapid and enormous growth of external debt (again, particularly in Latin America), the shortening of maturities as more and more of that debt was owed to the world capital market rather than to international financial institutions, the sudden and spectacular rise in dollar interest rates, worldwide dollar deflation, and the political crisis in Latin America. All of these events were primary ingredients.

From 1971 to 1982, the total external debt of the developing countries grew, in nominal terms, by 600 percent, and debt service by 1,100 percent. (Estimates based on the 1983 *World Debt Tables* of the World Bank.) Even if we exclude dollar inflation during that period, growth was at an unsustainable rate, as it far exceeded the rate of growth of real output in the creditor nations. Nevertheless, by historical standards, the level of debt in 1982 was not extraordinarily high when measured against variables such as gross domestic product and exports. Debt service relative to debt, however, had doubled, with no commensurate increase in the ability of the countries to generate the requisite fiscal and trade surpluses to pay that service.

Moreover the countries borrowing most heavily were also those most heavily in debt; their debt service was enormous but still less than their annual borrowings. Once the ability to borrow began to wane, the heavy borrowers had to convert fiscal and trade deficits into surpluses virtually overnight, a trick that none of them could turn. The result was that country after country had to go hat in hand to the International Monetary Fund (IMF), seeking the blessing that would prevent the lines of credit from drying up entirely.

The great buildup of private international lending occurred during the 1970s and early 1980s and was closely related to, if not a consequence of, the oil price increase(s), which produced a virtual explosion of liquidity in the international commercial banks. Perhaps because of unanticipated inflation, and perhaps in part due to the surpluses of the Organization of Petroleum Exporting Countries (OPEC) following the oil price increase of 1973–74, real interest rates on dollar-denominated external debt were very low and indeed frequently negative, giving the developing countries a rather strong incentive to incur that debt. When real interest rates are negative (and are expected to remain so), it is clearly impossible to have "too much" external debt.

To be sure, there was concern by economists and government officials, but it focused on the more narrowly defined recycling problem rather than on the ability of the developing countries to meet the interest service on their external debts. The recycling issue arose from the fact that the commercial banks were absorbing short-term liabilities (from a relatively concentrated group of depositors) while acquiring assets that were, by their very nature, long term (despite the particular contractual terms of any given loan), as the bulk of the loans were going to a limited number of the developing countries.

By the late 1970s and early 1980s, less and less was heard about the recycling problem. There were basically two reasons. First, the insatiable appetite of at least certain developing countries for foreign capital was clearly matched by the willingness of the larger commercial banks to add to their international exposure, and second, growing fiscal deficits in several of the industrialized countries were absorbing an ever larger portion of the OPEC surplus. So strong were these forces that the second oil shock, one much larger than the first in terms of the transfers involved, failed to reestablish any significant degree of concern with the recycling problem.

Three nearly simultaneous events in the early 1980s served to trigger the current international debt "crisis," which is, of course, precisely the doomsday scenario envisaged by the more pessimistic participants in the recycling debate. The first was the sharp recovery of the dollar beginning in late 1980, followed by the extraordinary strength of the dollar during much of 1982. Associated with the recovery were two important (and related) developments: dollar interest rates rose sharply, and dollar prices of many traded goods (particularly commodities that figured heavily in the exports of the debtor countries) fell abruptly, especially during the spectacular rise of the dollar from October 1980 through February 1981. As most of the debt of the developing countries was denominated in dollars, and much of it at the floating London interbank offered rate (LIBOR), the appreciation of the dollar and the rise in dollar interest rates implied an equivalent rise in debt service. Not only did the nominal interest service increase because of the rise in interest rates, but real interest service rose even more because of the decline in the dollar prices of many tradables. The latter effect comes about because countries obviously service their foreign debt by importing less or exporting more (in the final analysis); a decline in the dollar price of tradables implies an increase in the real burden of servicing foreign debt. In addition, there is some evidence that the appreciation of the dollar, coupled with the subsequent world recession, resulted in an adverse turn in the terms of trade facing the debtor countries. This latter effect came about because the appreciation of the dollar had, initially at least, a stronger downward effect on the prices of homogeneous commodities than on those of manufactures, and the former are very important exportables of most debtor countries.

Whereas appropriately defined real rates of interest on external debt had been negative during much of the 1970s for a number of developing countries, short-term real rates of interest on that debt rose abruptly to the 15–20 percent range at the end of 1980 and have remained very high ever since. Although it is difficult to have too much debt (in the short run, at least) when real rates of interest are negative, a debt service problem quickly emerges when real rates increase as they did.

Chilean data readily illustrate the point. The second column of table 6-1 indicates the annual rate of change of unit (dollar) values of Chilean imports and exports, and the third column indicates the behavior of

Table 6-1. *External Prices of Chilean Tradables and Interest Rates*
(percent)

Period	Annual rate of change— prices[a]	Interest rate[b]	Real interest rate[c]
1977	5.1	7.0	1.8
1978	6.1	6.4	0.3
1979	26.8	11.2	− 12.3
1980	16.6	13.9	− 2.3
1981	− 5.5	15.7	22.4
1982	− 8.6	13.3	24.0

a. Rate of change in a simple average of unit values of Chilean imports and exports as calculated by the United Nations Economic Commission for Latin America.
b. Annual averages of six-month LIBOR rates, based on U.S. dollars.
c. Defined against the prices of Chilean tradables.
Source: Gil-Diaz 1983.

dollar nominal interest rates. The fourth column combines the two into a real rate of interest on Chilean foreign debt. Note that that rate was very low or negative from 1977 through 1980 and then rose into the 20–25 percent range. Although nominal dollar interest rates rose somewhat, the main source of the increase in the real rate is the dollar deflation—the prices of Chilean tradables actually fell during 1981 and 1982. The same phenomenon occurred in most other debtor countries in 1981, and it was probably the most important single element in the making of the crisis. The dollar deflation was a direct consequence of the recovery of the U.S. dollar vis à vis other major currencies.

The second development was an intensification of the tendency toward greater fiscal deficits in the industrialized countries, a development that was exacerbated by the rapid decline in the OPEC current account surpluses that began in early 1981. Clearly the excess supply of funds available to the developing countries was shrinking; nevertheless, they were still able to finance their debt service (and then some) by rollovers of the principal and further borrowing that more than covered interest payments. The change in real interest rates that began in late 1980 did not immediately provoke the crisis, but competition for international funds was plainly making it more difficult for the developing countries to maintain their level of foreign borrowing. Even without further developments, it was but a matter of time until the debt crisis.

The third development exposed the underlying rot for all to see and precipitated the crisis. That development was the South Atlantic conflict of May–June 1982. As is well known, several major U.S. banks had an exposure in Latin America well beyond their capital and reserves; such an exposure could be considered prudent only if the United States could reasonably be expected to come to the aid of any Latin American country with large debts to U.S. banks when that country encountered a payments difficulty. The decision by the United States to support Britain against Argentina in the South Atlantic conflict, however, exploded the credibility of that assumption. The bankers, unnerved by the event, began immediately to restrict the flow of loans to Latin America. Mexico, whose reserve position was very fragile after the February 1982 devaluation, was the first country forced to suspend payment, but Argentina, Chile, Brazil, and even Venezuela suffered the same fate.

Thus the debt crisis resulted from a number of factors no single one of which would have been sufficient alone. The crisis has been particularly intense owing to the fact that much of the borrowing helped, directly or indirectly, to sustain fiscal deficits; as that borrowing declined, the fiscal deficits had to be turned into surpluses to generate the local currency required to buy the dollars to service the debt. Countries such as Argentina and Brazil have found it extremely difficult to undertake the fiscal reforms that are required of them and have turned more and more to inflation as a source of finance. In the process, control of international capital flows has been tightened (as the country tries to avoid runs on its own currency), with the effect that governments have no access whatsoever to the very substantial foreign currency earnings accruing to their citizens on their foreign investments. Governments increasingly find themselves being abruptly cut off from such funds, and this aspect makes the current debt crisis particularly dangerous.

Latin American Public Finance during the 1970s

In this section we look at the revenues, expenditures, and deficits of Latin American governments during the 1970s and, when data are available from our source, the *Government Finance Statistics* of the IMF, during the early 1980s.[1] We also look at the main expenditure items in order to detect the sources of growth in the aggregate.

Because we are primarily interested in the connection between public expenditure and foreign indebtedness, we have taken the rather unusual step of presenting these figures in current U.S. dollars. To do so we used the market exchange rates as they are recorded in the *International Financial Statistics (IFS)* of the IMF. Since we are dealing with flow data, we use the average market exchange rate in each period. The presentation of data in current U.S. dollars has two implications: the U.S. inflation imparts a positive trend to all series, and the figures reflect the volatility of Latin American exchange rates.

The reason for looking at the data in current U.S. dollars rather than in units of constant domestic purchasing power, as is customary, is that, with free access to the world capital market, it is the current dollar value of expenditures, and not its size in terms of units of constant domestic purchasing power, that affects the extent of foreign borrowing. The interested reader could easily relate these series to foreign debt data in other sections of this book.

Finally, we should note that the four main expenditure items that we have considered here—general public services, defense, capital expenditure, and our aggregate "social, economic, others"—do not add up, in general, to the figure we present under the heading "total expenditure and net lending." In consequence, the reader should not expect to see the average rate of growth of the latter equal to a weighted average of the average rates of growth of our four expenditure items.

General Patterns

Revenues have been growing faster, on average, than expenditures in four out of five countries surveyed, Venezuela being the exception, with both items growing at the same pace.

The ranking of different expenditure items in terms of growth rates varies widely across countries. Some patterns emerge clearly, however, from table 6-2. First, the aggregate "social, economic, others" is a very fast-growing item. It ranks first in Argentina and Brazil and second in Chile and Mexico. Capital expenditure, on the other hand, is a slow-growing item in the southern cone countries. It ranks fourth of four items in Argentina and Brazil and third in Chile. Third, defense has been a fast-growing item in Chile and Argentina only. Two striking features of these rankings are their similarity in the cases of Argentina and Brazil and their perfect disparity between Chile and Venezuela.

Argentina

Time series in Argentina reflect the highly unstable nature of its economic behavior during the 1970s and early 1980s. Except in 1975, when a series of "maxi" devaluations by former economic ministers Gomez Morales and Rodrigo reduced the dollar value of revenues about 49 percent, they have been growing all along the period (see table 6-3). Expenditures, on the other hand, suffered two contractions, the first in 1975, for the reason explained above, and the second in 1977, when the

Table 6-2. *Growth of Revenues and Expenditures in Selected Latin American Countries, 1973–80*

Item	Argentina	Brazil	Chile	Mexico	Venezuela
Total revenue and grants (percent)	36.7	21.4	23.3	27.5	32
Total expenditure and net lending (percent)	34.7	20.9	15.1	26.4	32
General public services (percent)	36.2	19.5	2.5	0.4	30.4
Rank[a]	3	2	4	4	1
Defense (percent)	37.9	11.3	15	17.5	13.5
Rank[a]	2	3	1	3	4
Social, economic, other (percent)[b]	43.4	23.7	11.4	24.4	22
Rank[a]	1	1	2	2	3
Capital expenditure (percent)	33.5	10.4	5.5	29.2	23.3
Rank[a]	4	4	3	1	2

a. According to growth rate.
b. Education, health, social security and welfare, housing and community amenities, other community and social services, economic services, other purposes.
Source: Tables 6-3 through 6-13.

Table 6-3. *Total Revenues and Grants, Total Expenditures and Net Lending, and Deficit in Argentina, 1973–80*

Year	Total revenue and grants		Total expenditure and net lending		Deficit (US$ billions)
	US$ billions	Percentage change	US$ billions	Percentage change	
1973	4.68	42.16	6.50	56.51	1.81
1974	8.54	82.43	11.46	76.61	2.92
1975	4.37	48.81	8.44	−26.33	4.07
1976	6.63	51.63	10.51	24.54	3.89
1977	7.26	9.56	8.77	−16.63	1.42
1978	10.55	45.23	12.66	44.38	2.11
1979	17.88	69.50	20.70	63.49	2.82
1980	26.64	49.00	32.14	55.34	5.51
Average	—	36.70	—	34.70	—

Sources: International Monetary Fund, *Government Financial Statistics* and *International Financial Statistics*, various issues.

Table 6-4. *Expenditure in Argentina, by Function, 1973–80*

Year	General public services US$ billions	General public services Percentage change	Defense US$ billions	Defense Percentage change	Social, economic, other[a] US$ billions	Social, economic, other[a] Percentage change	Capital expenditure US$ billions	Capital expenditure Percentage change
1973	0.64	74.47	0.64	74.47	4.89	103.8	1.06	24.6
1974	0.90	40.82	0.79	23.22	8.65	76.9	1.69	58.4
1975	0.55	−39.21	0.60	−23.58	5.09	−41.2	1.04	−38.4
1976	0.74	35.94	1.02	69.93	8.50	67.0	2.68	158.0
1977	0.75	0.4	0.93	−8.73	6.91	−18.7	2.23	−16.7
1978	1.06	42.54	1.59	70.77	10.71	55.0	2.64	18.5
1979	1.80	69.63	2.64	66.01	15.96	49.0	3.60	36.1
1980	2.98	65.10	3.48	31.49	24.81	55.5	4.59	27.7
Average	—	36.20	—	37.90	—	43.4	—	33.5

a. Education, health, social security and welfare, housing and community amenities, other community and social services, economic services, other purposes.

Sources: International Monetary Fund, *Government Financial Statistics* and *International Financial Statistics*, various issues.

recently installed military government tried, with some initial success, to reduce the size of public bureaucracy.

The fastest-growing item during the period was the aggregate "social, economic, other." Within this aggregate, the leading item was what the IMF *Government Finance Statistics* presents as "other purposes," with a growth rate of 107.3 percent.

The defense average growth rate ranks second among the four aggregates displayed in table 6-4. It is also the more volatile item, reflecting both the timing of the limits conflict with Chile and the changing political influence of the Argentine military.

Finally, Argentina shares with Brazil and Chile, the other southern cone countries in the group, a pattern of slow-growing capital expenditures.

Brazil

Brazil shows the smoother set of time series within the group of countries surveyed in this study. Figures for the central government are displayed in tables 6-5 and 6-6 and figures for state and local governments in table 6-7. The central government's revenues presented a slightly larger average rate of growth than expenditures. The opposite was true of state governments.

An interesting feature of the central government's aggregate figures is the negative trend in growth rates for both revenues and expenditures. No definite trend was observed in the rates of growth of both items at the state government level. With respect to the components of central government expenditure, there are two fast-growing items, general public services and "social, economic, other," and two slow-growing ones, defense and capital expenditure. "Social, economic, other" ranks first, in accordance with the leading role this aggregate plays in explaining expenditure growth in our group of countries. Capital expenditure shows the same slow growth pattern of the other two southern cone countries, Argentina and Brazil, and within this group, Brazil is the only exception with respect to high defense spending growth.

It is interesting to note that the only item that clearly follows the trend of decrease observed in aggregate expenditure growth is "social, economic, other." The other three items show more volatile behavior. State governments' expenditures also show a decreasing growth rate.

Chile

In Chile, much as in the other countries, central government revenues have grown at faster rates than expenditures over the 1973–80 period.

Table 6-5. *Total Revenues and Grants, Total Expenditures and Net Lending, and Deficit of Brazil's Central Government, 1973–79*

Year	Total revenue and grants		Total expenditure and net lending		Deficit (US$ billions)
	US$ billions	Percentage change	US$ billions	Percentage change	
1972	11.12	23.3	11.36	20.4	0.24
1973	15.44	38.8	15.18	33.6	−0.26
1974	20.41	32.2	19.3	26.0	−1.28
1975	24.20	18.6	24.76	29.4	0.55
1976	30.14	24.5	30.45	23.0	0.31
1977	33.86	12.3	35.18	15.5	1.32
1978	39.05	15.3	41.08	16.8	2.04
1979	41.39	6.0	41.92	2.0	0.53
Average	—	21.4	—	20.9	—

Sources: International Monetary Fund, *Government Financial Statistics* and *International Financial Statistics*, various issues.

Data relating to the Chilean government revenues and expenditures appear in table 6-8. This tendency results in surpluses for 1979 and 1980 of about $1 billion and $1.5 billion.[2] It must be considered throughout that central government data give a narrow definition of the public sector. Although these data include several official agencies, they leave out important public enterprises such as Corporación Nacional del Cobre (copper) and Linea Aerea Nacional (airlines). Therefore these figures are significant more in relation to the evolution of the government finances over time than in relation to the absolute level of the aggregates.

In the 1975–78 period the central government registered only minor surpluses and deficits. Nevertheless, in 1979–80 it achieved significant surpluses, probably with the intention of paying off part of its domestic outstanding debt. The composition of Chilean government expenditure over the 1973–80 period was rather peculiar (see table 6-9). The relative average growth of expenditures for social and economic purposes and capital was the lowest among the countries under consideration (aggregate expenditure was also relatively low). General public services spending was specially reduced during 1974–75 as a consequence of the government's efforts to reduce the size of the public sector. Important decreases in other expenditure items in 1975 are also explained (at least in part) by the huge devaluation experienced in that year. In the 1976–77 period, all expenditure grew significantly, especially social and economic spending in 1977. By 1978 public spending in general had slowed down. Social and economic spending, however, kept rising rapidly.

Table 6-6. Expenditure in Brazil's Central Government, by Function, 1973–79

Year	General public services US$ billions	General public services Percentage change	Defense US$ billions	Defense Percentage change	Social, economic, other[a] US$ billions	Social, economic, other[a] Percentage change	Capital expenditure US$ billions	Capital expenditure Percentage change
1972	1.37	4.6	0.84	11.4	8.22	33.0	1.38	12.4
1973	1.40	2.8	1.09	29.8	10.92	32.8	1.52	9.9
1974	2.14	52.1	1.28	17.2	14.32	31.1	2.15	41.7
1975	2.62	22.7	1.38	7.6	19.22	34.2	3.06	42.5
1976	4.04	54.1	1.78	29.2	21.63	12.5	4.13	34.9
1977	4.49	11.2	1.83	2.9	25.6	18.4	4.01	-3.0
1978	5.63	25.4	2.04	11.5	31.2	21.9	3.90	-2.8
1979	4.68	-16.9	1.65	-19.3	32.92	5.5	1.87	-52.1
Average	—	19.5	—	11.3	—	23.7	—	10.4

a. Education, health, social security and welfare, housing and community amenities, other community and social services, economic services, other purposes.

Sources: International Monetary Fund, Government Financial Statistics and International Financial Statistics, various issues.

Table 6-7. *Revenues, Expenditures, and Deficits of Brazil's State and Local Governments, 1973–79*

Year	State governments' total revenue and grants		State governments' total expenditure and net lending		Deficit (US$ billions)	Local governments' deficit (US$ billions)
	US$ billions	Percentage change	US$ billions	Percentage change		
1972	5.61	17.8	5.80	22.1	0.19	0.05
1973	7.62	35.8	7.87	35.7	0.24	0.08
1974	9.87	29.4	10.28	30.7	0.41	0.15
1975	11.04	11.9	12.30	19.6	1.26	0.22
1976	11.37	3.0	13.13	6.8	1.76	0.25
1977	13.28	16.9	13.97	6.4	0.69	0.23
1978	12.11	−8.8	17.31	23.9	1.72	0.29
1979	17.05	40.8	18.38	6.2	1.33	0.07
Average	—	18.3	—	18.9	—	—

Sources: International Monetary Fund, *Government Financial Statistics* and *International Financial Statistics*, various issues.

Table 6-8. *Revenues and Expenditures of Chile's Central Government, 1973–80*

Year	Total revenue and grants		Total expenditure and net lending		Deficit (US$ billions)
	US$ billions	Per-centage	US$ billions	Per-centage	
1973	2.94	—	3.70	—	0.76
1974	3.13	6.5	3.73	0.8	0.6
1975	2.54	−19.0	2.53	−32.2	−0.01
1976	3.14	23.9	3.01	19.0	−0.13
1977	4.25	35.2	4.40	46.2	0.15
1978	5.97	16.9	4.99	13.4	0.02
1979	7.07	66.4	6.07	21.8	−1.0
1980	9.41	33.1	7.87	29.5	−1.55
Average	—	23.3	—	15.1	—

Sources: International Monetary Fund, *Government Financial Statistics* and *International Financial Statistics*, various issues.

Table 6-9. *Expenditure in Chile's Central Government, by Function, 1973–80*

Year	General public services US$ billions	General public services Per-centage	Defense US$ billions	Defense Per-centage	Social, economic, other[a] US$ billions	Social, economic, other[a] Per-centage	Capital US$ billions	Capital Per-centage
1973	0.6	—	0.4	—	2.65	—	0.78	—
1974	0.4	−36.8	0.5	39.8	2.82	6.4	1.13	44.9
1975	0.3	−19.0	0.3	−37.3	1.92	−31.9	0.49	−56.6
1976	0.4	28.1	0.4	16.8	2.01	4.69	0.43	−11.7
1977	0.5	35.7	0.5	35.5	3.34	66.2	0.50	16.1
1978	0.6	4.3	0.6	20.0	3.73	66.7	0.61	22.7
1979	—	—	—	—	—	—	0.71	16.7
1980	—	—	—	—	—	—	0.76	6.6
Average	—	2.5	—	15.0	—	11.42	—	5.53

Note: Dashes indicate that data are unavailable.

a. Education, health, social security and welfare, housing, other community and social services, economic services, and other purposes.

Sources: International Monetary Fund, *Government Financial Statistics* and *International Financial Statistics*, various issues.

It is noteworthy that, in growth, official capital expenditures are always below aggregate spending except in 1978. This tendency may well be misleading, however, because, as noted above, several public enterprises are excluded from these figures. Finally it is also noteworthy that both expenditures and revenues show the lowest average growth in the group of countries considered.

Mexico

Although it is also observed in the Mexican case that the relative increase in revenues is slightly higher, on average, than that of expenditures, the deficit of the central government shows substantial increases in the 1972–80 period. Data relating to the central government finances appear in table 6-10. This behavior is explained by the changes in economic policies in the 1970s. A very expansionist policy was clearly pursued until 1975, which concluded with a significant devaluation at the end of 1976. The low deficits registered in 1977 and 1978, then, reflect the implementation of the adjustment program undertaken after the devaluation. In 1978 another fiscal expansion began, probably one of a higher magnitude, and continued until 1981. The reduction of all figures

Table 6-10. *Revenues and Expenditures of Mexico's Central Government, 1972–80*

Year	Total revenue and grants US$ billions	Total revenue and grants Per-centage	Total expenditure and net lending US$ billions	Total expenditure and net lending Per-centage	Deficit (US$ billions)
1972	4.68	—	6.04	—	1.4
1973	5.59	19.5	7.8	29.0	2.2
1974	7.64	36.8	10.4	33.3	2.7
1975	10.70	40.0	15.0	44.0	4.3
1976	10.96	2.4	15.1	0.8	4.2
1977	10.68	−0.2	13.4	−11.4	2.7
1978	14.19	32.9	16.9	26.6	2.8
1979	19.23	35.7	23.7	40.0	4.5
1980	29.42	52.8	35.2	48.6	5.8
Average	—	27.5	—	26.4	—

Note: Data for 1972 percentages are not available.

Sources: International Monetary Fund, *Government Financial Statistics* and *International Financial Statistics*, various issues.

in table 6-7 during 1977 had the monetary causes implied by the devaluation, and a similar effect was probably observed in 1981.

Until 1975 the most important expenditure item of the government, in levels and rates of growth, was social and economic spending (see table 6-11). General public services and capital expenditure also showed significant increases, increases in the latter being of a higher level. Although defense spending shows a high growth rate on average, its share in total spending is not significant by comparison with the figures for the other countries.

The effects of the devaluation and the adjustment program implemented in 1976 were felt most in government public service and capital expenditures. Social and economic spending fell insignificantly in 1977. Nevertheless, the spending level in general public services kept falling until 1979, and that of capital rose after 1977 at the highest level. Even though this definition of government excludes many huge public enterprises—for example, PEMEX (petroleum), CFE (electricity), twenty-one steel enterprises, and seventeen chemical companies—the government's capital expenditures have, on average during 1973–79, the highest growth rate, whereas spending for general services has the lowest.

Venezuela

The central government in Venezuela registered important deficits, especially in 1977–78. Data relating to Venezuelan government finances appear in table 6-12. The same qualification expressed about the definition of government used for the other countries applies here: the Venezuelan data exclude many important publicly owned enterprises—such as Petróleos de Venezuela (petroleum) and Petroquímica de Venezuela (petrochemical plants). Government expenditure consistently increased over the 1972–81 period although at very different rates. The highest sustained increase seemed to take place starting in 1980. Notice that monetary factors could not affect these figures as much as in the other cases, because the exchange rate remained fixed during practically the whole period. It is noteworthy that the benefits from the world oil shock to Venezuela were immediately reflected in the 1974 increase in spending (and revenue) figures.

Regarding the composition of government expenditure (table 6-13), the highest growth was registered by general public services, whereas defense had the lowest. Furthermore, the latter's level was relatively unimportant. Expenditure on social and economic activities showed rather significant increases until 1977 and slowed down later in 1978–79. The general slowdown in government spending, however, was most

Table 6-11. *Expenditure in Mexico's Central Government, by Function, 1972–80*

Year	General public services US$ billions	Per- centage	Defense US$ billions	Per- centage	Social, economic, other[a] US$ billions	Per- centage	Capital US$ billions	Per- centage
1972	0.5	—	0.2	—	0.9	—	1.61	—
1973	0.6	15.8	0.3	24.1	5.9	37.2	2.06	28.0
1974	0.7	20.0	0.4	35.4	8.3	40.7	2.52	22.3
1975	1.1	50.3	0.5	23.8	11.1	33.7	3.0	19.0
1976	1.2	11.7	0.5	5.3	11.2	1.0	3.43	14.4
1977	0.5	−55.0	0.4	−17.7	10.1	−9.8	2.82	−17.8
1978	0.4	−32.1	0.5	18.5	11.2	10.9	4.03	42.7
1979	0.3	−7.3	0.6	31.5	14.7	31.3	6.83	69.6
1980	—	—	0.8	19.2	22.1	50.3	10.61	55.4
Average	—	0.36	—	17.5	—	24.4	—	29.2

Note: Dashes indicate that data are unavailable.

a. Education, health, social security and welfare, housing, other community services, and economic services.

Sources: International Monetary Fund, *Government Financial Statistics* and *International Financial Statistics*, various issues.

Table 6-12. *Revenues and Expenditures of Venezuela's Central Government, 1972–81*

Year	Total revenue and grants		Total expenditure and net lending		Deficit (US$ billions)
	US$ billions	Per-centage	US$ billions	Per-centage	
1972	3.0	—	3.1	—	0.13
1973	3.95	31.4	3.7	17.8	−0.3
1974	10.4	162.0	9.8	164.0	−0.6
1975	9.9	−4.3	9.8	0.5	−0.1
1976	9.3	−6.0	10.6	8.5	1.3
1977	10.0	7.5	12.3	15.9	2.3
1978	10.0	−0.2	12.7	3.3	2.7
1979	12.0	19.8	11.8	−7.8	−0.2
1980	15.7	31.1	16.1	37.1	0.4
1981	22.8	46.6	24.3	48.2	1.5
Average	—	32.0	—	32.0	—

Note: Data for 1972 percentages are not available.

Sources: International Monetary Fund, *Government Financial Statistics* and *International Financial Statistics*, various issues.

important in capital expenditure: negative rates of growth were registered in 1979 and 1980, whereas a positive but low growth took place in 1978. Until that time capital expenditure had shown the most rapid increases.

There are thus two major characteristics of government spending in Venezuela during the 1972–80 period. Until 1977, total expenditure increases were sustained (though at varying rates), and capital accumulation appeared to be the major concern of government fiscal expansion. In addition, social and economic activities seemed to be important targets during the period. After 1977 there was a generalized slowdown in total expenditure—which seems to have ended in 1981—and a change in the major concerns of government policy, away from capital spending and toward current expenditure, mainly in general public services.

Money Creation and Government Finance

The manner in which money creation is linked to public sector deficits, and the degree to which it is, are complex questions. Not all central bank expansion takes the form of credit to the government, nor does all credit

Table 6-13. *Expenditures in Venezuela's Central Government, by Function, 1972–81*

Year	General public services US$ billions	Per-centage	Defense US$ billions	Per-centage	Social, economic, other[a] US$ billions	Per-centage	Capital US$ billions	Per-centage
1972	0.2	—	0.3	—	2.4	—	0.74	—
1973	0.2	16.5	0.3	6.7	2.73	13.8	0.90	21.7
1974	0.4	54.1	0.5	43.2	4.57	67.4	1.70	89.3
1975	0.6	50.3	0.5	18.1	5.54	21.2	1.90	12.0
1976	0.6	12.8	0.4	−16.6	6.1	10.1	2.95	55.1
1977	0.8	33.2	0.6	26.2	8.4	37.7	4.17	41.3
1978	1.0	17.1	0.6	10.4	8.9	6.0	4.49	7.8
1979	1.0	1.1	0.7	12.0	8.2	−7.9	2.75	−38.7
1980	1.6	58.3	0.8	8.3	10.5	28.0	2.69	−2.2
Average	—	30.4	—	13.5	—	22.0	—	23.3

Note: Data for 1972 percentages are not available.

a. Education, health, social security and welfare, housing, other community services, economic services, and other purposes.

Sources: International Monetary Fund, *Government Financial Statistics* and *International Financial Statistics*, various issues.

to the government come from the central bank. Much money is created, in some countries, to finance off-budget expenditures such as interest subsidies (for example, in Brazil) or to aid ailing private banks (for example, in Chile and Argentina). Finally, the relation between deficits and money creation is subject to great and frequent change, making it difficult to formulate any generalizations.

To estimate the amount of resources provided to the public sectors of Argentina, Brazil, Chile, Mexico, and Venezuela by their monetary authorities, we combined direct and indirect financing. Direct financing consists of the change in central bank claims on government (line 12a of the *IFS*). Indirect financing comes about because central banks lend to commercial banks, which in turn lend to public sectors. To obtain an estimate of this indirect finance, we constructed the net claims of the commercial banks on the public sector (commercial bank claims on government, line 22a, plus commercial bank claims on the rest of general government, line 22b, minus government deposits in commercial banks, line 26d), and compared it with central bank credit to commercial banks (line 26g). When changes in commercial bank claims on the public sector exceeded the change in central bank claims on commercial banks, we used the latter as the amount of indirect finance, and vice versa. It is unlikely, then, that either private saving or central bank lending to the private sector is included in our measure of indirect finance. The sum of the direct and indirect provision of resources appears in tables 6-14 and 6-15 under the heading ΔCG. Tables 6-14 and 6-15 also show the change in reserve money (labeled ΔRM, line 14 in the *IFS*) and the ratio of ΔCG to ΔRM. As can be seen, the ratios fluctuate enormously, indicating that contemporaneous monetary expansion is not highly correlated with central bank lending to the public sector. In Argentina, claims on the public sector have increased every year during the 1972–82 period except for 1977, the average ratio being about two-thirds. In Brazil, the pattern has been highly erratic, and the average ratio is slightly negative; only in 1982 did direct plus indirect central bank claims on government expand by a greater amount than reserve money. The Brazilian case is obviously a special one in that central bank lending is largely to the Banco do Brazil, which then extends subsidized credit to both the public and the private sector.

In Chile there was a sharp contraction of lending to the public sector in 1980 and 1981 but also a sharp decline in the stock of reserve money in 1981 and 1982. During an earlier period (1973–75), lending to the government far exceeded money creation, indicating that credit to the private sector was severely squeezed. During the 1977–80 period, central bank claims on government grew by only one-third as much as reserve money;

Table 6-14. *Changes in Central Bank Credit to Government and Flows of Reserve Money: Argentina, Brazil, and Chile*

	Argentina[a]			Brazil[b]			Chile[c]		
Year	ΔCG	ΔRM	ΔCG/ΔRM	ΔCG	ΔRM	ΔCG/ΔRM	ΔCG	ΔRM	ΔCG/ΔRM
1972	7	6	1.17	0.4	5.2	0.08	53	39	1.36
1973	24	108	0.22	3.5	15.0	0.23	605	251	2.41
1974	30	75	0.40	−13.0	14.8	−0.88	2,917	692	4.22
1975	160	349	0.46	−9.9	17.4	−0.57	14,394	2,565	5.61
1976	468	1,960	0.24	5.5	40.0	0.14	23,788	10,254	2.32
1977	−57	1,103	−0.05	33.3	56.1	0.59	41,252	15,391	2.68
1978	1,669	3,504	0.48	25.2	73.2	0.34	12,860	16,637	0.77
1979	1,705	6,095	0.28	74.6	206.4	0.36	22,296	19,471	1.15
1980	15,060	10,386	1.45	64.6	261.0	0.25	−48,640	25,359	−1.92
1981	54,478	27,794	1.96	−163.8	502.0	−0.33	−62,647	−8,381	7.47
1982	112,297	381,847	0.29	1,504.2	1,004.3	1.50	16,466	−21,006	−0.78

Note: ΔCG = sum of the direct and indirect provision of resources (see text). ΔRM = change in reserve money.
a. In billions of current pesos.
b. In billions of current cruzeiros.
c. In millions of current pesos.
Sources: International Monetary Fund, *Government Financial Statistics*, various issues.

Table 6-15. *Changes in Central Bank Credit to Government and Flows of Reserve Money: Mexico and Venezuela, 1972–82*

Year	Mexico[a]			Venezuela[b]		
	ΔCG	ΔRM	$\Delta CG/\Delta RM$	ΔCG	ΔRM	$\Delta CG/\Delta RM$
1972	23.1	24.2	0.95	30	619	0.05
1973	22.7	17.6	1.29	65	1,363	0.05
1974	34.8	30.1	1.15	−1,279	2,722	−0.47
1975	32.5	35.5	0.92	−872	4,009	−0.22
1976	24.3	−9.9	−2.45	−1,743	2,558	−0.68
1977	148.4	165.0	0.90	−201	3,517	−0.06
1978	58.2	84.9	0.69	−3,529	2,078	−1.70
1979	109.0	132.7	0.82	1,148	2,791	0.41
1980	159.0	208.2	0.76	−1,538	1,613	−0.95
1981	284.8	323.3	0.88	372	4,630	0.08
1982	1,459.5	1,023.6	1.43	3,165	5,203	0.61

Note: ΔCG = sum of the direct and indirect provision of resources (see text). ΔRM = change in reserve money.

a. In billions of current pesos.

b. In billions of bolivars.

Sources: International Monetary Fund, *Government Financial Statistics*, various issues.

this was the period of accumulation of international reserves in that country, with 1982 being a year of major decumulation.

The Mexican case is much more stable (until 1982). In most years, the growth in claims on government was very close to the growth in reserve money, the major exception being 1976, when the devaluation caused a flight from the peso and hence an actual decline in reserve money. With the onset of the debt crisis in 1982, however, the government began to rely more heavily on the central bank for financing.

Venezuela presents a picture similar to that of Brazil (but for different reasons). Reserve money has grown steadily and systematically, but very little of that growth has been captured by the government. This situation sharply contrasts with that of Mexico, where in most years the bulk of the money created in the central bank was passed directly to the fiscal authorities.

The generalizations that the data permit are quite limited. All five countries except Venezuela have made heavy use of the central bank for fiscal purposes. This practice seems to have accelerated in 1982 with the onset of the debt crisis; central bank direct and indirect lending to governments increased very sharply in all five countries, including Venezuela. Second, new central bank credits to governments exceeded reserve money creation in 1982 in all five countries except Argentina and Vene-

Table 6-16. Ratios of Money Creation to GDP and of Inflation Tax to GDP and Total Revenue: Argentina, Brazil, and Chile (percent)

Year	Argentina $\frac{\Delta RM}{GDP}$	Argentina $\frac{TAX}{GDP}$	Argentina $\frac{TAX}{TAX+REV}$	Brazil $\frac{\Delta RM}{GDP}$	Brazil $\frac{TAX}{GDP}$	Brazil $\frac{TAX}{TAX+GDP}$	Chile $\frac{\Delta RM}{GDP}$	Chile $\frac{TAX}{GDP}$	Chile $\frac{TAX}{TAX+GDP}$
1972	2.6	3.5	23.7	1.2	0.8	8.5	9.8	9.1	32.1
1973	29.2	7.0	38.6	2.6	0.8	8.1	12.2	14.2	41.2
1974	13.0	9.4	39.5	2.0	2.0	16.7	6.6	9.3	26.7
1975	19.8	31.2	74.0	1.6	1.7	16.1	6.2	7.4	21.5
1976	25.8	25.5	67.8	2.5	2.2	17.8	7.8	5.7	16.6
1977	4.7	13.3	50.0	2.3	2.1	17.7	5.5	3.6	10.5
1978	5.8	8.8	38.2	2.1	1.9	16.3	3.9	2.3	6.2
1979	3.7	5.3	27.7	3.4	3.1	26.6	3.1	2.9	6.7
1980	3.0	3.3	19.0	2.2	3.0	22.2	2.8	2.3	5.7
1981	4.0	4.3	—	2.1	2.8	23.8	-0.7	0.7	—
1982	24.9	13.1	—	2.1	2.5	—	-1.8	1.2	—

Note: ΔRM = change in reserve money. GDP = gross domestic product. TAX = inflation tax. REV = revenue. Some data were unavailable, as indicated by the dashes.

Sources: International Monetary Fund, Government Financial Statistics, various issues.

zuela (in Argentina much of the enormous acceleration in money creation stemmed from the ruinous Carvallo plan for bailing out bankrupt
financial institutions; much the same sequence of events was to unfold in
Chile in 1983). Prior to the debt crisis, however, reliance on central bank
financing was erratic in all countries except Mexico.

The above data indicate only qualitative behavior, not the magnitude
of the financing, nor do they indicate the consequences for inflation.
Indeed, reliance on central bank financing need not be inflationary if the
resources transferred to the government do not exceed the normal
growth in the demand for reserve money. Indeed, if the central bank does
not allocate that growth to the government, the result will be a buildup
for international reserves, which is essentially lending abroad, a phenomenon that occurred in all five countries during the second half of the
1970s and in 1980.

Tables 6-16 and 6-17 give a better idea of the magnitude of central bank
finance, and the consequences for inflation, by presenting the growth of
reserve money as a fraction of GDP, distinguishing between growth in that
money and the "inflation tax." Reserve money is always a very small
fraction of GDP, so that, in the absence of inflation, the growth in that stock
relative to the level of GDP will be correspondingly small. Tables 6-16 and
6-17 indicate, however, that some countries have made very heavy use of
reserve money growth. During the 1973–76 period in Argentina, growth
in reserve money averaged about 20 percent of GDP—a level that cannot
be sustained without igniting a very high rate of inflation—and returned
to that level in 1982. The growth of reserve money in Brazil and Venezuela has been stable in the neighborhood of somewhat more than 2
percent of GDP. In Chile it has fluctuated widely, as it has in Mexico, in the
latter country reaching more than 10 percent of GDP in 1982.

The growth in reserve money indicates the *potential* (or sometimes the
consequences) for central bank finance of fiscal deficits (or the acquisition
of international reserves). This growth includes both the increased demand for reserve money because of normal economic growth and the
replacement demand that comes about because of inflation. Inflation
depreciates the real value of the stock of reserve money, so money
holders must demand more of it simply to sustain their holdings in real
terms. The latter source of demand is identified as *TAX* in tables 6-16 and
6-17; the ratio of *TAX* to *GDP* is simply the inflation rate (as measured by
the various CPIs) multiplied by the beginning-of-year stock of reserve
money, the product being expressed as a fraction of *GDP*. The third
column in each country panel of table 6-10 presents *TAX* as a fraction of
normal revenues (*REV*) plus the inflation tax. The excess of the column
labeled Δ*RM/GDP* and that labeled *TAX/GDP* is the change in reserve
money in *real* terms expressed as a fraction of *GDP*.

Table 6-17. Ratios of Money Creation to GDP and of Inflation Tax to GDP and Total Revenue:
Mexico and Venezuela

	Mexico			Venezuela		
Year	$\frac{\Delta RM}{GDP}$	$\frac{TAX}{GDP}$	$\frac{TAX}{TAX + REV}$	$\frac{\Delta RM}{GDP}$	$\frac{TAX}{GDP}$	$\frac{TAX}{TAX + REV}$
1972	4.0	0.4	4.0	0.9	0.2	0.8
1973	2.5	1.8	15.3	1.6	0.4	1.6
1974	3.4	1.9	15.1	2.7	0.9	1.6
1975	3.3	1.2	9.0	3.2	0.7	1.6
1976	−0.7	2.4	16.1	1.8	0.7	1.9
1977	9.4	2.2	14.1	2.2	0.9	2.4
1978	3.9	2.3	13.6	1.2	0.8	2.4
1979	4.6	2.8	15.8	1.3	2.1	6.1
1980	5.4	4.1	19.4	0.7	1.9	4.9
1981	5.6	3.8	—	1.6	1.0	—
1982	10.4	10.5	—	1.5	0.7	—

Note: ΔRM = change in reserve money. TAX = inflation tax. REV = revenue. Revenue data are unavailable for 1981 and 1982.
Sources: International Monetary Fund, Government Financial Statistics, various issues.

Tables 6-16 and 6-17 indicate that all countries except Venezuela have relied heavily on the inflation tax, particularly Argentina (and also Chile during the first half of the 1970s). During 1975 and 1976, Argentine collections of the inflation tax accounted for more than 25 percent of its GDP (and half or more of total resources available to the government)! The tax has been important in both Brazil and Mexico since the early 1970s; again, Venezuela is the exception. In Argentina and Mexico, the inflation tax increased sharply in 1982 (unfortunately, revenue data are not available for 1981 and 1982 for those countries); in the other three countries, the change is modest.

The data give some support to the idea that the debt crisis has forced governments to rely more heavily on the inflation tax as a source of finance, but we must be careful in evaluating this finding. Clearly the governments of Argentina, Brazil, and Chile were using the inflation tax as an important source of revenue long before the debt crisis. Indeed, it appears that in some countries (with the exception of Chile and possibly Venezuela), the low level of reliance on the inflation tax was a direct consequence of the ready availability of funds on the international capital market. That a drying up of those funds would cause the governments to revert to their old ways should surprise no one.

Gross versus Net Debt and Implicit versus Actual Amortization

In evaluating the implications of the enormous increase in Latin American external debt—particularly in the countries under consideration— over the past decade, we must take into account the world inflation and the special circumstances of each of the countries involved. Dept service is always at the expense of domestic consumption (and investment) of tradables, even if the debt service is covered entirely or in part by new borrowing. Consequently, it is the price of tradables that is relevant for converting nominal external debt into real debt. Moreover, as most of that debt is denominated in dollars, it is the dollar price of tradables that is relevant for this purpose.

The dollar prices of tradables have risen a great deal over the past decade for all countries but particularly for Mexico and Brazil. Part of the reason is the general world inflation, but the prominence of oil in the tradables of Mexico and Brazil has magnified the price increase for these countries. The two countries are in quite different circumstances, of course—Brazil is an oil importer, whereas Mexico is a major oil exporter. Mexico can take double advantage by exporting more, whereas Brazil can benefit only by contracting its imports. Nevertheless, by this means and others Brazil will, in the final analysis, service its external debt.

When the nominal magnitudes of external debt are deflated by country-specific price indexes for tradables, the reduction is very great indeed. The results of the exercise are contained in table 6-18. The growth rate of foreign debt is greatly reduced, and service of it begins to appear much more feasible. Another factor, however, offsets the first. The world inflation, among other things, has resulted in much higher than normal interest rates; indeed, much of the interest payments are actually amortization. Worse still, the debt is more and more owed to the private capital market (as opposed to international financial institutions), where interest rates are normally higher and maturities shorter. The consequence, reported in table 6-19 below, is that debt service rates—interest plus amortization—have increased by an amount that more than offsets the inflation-induced decline in real external debt. The two effects are, of course, opposite sides of the same coin.

The outcome is that external debt service is so enormous that none of the five countries can be expected to meet that service from trade surpluses alone (with the possible exception of Venezuela and the even more remotely possible exception of Mexico). This issue is taken up in further detail in a later section, but it seems most unlikely that any of the countries in question can trade their way out of the debt problem.

In the remainder of this section, we shall analyze each country's situation individually. For the most part, the results speak for themselves. In table 6-19, adjustments for interest and amortization rates are made; the column labeled "difference" is the increase in debt service owing to the rise in interest rates and shortening of maturities. The column labeled "current account adjustment" is the part of interest payments that is really amortization and that should be shifted from the current to the capital account of the balance of payments. In table 6-18, the debt and amortization figures are adjusted for inflation. The results of table 6-18 are self-explanatory.

Brazil

One of the key elements of Brazil's external debt problem is the evolution of its interest payments. The average interest rate on new commitments has risen from 7.2 percent in 1972 to 14.6 percent in 1981 (according to the World Bank's *World Debt Tables*). If we consider a real interest rate of 3 percent and assume that this is a reasonable estimate of the perceived real rate at the time when the major increase in indebtedness began (in the second half of the 1970s), we can calculate the interest payments that would have been made if this rate had been realized. The actual nominal interest rate increased as a result of world inflation,

Table 6-18. *Adjustments of Debt and Amortization for Inflation*
(millions of current dollars)

Year	Total government nominal debt[a]	Deflator[b]	Government real debt	Total nominal amortization	Total real amortization	Nominal borrowing[c] Gross	Nominal borrowing[c] Net	Real borrowing[d] Gross	Real borrowing[d] Net
				Argentina					
1976	3,150	212	1,486	774	351	1,883	1,279	887	536
1977	4,429	219	2,022	907	415	1,236	604	948	533
1978	5,033	197	2,555	1,976	999	3,330	1,715	664	-335
1979	6,748	304	2,220	1,261	415	2,704	1,809	788	373
1980	8,557	330	2,593	1,730	524	2,776	1,630	785	261
1981	10,128	357	2,854	1,844	517	1,411	319	1,986	1,419
				Brazil					
1976	23,080	228	10,101	3,547	1,522	8,217	5,696	1,156	-396
1977	28,776	296	9,705	4,833	1,630	10,007	6,343	4,081	2,451
1978	35,119	289	12,156	7,265	2,515	16,539	11,347	4,478	1,963
1979	46,466	329	14,119	9,902	3,009	11,524	5,016	2,343	-667
1980	51,482	383	13,452	11,580	3,026	11,067	4,274	3,787	761
1981	55,756	392	14,213	13,196	3,364	14,948	7,857	6,110	2,746
				Chile					
1976	4,498	175	2,570	753	430	509	-134	53	-377
1977	4,364	199	2,193	942	473	1,120	291	704	231
1978	4,655	192	2,424	1,331	693	2,357	1,270	707	14
1979	5,925	243	2,438	1,722	709	2,940	1,623	770	61
1980	7,548	302	2,499	2,154	713	3,326	1,865	1,405	692
1981	9,413	295	3,191	2,939	996	4,945	3,148	2,770	1,774

(Table continues on the following page.)

Table 6-18 *(continued)*

Year	Total government nominal debt[a]	Deflator[b]	Government real debt	Total nominal amortization	Total real amortization	Nominal borrowing[c]		Real borrowing[d]	
						Gross	Net	Gross	Net
Mexico									
1976	11,580	199	5,819	1,892	951	5,503	4,350	1,581	630
1977	15,930	247	6,449	3,073	1,244	7,066	4,828	3,939	2,695
1978	20,758	227	9,144	5,603	2,468	9,265	4,857	439	-2,029
1979	25,615	360	7,115	9,199	2,555	10,739	3,672	134	-2,421
1980	29,242	623	4,694	6,991	1,122	8,375	4,349	389	-733
1981	33,591	848	3,961	7,474	881	12,907	9,125	-569	-1,450
Venezuela									
1976	2,192	416	527	341	82	1,054	769	192	110
1977	2,961	465	637	739	159	2,071	1,466	474	315
1978	4,427	465	952	616	132	2,822	2,466	274	142
1979	6,893	630	1,094	1,342	213	3,802	2,912	68	-145
1980	9,805	1,033	949	2,670	259	2,803	1,068	218	-41
1981	10,873	1,198	908	2,722	227	1,831	479	267	40

a. Figures for Argentina and Venezuela refer to public sector debt, whereas for the other countries they refer to total outstanding debt. Figures correspond to the beginning-of-year stock.

b. The deflators correspond to the simple average of export and import unit values as they appear in the "world tables," World Bank (1980), until 1978. Afterward the deflators were updated with the available information about export and import unit values as they appear in the *International Financial Statistics*, IMF.

c. From the first column and total (true) amortization.

d. From the third and fifth columns.

Sources: World Bank (1980); International Monetary Fund, *International Financial Statistics*, various issues.

however, and possibly also because of rises in the real rate. Therefore the explicit interest payments that result from the increase in the nominal interest alone, above the 3 percent level, should be regarded as implicit principal repayments that, had real interest rates stayed constant, would have been avoided. This implicit amortization amounted to more than $6 billion in 1981, six times the level of 1976 (see table 6-19).

The above-mentioned component of interest payments actually represents a capital account item rather than a current account item. If the capital and current accounts are corrected by this factor, we find that Brazil's capital surplus and current account deficit is significantly reduced. This correction is, of course, most significant in the later years. Both accounts, for example, are cut in half, when corrected, in 1981 (see table 6-19).

In assessing the external position of borrower countries, we must recognize that the stock of foreign debt in real terms has grown much less rapidly than in nominal terms. If the stock in nominal terms is deflated by an average of import and export unit values, the corresponding real debt service is an approximation of the sacrifice that the country has to make in terms of traded goods in order to enjoy the benefits of the borrowed capital. By using an index of this kind, we can see that, although nominal indebtedness in Brazil as of 1981 was more than ten times that of 1972, the real indebtedness has only slightly more than doubled over the same period (see table 6-18). On the other hand, during most of the years between 1976 and 1981, there was positive net new borrowing, and in all years the gross real new borrowing was positive (see table 6-18). The Brazilian foreign borrowing, in other words, not only covered interest payments on previous debt but also more than offset the negative effect that international inflation had on the real value of Brazil's outstanding debt.

In addition to the amortization implicit in the increase in the nominal interest rates, principal repayments were also increased by a reduction of the loan maturities. It is reasonable to assume that long-term borrowing implies annual amortization of about 10 percent of the outstanding debt per year. The difference between the actual debt service and a hypothetical debt service, if we assume both a (real) interest rate of 3 percent and amortization of 10 percent of the stock of debt, indicates about how much extra was paid in contrast to the amount that would have been paid if the interest rate had not increased and the maturities had not shortened. In the Brazilian case, this calculation indicates that by 1981 the debt service actually paid was about twice the hypothetical figure (see table 6-19). The implication is that the combined effect of increasing nominal interest rates and shortening maturities was responsible for a doubling of Brazil's

Table 6-19. Adjustments for Interest Rates and Amortization Periods
(millions of current dollars)

Year	Foreign debt[a]	Debt service			Hypothetical debt service			Difference	Current account adjustment
		Interest	Amortization	Total	Interest[b]	Amortization[c]	Total		
Argentina									
1976	3,150	264	604	869	95	315	410	459	170
1977	4,429	318	722	1,040	133	423	556	484	185
1978	5,033	503	1,615	2,117	151	503	654	1,463	352
1979	6,748	568	895	1,463	202	675	877	586	366
1980	8,557	841	1,146	1,987	257	856	1,113	874	584
1981	10,187	1,058	1,092	2,150	306	1,019	1,325	825	752
1982	10,506	—	—	—	315	1,051	1,366	—	—
Brazil									
1976	23,080	1,718	2,521	4,239	692	2,308	3,000	1,239	1,026
1977	28,776	2,032	3,664	5,696	863	2,878	3,741	1,955	1,169
1978	35,119	3,127	5,192	8,319	1,054	3,512	4,566	3,753	2,073
1979	46,466	4,750	6,508	11,258	1,394	4,647	6,041	5,217	3,394
1980	51,482	6,331	6,793	13,124	1,544	5,148	6,692	6,432	4,787
1981	55,756	7,778	7,091	14,869	1,673	5,576	7,249	7,620	6,105
1982	63,613	—	—	—	1,908	6,361	8,269	—	—
Chile									
1976	4,498	245	643	888	135	450	585	303	110
1977	4,364	244	829	1,074	131	436	567	507	113

1978	4,655	384	1,087	1,471	140	466	606	865	244
1979	5,925	583	1,317	1,899	178	593	771	1,128	405
1980	7,548	919	1,461	2,380	226	755	981	1,399	693
1981	9,413	1,424	1,797	3,221	282	941	1,223	1,998	1,142
1982	12,561	—	—	—	377	1,256	1,633	—	—
Mexico									
1976	11,580	1,086	1,153	2,239	342	1,158	1,505	734	739
1977	15,930	1,313	2,238	3,552	478	1,593	2,071	1,481	835
1978	20,758	1,818	4,408	6,226	623	2,076	2,699	3,527	1,195
1979	25,615	2,855	7,112	9,966	768	2,562	3,336	6,630	2,087
1980	29,242	3,842	4,026	7,868	877	2,924	3,801	4,607	2,965
1981	33,591	4,670	3,782	8,482	1,008	3,359	4,367	4,115	3,692
1982	42,716	—	—	—	1,281	4,272	5,553	—	—
Venezuela									
1976	2,192	122	285	407	66	219	285	122	56
1977	2,961	223	605	827	89	296	385	442	134
1978	4,427	393	356	750	133	443	576	174	260
1979	6,893	659	890	1,548	207	689	896	652	452
1980	9,805	1,229	1,735	2,964	294	981	1,275	1,689	935
1981	10,873	1,696	1,352	3,049	326	1,087	1,413	1,636	1,370
1982	11,352	—	—	—	341	1,135	1,476	—	—

Note: Dashes indicate that data are unavailable.

a. Beginning-of-year stock of public sector debt for Argentina and Venezuela and beginning-of-year total debt for other countries.

b. Assumes an interest rate of 3 percent (see text).

c. Assumes an amortization rate of 10 percent of outstanding debt (see text).

Sources: World Bank (1980); International Monetary Fund, *International Financial Statistics*, various issues.

debt service. Therefore the trade surplus that must be generated in order to avoid default was doubled by factors that may be regarded as external to Brazil.

Mexico

High interest payments on external debt also played a dramatic role in the evolution of the Mexican foreign debt problem. Between 1972 and 1981, the average interest rate on new commitments increased from 6.9 percent to 15.1 percent, and the interest charged by private creditors went from 7 percent to 16.1 percent. The debt service due to higher nominal interest rates was increased further by the fact that the participation of private creditors on total loans to Mexico grew from 64 percent in 1972 to 88 percent in 1981. (A similar change also occurred in Brazil.) Assuming once again that 3 percent is a reasonable figure for the long-run real interest rate, the result is that, by 1980–81, the implicit amortization due to nominal interest increases accounted for about 10 percent of the total stock of debt outstanding, and in 1981 it was nearly ten times as large as it had been in 1974. If the capital account surplus and the current account deficit are adjusted by this implicit amortization, they decrease from $19.3 and $12.8 billion to $15.6 and $9.1 billion, respectively, in 1981 (see table 6-19).

In Mexico the stock of foreign debt grew most rapidly between 1977 and 1981. This growth was matched, however, by the oil boom, which consisted of both a tremendous increase in the proven reserves and a doubling of the international price. When we assess the international debt position, we must consider two points: first, some of the debt was contracted only in order to anticipate higher consumption that would be made possible by the newly found wealth. Second, the stock of real debt was significantly reduced (with respect to the nominal stock) because of the oil price rise and oil's growing participation in the Mexican exports. Indeed, net real new borrowing may actually have been negative after 1978, although gross real borrowing was positive for most of the period (see table 6-18). As in the Brazilian case, borrowing was sufficient to cover at least all real total amortization.

The change in the average maturity of the loans to Mexico also plays an important role in the debt problem. The average maturity from all creditors on new public debt commitments went from 13.7 years in 1972 to 7.8 years in 1981. Actual amortization was about twice what it would have been if the interest rate had been 3 percent and amortization 10 percent (see table 6-19).

As in the Brazilian case, the increase in debt service implies that a much larger trade surplus must be generated to achieve equilibrium in the balance of payments, if no further lending is forthcoming. The two cases show an important difference, however: the increase in the prices of Mexican traded goods comes from an increase in the price of its *exportables*, whereas the main increase in the prices of Brazilian traded goods comes from its *imports*—oil being probably the most significant price change. Therefore, with no more foreign borrowing available, the adjustment will probably imply an increase in exports in the first case and a reduction of imports in the latter.

Argentina

Although the average interest rate on new public debt commitments has not risen as much as for the other countries, the rate of interest on Argentine borrowing was already higher than for the other countries in 1972. In addition, interest on loans from private creditors (and the share of these in total indebtedness) has increased from 8.6 percent in 1972 to 13 percent in 1981 (and that share increased from 69 percent in 1972 to 82 percent in 1981). Therefore, when the implicit amortization is calculated using an assumed 3 percent long-run interest rate, the amount proves to be significant, reaching nearly 10 percent of total debt in 1980–81. For the same period, when the current account is corrected by the implicit principal repayments, the deficit is substantially reduced (see table 6-19).

The price index of traded goods in Argentina, in contrast with Brazil, Mexico, and Venezuela, has increased little. It grew significantly from 1978 to 1981 (about 80 percent) but declined sharply in 1981. Therefore, the stock of Argentina's debt in real terms has not been affected by inflation as much as the stock of debt in Brazil, Mexico, and Venezuela. In the second half of the 1970s, net real borrowing was negative only in 1978, whereas the gross equivalent was always positive, so that, in general, foreign indebtedness was enough to cover the real (implicit and actual) amortization (see table 6-18).

The maturities on new public debt commitments have lengthened somewhat during the period 1972–81 in Argentina, in contrast to the rest of the countries, but they have been quite variable. Amortization (actual and implicit) has increased mainly because of the effect of higher interest rates. Actual amortization has been below the hypothetical figure implied by the assumed 10 percent annual rate. The result is that the service of Argentine debt, relative to the hypothetical figure (assuming 3 percent interest and 10 percent amortization), amounted to about 10 percent in 1980–81, a lower percentage than in the countries discussed above (see table 6-19).

The implication is that, although Argentina has also been hurt by high rates of interest on its debt, the corresponding maturity terms have been relatively favorable. The price of its exports, however, has not grown to match the growth in the debt service; should this situation continue, the required adjustment (in case no further indebtedness is made possible) would imply an enormous reduction in imports.

Venezuela

The total foreign indebtedness of Venezuela has not reached the absolute levels that we saw in the cases of Brazil and Mexico but is important in relation to its GNP—about 17 percent as of 1981. In addition, the participation of private creditors in the total debt is extremely high: 97 percent in 1981 (versus 71 percent in 1972). The effect of higher interest rates on the debt service payments is therefore especially important; indeed, the average interest rate on new commitments from private creditors nearly tripled between 1972 and 1981. The above-mentioned factors result in an implicit amortization (again, if we assume a 3 percent long-term interest rate) of about 13 percent of the outstanding stock of foreign debt in 1981. The Venezuelan capital and current accounts, unlike those of Brazil and Mexico, are not regularly in surplus and deficit, respectively; in fact, the (unadjusted) capital account shows net outflows in some years, and when it is adjusted by the implicit amortization, it is mainly negative.

As in the Mexican case, the important foreign debt contracting was matched by an oil boom that began in 1974. Because of that boom, *real* debt has grown far less than its nominal counterpart; indeed, it may even be argued that real debt has stayed at a more or less constant level since 1972 (see table 6-18). The greatest increase in real foreign debt occurred in 1975–77, but it is mainly a result of the reduction in real terms during 1973–74. In the 1978–81 period, the gross real borrowing was about equal to (actual plus implicit) amortization (see tables 6-18 and 6-19).

In addition to the implicit amortization coming from the increase in interest rates, the average maturity of the loans to Venezuela also declined, as in the other countries. These two developments have made the service of the debt double with respect to the hypothetical service, which assumes a 3 percent interest rate and an amortization rate of 10 percent (see table 6-19). If Venezuela can borrow no additional funds, its prospect of running a trade surplus that offsets the debt service may be brighter than in the cases of Brazil and Mexico. The reason is Venezuela's tremendous oil export potential and stock of debt, which in absolute terms is not as high as that of the other two countries.

Chile

The implicit amortization due to high interest rates on Chile's external debt also provoked an important increase in its debt service. This increase was fueled not only by a general interest rate rise but also by a dramatic change in the participation of private debt in the total stock, which went from 13 percent in 1972 to about 65 percent in 1981. Private debt comes from private sources, whose share in public debt also increased significantly in the 1977–81 period. These factors help explain why in 1977 the implicit amortization was only about 5 percent of the total outstanding debt in 1978, whereas it reached 12 percent in 1981. This situation is also reflected in a reduction of the capital account surplus and the current account deficit of about 25 percent each in 1981 once both amounts have been adjusted for the implicit amortization in interest payments (see table 6-19).

As with Argentina, the real stock of debt is far less affected by inflation of Chilean tradables than it is in the case of the other countries. The only negative real borrowing takes place in 1976 and is due to a reduction in nominal debt; most of the increase in external indebtedness took place in 1980–81 (see table 6-18). As with Brazil and Mexico, gross borrowing was more than enough to offset debt service.

The average maturity from all creditors on loans to Chile declined from 13.5 years in 1972 to 10.7 in 1981. When the change of maturities is taken into account, the actual debt service was nearly twice as great as the hypothetical service, in contrast with the situation in Mexico, Brazil, and Venezuela (see table 6-19). Debt service in the case of Chile is a more serious problem than in the other four countries because Chile's foreign debt is nearly 85 percent of GDP—roughly double the relative debt of Mexico and Argentina. In addition, since January 1983 nearly all of the debt has become a liability of the government. The fiscal problem in Chile is therefore clearly a very intense one. Chile's ability to service its foreign debt plainly does not lie exclusively in trade; obviously more lending will be required.

Post–Debt Crisis Adjustment

The debt crisis burst on the world in August 1982 with the Mexican announcement that a suspension of payments was unavoidable. It quickly spread to other nations, particularly Latin American countries. The crisis was brought on by a number of factors, but the immediate cause was a growing reluctance on the part of the banking community to extend new credits, credits with which the debtor countries had been paying both interest and amortization. No immediate adjustment could be made to the sudden unavailability of funds in the international capital market. Rescheduling was the only possibility in the short run. Rescue packages were forthcoming from the Bank of International Settlements (BIS), the U.S. Treasury, and the International Monetary Fund. The World Bank has since instituted its structural adjustment loan program. None of these short-run measures, however, can substitute for adjustment at the country level.

In this section, we examine the adjustments that have been made by Argentina, Brazil, Chile, Mexico, and Venezuela. In all cases, we find that a very considerable amount of progress has been made, but it has taken the form of accelerating the inflation rate (to collect more inflation tax), curtailing imports (at the expense of domestic industrial activity and employment), and appealing to the IMF for assistance. We conclude that these adjustments are insufficient *if* major lending does not continue; indeed, in most cases, no conceivable amount of domestic adjustment will replace the need for more borrowing. Unless some miracle reduces the ratio of debt service to debt, major defaults will be avoided only by writing down existing loans or by lending more funds.

Argentina, 1981–83

During the last three years, Argentina has gone through a very complex process of political change, including the inauguration of a new constitutional government last December. These developments have had an impact on its ability and willingness to impose the fiscal and monetary discipline required to adjust the economy to the current world capital market situation.

The Argentine case is noteworthy in that most of the difficulty seems domestic in nature. As the country is nearly self-sufficient in oil, it was not seriously affected by the two oil shocks of the last decade. The need for capital inflows to foster economic development is far less acute than in other countries of the region (for example, Brazil); mere avoidance of recurrent politically motivated capital outflows would ensure sufficient development.

At the end of 1980, the approaching change of command in the military government led to a major crisis from which the country has yet to emerge. Between 1978 and 1980, the country attracted foreign resources, channeled through the international banking system, in order to finance an ever-growing public sector. This capital inflow led to the sharp appreciation of the peso and growing trade deficits, as shown in table 6-20. The appreciation of the peso generated not only a change in domestic relative prices but also an increase in real interest rates for both the exporting and import-competing sectors of the economy, which resulted in widespread bankruptcy. The economic policy changes introduced since 1981 have been more closely related to these domestic developments than to the state of the world capital market.

During the second and third quarters of 1981, the trade balance began to recover, and since the first quarter of 1982, it has consistently been in surplus. Such adjustment, however, has not been made on the basis of fiscal austerity. As table 6-21 shows, public expenditure has been rising since 1980. Although the new civilian government has announced its intention to reduce spending, significant measures are yet to be taken.

The adjustment that has been realized to date essentially consists of a massive transfer of resources to the public sector, implemented by means of private credit rationing and a huge increase in inflation tax collections. The proportion of domestic credit directed to the government gives a clear picture of the increasing pressure of the public sector on the domes-

Table 6-20. *Trade Balance for Argentina, 1980–83*
(millions of U.S. dollars)

Year and quarter	Exports (f.o.b.)	Imports (c.i.f.)	Balance
1980			
1	2059.6	2282.2	−226.6
2	1927.3	2290.7	−363.4
3	2035.5	2782.1	−746.6
4	2002.2	3190.4	−1188.2
1981			
1	1989.9	2614.0	−624.1
2	2848.2	2622.0	226.2
3	2719.2	2196.0	523.2
4	1585.7	1999.0	−413.3
1982			
1	2170.2	1484.0	686.2
2	2346.1	1333.0	1013.1
3	1622.6	1217.0	405.6
4	1483.7	1306.0	177.7
1983			
1	1933.7	977.0	956.7
2	2106.9	1184.6	922.3

Note: f.o.b. = free on board. c.i.f. = cost, insurance, freight.
Sources: International Monetary Fund, *International Financial Statistics*, various issues.

Table 6-21. *Basic Data for Argentina, 1980–83*

Year and quarter	Public expenditure (1982 US$ billions)	Government credit/ total credit (percent)		Real GDP (1980Q1 = 100)	Consumer prices (twelve-month percentage change)
		Stock	Flow		
1980					
1	1.114	14.0	—	100.0	—
2	1.224	11.8	0.9	100.83	—
3	1.326	13.0	19.4	104.78	—
4	1.288	15.3	26.3	106.43	—
1981					
1	1.196	14.8	12.9	100.28	—
2	1.363	16.7	21.3	100.83	89.3
3	1.652	21.1	36.1	93.67	112.8
4	1.812	26.9	42.3	92.19	122.7
1982					
1	1.090	29.0	38.6	92.38	147.2
2	1.171	28.4	25.9	90.54	129.7
3	1.343	24.3	17.5	91.00	156.4
4	1.808	25.4	28.9	92.29	202.9
1983					
1	1.598	32.4	48.2	92.93	244.7
2	—	34.3	39.4	93.21	313.5
3	—	—	—	—	338.7

Note: Dashes indicate that data were not available at the time of writing.

Sources: International Monetary Fund, *International Financial Statistics* and *Government Financial Statistics*, various issues.

tic capital market. This development is clearly revealed in table 6-21, which shows the ratio of the stock credit to the government to total domestic credit, the ratio between the respective flows, and the time pattern of the inflation rate, measured by the CPI.

As should be expected, this type of adjustment has had devastating effects on economic activity. Table 6-21 also shows the declining trend of the GDP since 1981. A direct consequence of this process has been the sharp fall of imports, which accounts for most of the observed adjustment in the trade balance. This adjustment is still well below the level necessitated by the present debt service schedule. Owing to the military government's political inability to carry out the IMF-sponsored austerity program after the South Atlantic conflict, and the unwillingness of the new civilian government to accept that program, the Argentine case is one of the most troublesome spots in the map of the debt crisis. Moreover, the sort of adjustment realized so far (particularly the lack of fiscal austerity) will not be politically viable for much longer.

Brazil, 1981–83

An understanding of the difficulties currently faced by Brazil in its current adjustment to the international capital market developments since mid-1982 requires a brief account of the initial conditions. Before the 1973 oil shock, Brazil constituted one of the major success stories in the developing world. The average rate of growth of real GDP was about 10 percent per annum and that of exports was 20 percent. The maximum figures for both variables since 1970 occurred in 1973: 14 percent for GDP and 55 percent for exports. At that time, the bright economic performance, the small size of the foreign debt ($12.5 billion), and a high level of international liquidity made it possible temporarily to avoid the unavoidable: adjustment to a higher oil price. Despite stagnation in the world economy, Brazil was able to sustain an average GDP growth rate of 8.6 percent and an export growth rate of 24.9 percent during the 1973–77 period. In 1979 a new oil shock coupled with rising international real interest rates put an end to this process.

After a $5 billion loss of international reserves between 1978 and 1980, a rather drastic revision of monetary policy was introduced in 1981 (see table 6-22). Interest rates were freed, and under the assumption of unrestricted (although expensive) access to the international capital market, additional measures were taken with the explicit objective of increasing domestic real interest rates in order "to stimulate demand for foreign resources (in the short run), and in the medium and long run to increase domestic savings" (Langoni 1981). At the expense of a nearly 10 percent

Table 6-22. *Basic Data for Brazil, 1980–83*

Item	1980	1981	1982	1983
Exports (US$ billions)	20,132	23,293	20,175	21,899
Imports (US$ billions)	22,955	22,091	19,395	15,408
Oil imports (US$ billions)	9,405	10,600	9,566	7,800
Trade balance (US$ billions)	−2,823	1,202	780	6,491
Inflation (percent)	86.4	100.0	97.9	172.9
Devaluation (percent)	—	—	95.8	286.2
Monetary growth (percent)	—	—	86.8	89.1

Note: Dashes indicate that data were not available.

Sources: International Monetary Fund, *International Financial Statistics* and *Government Financial Statistics*, various issues.

decline in industrial output, the $2.8 billion trade deficit was turned into $1.2 billion and $0.8 billion surpluses in 1981 and 1982, respectively. With this strategy of medium- and long-term reduction of the growth in foreign indebtedness Brazil confronted the disruption of the world capital market in 1982.

Since the debt-restructuring agreement signed with the IMF on February 25, 1983, a substantial deepening of the adjustment process has taken place. The cruzeiro was devalued by 30 percent at the end of that month and the accumulated devaluation for 1983 was 286 percent, compared with a 211 percent increase in the general price level. The implied "real" devaluation is nearly 30 percent. A $6.5 billion trade surplus was achieved in 1983, although the monthly trade balance data indicate a decay in that balance since midyear. Given the present conditions in the international capital market, the adjustment still seems to be below the required level in magnitude; consequently a $9 billion trade surplus has been targeted for 1984.

During the first eleven months of 1983, public expenditure fell by 5.5 percent, and revenues increased by 1.9 percent. Accordingly, the monetary base grew by only 98 percent (implying a decline, in real terms, of the monetary base by 40 percent), as far less revenue was collected by money creation. According to *Conjuntura econômica* (Fundação Getulio Vargas 1984), the nominal deficit target on which Brazil and the IMF had agreed for 1983 had been met.

An important aspect of the adjustment in Brazil was the decline in imports, which accounted for 61 percent of the trade balance improvement. Much of the decline was in crude petroleum, the imports of which fell by 18.5 percent. Associated with this improvement on the trade front was a decline in industrial employment of 3.7 percent from January to August of 1983. As that sector had been seriously depressed since early 1981, this development cast some doubts on the political viability of the current adjustment process in Brazil.

Chile, 1981–83

The Chilean economic adjustment was quite different from that in the other Latin American economies considered here. The reason lies in the roots of the problem, which are peculiar to Chile. One key difference is that the crisis in Chile was not associated with a huge government deficit; indeed, the government ran a surplus in 1980–81 and only a small deficit in 1982. Nevertheless, the current account deficit as a proportion of GDP reached 14 percent in 1981 and 10 percent in 1982.

The current account and trade deficits of 1980 and 1981 (table 6-23) can be explained (aside from the rise in interest rates and the fall in the price of copper) by an excess of domestic private absorption over income. Indeed, if we look at the financial flows, we see that only about half of the growth in credit to the private sector in these two years came from an increase in quasi-money, whereas the remainder matched the rise in the net foreign liabilities of the financial system. During 1982 the current account deficit was cut in half and the trade balance became positive, and the tendency continued in 1983. At least two factors help explain the 1982 turning point in the trade balance. First, the devaluation in June 1982, when the peg to the U.S. dollar was abandoned and the basket peg began. Second, the severe recession of 1981–83, which can be linked to several factors, including the incredibly high levels of the real interest rates since early 1981. In a related development, the unemployment rate—one of the major concerns of the adjustment program—reached a peak of 25 percent (in Santiago) by mid-1982.

Although it may be thought that the government deficit of 1982 (the first since 1978) responded to the recession, this deficit clearly reflected the reduction in tax collections and in copper revenues. In fact, total government expenditure (measured in U.S. dollars) was the same as in 1981. On the other hand, in 1982 there was an important increase of credit to the private sector from both the central and the commercial banks. It is not clear how this increase in credit was financed, as the flow of quasi-money was about equal to that of the previous year. "Net foreign" and "other net" liabilities show the largest increases of the financial system liabilities.

An obvious conclusion from the discussion thus far is that the Chilean financial problems arose more from excessive expenditure in the private sector than from fiscal imbalances. The low rate of internal saving made necessary the use of external saving, which is reflected in the current and trade accounts of 1980–82. As external debt service also rose because of general shortening of maturities and higher interest rates, larger domestic savings will be needed to generate a trade balance high enough to cover future debt service and imports. From this point of view, the Chilean adjustment problem is no different from that of other Latin American countries.

During 1983, the adjustment of the economy in Chile seems to be well under way, even though it is occurring at a high cost in terms of domestic welfare. Until October 1983, a trade surplus of nearly $1 billion had been achieved, mainly at the expense of imports (which fell 26 percent on top of the 44 percent decline in 1982). The flow of credit from the domestic

Table 6-23. *Selected Economic Indicators, Chile, 1980–83*

Item	1980	1981	1982	1983	Range[a]
Trade balance (US$ billion)	-764	-2.677	63	986	(to Oct.)
Percent change					
In exports	22.7	-18.5	-3.4	0.8	(to Oct.)
In imports	30.5	19.1	-44.1	-26.1	(to Oct.)
Current account (US$ billion)	-1.971	-4.733	-2.304	—	
Capital account (US$ billion)	3.165	4.698	1.215	—	
Change, intl. reserves (US$ billion)	1.244	0.067	-1.165	—	
Percentage change					
In monetary base	37.9	-8.7	-25.5	-5.5	(to Sept.)
In money, M_1	77.1	-8.6	-7.9	9.6	(to Sept.)
Fiscal def./GDP (percent)	-5.5	-1.1	2.7	—	
Currency account def./GDP (percent)	7.1	14.1	7.9	—	
Copper price (cents/pound)	99.2	79.0	67.1	73.9	(to Nov.)
Inflation (CPI)					
Average	35.1	19.7	9.9	27.3	
December–December	31.2	9.5	20.7	23.1	

Exchange rate (pesos/dollar)	39.0	39.0	50.9	78.8 (to June)
Percentage change in GDP	7.8	5.7	-14.3	-7.0 (to Aug.-Oct.)
Unemployment rate (Santiago, Oct.-Dec.)	10.1	11.0	21.9	17.7 (to Nov.)
Real interest rate[b]	5.4	29.1	23.9	3.7
Flow of financial system credit				
To public sector (billion pesos)	5.1	-36.0	84.8	-18.1 (to Sept.)
To private sector (billion pesos)	207.2	204.3	354.2	-45.9 (to Sept.)
Change in net foreign liabilities, excluding intl. reserves (US$ billion)	79.7	89.8	158.4	-105.5 (to Sept.)
Central bank intl. reserves (US$ billion)[c]	4.074	3.775	2.578	1.998 (to Nov.)
Financial system flow of quasi-money (billion pesos)	120.8	98.8	94.0	-16.9 (to Sept.)
Other net liabilities (billion pesos)	-34.9	-29.1	163.7	97.2 (to Sept.)

Note: Dashes appear in the column for 1983 where the range extended from December to December. Blank cells in the last column indicate that data were not available.

a. 1983 only.
b. Short-term deposit rates (monthly) corrected by CPI inflation and annualized.
c. Excludes the use of credit from the IMF.
Source: Banco Central de Chile, *Boletín mensual,* November and December 1983.

173

financial system to both private and public sectors was negative in 1983. As of November 1983, international reserves (excluding IMF credit, which was reactivated in August) stood at $1.998 billion, or nearly $600 million below the level of December 1982; however, they had been increasing since April 1983.

An external debt renegotiation agreement reached in July 1983 included a new loan for $1.3 billion, a medium- and short-term debt rescheduling of $3.4 billion, and a short-term rollover (to December 1984) of $1.8 billion (Brau, Williams, and others 1983). If we assume that the current account deficit was in fact cut by one-half in 1983, relative to 1982, this agreement provides Chile—at least in the short run—with sufficient external liquidity. As in other cases in Latin America, however, the question remains as to how long the low level of consumption can be sustained. The need to generate large trade surpluses in the next three years is evident from the terms of the renegotiation agreement. Finally, important external obligations must be met during 1987–88 (owing to the new loan and the medium- and short-term debt reschedulement).

Mexico, 1982–83

The financial crisis that had been building up since 1980 culminated in 1982 (see table 6-24). The balance-of-payments situation in 1981 gives a clear picture of the Mexican financial crisis at that time. The current account deficit reached a record of $14 billion, with the "errors and omissions" deficit at a record $10 billion. These two outflows were nearly totally offset by an extraordinary inflow of capital, so that there was but a minor decline of international reserves. The enormous deficit in the current account has been attributed to a variety of causes, including the high government deficit, the fall of the international oil price, and the increase in debt service payments. On the other hand, the deficit in the "errors and omissions" account reflects private capital outflows due to the perceived increase in exchange and political risk. The exchange risk is also evident from the increase in savings channeled through dollar-denominated assets in Mexican banks. Although the nominal exchange rate was "sliding" down (slowly depreciating) in a controlled fashion, the perspectives concerning the balance-of-payments situation, and the "confidence crisis," made the devaluation rate appear insufficient, so that capital flight went on.

In 1982, the major devaluation of February (from twenty-seven to forty-five pesos per dollar) marked the beginning of a series of confusing and contradictory policy developments, which resulted in an acceleration of the capital flight, despite the devaluation. There was, however, an

Table 6-24. *Mexico: Selected Economic Indicators*

Item	1980	1981	1982	1983	Range
Imports, f.o.b. (US$ billion)	18.896	24.037	14.489	6.485	(to Oct.)
Trade balance (US$ billion)	−2.830	−4.099	6.885	10.766	(to Oct.)
Service account (US$ billion)	−5.607	−10.089	−10.110	−7.645	(to Oct.)[a]
Errors and omissions (US$ billion)	−3.933	−8.840	−6.157	0.289	(to Sept.)
Change, intl. reserves (US$ billion)	−0.749	−1.106	3.011	2.556	(to Sept.)
Exchange rate (pesos/dollar)					
Preferential	22.95	24.52	54.99	119.80	(to Dec.)
Free	22.95	24.52	61.52	150.79	(to Dec.)
Percentage change[b]					
In monetary base	40.5	44.8	98.0	45.5	(to Nov.)
In central bank claims on govt.	33.1	47.2	137.5	77.3	(to June)
In claims on govt./mon. base	85	86	103	101	(to June)
In money, M_1	32.2	33.1	64.9	29.0	(to Nov.)
In quasi-money	39.2	59.0	73.5	67.6	(to June)
In industrial production	9.8	8.8	−1.9	−7.0	(to June)
In real GDP	8.3	8.0	−0.2	—	—
Inflation (CPI)	26.4	27.9	59.0	101.9	(to Dec.)
Fiscal def./GDP (percent)[c]	7.7	14.8	18.6	—	—
Current account def./GDP[c]	4.0	5.9	1.7	—	—
Short-term interest rate[d]	27.25	32.75	59.50	54.70	(to Dec.)

Note: Dashes in the column for 1983 indicate that data were not available. Dashes in the last column indicate full range (January to December).

a. Financial service only.

b. Annual relative change at the end of the period indicated.

c. From a speech by IMF Western Hemisphere director, reproduced in Banco Central de Chile, *Boletin mensual*, November 1983.

d. End of period rate on three-month certificates of deposit.

Source: International Monetary Fund, *International Financial Statistics*, and Banco de Mexico, *Indicadores económicos*, various issues.

important effect on the trade balance, which turned positive in the second quarter of 1982—mainly at the expense of reduced imports, which in turn derived from the imminent recession. Many private firms had difficulty in servicing their foreign debt, and the scarcity of foreign exchange constrained the purchase of imported intermediate goods. This situation resulted in a decline of industrial production beginning in the third quarter of 1982.

In August 1982, a two-tier exchange system was imposed with the intention that the capital account (or the speculative movements) would take place at a freely determined rate and the service account and part of the trade account (imports) at the lower rate of about 48 pesos per dollar. As it was recognized that this measure might accelerate capital flight, it was also decided to make dollar-denominated assets in Mexican banks payable only in pesos (at a rate of 69.5 pesos while the free market was fluctuating between 100 and 120 pesos per dollar).

In August 1982, Mexico also declared itself temporarily unable to service its foreign debt and obtained a postponement of principal repayments. At the same time, negotiations for a restructuring of foreign debt maturities began, and Mexico engaged in talks with the IMF. On September 1, 1982, the nationalization of commercial banks was decreed and controls on the foreign exchange market were imposed, with adverse effects on the already low level of private production and investment; property rights had become unclear. In addition, the private banks owned a large portion of the Mexican industrial sector shares, and what was going to be done with them has never been explained.

In 1982, the public sector deficit rose to 18.6 percent of GDP, and deficits in the service and "errors and omissions" accounts amounted to more than $10 billion and $6 billion, respectively. The trade account surplus reached nearly $7 billion, but growth of real GDP was negative (-0.2 percent), and the inflation rate (average CPI) was 60 percent. In December, just after the new administration took office, foreign exchange operations were liberalized, with a controlled rate of 150 pesos per dollar and a preferential rate of about 96 pesos (which would eventually catch up to the higher rate) for debt service payments and some imports.

The main objectives of the adjustment program undertaken by the new administration, in agreement with the IMF, were a reduction of the public sector deficit in 1983 to 8.5 percent of GDP and the reduction of inflation and of the current account deficit. The latter target implies lower imports, higher oil exports, and a debt rescheduling. The assumption was that GDP growth, in real terms, would be zero.

Available data suggest that the main objectives of the program are being met (see Buira 1983; International Monetary Fund 1984). There was a trade balance surplus of $10.8 billion until October of 1983 (mainly a result of lower imports, whose value declined by 40 percent with respect to 1982). An agreement concerning public sector debt amortization was reached in order to postpone $20 billion of repayments due from August 1982 to December 1984. There was also new financing from U.S. syndicated sources in the amount of $5 billion and from official sources of $2 billion to $2.5 billion (Brau, Williams, and others 1983).

The growth rate of the nominal monetary base and of the money stock have been declining (to about 46 percent and 29 percent, respectively, by November 1983), suggesting in view of the close relationship between monetary and fiscal policy that exists in Mexico, that the growth in the public sector deficit has been slowing down. Inflation has also declined, although it was still about 100 percent on average in 1983. There is also some evidence of a very important decline in production, indicating that real GDP probably fell significantly in 1983. Indeed, industrial production was about 10 percent lower in the first semester of 1983 than it had been a year earlier. Increasing unemployment is also reflected in the coverage of workers by the Social Security Institute.

The adjustment policy has a number of drawbacks, including the serious recession and the postponement of debt repayments. The restructuring of debt mentioned above implies that obligations for the $20 billion will have to be met starting in 1987 and for the $5 billion starting in 1986. Very high debt service payments will be due in those years unless other arrangements are made. Other dangers are present, such as private sector distrust of economic policy and the possibility that the government will be unable to reach agreements with the labor unions. In short, the adjustment program requires an important reduction in consumption that may or may not be feasible, in view of the rates of growth experienced in recent decades.

Venezuela since 1982

The adjustment facing the Venezuelan economy is rather different from that in other debtor countries. Venezuela did not experience significant external imbalances until 1982, and inflation and monetary expansion have not been as high as in other cases in Latin America. In fact, the trade account registered a surplus (albeit declining) until 1982 (see table 6-25), and it does not seem likely to have turned into a deficit in 1983. In the first quarter of 1983, foreign assets of the central bank stood at $8.6 billion, whereas total external debt was on the order of $34–35 billion. Nevertheless, in February of that year, it was decided to abandon the convertibility of the bolivar (which had been fixed at the rate of 4.3 Bs/dollar for years) in order to impose a three-tier exchange rate system. This system consisted of a low rate of 4.3 Bs/dollar for public and some private debt service payments and some "essential" imports, another rate of 6 Bs/dollar for "necessary" imports, and a free rate for all other foreign exchange transactions. Shortly thereafter, the finance minister began negotiations to convert short-term debt into medium-term debt.

At the same time, the government announced its economic adjustment plan, which was at variance with many of the recommendations made by the IMF. The plan's main features were:

- Indefinite maintenance of the three-tiered exchange rate system and stabilization of foreign exchange outflows to sustain central bank reserves at $8–9 billion

Table 6-25. *Venezuela: Selected Economic Indicators, 1980–83*

Item	1980	1981	1982	1983	Range
Trade account (US$ billion)	8.714	7.840	3.199	—	
Imports, f.o.b. (Bs billion)	45.375	50.682	50.056	8.887	(to Mar.)
Exports (Bs billion)	82.507	86.388	70.583	51.941	(to Sept.)
Percentage change					
In imports	8.7	11.5	8.6	—	
In exports	34.6	4.8	−18.0	—	
Current account (US$ billion)	4.728	4.000	−3.455	—	
Capital account (US$ billion)	0.164	−1.882	−2.182	—	
Short-term capital (US$ billion)	−1.896	−2.692	−4.567	—	
Errors and omissions (US$ billion)	−1.129	−2.139	−2.526	—	
Change, intl. reserves (US$ billion)	3.823	−0.012	−8.215	—	
Percentage change[a]					
In monetary base	6.6	17.1	17.5	66.3	(to Sept.)
In money, M_1	18.3	9.5	5.6	26.5	(to Sept.)
In central bank claims on govt.	−21.3	83.4	79.6	15.2	(to Sept.)
In claims on govt./mon. base	8.0	12.4	19.0	22.0	(to Sept.)
In GDP	−1.7	0.4	0.6	—	
Unit value of oil exports	100	116.1	116.1	98.1	
Inflation (CPI)	21.5	16.0	9.6	5.7	(to Sept.)
Exchange rate	4.3	4.3	4.3	4.3	
Preferential	—	—	—	6.0	
Free	—	—	—	8.0–9.0	(to Sept.)
Flow of credit to govt. from central bank					
(Bs billion)	−0.65	1.736	3.039	—	
Jan.–Sept.	—	—	3.558	1.641	

Note: Dashes for 1983 indicate that data were not available. Blank cells in the last column indicate full ranges (January to December).

a. Annual relative change at the end of the period indicated.

Source: International Monetary Fund, *International Financial Statistics*, various issues.

- Ultimate unification of the exchange rates at a level of less than 7 Bs/dollar
- Budget reductions (not specified) not including reductions in wages in state enterprises or in the public sector payrolls
- Price controls to remain after the (decreed) general price freeze of sixty days, which began with the devaluation
- Reduction of 1983 imports by $4 billion (25 percent), mainly by prohibiting the entry of many luxury products
- Inflation at about 15 percent in 1983
- Negotiations to refinance about $10 billion in foreign debt due in 1983 in order to convert it into five- to seven-year loans.

In March 1983 Venezuela declared a deferral on amortization of public external debt (which was subsequently extended to October 1983); the short-term debt involved was about $11 billion. Nevertheless, interest payments were not going to be suspended. Total public sector debt at that time stood at $27 billion, whereas private sector debt was on the order of $7–8 billion. Private sector debt payments would be eligible for the preferential exchange rate (4.3 Bs/dollar) only if principal payments were to take place over a three-year period starting in January 1984.

A key difference between the Venezuelan crisis and others is that the central bank was holding a significant amount of reserves at the time the adjustment program started and negotiations for debt rescheduling began. Indeed, in March 1983, reserves at the central bank were more than 25 percent of total external debt and more than 30 percent of public sector foreign debt. Although Venezuela had to meet obligations of about $10 billion during 1983, private capital flight may well have been the factor that finally pushed the government to impose exchange restrictions and to announce the adjustment plan. In 1982, the short-term capital and errors and omissions accounts showed outflows of $4.6 and $2.5 billion, respectively, whereas the overall balance of payments resulted in a fall of $8.2 billion of international reserves. In addition, there is evidence of a further fall of more than $1 billion in January and February of 1983. The Venezuelan authorities thus seem to have acted in February 1983 *in anticipation* of a liquidity crisis such as had occurred in Brazil and Mexico by implementing an economic policy package before they were forced to do so under IMF conditions.

As of April 1983, capital flight had ceased and international reserves were above their February levels. There is evidence of an increase in the trade surplus, mainly at the expense of lower imports, which was used to finance public sector debt service. In the foreign exchange market, the preferential rates remain at 4.3 and 6 Bs/dollar, and the free rate fluctuated at about 8–9 Bs/dollar.

In July 1983, some government officials were reportedly projecting GDP reductions of about 2.2 percent and 2 percent during 1983 and 1984, respectively, together with significant declines in domestic gross investment. The balance-of-payments deficit is believed to have reached $4 billion in 1983, despite the contraction of imports. In addition, inflation was being projected at 20 percent and 30 percent for 1983 and 1984 and international reserves fell to $7.5 billion at the end of 1983.

By September 1983, it was evident that Venezuela would not reschedule its foreign debt until the new administration took office the following January. In the same month, creditor banks reportedly stated that they would not consider rescheduling Venezuela's debt until all public sector interest payments had become current.[3] Despite the intentions embodied in the plan, the private sector had not, as of September 1983, been able to obtain dollars at preferential rates to meet its debt service obligations. If this situation continues, the total amount of Venezuelan debt in need of rescheduling in 1983–84 could be on the order of $23 billion.

Trading the Way Out

Under the world's normal capital market conditions, the capacity of the countries discussed above to service their foreign debts is seldom questioned. Except for Chile, where the foreign debt–GDP ratio is about 85 percent, all of them present rather "normal" levels of foreign indebtedness by historical standards. If real interest rates and maturity terms were also in accordance with historical precedents, we would certainly not speak of a "debt problem" today. The problem, of course, is that, under the present capital market conditions, these countries are being asked to pay nominal interest rates in excess of 10 percent (real rates being even higher), and amortization rates in excess of 20 percent. For the worst case—that of Chile—this requirement implies debt service payments close to 25 percent of GDP, and for the group in general it is a burden very difficult or impossible to sustain without serious domestic political distress.

In the recent past, all of the countries in question have demonstrated a rather impressive ability to generate substantial trade surpluses, but these surpluses are still below the levels required by the present world capital market. The adjustment realized so far has been facilitated by the huge U.S. trade deficit but has also been harmed to some extent by protectionist policies, particularly those of the European Economic Community.

Unfortunately, many domestic policies implemented by these countries do not contribute to facilitating the always difficult process of adjustment. There is no doubt that adjustment in this context means increased savings. A very popular economic policy instrument used to generate trade surpluses, however, has been to restrict imports. This measure has had the adverse effect of precipitating a reduction in industrial activity and has also increased unemployment rates; on the other hand, exports have not increased and have even fallen below previous levels in some cases. In sum, the adjustment has mainly consisted of sharp reductions in imports. Perhaps the most important policy mistake has been the closing of domestic capital markets, thereby insulating residents from the strong incentives to save that were afforded by the world capital market's efforts to finance the U.S. budget deficit. Clearly there is a way out of the debt problem: the banks can roll over the present debt in order to bring the maturity profile into a feasible configuration.

On the trade side of the problem, developed countries, in particular those of the European Economic Community, will have to ease their protectionist policies. Finally, the countries that are in trouble will have to avoid insulating their residents from the incentives to save. The normalization of the world capital market is also imperative, not only to make feasible the service of present debts, but also to make available in the future the resources that will be needed to finance the development of the region.

Notes

1. Information about these governments does not, however, give an adequate picture of the financial status of the whole public sector, which includes various parastatals not covered by the available statistics.

2. "Billion" means "thousand million."

3. By mid-September the government was expected to request that the standstill on interest payments be extended for 120–180 days; it was due to expire at the end of the month. Arrears of the public sector stood at about $85 million, but private sector arrears exceeded $400 million.

References

Brau, E., R. C. Williams, and others. 1983. *Recent multilateral debt restructurings with official and bank creditors.* Occasional paper 25. Washington, D.C.: International Monetary Fund (IMF).

Buira, Ariel. 1983. The exchange crisis and the adjustment program in Mexico. In J. Williamson, ed. *Prospects for adjustment in Argentina, Brazil, and Mexico.* Washington, D.C.: Institute for International Economics.

Fundação Getulia Vargas. 1984. *Conjuntura econômica* (January).

Gil-Diaz, José. 1983. DEI ajuste a la deflación: La politica economica entre 1977 y 1981 (Chile). Washington, D.C.: International Monetary Fund; processed.

International Monetary Fund (IMF). 1984. *International Financial Statistics* (January).

Langoni, Carlos G. 1981. The strategy of foreign sector adjustment. Seminar on the outlook of the world economy. Brasilia: Banco do Brazil.

World Bank. 1980. *World Tables.* 2d ed. Washington, D.C.

Chapter 7

Government Deficits, the Real Interest Rate, and Developing Country Debt: On Global Crowding Out

Deepak Lal and Sweder van Wijnbergen

THE TWO MAJOR PROBLEMS in the global economy clouding the future prospects of developing countries are those of rising protectionism in industrial countries and the debt crisis. Many observers hope that the current recovery will be sustained and will resolve these problems. Against this cyclical view of current problems, the present chapter explores other explanations suggesting that these problems will not disappear with the cyclical upturn and will require more fundamental changes in policies in both developed and developing countries.

Development economics has traditionally emphasized the trade linkage between developed and developing countries, namely that growth in developed countries is a major determinant of exports and therefore of the growth of developing countries. This so-called engine-of-growth view of the role of trade in development (as propounded for instance by Lewis 1980) has been empirically questioned by Kravis (1970) for the nineteenth century and by Riedel (1984) for the post–World War II development experience. The far-reaching changes in the composition of developing country exports (toward manufactures and away from primary products) in the post war decades have meant that domestic supply rather than foreign demand factors have been the major determinant of developing country export performance and thus of their growth (see Lal 1983, chap. 2). This statement does not mean that the rising protectionism of developed countries (triggered in part by their poor economic performance in the 1970s) may not pose a serious future threat to the growth of developing countries' exports and income. These risks and their consequences, however, have been discussed relatively frequently. In contrast, another important link between developed and developing countries is emerging and is the focus of this chapter.

Although the trade link may have become weaker, the integration of world capital markets and the explosion in commercial bank lending in the 1970s, stimulated by the recycling of financial surpluses in the Organization of Petroleum Exporting Countries (OPEC) that arose from the two oil price shocks of the past decade, have provided another important and growing link between economic prosperity and growth in developed and developing countries. This chapter is concerned with charting and analyzing the implications of certain trends in global savings and investment balances and with determining how these are affected by public policies, in particular fiscal policies, in both developed and developing countries.

The two problems of protectionism and debt that currently plague the global environment and thence the prospects for developing countries, are in turn linked to certain longer-term trends and "structural" weaknesses of developed and developing countries that have been exposed by the supply shocks of the 1970s. These are the possibility of an emerging global shortage of savings; a fiscal problem of rising structural public sector deficits in both developed and developing countries associated with certain structural features: the aging of the population in developed countries and its "greening" in developing countries; the real wage resistance of workers in many industrial countries; and the explosive growth in social expenditures in most countries of the Organisation for Economic Co-operation and Development (OECD).[1]

In the first part of the chapter we chart these trends and structural weaknesses. In the second through the fourth parts we outline their interrelationships. In the fifth part we present a simple three-region model of global saving-investment balance, which is calibrated with data for the 1970s, and in the final part we summarize our postulated global interactions.

Trends in OECD Real Wages, Social Expenditures, and Fiscal Deficits

The deteriorating economic performance of the global economy and the industrialized countries in particular is well documented (see OECD 1983). Two structural aspects of industrialized economies were exposed by the supply shocks of the 1970s. The first was the real wage growth that workers in industrial countries had come to expect as a right and that they were willing to enforce at the cost of a declining share of profits in the late 1960s. The second was the commitments that most OECD governments had increasingly made to various groups to serve their notions of social justice.

Both features influenced public policy in the postwar decades. According to a common belief, except for minor recessions that could be smoothed by suitable demand management policies, the postwar boom would be unending. Its continuation would allow both increased real wages and social expenditures to be financed without the need for difficult choices concerning tradeoffs between wages and profits or between consumption and investment (see Crosland 1950 for the classic statement of this view). Increasingly since the 1960s, microeconomic interventions (industrial subsidies, regional subsidies, and in the 1970s various forms of protectionism) to maintain workers in particular occupations and locations at income levels above the value of their marginal product were justified as a legitimate tradeoff between "economic security" and economic growth. (For a rough quantification of these microeconomic distortions for Europe, see Curzon-Price 1982.)

The supply shocks of the 1970s and the universal slowing down of productivity growth in the OECD countries exposed the unreality of these assumptions and the unviability of the policies they had engendered. Most obvious and best analyzed were the discrepancies between the real wage that workers expected and the lowering of the "full employment wage" caused by both the terms-of-trade losses suffered by the OECD countries in the 1970s and by their worsened growth prospects stemming from the productivity slowdown. Sachs (1979, 1983) has shown (see tables 7-1 and 7-2) how slowly the real wage in different industrial economies and particularly in Europe adjusted downward toward the new "equilibrium" real wage. The United States was an exception, as it succeeded in creating 20 million extra jobs in the 1970s, whereas in Western Europe employment changed by only 2 million. With the maturation of the baby boom generation, the labor supply increased, producing levels of unemployment unprecedented since the 1930s. The distortion in relative factor prices resulting from the relative rigidity of real wages provided producers with an incentive to substitute capital for labor (see Scott and Laslett 1978) while the accompanying squeeze on profits attenuated the means to finance investment to create future employment and growth. The rise in commodity prices and the associated structural changes in the economy, moreover, led to a reduction in the "effective" capital stock as the expected return on capital employed in oil-intensive and other raw material–intensive industries declined (see Baily 1981 and Bruno 1982, 1984).[2] Actual profits in manufacturing also declined (see table 7-3).

In these circumstances, conventional demand management policies cannot avoid the transitional unemployment that would in any case be caused by a higher real wage adjusting only slowly toward that "warranted" by the changed circumstances. The conventional method of reducing such transitional unemployment is premised on the assumption

Table 7-1. *Rates of Growth in the Product Wage and in Labor Productivity for the Manufacturing Sector and the Aggregate Economy, by Country, Selected Periods, 1962–78*
(annual average in percent)

Sector, measure, and period	Canada	France	Ger-many	Italy	Japan	United Kingdom	United States
Manufacturing							
Product wage							
1962–69	5.0	4.8	5.6	7.4	10.8	4.6	3.4
1969–73	3.6	7.0	7.5	9.7	12.6	5.6	3.6
1973–75	0.1	6.2	6.8	4.4	0.6	4.6	0.1
1975–78	n.a.	4.8	5.4[a]	2.0	8.9	−1.4	3.0
Labor productivity							
1962–69	4.5	6.3	5.9	6.8	11.2	4.5	3.1
1969–73	4.4	5.4	4.8	6.9	8.7	4.1	3.2
1973–75	−0.4	2.8	5.2	0.4	−1.8	−1.3	−0.3
1975–78	4.5	6.1	5.0	4.1	7.3	1.2	3.0
Aggregate economy							
Product wage							
1962–69	3.6	5.1	5.0	7.8	8.5	3.2	3.1
1969–73	2.0	5.5	6.3	7.9	12.2	3.7	2.6
1973–75	1.5	5.1	4.8	6.0	8.6	4.9	0.2
1975–78	1.8	5.2	2.7	1.2	2.7	1.5	2.3
Labor productivity							
1962–69	3.3	5.2	5.3	7.4	9.9	3.1	2.7
1969–73	3.2	5.7	5.2	6.6	9.1	3.9	2.6
1973–75	0.7	2.6	4.0	3.0	3.9	0.7	0.3
1975–78	2.0	5.0	4.5	1.3	4.1	2.0	2.1

Source: Sachs (1979).

Table 7-2. *Annual Percentage Changes in Real Hourly Compensation for Manufacturing, Selected Periods, 1960–82*

Country	1960–73	1973–79	1979–81	1980	1981	1982
Canada	2.8	2.5	−0.6	−1.0	−1.1	0.8
France	5.3	4.3	1.8	2.8	0.8	3.0
Germany	6.4	5.3	2.2	2.9	1.5	−0.3
Japan	8.2	2.3	0.5	−1.5	2.5	2.1
United Kingdom	3.7	3.7	3.8	4.9	2.7	2.4
Unites States	1.8	0.9	−0.9	−1.6	−0.1	0.2

Source: Sachs (1983).

Table 7-3. *Real Rates of Return on Corporate Capital,*
by Country, 1962–76
(percent)

Year or period	Canada	France	Germany	Italy	Japan	United Kingdom	United States
1969	9.8	11.5	20.7	12.2	30.6	10.1	10.2
1970	6.6	11.5	18.2	11.5	28.1	8.7	8.1
1971	8.4	10.6	15.6	9.4	23.5	8.7	8.4
1972	9.4	12.3	13.4	9.9	20.2	8.6	9.2
1973	11.4	11.8	12.9	n.a.	15.7	7.2	8.6
1974	11.4	10.8	12.7	n.a.	13.1	4.0	6.4
1975	8.2	5.2	10.0	n.a.	13.9	3.4	6.9
1976	8.1	n.a.	11.4	n.a.	n.a.	3.6	7.9
Average							
1962–64	7.9	9.7	19.3	10.4	28.2	11.9	12.0
1965–69	9.6	10.0	19.5	11.4	27.9	10.6	12.2
1970–73	9.0	11.6	15.0	10.3	21.9	8.3	8.6
1974–76	9.2	8.0	11.4	n.a.	13.5	3.7	7.1

n.a. = not available.
Source: Sachs (1979).

that workers suffer from some money illusion and that a lower real wage
and unemployment rate can therefore be obtained by boosting demand
and the inflation rate. With the disappearance of money illusion, however, there is no long-run tradeoff and possibly not even a short-run
tradeoff between inflation and unemployment. The increased labor militancy in Europe in the late 1960s was illustrated by the explosion in
money wages in the 1964–70 period, particularly in West European
countries (see figure 7-1 and Phelps-Brown 1983; Sachs 1979; and Soskice
1978) at a time when productivity was slowing down. This militancy can
be taken as a sign that, with rising inflation, workers' money illusion had
progressively disappeared, and since the 1960s workers were willing to
strike to maintain their *real* wage. The resulting unemployment can then
be ascribed to the rigidity of real wages rather than to a lack of effective
demand.[3]

The social commitments of governments posed equally serious problems. Regardless of whether or not the level and coverage of social
commitments were justified in view of the growth expectations of the
post–World War II Golden Age, the worsened prospects in the 1970s
required some downward adjustment in the levels and coverage of these
social benefits even with *unchanged social preferences concerning equity*.[4]
Instead, until the late 1970s, social expenditures grew rapidly in most
OECD countries, with most of the growth being due to improved levels of

Figure 7-1. *The Origins of Trade Union Power*

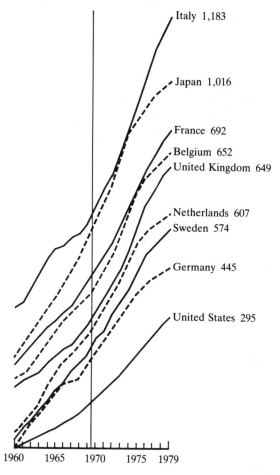

Note: Rise of hourly rates or earnings, mostly in manufacturing, in nine countries of the OECD, 1960–79, showing change in rate of rise about 1969–70. (Ratio scale: number at end of each curve gives average hourly rates or earnings in the first three quarters of 1979, expressed as an index in which 1960 = 100.)

Source: Phelps-Brown (1983:156).

benefits (see figure A1-2, table A1-3, and appendix 1 in this book for a summary of the evidence). In light of the recent project evaluation literature (Lal 1974, 1980; Little and Mirrlees 1974), a "critical consumption level" of income can be defined, at which a marginal increase in publicly funded income transfers is considered socially as valuable as a marginal change in public revenue. The worsened growth prospects of the 1970s required a downward adjustment in this critical consumption level. The net effect of both a real wage and a critical consumption level higher than warranted by the new circumstances is a socially suboptimal consumption-savings balance for the economy. There would now be a premium on domestic savings such that a rational government should attempt to raise the domestic savings level through fiscal policy.

Instead, the emergence of a social premium on savings also saw the growth of large fiscal deficits in many OECD countries (see figure A1-4). The decomposition of these deficits into their cyclical and structural components is controversial, although we cannot assume—as people usually do—that deviations of actual GDP in the 1970s from the trend levels based on performance in the 1960s represent a cyclical shortfall that can be corrected by expansionary fiscal policy. The cyclical adjustments should be made with reference to the peaks of the *cycles* in the 1970s and not to the *hypothetical trend* that would have occurred if overall economic performance had matched that in the Golden Age of the 1950s and 1960s. Putting the matter differently, in making the cyclical adjustments to the deficits, we cannot assume that the natural rate of unemployment has remained at its 1960s levels in most OECD countries. If it has drifted upward, the cyclical element in the budget deficits will be lower than has been estimated by many commentators.[5]

Even in terms of conventional accounting in the 1980s, however, the fiscal deficits in some OECD countries, particularly in the United States, have an increasing structural component (see figure 7-2). It is to the causes and implications of these structural deficits that we now turn.

The Financing of Social Expenditures, Budget Deficits, and Crowding Out

The implications of the rising budget deficits in OECD countries are best seen by examining their relationship to gross domestic savings in the area over time (see figure 7-3). In 1970, OECD budget deficits absorbed less than 1 percent of gross savings; by 1975 this figure had risen to 44 percent and by 1983 to nearly 52 percent. The relationship with respect to the more nebulous notion of net savings was even worse (see figure A1-9). The resulting crowding out of private expenditures, particularly investment, that this public draft on available domestic savings represents is the most serious long-term trend in these countries. In subsequent parts of this chapter, we explore its implications for the global savings-investment balance and for world interest rates and thereby outline its effects on developing countries.

Figure 7-2. *Budget Deficit in the United States, 1980–89*

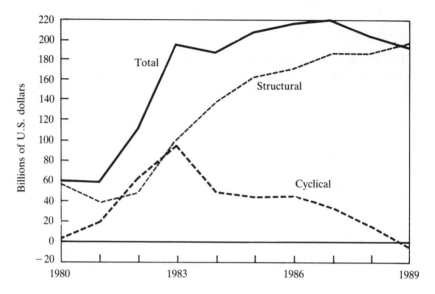

Source: Derived from data in Council of Economic Advisers (1983).

Figure 7-3. *Budget Deficit in the OECD Countries, 1974–84*

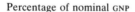

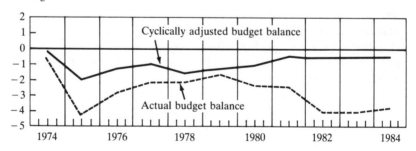

Note: For definitions and methods of calculation, see annex on sources and methods in OECD (1983). Data for 1983 and 1984 are OECD forecasts.
Source: OECD (1983, December).

A substitution of public for private uses of available domestic savings in itself poses no problem if the social value of these alternative uses is equated at the margin. There are some grounds, however, for questioning whether this is currently the case.

Social Expenditures

The increased pressure on budgets is due to increases in expenditure on social security (public pensions) and public health provision, representing improved levels of benefits as well as extensions in their coverage (see OECD 1984, and appendix 1 in this book). These expenditures are the equivalent of providing public insurance for expenses incurred on private illness and the possibility of fluctuations in income over the life cycle. They thus provide wealth holders with an asset (whose "value" is equal to the present expected value of the programmed benefits) that is a substitute for private capital in their portfolios. If these public entitlements were funded through the accumulation of public capital, and its efficiency were no worse than that of private capital, the publicly provided capital asset would simply substitute for a privately provided one in the portfolio of wealth holders. There would be no adverse effects on the overall consumption-savings balance, the long-run capital stock, and the intertemporal welfare of the economy.

Most of the expenditures of a social insurance type in OECD countries, however, are funded through pay-as-you-go schemes, which tax current workers in order to transfer entitlements to the old and the sick. The reduction in the privately held capital for these insurance purposes is not then matched by any offsetting capital accumulation by the government. There is merely a publicly enforced transfer of income from the working population to the old and sick. It can be shown (see Johnson 1981 and others) that pay-as-you-go social security systems can substitute for physical capital in private portfolios and can thus reduce the long-run equilibrium capital stock if the size of bequests left by one generation to the next is not subject to economic choice and if each generation does not put the same weight on its children's welfare as on its own. If, however, each family is linked to the infinite future because of an altruistic concern for its children, who in turn are concerned about the welfare of their chidren, and so forth, then in effect we have a one-consumer "infinite horizon" model of the choice of the optimal intertemporal time path of consumption. Once this choice has been made—in view of technology and tastes—a government-enforced intertemporal transfer will have no effect on the optimal choices of these infinitely lived consumers (if capital markets are efficient). Private actions will completely offset public ones to yield the same intertemporal outcomes with or without a pay-as-you-go insurance scheme.

There are various reasons why this link between the present and the infinite future may be snapped, however (see Buiter and Tobin 1980): for example, some consumers may have tastes that do not make it optimal to leave any bequests; some consumers may plan not to have any children; consumers may not care at all about the welfare of their children; and there may be capital market imperfections due, most importantly, to the difficulty of borrowing against human capital. Then the effect of increased social security wealth on reducing savings and thence on the long-run equilibrium capital stock will be reintroduced. Unfortunately the empirical evidence on the effects of social security on savings is inconclusive (see Feldstein 1983; Thompson 1983), but there seems to be support for some reduction in savings resulting from increased social security payments.

Bond Financing of Fiscal Deficits

Apart from the "wealth illusion" effect on savings of recent public expenditure increases financed by taxation of the working population, there is a further reason for concern. Increased expenditures are typically funded in OECD countries (particularly the United States) through bond-financed budget deficits, with further distortionary effects on the consumption-savings balance in OECD countries. Besides current taxation, there are essentially only two ways of financing the increased social expenditures—through the seigniorage of printing money or through bond financing and the implicit future taxes needed to pay the interest on a growing stock of public debt. It has been argued (Barro 1974; Friedman 1978) that the effects of public spending on the consumption-investment balance in the economy are fully measured by the level of public expenditure; the form of financing—through explicit taxation or the hidden taxes of inflation (associated with the printing of money) or borrowing from the public (bond financing)—is deemed to be immaterial. This so-called Ricardian equivalence theorem concerning debt neutrality is based on assumptions very similar to those that cause pay-as-you-go social security systems to have no effect on the level of savings. Thus if public expenditure rises by say $x billion and is funded either by current taxes of $x billion or by issuing government consols of $x billion with an interest rate of r percent, then, according to the Ricardian equivalence theorem, there will be no effect on the consumption-investment mix of the economy. Rational wealth holders will notice that the present value of the future taxes (annually $rx billion) that they have to pay exactly equals a current tax burden of $x billion.[6] Once again, there will be no difference in the effects of tax or bond financing on savings, as every wealth holder voluntarily negates the involuntary intergenerational transfer associated with bond financing by reverse changes in intergenerational bequests. As before, if for some reason this private intergenerational link is weak, or else the public suffers from some form of debt illusion and considers government bonds as part of its net wealth, then the expansion of the interest-bearing public debt will lead to a substitution of bonds for real capital in portfolios and thence to a decline in aggregate savings and the long-run capital stock. Although again the econometric evidence is equivocal, Buiter and Tobin remark after surveying it: "On the basis of currently available theoretical models and empirical evidence our provisional conclusion is that the case for debt neutrality is not well established" (1980:58). The most recent, empirical test of the hypothesis by Koskela and Viven for nine OECD countries for the period 1964–79 seems to reject the debt neutrality hypothesis fairly convincingly, as does our own test in the fifth section of this chapter.

Thus at this stage we may tentatively accept two links in our chain of reasoning concerning the global economy while noting that the evidence for them is equivocal. *First, the expansion of social security and other social insurance–type schemes in pay-as-you-go systems will tend to diminish domestic savings. Second, the financing of this increased public expenditure through bonds rather than through taxation is further likely to crowd out private investment and to reduce the long-run capital stock of the economy, thereby further raising the social premium to be attached to savings in the OECD countries.*

Additional problems connected with the funding of higher social expenditures through bond-financed budget deficits have to do with their effects on inflation. Of the three ways of financing increased public expenditure—taxation, bonds, and the printing of money—the last is considered to have a by-product cost not associated with the others, namely the efficiency costs of inflation. Sargent and Wallace have recently argued that bond financing of public expenditures may also be inflationary. The argument runs as follows. Suppose that the only way to finance the budget deficit is through money creation or the issuing of government bonds. Suppose further that the public's demand for government bonds is such that the additional bonds will only be held at a real interest rate that is greater than the economy's real trend rate of growth.[7] Finally, suppose that the monetary authorities are concerned with controlling an ongoing inflation and to do so adopt targets for the expansion of base money in the economy. In that case they will have to fund the budget deficit by allowing an expansion in the real stock of bonds held by the public. In order to hold down the growth of base money, they will have to finance the principal and interest paid on these bonds by selling still more bonds, and as the real rate of interest on the bonds is greater, by hypothesis, than the real growth rate of the economy, the real stock of bonds will grow faster than the economy. The demand for the stock of bonds relative to GDP, however, must have an upper limit; when that limit is reached, the only way to finance the principal and interest due on the existing stock of bonds is by printing money, that is, by monetizing the deficit, thus creating the inflation required to obtain the seigniorage from the inflation tax.[8] Bond financing of deficits under these circumstances cannot avoid the inflationary consequences that the alternative form of financing through money creation would entail. Moreover, to the extent that this future rise in inflation is anticipated, as it will be if agents have rational expectations, then not merely the future but also the current level of inflation will rise. Tight money and bond-financed fiscal deficits cannot then prevent an inflationary outcome.

The Global Capital Market and Real Interest Rates

The discussion thus far has implicitly taken as its context a closed national economy. The increased worldwide financial integration of the 1970s was aided and accompanied by the general movement to flexible exchange rates and the concomitant removal of exchange controls in most OECD countries. The result has been that, in the 1970s, capital movements themselves became a major determinant of exchange rates, which were determined as much by national savings and investment balances, and by the portfolio choices of international lenders, as by the underlying "real" trade balances of the respective national economies.

Global Financial Integration

The resulting relatively integrated international financial market can then most usefully be considered as a closed *world* economy, where, to maintain flow equilibrium, the ex ante global savings-investment imbalances are mediated through changes in world interest rates that lead to an ex post equality of global savings and investment. If we look at the same issue from the purely financial (stock equilibrium) side, we see at any point in time a given stock of different national financial assets, including national monies being held in the portfolios of an international body of lenders, such that the structure of real exchange and interest rates is determined by the relative supplies and demands for these assets. Furthermore, as a useful simplification we can group countries in three "regional" aggregates in the world economy—the industrialized world (OECD), the oil-exporting countries (OPEC), and the oil-importing developing countries.

Historically, most capital flows have moved from developed to developing countries. In the 1970s, however, OPEC countries emerged as major suppliers of capital to the world economy as a result of the rise in the financial surpluses stemming from the two oil price rises in that decade. The intermediation of the resulting international financial surpluses and deficits was performed, it seemed very successfully, by the offshore branches of mainly U.S. and U.K. commercial banks. Whereas until 1974 the major sources of external capital for most developing countries were official capital transfers and direct foreign investment, the recycling of the OPEC surpluses reopened the market for commercial credit to them for the first time after their defaults in the 1930s.

Given the historically low interest rate (whose determinants we discuss below) during the mid-1970s, it was reasonable for many developing countries to borrow abroad to finance investment and even consumption (using current estimates of the expected costs of future repayments of the debt). The accumulated debt, however, became a problem when, after the second oil price shock and the unexpected tightening of monetary policy in the United States, real interest rates instead of remaining at their previous low levels increased to historically very high levels. This rise was a major cause of the debt crisis.

In explaining the divergent behavior of real interest rates after the two oil shocks it is important to chart the trends in global savings and investment balances in the 1970s, as well as in the three regions, as there have been important changes in capital-importing and capital-exporting status during the 1970s. These changing regional balances between savings and investment in turn reflect the effects of particular public policies, primarily fiscal and monetary policies. Table 7-4 provides a rough indication of regional and global savings during the 1970s.

Trends and Determinants of World Interest Rates

What, then, explains the behavior of real interest rates during the 1970s? In a perfectly competitive economy, where all taxes were lump sum and there was no money illusion, the real interest rate on financial assets would equal (a) the cost of capital to the firm and thence the marginal productivity of capital, and (b) the real return to savers. If the underlying technology (marginal productivity) and tastes (rates of time preference and degrees of risk aversion) remained unchanged, then the

Table 7-4. *Domestic Savings Ratios, by Region and Total, for Three Regions*

Year	Developing country S_i	OECD S_i	OPEC S_i	Total S_i
1952	n.a.	15.0	n.a.	n.a.
1953	n.a.	15.6	n.a.	n.a.
1954	n.a.	16.2	n.a.	n.a.
1955	n.a.	16.7	n.a.	n.a.
1956	n.a.	17.3	n.a.	n.a.
1957	n.a.	17.3	n.a.	n.a.
1958	n.a.	16.4	n.a.	n.a.
1959	n.a.	16.9	n.a.	n.a.
1960	n.a.	17.4	n.a.	n.a.
1961	n.a.	17.7	n.a.	n.a.
1962	n.a.	17.8	n.a.	n.a.
1963	n.a.	18.0	n.a.	n.a.
1964	14.4	18.5	n.a.	n.a.
1965	15.4	18.7	n.a.	n.a.
1966	14.9	18.5	n.a.	n.a.
1967	15.4	18.1	n.a.	n.a.
1968	15.8	18.3	n.a.	n.a.
1969	16.7	18.9	n.a.	n.a.
1970	16.6	19.4	n.a.	n.a.
1971	15.9	19.8	n.a.	n.a.
1972	16.8	20.4	45.1	20.2
1973	17.3	21.4	47.8	21.2
1974	15.7	19.8	71.7	20.7
1975	16.5	19.4	56.8	20.0
1976	19.0	18.8	61.7	20.0
1977	18.9	19.2	56.1	20.2
1978	19.0	20.6	47.7	21.0
1979	19.4	20.2	58.5	21.1
1980	19.0	19.5	65.4	20.8
1981	n.a.	19.4	55.5	n.a.

n.a. = not available.
Source: Derived from data in appendixes 1 and 2 of this volume.

nominal interest rate would rise by the rate of inflation, leaving the real rate of interest unchanged. This so-called Fisher neutrality of inflation on interest rates was questioned by Tobin (1965) and Mundell (1963), who argued that in an economy with non-interest-bearing money, inflation (being a tax on money) reduces the demand for money balances and, for a given stock of other financial assets (backed by real ones), increases the relative price of bonds and thus leads to a lower real interest rate. This portfolio composition effect of inflation leads to a fall in the marginal product of capital (higher capital intensity of production) because of the lower real interest rate, the lowering of the real interest rate being the result of a rise in nominal interest rates that is less than the rate of inflation.

Darby (1975) and Feldstein (1983) in turn emphasize the effects of income and corporate taxes to show that they lead to a rise in nominal interest rates greater than inflation and hence to a rise in pretax real interest rates, a rise in the marginal productivity of capital and thus a lowering of the capital intensity of production.[9] The basic argument of Darby and Feldstein is straightforward. Suppose that savers expect a constant real return of 3 percent. Their interest payments are taxed at the rate of 50 percent, and the tax system is unindexed. Then initially, with no inflation, the nominal and real interest rates (which will be the same) that are required by savers in equilibrium will be 6 percent. Now, suppose there is inflation of 10 percent. To obtain a real net-of-tax rate of interest of 3 percent, savers would accept only a nominal interest rate that yielded a net-of-tax nominal return of 13 percent, which means a pretax nominal interest rate of 26 percent.[10] The nominal interest rate would have had to rise by more than the inflation rate.

Various other aspects of the interaction of existing tax systems with inflation work against the Fisher neutrality hypothesis. In general, inflation distorts the measurement of profits, interest payments, and capital gains. The provision in most income tax codes for the deduction of mortgage interest and other nominal interest payments to derive taxable income introduces a bias toward the expansion of consumer debt, toward increased demand for housing, and against physical capital formation during an inflation.[11] The corporate tax treatment of depreciation, where depreciation for tax purposes is limited to the original or "historic cost" of the firm's capital stock, causes the effective tax rate on corporate income to rise with inflation as the real value of depreciation allowances is reduced. Similarly, firms that use first in, first out (FIFO) inventory accounting will be reporting mythical profits with inflation, as they will be deducting the acquisition and not the replacement cost of inventories. (See Feldstein 1983 for these and other arguments.)

For all these institutional reasons, the Fisher neutrality hypothesis may not hold. Finally, as Fisher himself recognized, the assumption of a complete lack of money illusion in financial markets may be invalid. Thus Fisher states:

> The money rate and the real rate are normally identical; that is, they will . . . be the same when the purchasing power of the dollar in terms of the cost of living is constant or stable. When the cost of living is not

stable, the rate of interest takes the appreciation or depreciation into account to some extent, but only slightly and, in general, indirectly . . . , that is . . . , when prices are falling, the rate of interest tends to be low, but not so low as it should be to compensate for the fall. . . . Men are unable or unwilling to adjust at all accurately and promptly the many interest rates to changing price levels. . . . The erratic behavior of real interest rates is evidently a trick played on the money market by money illusion. . . . The money rate of interest and still more the real rate are attacked more by the instability of money than by those more fundamental and more normal causes connected with income, impatience and opportunity. [1930:43, 415, 451]

The historical evidence (surveyed, for instance, for the United States in Summers 1983, and summarized in table 7-5 for short-term interest rates) does not support Fisher neutrality. Nor does it support either the Tobin-Mundell or the Darby-Feldstein position unequivocally. Nominal interest rates have exhibited both greater than and less than unitary response to inflation in different periods. Clearly explaining the behavior of nominal and real interest rates will require that all the following factors be taken into account: (a) the qualifications mentioned by Fisher, based on some money illusion in financial markets; (b) the real balance effects on the marginal product of capital and real interest rates of inflation, as emphasized by Tobin and Mundell; (c) the effects on nominal interest rates of inflation in economies with income and corporate taxes, as emphasized by Feldstein and Darby; and (d) changes in underlying technology and tastes.

Wilcox (1983) has attempted to develop and test a model incorporating some of these factors for U.S. short-term rates for the period 1952–79 in order to explain the low rates in the early 1970s and *mutatis mutandi* the higher rates in the late 1970s. He emphasizes the important interactions between the supply shocks flowing from the changing relative prices of primary commodities (particularly energy) and changes in expected rates of inflation during the postwar decades.

The energy shock's main effect was to reduce the net demand for capital, as many studies (for example, Hudson and Jorgenson 1978) have found empirically that energy and capital are "cooperative" in production.[12] This statement is also borne out by the dramatic fall in the growth rate of investment and its share of total output in industrial countries after relative energy prices rose by about 60 percent in 1973. Thus, all other things being equal, the negative supply shocks of the 1970s would have reduced real interest rates. In contrast, until 1973 the industrial countries were faced with a positive supply shock flowing from a fall

Table 7-5. *Trends in Inflation and Interest Rates, by Decade,
1860–1979*
(percent)

Period	Average yield on commercial paper[a]	Average inflation rate[b]	Average real interest rate
1860–69	7.1	5.5	1.5
1870–79	6.5	−3.4	9.8
1880–89	5.1	−2.1	7.2
1890–99	4.6	0.3	4.2
1900–09	4.8	2.5	2.3
1910–19	7.7	8.3	−3.6
1920–29	5.1	−0.9	6.0
1930–39	1.5	−2.0	3.6
1940–49	0.9	5.5	−4.6
1950–59	2.6	2.2	0.4
1960–69	4.6	2.5	2.1
1970–79	7.2	7.4	−0.2

Regression of twelve ten-year averages
$$R_t = 4.43 + 0.05\pi_t$$
$$(0.69) \quad (0.16)$$
$$\bar{R}^2 = -0.09$$

Note: Computed as an arithmetic average of monthly data.

a. For 1860 through 1918, the data correspond to the two- to three-month rate in
MacCaulay (1938). From 1919 to 1979 I used the four- to six-month paper rates from the
Federal Reserve.

b. For 1860 to 1918 the figures are derived from the Warren-Pearson wholesale price
index. For 1919 to 1979 I used the nonseasonally adjusted consumer price index.

Source: Summers (1983:213).

in the relative price of primary commodities, mainly energy. Between
1950 and 1970, for instance, the relative price of Saudi crude oil declined
by 55 percent. This drop put upward pressure on the real interest rate, as
the positive supply shock would raise the net demand for capital.

The steadily rising expected inflation rate, in contrast, put downward
pressure on real interest rates. The net effect was dominated by the
positive effect of the favorable supply shock, and so there was a marginal
rise in real interest rates. In the 1970s the negative supply shock reinforced the downward pressure on real interest rates stemming from an
acceleration in the expected inflation rate, so real interest rates became
negative.[13]

To the above-mentioned factors we need to add the shifts in global savings balances that occurred as a counterpart to the oil price rise and the changing state of the public finances in many industrialized countries. Tables A1-3 and 7-4 suggest several points.

- The rise in OPEC savings was matched by falls in savings in the other two regions, so that there was no marked deterioration in the overall global savings rate; but as the composition of global savings shifted toward a region with a higher ex ante savings rate, this shift in itself would have put downward pressure on real interest rates.
- The explosion in commercial bank lending after the first oil shock led to a recycling of the OPEC financial surpluses, in effect to cover incipient budget deficits in both developed and developing countries.
- As the OPEC surplus fell during the 1970s, the public sectors in many developed and developing countries increased their draft on domestic global savings very substantially by running large actual budget deficits.[14]

Furthermore, in many industralized countries, particularly the United Kingdom and the United States, an inflationary explosion yielded substantial revenue from the inflation tax to cover the public sectors' borrowing requirements. This inflationary tax hit public debt holders particularly hard. In the United Kingdom the public debt in real terms was reduced by half (the ratio of public debt to GDP was 95 percent in 1970 and 58 percent in 1979), even when nominal debt was rising to cover the actual public sector deficit (see appendix 1 in this book). As governments were able to extort the inflation tax from bondholders in the mid-1970s, it would appear that the inflation was unanticipated by the capital markets.

Although these factors—a decline in the marginal product of capital and thus in demand for investment at a time when global savings did not fall markedly; a rise in the expected rate of inflation; and the success in recycling the OPEC surpluses to finance the increased public expenditure needs of industralized and many developing countries—all led to historically low real rates of interest, what explains their subsequent rise?

The supply factors, particularly changes in the real price of energy in the early 1980s, and other primary commodities, exerted a favorable supply shock in OECD countries, which could have been expected to raise real interest rates. In addition, the disinflationary policies that most industrial countries had to pursue meant that expected inflation fell, and this drop would also have put upward pressure on real interest rates. A third factor, however, which though speculative may be of some importance, was that the inflationary expropriation of bondholders in the 1970s reduced (if it did not completely remove) money illusion in capital markets. Thus from figure 7-4 it would appear that until 1980 expected inflation in the United States was below the actual, but this pattern has since been reversed, so that subsequently the actual budget deficits (particularly in the United States and the United Kingdom) could not be financed by the inflation tax. This development in turn, however, meant that money would have to remain tight, putting further upward pressure on short-term rates. Meanwhile the loose fiscal policy reflected in large budget deficits needed to be financed through borrowing. The resulting crowding out of private expenditures could also be expected to exert pressure on real interest rates, if for no other reason than that, as the share of government debt in private portfolios rises, it will only be held at a lower price (that is at higher interest rates). Moreover, taking into account the argument that bond financing of growing public expenditures may worsen expectations of future inflation, lenders fully cured of money illusion may now be including a risk premium to cover the future possibility of another inflationary upsurge, as governments unable to finance further public expenditures (including an increasing interest rate burden on the growing public debt) in the future may be forced to monetize the resulting budget deficits.[15] In a nutshell, therefore, given the disappearance of money illusion in financial markets in the 1970s, and growing public expenditure that cannot be financed through either raising taxes or printing money now, short-term interest rates will be high because money today is tight, and long-term rates will be high because people expect money to be looser and hence inflation to be higher in the future, because money today is tight!

Third World Debt, Infrastructural Investments, and Fiscal Deficits

The final link in our chain of reasoning concerns the public finances in developing countries and the role of foreign borrowing in development.

Historically (see Lewis 1978), the flow of international capital has not *necessarily* been from rich to poor countries nor from those with high domestic savings rates to those with low domestic savings rates. In the nineteenth century, per capita income was higher in the major borrowing countries (the United States, Australia, and Argentina) than in the lending countries (the United Kingdom, France, and Germany).

The major determinants of foreign borrowing were differences in rates of population growth and the associated urbanization. Urbanization in the nineteenth century was the decisive factor, according to Lewis: "Those whose urban populations were growing by less than 3 percent per

Figure 7-4. *Interest Rates, Inflation, and Borrowing in the United States,*
1961–84

Short-term interest rates
(on ninety-one-day Treasury bills)

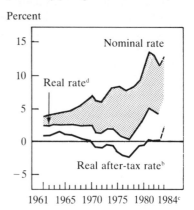

Long-term interest rates
(on twenty-year government bonds)

Inflation
(annual percentage change in consumer prices)

Federal government borrowing
(percent of total credit flows)

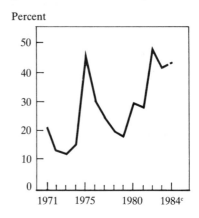

a. Deflated by the GNP deflator.
b. Assuming a 35 percent average marginal tax rate for bond buyers.
c. Forecast.
d. Deflated by a four-year moving average of the GNP deflator.
Source: Economist (May 5, 1984:21).

annum (France 1.0, England 1.8, and Germany 2.5) loaned, and those whose urban populations were growing by more than 3 percent per annum (Australia 3.5, United States 3.7, Canada 3.9, Argentina 5.3) borrowed" (1978:39).

Urbanization, moreover, is expensive in terms of capital because of the capital intensity of the infrastructure required to provide housing, transport, sanitation, and water supplies as well as the need for skill-intensive (and thus human capital–intensive) labor in social services such as health and education. Not only is the per capita provision of these infrastructure services higher in urban areas than in rural areas, but their provision tends to require both more highly priced labor and more capital per unit of provision than does a similar rural infrastructure.

Moreover, as much of this physical and human infrastructure has public goods characteristics, public provision is a common feature irrespective of the form of political and economic organization in different countries. The resulting positive link between the growth of public expenditure and urbanization is a well-documented statistical relationship in both current developed and developing countries (see appendix 2 in this book).

In many currently developing countries, apart from the pressures for urbanization associated with a growing population's pressure on available land resources, industrialization—whether it is an efficient natural stage in economic development or the hot house kind associated with the promotion of import substitution—would, as in the past evolution of currently developed countries, also have led to increased urbanization and the associated growth of public expenditure to finance urban infrastructure.

Equally important for the growth of public expenditure are the effects of the demand for social services, in particular education, associated with the greening of the population. Although the *public* provision of education is not necessarily essential, it has increasingly been accepted as such in developing (and developed) countries. This is another source of pressure on the public finances in many developing countries. Moreover, these social expenditures, as well as expenditures on infrastructural development in developing countries, differ from expenditures related to health and social security in developed countries in one essential respect. As they are complementary to other inputs in the production process, they raise the long-run productivity of the economy more than do the pure transfer-type effects of developed country social expenditures on the health care and pensions of the "aged."

Although for the reasons given above there are inevitable pressures for the growth of public expenditures in present-day developing countries, the financing of this expenditure need not pose a problem for the government if domestic savings are sufficient and can be mobilized by governments in the form of tax revenues. Most developing countries have raised domestic savings rates steadily since the 1950s (see appendix 2 in this book). The exception is Africa, where domestic savings rates, having peaked at about 15 percent at the end of the 1960s, have collapsed in the 1970s.

Within the life cycle framework, the greening of the working population can be expected to lead to a rise in domestic savings rates for exactly the obverse of the reasons discussed in our second section, which implied that the aging of the population in developed countries would tend to depress domestic savings rates. On the other hand, the higher (young) dependency ratio associated with the greening of Third World population would be expected to depress savings rates. The most recent empirical evidence, however, shows that "in no case was there any statistically significant adverse effect of the young dependency rate on aggregate saving in any group of LDCs and, in many cases, the relevant coefficient was observed to have a positive sign" (Rati Ram 1984:234; also see Rati Ram 1982). Unfortunately, little more can be said about the reasons for the remarkable savings performance of Asian and Latin American countries since the 1960s. In this area further research is badly needed.[16]

Although taxes have been raised in many developing countries, these have proved to be insufficient to meet the rise in public expenditures. Where overt taxation has been insufficient to cover rising public expenditure, covert taxation, usually in the form of the "inflation tax," has been common, particularly in Latin America (see chapter 6 in this book and Harberger and Edwards 1980). Data on the true fiscal deficits, which are financed by money or bond creation, particularly for Latin American countries, are not available (see appendix 2 in this book).[17] Tables 7-6 and 7-7, however, which were derived by Harberger and Edwards from the *International Financial Statistics* of the International Monetary Fund, give us some idea of the differences between developing economies with regard to the use of the inflation tax to finance public sector expenditures.

The opening up of the commercial loan markets to developing countries in the late 1960s, and the availability of cheap and plentiful commercial credit after the 1973–74 oil price rise, allowed a rising proportion of the growing public expenditure and incipient fiscal deficits to be financed by commercial borrowing rather than by the inflation tax (see chapter 6 in this book). With low and even negative rates of interest on the loans, it was not imprudent to borrow to finance even public consumption, as the real rates of interest were likely to have been below the country's social rate of time preference, if we assume that the decision took into account risk and the future ability to repay the loans.

Although there was undoubtedly some waste involved in the public

Table 7-6. *Cases of Acute and Chronic Inflation*

Economy	Year	β (percent)	γ	λ (percent)	π (percent)
		Cases of acute inflation			
Indonesia	1966–68	2.0	0.542	145	128
Bolivia	1954–57	4.4	0.800	81	120
Chile	1973–76	33.0	0.850	433	365
Uruguay	1966–68	1.7	0.215	40	89
Uruguay	1972–75	3.0	0.234	95	80
Argentina	1975–76	13.3	0.394	220	310
Median	—	3.7	0.467	120	124
		Cases of chronic inflation			
Argentina	1954–74	2.6	0.333	27	26
Uruguay	1954–65;				
	1969–71	1.2	0.120	26	21
Chile	1959–72	2.9	0.477	41	28
Brazil	1954–76	2.0	0.300	43	29
Iceland	1973–79	3.6	0.140	40	38
Ghana	1975–79	5.6	0.675	56	61
Uganda	1973–79	n.a.	n.a.	n.a.	n.a.
Zaire	1974–79	8.6	0.676	60	58
Israel	1973–79	3.2	0.277	41	35
Colombia	1973–79	1.0	0.138	24	29
Peru	1975–79	3.9	0.352	49	38
Median	—	3.1	0.320	41	35

n.a. = not available.

Note: Data are median observations of the indicated variable during the period specified.

β = net increase, during the year, of banking system credit to the public sector, expressed as a percentage of the year's GDP. Thus, if the public sector's borrowings from the banking sector stood at 200 at the beginning of the year, and went to 300 by year's end, the net increase would be 100. If GDP of the year were 800, then β would be 12.5 percent (= 100/800).

γ = fraction of total banking system credit going to the public sector. Thus, if at the beginning of the year total bank credit were 400, and if at the end it were 500, then (using public sector credit figures from above) γ would be 0.50 (= 200/400) at the beginning of the year and 0.60 (= 300/500) at the end. In the tables presented in this paper γ is always measured from end-of-year data. Whenever the public sector is a net lender to the banking system, γ is simply recorded as < 0.

λ = percentage increase during the year in total domestic credit of the banking system. This, with the figures just presented, would be 25 percent [= (500/400) − 1].

π = rate of inflation.

Source: Harberger and Edwards (1980).

Table 7-7. *Control Group: Stable Exchange Rate Economies*

Economy	Year	β (percent)	γ	λ (percent)	π (percent)
Taiwan	1960–72	0.5	0.267	0.186	0.030
Honduras	1954–70	0.2	0.288	0.121	0.012
Haiti	1954–70	0.5	0.680	0.077	0.014
Jamaica	1954–65	0.3	<0	0.218	0.021
Iran	1960–70	1.8	0.345	0.202	0.016
Thailand	1954–70	0.1	0.251	0.119	0.021
Portugal	1954–70	0.2	0.164	0.110	0.030
Guatemala	1954–70	0.3	0.174	0.114	0.006
El Salvador	1954–70	0.5	0.093	0.103	0.015
Dominican Republic	1954–70	0.6	0.379	0.157	0.003
Morocco	1960–70	0.3	0.439	0.102	0.030
Iraq	1954–70	1.4	0.246	0.266	0.082
Nigeria	1960–70	1.8	0.248	0.417	0.052
Malaysia	1954–70	0.8	0.017	0.190	−0.001
Sudan	1954–70	2.6	<0	0.254	0.024
Trinidad and Tobago	1954–65	0.4	0.070	0.143	0.021
Median	—	0.5	0.247	13	2.1
First quartile	—	0.3	0.082	11	1.3
Third quartile	—	1.1	0.317	21	3.0

Note: Data are median observations of the indicated variables during the period specified.

β = net increase, during the year, of banking system credit to the public sector, expressed as a percentage of the year's GDP. Thus, if the public sector's borrowings from the banking sector stood at 200 at the beginning of the year and went to 300 by year's end, the net increase would be 100. If GDP of the year were 800, then β would be 12.5 percent (= 100/800).

γ = fraction of total banking system credit going to the public sector. Thus, if at the beginning of the year total bank credit were 400 and if at the end it were 500, then (using public sector credit figures from above) γ would be 0.50 (= 200/400) at the beginning of the year and 0.60 (= 300/500) at the end. In the tables presented in this paper γ is always measured from end-of-year data. Whenever the public sector is a net lender to the banking system, γ is simply recorded as < 0.

λ = percentage increase during the year in total domestic credit of the banking system. This, with the figures just presented, would be 25 percent [= (500/400) − 1].

π = rate of inflation.

Source: Harberger and Edwards (1980).

investments financed by foreign borrowing, by and large much of the public investment is likely to have had social rates of return above the real cost of borrowing (see Sachs 1981).

Problems arose because most of the borrowing was made by countries with weak fiscal systems through commercial bank loans of short maturity and with a floating rate of interest. If the world environment had been stable and real interest rates had remained at their mid-1970s levels, or if the government had had complete fiscal control, the uses (long-gestation projects or consumption) to which the borrowed funds were put might have been justifiable. If the loans could be rolled over (as they were for a time) at relatively low real interest rates, both public consumption and, of course, investment would have been justifiable even if the government's fiscal powers were weak.[18]

The changes in world capital markets in the late 1970s, however, exposed the fiscal weaknesses in the major borrowing countries. The liquidity crisis precipitated by the Mexican government's inability to continue debt service in 1982 was essentially a crisis of confidence in the ability of the *public sector* in many borrowing countries to generate the requisite net resources (either by cutting back public expenditures or by raising taxation) to meet the rising cost of real public debt service. The resulting rise in the incipient public sector deficits was once again financed by levying the inflation tax (see chapter 6 in this book). At the same time, attempts were made to cut back public expenditures, usually by cutting back on the infrastructural public investment, which in the long run is necessary for the development of borrowing countries' economies.

We thus have an interrelated global economy such that the financing of public expenditures in both developed and developing countries impinges on the pool of global savings and thus on world interest rates. Our next section formalizes and integrates this aspect of global interactions together with the conventional interrelationships with reference to the terms of trade between developed and developing countries.

A Model of Global Crowding Out

We use a simple three-region, three-commodity model, with each region completely specialized in the production of its "own" good. The three regions are OPEC, which produces only oil, the OECD, and the developing countries; the last two each produce a final good consumed by all other countries. There is, by assumption, no direct consumption of oil and no use of oil at all in OPEC itself, but developing countries and the OECD use oil as a factor of production.

The OECD

Consider first the OECD block of the model. With Cobb-Douglas technology we can write output supply (measured by GDP) as a function of the real product wage *WOE*, the real price of oil in terms of OECD goods, *PROIL*, the capital stock *KOE*, and the rate of technological progress ρ:

(7.1) $$XOE = CO^{\epsilon\rho t} \, WOE^{C_1} \, PROIL^{C_2} \, KOE^{C_3}.$$

Estimation of (7.1) after taking log differences gives:[19]

$$\Delta\log XOE = -.14 \, \Delta\log WOE - .03 \, \Delta\log PROIL$$
$$(.47) \qquad\qquad (1.28)$$

$$+ .02 \, \Delta\log KOE + .038.$$
$$(.47) \qquad\qquad (2.42)$$
$$r^2 = .301$$

The derived demand for oil imports, *OILOE*, can be similarly derived and will depend on output and the real price of oil in terms of OECD goods:

(7.2) $$OILOE = e^{C_{21}} \times XOE^{C_{22}} \times PROIL^{C_{23}},$$

which, when estimated in loglinear form, gives:

$$\log(OILOE) = 4.65 + .49 \times \log XOE$$
$$(1.39) \quad (2.31)$$

$$- .20 \times \log PROIL.$$
$$(6.18)$$
$$r^2 = .891$$

Neither equation presents surprises. Output depends negatively on real product wages and the real price of oil and positively on the capital stock; the rate of technological progress is estimated at 3.8 percent, not an unreasonable number. Real oil imports depend positively on output but negatively on the real price of oil.

Real tax revenues are a function of real output:

(7.3) $$TAX = -213519 + .23 \times XOE.$$
$$(2.03) \quad\quad (12.7)$$
$$r^2 = .953$$

Private consumption depends on the real interest rate and on real disposable income. Issues of crowding out arise here first. If the private sector is completely indifferent when asked to choose between different ways of financing the deficit, that is, if a strong version of the Ricardo equivalence theorem holds, disposable income equals income minus government expenditure, giving rise to the following consumption function:

$$(7.4\text{NCO}) \qquad PCON = -28717 + .85 \times YDNC$$
$$(.86) \qquad (11.7)$$
$$+ 7799 \times RRATE,$$
$$(.77)$$
$$r^2 = .961$$

where PCON is real personal consumption, GCON and GINU are real government consumption and investment, respectively, RRATE is the real interest rate, and NCO stands for "no crowding out." Disposable income YDNC equals GDP plus interest earnings on foreign assets minus government expenditure:

$$YDNC = XOE + RRATE \times FAROE(-1) - GCON - GINV.$$

If, however, the private sector does *not* recognize that bond issues give rise to future tax liabilities with a discounted value equal to the value of the issue, *then* a proper measure of disposable income is income minus tax revenues, giving rise to the following private consumption equation:

$$(7.4\text{CO}) \qquad PCON = -433675 + .86 \times YDC$$
$$(-1.8) \qquad (17.1)$$
$$+ 11442 \times RRATE,$$
$$(1.7)$$
$$r^2 = .981$$

where CO stands for "crowding out."

Here disposable income is defined as:

$$YDS = XOE + RRATE \times FAROE(-1) - TAX$$
$$- OIL \times PROIL.$$

This procedure suggests that we try a natural test to determine whether or not there is crowding out: by including income minus government expenditure (YDNC) *and* government expenditure minus tax revenues in the equation, (7.4NCO) and (7.4CO) become special cases. If the coefficient on the government deficit equals *zero*, (7.4NCO) is relevant, but if it equals *one*, (7.4CO) emerges. In other words, if the coefficient is not significantly different from zero, crowding out is not a problem; if it is not significantly different from one, crowding out *is* a problem. The results when we ran this regression were:

(7.5) $PCON = -509700 + .85\,X(YDNC)$
                              (2.43)   (19.7)

                    $+ 1.72X(GCON + GINV - TAX)$
                    (3.67)

                    $+ 15938\ RRATE.$
                    (2.48)
                                                $r^2 = .989$

Clearly the coefficient on the deficit is significantly larger than zero but not significantly different from one at normal confidence levels (for example, 5 percent). This result clearly demonstrates that crowding out *is* a problem; the data do not support the Ricardo equivalence theorem.

We could finish the OECD block by running an investment equation and could derive the current account as the difference between aggregate savings and investment; instead we choose to go the other way around and use a current account (CA) equation that will, after the appropriate substitutions, give us investment.

In the no-crowding-out case, the CA is independent of the government deficit. We accordingly ran the following equation:

(7.6NCO) $CAROE = -6916 + .023 \times XOE + 4998$
                    (.67)   (1.2)   (1.74)

                    $\times RRATE - 158047 \times PROIL$
                                  (3.00)

                    $- 158047 \times PROIL,$
                    (3.00)
                                                $r^2 = .666$

which shows a positive dependence on the real interest rate and GDP and a strong negative dependence on the real price of oil in terms of OECD goods.

The crowding-out version should depend on the deficit, which gives us an equation such as the following:

(7.6CO) $CAROE = 11128 + .03 \times YDC + 4056 \times RRATE$
                    (.09)   (.91)   (1.02)

                    $+ .11\ (TAX - GCON - GINV)$
                    (.44)

                    $- 137188 \times PROIL.$
                    (2.17)
                                                $r^2 = .688$

Finally we have to make an assumption regarding the share of total OECD expenditure that falls on OECD goods. We assume that investment uses OECD goods only, whereas the consumption share will depend on relative prices:

$$(7.7) \qquad ADOE = INVOE + .95 \times (PRLDC)^{DEOE}$$
$$\times (PCON + GCON).$$

Investment $INVOE$ can be obtained from the savings-minus-investment-equals-the-current-account identity:

$$(7.8) \quad INVOE = TAX - GCON + YDC - PCON - CAROE.$$

(government	(private	(current
savings)	savings)	account)

OPEC

The OPEC part of the model is more simplified than the OECD part. In particular we do not distinguish between the government and the private sector but look at aggregate income, savings, and expenditure. OPEC sets the price of oil in terms of OECD goods, $PROIL$, as a policy variable and supplies all oil demanded at that price. Accordingly, the income equals:

$$(7.9) \qquad YDOPEC = PROIL \times OILOE + OILLDC$$
$$+ RRATE \times FAROPEC(-1),$$

where $FAROPEC$ represents the value of net claims on the rest of the world (in terms of OECD goods).

Net savings and investment behavior are summarized in a current account equation:

$$(7.10) \qquad CAROPEC = 18128 + .31 \times YDOPEC$$
$$\qquad\qquad (.86) \quad (2.47)$$

$$+ 4513 \times RRATE.$$
$$(1.52)$$
$$r^2 = .792$$

Simple accounting then gives us total OPEC expenditure ($YDOPEC - CAROPEC$), all of which is assumed to fall on OECD goods:

$$(7.11) \qquad ADOPEC = YDOPEC - CAROPEC.$$

Finally, the current account equals net foreign asset accumulation:

$$(7.12) \qquad FAROPEC = CAROPEC + FAROPEC(-1).$$

The Developing Countries

Developing country output is introduced as an exogenous trend mainly because the lack of good factor price and capital stock data precludes explicit estimation of an aggregate supply curve. The parameters were obtained by running the log of real output on a time trend:

$$(7.13) \qquad XLDC = \exp(14.3) \times \exp(.05 \times \text{time}).$$

$$r^2 = .986$$

The developing country current account equation performs remarkably well:

$$(7.14) \quad CAFLDC = -170559 + 5606 \times (RRATE - CHCORR)$$
$$\qquad\qquad (2.02) \quad (3.20)$$

$$+ .07 \times YDLDC/PRLDC - 42940$$
$$(.87) \qquad\qquad\qquad (.74)$$

$$\times PROIL/PRLDC.$$

$$r^2 = .693$$

$CAFLDC$ is the real current account surplus in terms of developing country goods, $YDLDC/PRLDC$ is real developing country income in terms of developing country goods, and $PROIL/PRLDC$ is the real price of oil in terms of developing country goods. The variable $CHCORR$ measures the influence of gradual relative price changes on the real cost of borrowing (compare Dornbusch 1983, Svensson and Razin 1983, or van Wijnbergen 1984 for an extensive discussion of this effect):

$$CHCORR = [PRLDC - PRLDC(-1)]/PRLDC(-1).$$

Developing country income (in terms of OECD goods) equals (7.13) minus real interest payments on foreign debt and minus the value of oil imports:

$$(7.15) \qquad YDLDC = XLDC \times PRLDC + RRATE$$
$$\times FARLDC(-1) - OILLDC \times PROIL.$$

Developing country expenditure can be obtained by combining (7.13) and (7.14); we assume zero price elasticity in developing country demand for OECD goods, which, when combined with (7.14) and (7.15), gives us developing country demand for OECD goods:

$$ADLDC = SCLDC \times (YDLDC - CAFLDC \times PRLDC).$$

Oil imports are a linear function of output, time, and the real price of oil.

Finally, increases in debt equal the current account deficit (or, as defined here, increases in net foreign assets equal the CA surplus):

(7.16) $FARLDC = CARLDC + FARLDC(-1)$.

Closing the Model

The two main endogenous variables are the world rate of interest and the OECD/developing country terms of trade, *RRATE* and *PRLDC*. *PRLDC* is defined as the developing countries' final goods terms of trade with respect to the OECD.

The model is closed by requiring OECD goods market clearing:

(7.17) $XOE = ADOE + ADOPEC + ADLDC$

and by requiring that the world current account equal zero:

(7.18) $CAROE + CAROPEC + CAFLDC = 0$.

Loosely speaking, (7.17) determines relative prices and (7.18) ties down the world interest rate.

Analysis of the Model in Operation

After suitable substitution in the above equations, we can reduce the model to two basic equations, with two variables, the real interest rate *RRATE* and the developing country/OECD terms of trade *PRLDC*.

The first equation says that the world current account should equal zero.

(7.19) $CA(RRATE, PRLDC) = 0$.
                    $(+)$ $(-)$

Higher interest rates will lead to an ex ante world current account surplus, but higher developing country/ OECD terms of trade will lead to a deficit, because the latter imply a transfer from high to low savers. We depict this relation in a diagram with *RRATE* on the vertical axis and *PRLDC* on the horizontal one (figure 7-5).

The curve, labeled *CA* in figure 7-5, slopes upward: higher interest rates would lead to an ex ante CA surplus; a terms-of-trade improvement for developing countries transfers income to high spenders and pushes the world CA back down.

The second equation sets excess demand for OECD goods equal to zero (see the curve labeled *GM* in figure 7-8):

(7.20) $GM(RRATE,\ PRLDC) = 0$.
                      $(-)$ $(+)$

Higher interest rates push down expenditure and so lead to excess supply; higher relative prices for developing goods will, however, shift demand to OECD goods and will thus cure the excess supply. This curve therefore also slopes upward. Stability analysis based on the assumption that an incipient CA surplus pushes down the interest rate and an excess demand for OECD goods pushes up their relative price indicates that the configuration in figure 7-5—(GM) steeper than (CA)—is stable; the other case (CA steeper than GM) is not. We therefore confine our attention to the case given in figure 7-5. To understand how the model works, we will consider the effects of two "shocks," an increase in government expenditure *not* financed by taxation or similarly a tax cut, and an increase in the real price of oil.

Consider first the deficit-financed increase in government expenditure (see figure 7-6). An increase in government consumption leads to excess demand for OECD goods and therefore shifts the goods market locus to the left. If there is *no* crowding out, private savings will offset the increased deficit, and the CA curve will *not* shift. This situation leads to an equilibrium, with lower interest rates and deteriorated terms of trade for developing countries. *PRLDC* goes down because of incipient excess demand for OECD goods; this drop transfers income from low net savers (developing countries) to high net savers (OECD) and therefore leads to a fall in interest rates (point B in figure 7-6).

If there *is* crowding out, however—if private savings are not accommodating the deficit—the world CA will have an incipient deficit that will push up interest rates (CA shifts *up*). This deficit will, if large enough, lead to an equilibrium perhaps at point C, where the world interest rate goes up *and* the developing countries' terms of trade deteriorate with respect to the OECD. In the crowding-out scenario, therefore, deficit-financed government consumption hits the developing countries twice, via both higher world interest rates and deteriorating terms of trade for final goods. This scenario looks very much like the world situation in the early 1980s.

Consider next an increase in oil prices. Higher oil prices transfer income to OPEC from developing countries and the OECD; OPEC has higher savings propensities than the other two groups, so there is an incipient world current account surplus: the CA curve shifts down (figures 7-7 and 7-8). Supply in the OECD may fall more than demand (although the reverse cannot be excluded), resulting in a leftward shift of GM. If demand falls more than supply, *GM* shifts to the right. The first case is given in figure 7-7, the second in figure 7-8.

In all cases the interest rate will fall, but the developing country/OECD terms of trade for final goods may either improve or deteriorate. The first scenario seems a plausible description of the aftermath of the oil price shocks of 1973–74.

Simulation Runs

The base run of the model tracks the in-sample data remarkably well. (See figures 7-9–11 and 7-12–13, which chart the actual and simulated current account surpluses of the three regions and the debt service payments of developing countries.)

We next perform two basic policy experiments with the model. In the first one, we add $400 billion (1980 U.S. dollars; "billion" means "thousand million") to aggregate government consumption in 1979 and 1980 under the assumption of *deficit financing*. In the no-crowding-out scenario, little happens (see figures 7-14 and 7-15–16).

Private savings increases substantially to offset the increased deficit (between 7 percent and 8 percent drop in private consumption in 1978 and 1980) and a small decrease in private investment (between 6 percent and 7 percent), to accommodate the increase in government expenditure. Accordingly, the CA is not really affected in either of the three regions, and no noticeable change in the interest rate or in the developing country interest payments on debt results.

The outcome is *very* different in the crowding-out scenario, however (the version of the model that was supported by our test above). Now private consumption does *not* fall, private saving does *not* accommodate the new deficit, and the OECD current account accordingly swings into deficit. To bring the world current account back into equlibrium, there is a 2.9 percentage point increase in the world real interest rate in 1979 and a 2.6 percentage point increase in 1980. The result is a dramatic fall in private investment, which declines by a whopping 26.3 percent in 1979 and 25.8 percent in 1980. This drop limits the CA deterioration in the OECD to about US$30 billion in both years. There is a dramatic effect on developing country real interest payments on debt, which increase by around US$24 billion in each year. In addition there is a small terms-of-trade deterioration for developing countries of about half a percentage point.

Similar results obtain in the second set of simulation runs, where we cut the marginal tax rate from 0.22 to 0.15. In the no-crowding-out scenario, there is no effect whatsoever on any variable except tax revenues, because the private sector accommodates one for one by saving the entire increase in disposable income. The results are very different, however, in the crowding-out version. Private savings do not go up one for one, with the result that the government deficit increases, so that incipient CA deficits and excess demand for OECD goods develop.

The terms of trade deteriorate for developing countries (by one percentage point). The real interest rate increases between two and three percentage points throughout the period (figure 7-17), leading to an increase of about $20 billion in real interest payments on debt for developing countries. The OECD current account deficit deteriorates, with as much as $36 billion in 1980 and somewhat smaller amounts (but always in excess of $16 billion). This development occurs despite a slowdown in investment (between 20 percent and 30 percent throughout the decade), leading to a cumulative shortfall in capital accumulation of 30 percent (the 1980 OECD capital stock is 30 percent below the base-run value).

A Summary of the Global Interactions

We have thus arrived at the following interdependent global system where there is a link between the actions and reactions of the public sectors in both developed and developing countries through their effects on world interest rates and the terms of trade of developing countries relative to the OECD. In both sets of countries, public expenditure is growing, partly driven by demographic trends—the aging of a relatively stable population, and the consequent need for increases in public spending on the health and social security of the aged in developed countries, and the greening of a growing population and the consequent need for related increases in human and physical infrastructural public expenditures in developing countries. This growth in global public expenditures in both sets of countries must be financed.

Increasingly in industrial countries tax resistance that has led to the adoption of indexed income tax systems is going to make it difficult for governments to raise adequate taxes to fund their social commitments. In other words, other things being equal, governments will have structural fiscal deficits. If these are financed through bonds, and if private savers do not raise their savings by the amount of this public dissavings, the increased public expenditure will raise the draft on a given pool of savings, so that real interest rates will rise and the developing countries' terms of trade will deteriorate with respect to the OECD. For a country with a large weight in the world economy, such as the United States, the rise in

(Text continues on p. 222)

Figure 7-5. *Diagrammatic Representation of the Model*

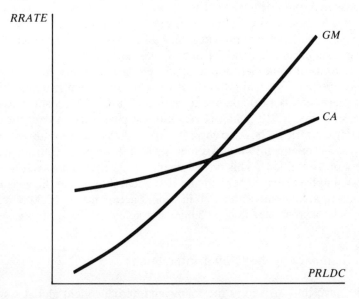

Figure 7-6. *Effects of Deficit-Financed Increase
in Government Expenditures*

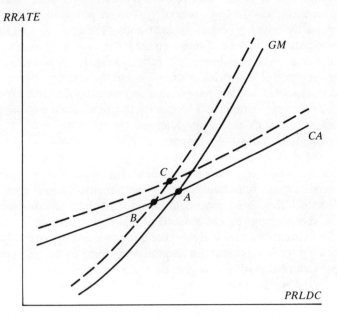

Figure 7-7. *A Dominant Supply Effect of an Oil Price Shock*

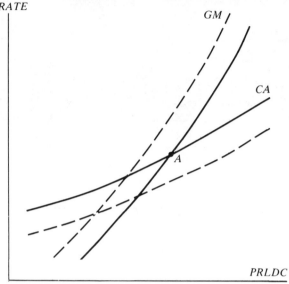

Figure 7-8. *A Dominant Demand Effect of an Oil Price Shock*

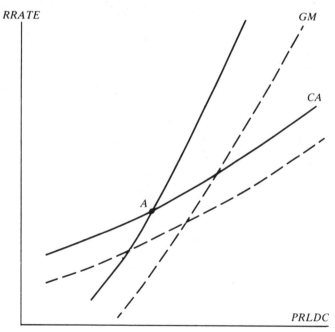

Figure 7-9. *Current Account Surpluses of OECD Countries, Actual and Simulated, 1971–80*

Billions of U.S. dollars

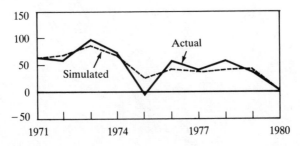

Source: World Bank data.

Figure 7-10. *Current Account Surpluses of OPEC Countries, Actual and Simulated, 1971–80*

Billions of U.S. dollars

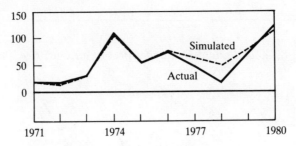

Source: World Bank data.

Figure 7-11. *Current Account Surpluses of Developing Countries, Actual and Simulated, 1971–80*

Billions of U.S. dollars

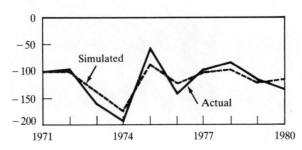

Source: World Bank data.

Figure 7-12. *Real Interest Rates, Actual and Simulated, 1971–80*

Percent

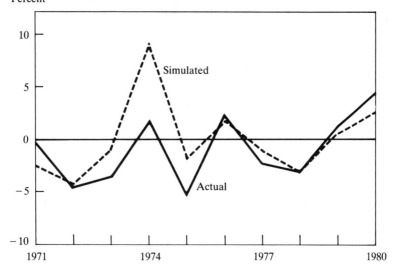

Source: World Bank data.

Figure 7-13. *Debt Service Payments of Developing Countries, Actual and Simulated, 1971–80*

Billions of U.S. dollars

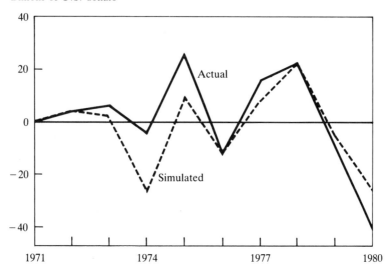

Source: World Bank data.

Figure 7-14. *Current Account Surpluses in Simulation 1,*
1971–80

Billions of U.S. dollars

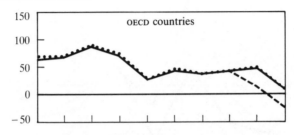

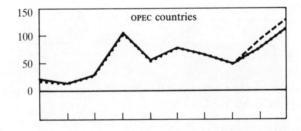

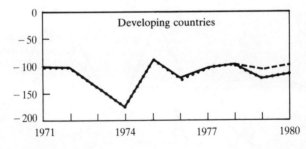

———— Base simulation

- - - - Crowding-out scenario

•••••• No-crowding-out scenario

Source: World Bank data.

Figure 7-15. *Debt Service Payments of Developing Countries in Simulation 1, 1971–80*

Billions of U.S. dollars

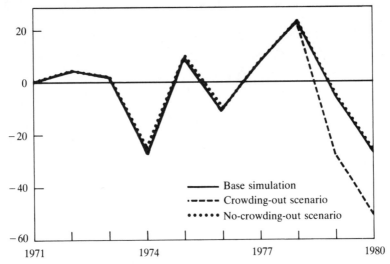

Source: World Bank data.

Figure 7-16. *Real Interest Rates in Simulation 1, 1971–80*

Percent

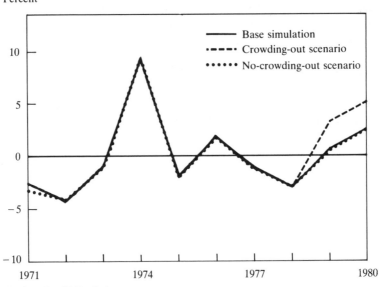

Source: World Bank data.

Figure 7-17. *Real Interest Rates in Simulation 2, 1971–80*

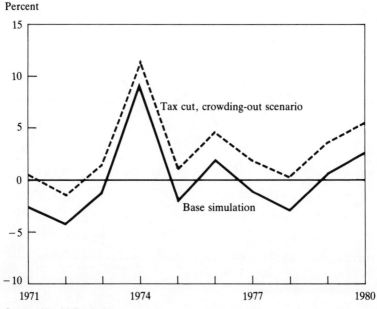

Source: World Bank data.

domestic interest rates also leads to an appreciation of its currency as a concomitant of the capital inflow that is induced, some of it from developing countries.

In developing countries, in view of the inherent weaknesses of the fiscal system and the pressure on the public finances flowing from the need for growing public sector infrastructural expenditures, the rise in world interest rates resulting from the structural public sector deficits in developed countries is likely to worsen the Third World's fiscal crisis, whereas the concomitant deterioration in developing countries' terms of trade with respect to the OECD will worsen their external transfer problem. The opportunity cost of financing infrastructure as well as other investments in developing countries would thus have been raised (via the interest rate linkages of the global market for savings) by the growth of transfer payments in developed countries. In an integrated global market for savings, the growth of "old age–related" social expenditures in developed countries financed through fiscal deficits is likely to crowd out, at the margin, the infrastructural developmental expenditures in developing countries that are required to provide some of the complementary goods necessary to raise the living standards of their poor, young, and growing labor forces.

Moreover, a major reason for the big buildup of debt by many Third World countries was the need to finance rising public expenditures and the associated incipient fiscal deficits. The debt crisis arose because the rise in interest rates, and thus the costs of public debt service, exposed the underlying fiscal weaknesses that the earlier buildup of debt by many Third World borrowers had masked. As this rise in interest rates was in part the result of the actual and expected structural fiscal deficits in industrial countries, the current and continuing debt crisis can be seen as stemming essentially from a global fiscal crisis, that is, from a crisis of the public sectors in both developed and developing countries.

Appendix A.   Rules for Optimal Foreign Borrowing

[This appendix is taken from Deepak Lal, "The Evaluation of Capital Inflows," *Industry and Development*, 1 (1978):2–19, and is reprinted with permission.]

A useful starting point is to consider the circumstances in which specific foreign borrowing is desirable. The borrowing could be at the implicitly subsidized effective interest rate (which takes account of the "softness" of the loans in terms of the "real" interest rate charged and of the terms of repayment), or at normal commercial terms, say, on the Eurodollar market. The same principles would apply in appraising the desirability of such borrowing[20] in both cases, and would take account of loans used to finance either current consumption or investment or combinations of the two. This problem has been analysed in detail elsewhere (Lal 1971) in terms of the cost-benefit framework, which takes aggregate current consumption as its *numéraire* for measuring social values (that is, the Dasgupta-Marglin-Sen framework), on the basis of alternative assumptions about such things as the grant element, excess import costs owing to the tying of aid to donor country imports on most types of foreign aid loans and grants, the proportions of the aid inflows supplementing domestic savings, and current consumption in the recipient country, and in terms of trade losses involved in repayments of interest and principal. The methodology essentially consists of comparing the net present value of a marginal investment project financed from internal sources with that financed from foreign sources; it also takes account of various domestic variables such as the changing scarcity of savings relative to current consumption and the Government's powers of controlling the level of consumption, the import content of current investment and the intertem-

poral pattern of social discount rates and social rates of return to
investment.[21] The condition for a foreign capital inflow to be socially
desirable is given by

$$(7.21) \quad \left[\frac{(1-\theta)(1+e)}{\theta} \right] - \left[\frac{(1-g)(1+e)(1+s_T)(1+i)^T}{\theta(1+d_0) \ldots (1+d_T)} \right]$$

$$\left[(1-\gamma_T)r_T \sum_{n=T}^{\infty} \frac{1}{(1+d_T) \ldots (1+d_n)} + \gamma_T \right] + \cdots$$

$$(1+ms_0)\left[(1-\gamma_0)r_0 \sum_{n=0}^{\infty} \frac{1}{(1+d_0) \ldots (1+d_n)} + \gamma_0 \right] \geq 0$$

where:

θ is the percentage of the capital inflow which is invested,

e is the percentage excess cost of imports owing to the tying of aid to the donor's imports,

g is the percentage of the inflow which is in the form of a grant,

i is the effective interest rate on the remaining $(1-g)$ percent of the capital inflow and assumes that the principal and interest are paid in a lump sum at the end of T years, the actual pattern of payments being converted to this assumed pattern to determine the effective interest rate,

s_n is the percentage terms of trade loss that the recipient has to suffer in year n, to increase exports required for financing imports or for effecting a capital transfer for repatriating interest, etc. in year n,

d_n is the social discount rate (consumption rate of interest) in year n,

γ_n is the percentage of domestic investment financed by reducing consumption in year n, with $(1-\gamma_n)$ the percentage from displaced investment,

r_n is the social return to investment in period n; that is, 1 rupee invested at date n yields a perpetual consumption stream of rupees (r_n), assuming for simplicity that there is no reinvestment from this consumption stream,

m is the import content of current investment.

To see the implications of this condition, assume that the whole of the capital inflow is invested ($\theta = 1$) and that the constraints on raising domestic savings and improving the rate of transformation of domestic into foreign inputs (via the terms of trade effects) remain fixed over the lifetime of the loan (this implies that r, d, s, and γ are constant over time, that is, in (7.21), $r_n = r$, $d_n = d$, $s_n = s$, and $\gamma_n = \gamma$), then the above condition for assessing the desirability of foreign capital inflows becomes:

(7.22)

$$\left[\frac{(1-\gamma)r}{d} + \gamma\right]\left[(1 + ms) - (1 - g)(1 - e)(1 + s)\frac{(1 + i)^T}{(1 + d)^T}\right] \geq 0.$$

From this it is obvious that, if the whole of the capital inflow is a grant ($g = 1$), then (7.22) is positive and, irrespective of the country's other characteristics, it should accept the inflow. Suppose, however, that at the other extreme there is no grant element in the capital inflow ($g = 0$) and, furthermore, that the country does not suffer any excess costs on its capital inflow-financed imports through aid tying (that is, that $e = 0$). Further assume that the import content of investment is unity[22] ($m = 1$); then it is obvious from (7.22) that a capital inflow will only be desirable if the effective interest rate it has to pay for the inflow is less than or equal to its social discount rate ($i \leq d$). While clearly if there are excess costs of tied imports ($e > 0$), the lower the effective interest rate on the inflow will have to be relative to the social discount rate in the economy. As the social discount rate is likely to be less than the social return to investment in most developing countries, where the level of savings is less than socially optimum, this suggests that even if the social rate of return to investment is as high as say 15 percent, in the postulated conditions, it will be worthwhile to borrow only at effective rates of interest that are less than the lower social discount rate, say, of 6 percent.[23]

If, however, the economy is faced by a complete savings bottle-neck (which means that in (7.21) above, γ_0 is zero), which is eliminated by the time the loan is repaid (which implies that by some date $t < T$, where T is the date by which the inflow (loan) has been paid back, $\gamma_t = 1$), and irrespective of the constraints in foreign trading (that is the value of s) the appropriate cut-off effective rate of interest for foreign borrowing will be higher than the social rate of discount, d, but for plausible values of the repayment period T, the social rate of return to investment r and the social discount rate d, it will have to be lower than the *social rate of return to investment r*. This can be seen, if we assume, for simplicity, that in (7.21) d and s are constant, $\theta = 1$, $m = 1$, $g = 0$, $e = 0$, and $\gamma_0 = 0$, but γ_t, $\gamma_{t+1}, \ldots \gamma_T = 1$. Then from (7.21) (see Lal 1971 for the derivation), the foreign capital inflow will be desirable as long as:

(7.23)

$$\frac{r_0}{d} \geq \left(\frac{1 + i}{1 + d}\right)^T$$

Thus for plausible values of the variables, say $T = 25$ years, $d = 5$ percent and $r = 15$ percent, the cut-off effective rate of interest, i, for which the loan is acceptable would be 9.7 percent, which is less than the social rate of return to investment r but greater than the social discount rate d.

Similarly, from (7.21) it can be shown (see Lal (1971)) that if, instead of the above assumptions, the economy is faced by a complete inelasticity of export earnings $(s_n \to \infty)$, with a continuing constant divergence between the actual and optimum level of savings (that is, $d_n = d < r_n = r$), a capital inflow at any effective rate of interest is desirable as long as with time the country is able to change its foreign trade structure to enable some transformation through foreign trade (that is, $s_t < s_n$, where $t > n$). Finally, it can also be shown that if the capital inflow has no grant element and entirely supplements domestic consumption, it will still be socially desirable as long as the effective rate of interest i on the borrowing is less than the social rate of discount d and the Government is not faced by a savings constraint of any kind when the loan is repaid (that is, the Government can choose whatever value it likes for γ_T).

It should therefore be apparent that while any inflow at an effective interest rate below the social discount rate d must be socially desirable whether it finances investment or consumption, inflows at even higher effective rates could be socially desirable under various circumstances, such as various structural features of the economy and expected changes in these over time. These features are normally taken into account in deriving shadow prices for project appraisal, and hence, in general, condition (7.21) can be interpreted as saying that valuing the net benefits from the capital inflow at shadow prices, the inflow is socially desirable if the discounted net present social value is positive, the discount rate being the social discount rate if the *numéraire* is aggregate consumption (*à la* UNIDO) or the accounting rate of interest (ARI) if the *numéraire* is savings (or more strictly uncommitted public income expressed in foreign exchange, *à la* LM).

Appendix B.   Data Description

The model assumes three regions—an aggregate OECD region, a developing country region, and an OPEC region—and three commodities: OECD goods, developing country goods, and oil. In general, the data used to estimate the model represent aggregates across a sample of individual countries within the three classifications. We used twelve OECD countries, eleven OPEC countries, and twenty-six developing countries to construct regional aggregates.[24] Thus although most (major) OECD and OPEC countries are included, it was not possible to achieve the same broad coverage for developing countries within the time constraints of the study. Developing countries were chosen on the basis of population size (we selected countries with 10 million or more residents), data availability, and contribution to adequate coverage across regions. Because of time constraints, centrally planned economies were excluded from the analysis. The omission may introduce problems in adding up and in current account and debt service computations. The simulation exercise covers the time period 1971 to 1980; forecasts were made through 1988.

OPEC countries were split into an "oil" segment and a developing country segment, so that the eleven OPEC countries became twenty-two countries—eleven OPEC and eleven developing countries. Output (GDP) for the oil segments was assumed equal to respective total oil production; the remainder of output (GDP less oil exports) was attributed to the developing country segments of the countries. Current account surpluses were set to be zero for the developing country segments (income was assumed equal to expenditures) and were set to the trade balance (total exports minus imports) for the OPEC segments. Total expenditures were computed as oil exports minus the current account surplus for the oil segments of the eleven countries and as the difference between the sum of new investment, government consumption, and private consumption (for example, total expenditures) and expenditures attributed to the oil segments for the non-oil (developing country) segments. Nominal GDP was apportioned between the two segments in shares equal to the ratios of real GDP. The end result of the process described above was twenty-two "countries"—eleven producing only oil and having large current account surpluses and eleven producing other developing country–type goods commonly produced by OPEC countries and having zero current account balances. The latter eleven countries were added to "real" developing countries in compiling developing country aggregate variables. The former countries were aggregated to construct pure OPEC measures.

Almost all data were drawn from the *International Financial Statistics* (*IFS*), which are complied by the IMF. Limited data items were drawn from *Government Financial Statistics* (*GFS*), likewise complied by IMF, and from miscellaneous other sources. These alternative sources are noted where appropriate.

The first section of the appendix describes each aggregate variable used in the model—what it represents, how it was computed, and where relevant data were obtained. The second section provides detailed information on data sources for each individual country; in some cases, data were interpolated or were drawn from alternative sources when information for specific time periods was not available in the *IFS* or *GFS* data base. These cases are noted country by country.

Discussion of Regional Aggregate Data

All data are in nominal millions of U.S. dollars unless otherwise noted.

OUTPUT SUPPLY $(XOE, XLDC)$. Measures of output supply are included for both OECD countries and developing countries. Output is measured in terms of real GDP for both regions. Data are drawn from the *IFS* data base (variable 99b.p or 99b.r, with rare exceptions noted in "Data Adjustments" below).

DISPOSABLE INCOME $(YDC, YDOPEC, YDLDC)$. The value for disposable income is computed using output measures, interest earnings on foreign assets, and oil expenditures/income (depending on the region). "Disposable income" is in general defined as output plus interest earnings minus oil expenditures. For OPEC, disposable income includes only the value of oil produced (its only output, all marketed) and foreign debt payments.

OIL IMPORTS/EXPORTS $(OILOE, OILLDC)$. In order to compute disposable income, measures of oil imports (OECD, developing countries) were required. Petroleum price indexes were obtained from the *IFS* data base (variable 76aa for Saudi Arabia was used for all OPEC countries). Crude petroleum consumption for the OECD region was derived from country-specific crude petroleum imports (variable 71aa when available) or simply from petroleum imports (variable 71a). Crude petroleum exports were obtained for OPEC countries (variable 70aa or 70a, crude and petroleum, respectively). Developing country oil consumption was computed simply as the difference between OPEC production and OECD consumption. Data quality was not judged adequate to estimate developing country consumption using country-specific *IFS* data sources. There are obvious problems with the measure used for developing country consumption—production from countries like Norway and Colombia are excluded, and Eastern Bloc consumption is ignored. Time limitations precluded a better solution. For purposes of the model, however, total petroleum consumption and production were constrained to be equal.

CURRENT ACCOUNTS $(CAROE, CAROPEC, CAFLDC)$. In general, current accounts are defined as the difference between total income (GDP) and expenditures (total investment plus private and government consumption) summed together with earnings from foreign assets. Measures of GDP, total annual investments, and private and government consumption were drawn from the *IFS* data base (variables 99b, 93e, 96f, and 91f, respectively). Total investment was split between the public and private sectors by first estimating government investment using *GFS* data for central, state, and local government investments and then attributing the difference between total and government investments to the private sector.

Current accounts were constrained to sum to zero across the three regions. Although base data were drawn from *IFS* and *GFS* sources for OPEC and the OECD regions, developing country current accounts were set equal to the negative sum of the OECD and OPEC holdings (like the oil consumption estimates).

An iterative process was used to compute the annual current account estimates used in the model; at any point in time, current account surpluses are equal to present-year differences in income and expenditures plus interest payments on past surpluses (foreign debt payments). These past surpluses are themselves based on past current account measures, which include foreign interest payments—and so on. Three iterations (current accounts to foreign debt payments) were used to estimate present-year values of current accounts and foreign assets, for example:

$$CA_n = CA_{\text{Base}} + (RRATE * FAR_n(-1)) \ (n = 1 \text{ to } 3)$$

where

$$FAR_{n+1} = \text{cumulative sum } (CA_n)$$
$$RRATE = \text{the real interest rate}$$
$$n = \text{region.}$$

The series converged quite quickly.

INCOME/LOSSES FROM FOREIGN ASSETS (*FAROE, FAROPEC, FARLDC*). As noted in the preceding paragraph, foreign assets in each year are computed as the cumulative sum of past current account surpluses in nominal terms times the real interest rate. Because of data constraints, the model assumed foreign assets previous to 1969 (the first year when foreign interest payments are valued in the model) to be negligible. Annual foreign assets are computed via the previously described three-step iterative process for the OECD and OPEC regions. Foreign debt for developing countries is defined as the sum of the OECD and OPEC foreign assets, insuring that total holding sum to zero.

AGGREGATE DEMANDS ($ADOE$, $ADOPEC$, $ADLDC$). The OECD region consumes only oil and the OECD commodity. Aggregate OECD demand for its own commodity is defined as total investment (new capital formation, *IFS* variable 93e) plus a faction of total consumption (government plus private consumption) determined by relative developing country/OECD prices, an estimated demand elasticity, and a constant (in this case 0.95) chosen to represent consumption propensity for own goods. Aggregate OPEC demand, assumed to fall entirely on OECD commodities, is simply defined as the difference between disposable income and the current account surplus. Aggregate developing country demand is defined similarly; we assumed a zero price elasticity of demand for OECD goods, which yields an OECD consumption factor of

$$SCLDC = \frac{(XOE - ADOE - ADOPEC)}{(YDLDC - CAFLDC * PRLDC)}.$$

PRICE AND WAGE INDEXES AND INTEREST RATES ($RRATE$, $PROIL$, $PRLDC$, WOE). $RRATE$ is the real interest rate in OECD terms. It is defined as

$$RRATE = IVRATE - GROWTH,$$

where $IVRATE$ is the Eurodollar rate in London (variable 60d) and $GROWTH$ represents the rate of inflation (computed using variables 99b.p and 99b).

$PROIL$ and $PRLDC$ are the ratios of oil price indexes to OECD price indexes and developing country price indexes to OECD price indexes, respectively. Price indexes are computed as the ratio of nominal GDP to real GDP (variables 99b and 99b.p).

WOE is defined as the ratio of the OECD wage index to the OECD price index. The wage index was drawn from *IFS* statistics (generally variable 65, 65ey, or 65..c) for each OECD country. The index was weighted by total population in each country (*IFS* variable 99) to compute an aggregate OECD wage measure.

REMAINING OECD-SPECIFIC MEASURES (TAX, KOE). Taxes were represented by government revenues (variable 81) from the *IFS* data base. KOE is gross fixed capital formation (variable 93e), likewise drawn from *IFS*.

EXCHANGE RATES. In all cases, the average period exchange rate (variable . . . rf from the *IFS*) was used to convert local currency to U.S. dollars.

Data Adjustments for Specific Countries

THE OECD COUNTRIES. For the United States, the *IFS* variable 93gf was used to compute government investment in 1970–71. Total domestic debt was computed as reported debt (*IFS* variable 88) minus debt held by monetary authorities (*IFS* variable 88aa) minus foreign and international debt holdings (*IFS* variable 88ca). The 1980 ratio between central, state, and local government investment was used to compute state and local government debt between 1972 and 1979. All debt values were interpolated in 1970–71.

For the Federal Republic of Germany, *IFS* variable 93e.c was used in place of 93e for measuring gross fixed capital formation. The 1980 ratio between central and local government investment was used to estimate local government investment between 1970 and 1977.

For France, the 1980 ratio between local and central government investments was used to estimate local government investments between 1970 and 1977.

For Belgium, petroleum imports were used in place of crude oil in 1970 and 1971. The 1980 ratio (local to central) was used to estimate local government investments between 1970 and 1977.

For Austria, in place of crude oil in 1970 and 1971, 32 percent of petroleum imports was used. Constant values were used (23,000, 76,000, and 16,000 million in local currency respectively) to estimate central, state, and local government investments between 1970 and 1972. Government debt figures were missing and were assumed equal to zero.

For the United Kingdom, government debt figures were missing in *IFS*. Comparable figures were drawn from Galli and Masera (1983). The 1980 ratio between local and central government investments was used to estimate the local component between 1970 and 1977.

For Japan, GNP in real terms was used in place of real GDP between 1977 and 1980. A 1980 value for government revenues was computed using the 1978–79 nominal growth rate. Government debt in 1980 was assumed equal (in real terms) to 1979 data. Variable 82v from the *IFS* was used for total government investment.

For Canada, central government investment only was used for government investment. Between 1970 and 1973, a constant value of 1,200 million in local currency was assumed. Thereafter, values were drawn from *GFS*.

For Finland, central government investment only is used for government investment. In 1970 and 1971, a constant value of 2,000 million in local currency was assumed. Thereafter, values were drawn from *GFS*.

For Italy, central government investment only is used. Values are interpolated between 1970 and 1972.

For the Netherlands, central government investment only is used. Values are interpolated between 1970 and 1972.

For Sweden, the 1978 ratio of central to local government investments is used to estimate local investments between 1970 and 1977.

OPEC COUNTRIES. For Libya, the consumer price index (*IFS* variable 64) is used for the non-oil segment in place of a GDP-based price index.

For Indonesia, variable 93 is used in place of 93e.

For Nigeria, total expenditures were set to 12,000 million in local currency in 1979 and 1980. The CPI was used in place of a GDP-based price index for the non-oil segment.

For Iraq, *IFS* variable 77a.d was used to compute total expenditures between 1976 and 1980. GDP was split fifty-fifty between current accounts and expenditures between 1978 and 1980. Investment data were missing between 1976 and 1980. A 15 percent annual growth rate was assumed for approximating required values. The CPI was used in place of a computed price index for the non-oil segment.

For the United Arab Emirates, total expenditures are assumed to be 34 percent of GDP in 1970 and 1971 (the same ratio as in 1972). Oil exports were missing in 1970 and 1971. Values were estimated by retaining the 1972 ratio between the oil and non-oil portion of GDP. Gross capital formation was assumed to be the same in 1970 and 1971 as in 1972.

For Saudi Arabia, national account expenditures were used to adjust GDP and expenditure estimates for the oil segment in 1974.

DEVELOPING COUNTRIES. For Sudan, values for GDP, consumption, new investment, and total expenditures were estimated for 1980 using 1978–79 growth rates. The CPI was used in place of GDP-based price indexes.

For Egypt, the CPI was used in place of a GDP-based price index in 1980. Estimates of GDP in 1979 and 1980 were drawn from World Bank sources.

For Hong Kong, the CPI was used in place of a GDP-based price index in 1979 and 1980.

For Ethiopia, the CPI was used in place of a GDP-based price index.

For Tanzania, the CPI was used in place of a GDP-based price index.

Notes

1. "Greening" means that both the population and the labor force are becoming younger.

2. Baily argues that the best available measure of the capital stock is the stock markets' valuation of capital services rather than conventional capital stock measures. By 1979 for the United States, Tobin's q, which measures the ratio of the market value to replacement cost of a business's capital stock, had declined by half since the late 1960s.

3. The inflationary context in which real wage rigidity and declining profit rates provide symptoms of "classical" rather than Keynesian unemployment is crucial in differentiating the policy choices available in the 1930s and 1970s. For as Bonnell (1981) has noted, the diagnosis of a profit squeeze, slowdown in productivity growth, and real wage growth in excess of productivity was also adduced by observers during the Great Depression. The real wage growth in the 1930s, however, was the result of relatively rigid *nominal* wages at a time when the price level was *falling*. Raising aggregate demand would thus stop the price fall, and any reversal of price trends—via the inflationary effects of increasing aggregate nominal expenditures by looser fiscal or monetary policy—would have *reduced* real wage growth. In the 1970s the rigidity of *real* wages in a period of inflation makes any inflationary expansion of aggregate demand to reduce unemployment by reducing the real wage impractical. See Sachs (1983) and the accompanying discussion by Gordon.

4. For a comparative analysis of this period over time and space, see Maddison (1982).

5. In addition a growing literature uses various forms of creative accounting to convert budget deficits into "real" surpluses by making adjustments for (a) the cyclical components, (b) the effects of inflation on the real value of public debt, (c) the effects of interest rate changes on the market value of the public debt, and (d) the net worth of the public sector. For an attempt along these lines to explain away the U.S. deficit, see Eisner and Pieper (1984). Most such exercises attempt to estimate the net effect of the deficit on Keynesian aggregate demand. For the reasons discussed above, as the 1970s unemployment in most industrial countries had a large "classical" element, the Keynesian demand expansion prescription would seem irrelevant at the present juncture. It is true that, in an inflationary period, inflation adjustment is required to assess the true net worth of the public sector or the fical stance of the government. Whether the revenues that the government implicitly extracts, by imposing a capital levy on holders of the existing stock of bonds in times of unanticipated inflation, should be netted out in determining the appropriate fiscal stance is open to question. Moreover, the actual nominal budget deficit does have implications for financial markets and particularly for expectations about the future supply of unindexed public debt insofar as these will influence the determination of current interest rates, which then feed through the usual channels into the "real" economy. These factors are discussed in the next two sections.

6. Thus if the capital market is perfect, the real rate of interest (r) on the newly issued government bonds (x) must be equal to wealth holders' rate of time preference. The present value of the infinite stream of interest payments and hence future taxes is thus:

$$\sum_{t=0}^{\infty}\left(\frac{rx}{[1+r^t]}\right) = \frac{rx}{r} = x.$$

7. This rule appears to have held in most industrialized countries since the late 1970s.

8. There is, however, a qualification to this argument; see McCallum (1984). The above-stated argument depends upon our assuming that the budget deficit is defined *inclusive* of interest payments. It breaks down if the deficits are defined *net* of interest. Also, the stock of bonds can grow indefinitely at a higher rate than that of output as long as the difference between the two is less than the rate of time preference.

9. These effects will be offset to the extent that countervailing factors in the tax system reduce the cost of borrowing to corporations and households by in effect allowing interest payments to be set off against taxes. For Third World borrowers and others not subject to OECD taxation, these offsets will obviously not apply.

10. If r is the real interest rate received by savers, i the nominal interest rate, t the rate of tax, and π the inflation rate, then

$$r = i\,(1-t) - \pi.$$

The numerical example given above is based on a determination of the value of i if $r = 0.03$, $t = 0.5$, and $\pi = 0$ or 0.1.

11. We are of course assuming that the Darby-Feldstein effect does not operate! For if nominal interest rates rise by more than the inflation rate, the net effects on borrowers who can deduct nominal interest payments can be quite complex. See Feldstein (1983).

12. See Berndt and Wood (1979). Energy, capital, and labor are cooperative in the technical sense that their cross-partials in the production function are positive. The definition of cooperation of factors of production is different from the usual definition of complementarity or substitutability in production, which refers to the sign of the partial of the demand for a factor with respect to the price of another factor at a given output level. Thus factors can be Hicksian substitutes yet cooperative.

13. Wilcox's estimates suggest that the negative supply shocks of the early 1970s reduced the after-tax real interest rates by one percentage point and the rise in expected inflation another one and one-half percentage points below his estimated steady-state expected after-tax real interest rate of 1.33 percent.

14. Many developing countries used the cheap short-term credits available in the early 1970s to fund increases in public expenditure, which were either in long-gestation investment projects or in various forms of consumption subsidies that were difficult to cut back when world capital market conditions changed. The cost of funding these expenditures rose substantially with the rise in interest rates and the shortening of maturities on foreign loans. The domestic fiscal deficits that then resulted are one of the more intractable elements in the current debt crisis (see below).

15. The econometric evidence on the effects of budget deficits and interest rates (see Galli and Masera 1983; Makin 1983) suggests that, although real rates of interest are affected in most industrial countries by monetary factors, there is little evidence *as yet* that fiscal factors are important. The temporal qualification is important, for as Galli and Masera conclude, "interesting movements in the two focus variables (real rates and the debt) have occurred only very recently and are therefore poorly captured in statistical models, which are necessarily estimated over a much longer sample period" (p. 27). Otherwise stated, before the 1970s most industrial countries maintained rough budgetary balances or else ran very small deficits that could plausibly be expected to be covered by a string of small surpluses in the future. There would not be any effects of fiscal policy on interest rates during this period. Only when enough time has ensued, with a string of large budget deficits expected to continue indefinitely, would we expect the econometric evidence to speak unequivocally, but of course by then it might be too late to take any remedial action!

16. The last survey was published in 1973, and certainly from reading it we would not have predicted the remarkable savings performance in most of the Third World in the 1970s.

17. The true fiscal deficit should cover what in the United Kingdom is called the whole public sector's borrowing requirement appropriately inflation adjusted. As in most Third World countries, the public sector extends well beyond the "fisc," published figures of the government deficit are highly imperfect indicators of the size of and trends in the public sector's borrowing requirement. This is another area calling for research.

18. See Lal (1971, 1978) for the principles by which the social desirability of foreign borrowing can be judged, given various constraints. The condition under which a foreign capital inflow would be desirable, as derived in Lal (1971), is reproduced in appendix 1.

19. The figures in parenthesis are *t* statistics. It should be noted that the insignificant and low value of the log *KOE* parameter reflects the productivity slowdown in the 1970s. As a result, the implicit production function for OECD countries estimated above cannot be used to make projections into the future.

20. Thus we are considering foreign aid inflows and foreign portfolio investment. The problems associated with direct foreign investment are complicated because such investment typically also includes access to new management and technology. We discuss this separately in Lal (1978).

21. It should be noted that the social discount rate in the UNIDO method is the consumption rate of interest in the Little-Mirrlees (LM) method, but there is no equivalent to the United Nations Industrial Development Organization (UNIDO) social rate of return to investment, which is in terms of consumption, in the LM method. The social rate of return of the text is not the LM accounting rate of interest (ARI), which is the marginal rate of return to investment in the economy in terms of savings (the LM *numéraire*).

22. The argument applies equally if the import content of investment is zero, as can be seen by putting $m = 0$ in (7.22). See Lal (1971).

23. Thus if the elasticity of social marginal utility is, say, 2, then the social discount rate will be twice the growth rate of per capita consumption of the economy, in terms of a constant elasticity social utility function. A realistic value for the growth rate of consumption in many developing countries is 3 percent per annum, which yields a value of 6 percent for the social rate of discount.

24. OECD countries include the United States, the United Kingdom, Canada, Japan, France, Belgium, Austria, Finland, Italy, the Netherlands, and Sweden. OPEC countries include Algeria, Indonesia, Iran, Iraq, Kuwait, Libya, Nigeria, Saudi Arabia, United Arab Emirates, Venezuela, and Mexico. Developing countries include Zaire, Ethiopia, India, Tanzania, Pakistan, Sri Lanka, Sudan, Ghana, Kenya, Zambia, Egypt, Thailand, Philippines, Morocco, Zimbabwe, Peru, Colombia, Turkey, Republic of Korea, Malaysia, Brazil, Argentina, Chile, Yugoslavia, Hong Kong, and Singapore.

References

Baily, M. W. 1981. Productivity and the services of capital and labour. *Brookings papers on economic activity* 1:1–50.

Barro, R. J. 1974. Are government bonds net wealth? *Journal of political economy* 82, no. 6 (November–December):1095–118.

Berndt, E., and D. Wood. 1979. Engineering and econometric interpretations of energy-capital complementarity. *American economic review* 69, no. 1 (March):342–54.

Bonnell, S. 1981. Real wages and employment in the Great Depression. *Economic record* 57, no. 158 (September):277–81.

Bruno, M. 1982. World shocks, macroeconomic response, and the productivity puzzle. In R. C. O. Matthews, ed. *Slower growth in the Western world*. London: Heinemann.

———. 1984. Raw materials, profits, and the productivity slowdown. *Quarterly journal of economics* 99, no. 1 (February):1–32.

Buiter, W. H., and J. Tobin. 1980. Debt neutrality: A brief review of doctrine and evidence. In G. M. von Furstenberg, ed. *Social security versus private saving*. Cambridge, Mass.: Ballinger. Reprinted as Cowles Foundation paper 505. New Haven: Yale University.

Crosland, A. 1950. *The future of socialism*. London: Jonathan Cape.

Curzon-Price, V. 1982. Government intervention as a factor in slower growth in advanced industrial nations. In R. C. O. Matthews, ed. *Slower growth in the Western world*. London: Heinemann.

Council of Economic Advisers. 1983. *Economic report of the president 1983*. Washington, D.C.: CEA.

Darby, M. 1975. The financial and tax effects of monetary policy on interest rates. *Economic inquiry* 13, no. 2 (June):266–76.

Dewhurst, J. A., and Associates. 1961. *Europe's needs and resources*. New York: Twentieth Century Fund.

Dornbusch, R. 1983. Real interest rates, home goods, and optimal external borrowing. *Journal of political economy* 91, no. 1 (February):141–53.

Eisner, R., and P. J. Pieper. 1984. A new view of the federal debt and budget deficits. *American economic review* 74, no. 1 (March):11–29.

Emi, I. 1963. *Government fiscal activity and economic growth in Japan, 1868–1960*. Tokyo: Kinokuniya.

Federal Reserve System. 1981. *Public policy and capital formation*. Washington, D.C.: FRS.

Feldstein, M. 1983. *Inflation, tax rules, and capital formation*. National Bureau of Economic Research Monograph. Chicago: University of Chicago Press.

Fisher, Irving. 1930. *The theory of interest*. Macmillan.

Friedman, M. 1978. The Kemp-Roth free lunch. *Newsweek*, August 7.

Furstenberg, G. M. von, ed. 1979. *Social security versus private saving*. Cambridge, Mass.: Ballinger.

Galli, G., and R. Masera. 1983. Real rates of interest and public sector deficits: An empirical investigation. Paper presented at the colloquium "Government policies and the working of financial systems in industrialised countries" of the Société Universitaire Européenne de Recherches Financières, Madrid, October 13–15.

Harberger, A. C., and S. Edwards. 1980. International evidence on the source of inflation. Paper presented at the Getulio Vargas Foundation's Conference on Inflation, Rio de Janeiro, December.

Hudson, E. A., and D. W. Jorgenson. 1978. Energy prices and the U.S. economy. *Natural resource journal* 18, no. 4 (October):877–98.

Johnson, L. 1981. Life cycle saving, social security, and the long-run capital stock. In Federal Reserve System. *Public policy and capital formation*. Washington, D.C.: FRS.

Koskela, E., and M. Viven. 1983. National debt neutrality: Some international evidence. *Kyklos* 36(4):575–88.

Kravis, I. B. 1970. Trade as a handmaiden of growth: Similarities between the nineteenth and twentieth centuries. *Economic journal* 80, no. 320 (December):850–72.

Lal, D. 1971. When is foreign borrowing desirable? *Bulletin of the Oxford University Institute of Statistics* (August).

———. 1974. *Methods of project appraisl—A review*. Baltimore, Md.: Johns Hopkins University Press.

———. 1978. The evaluation of capital inflows. *Industry and development* 1:86–103. Reprinted in World Bank Reprint Series 84. Washington, D.C.

———. 1980. *Prices for planning—Towards the reform of Indian planning*. London: Heinemann.

————. 1983. *The poverty of "development economics."* Hobart paperback 16. London: Institute of Economic Affairs.

Lewis, W. A. 1978. *The Evolution of the international economic order.* Princeton, N.J.: Princeton University Press.

————. 1980. The slowing down of the engine of growth. *American economic review* 70, no. 4 (September):555–64.

Little, I. M. D., and J. A. Mirrlees. 1974. *Project appraisal and planning for developing countries.* London: Heinemann.

McCallum, B. T. 1984. Are bond-financed deficits inflationary? A Ricardian analysis. *Journal of political economy* 92, no. 1 (February):123–35.

MacCaulay, Frederick. 1938. *Some theoretical problems suggested by the movements of interest rates, bond yields, and stock prices in the United States since 1856.* National Bureau of Economic Research Monograph. Chicago: University of Chicago Press.

Maddison, A. 1982. *Phases of capitalist development.* Oxford: Oxford University Press.

Makin, J. H. 1983. Real interest, money surprises, anticipated inflation, and fiscal deficits. *Review of economics and statistics* 65, no. 3 (August):374–84.

Matthews, R. C. O., ed. 1982. *Slower growth in the Western world.* London: Heinemann.

Mundell, R. 1963. Inflation and real interest. *Journal of political economy* (June).

Ohkawa, I., and M. Shinohara. 1979. *Patterns of Japanese economic development.* New Haven, Conn.: Yale University Press.

Organisation for Economic Co-operation and Development (OECD). 1983. *Economic outlook* 33(July) and 34(December).

————. 1984. Social expenditures: Erosion or evolution? *OECD observer* 126(January):3–6.

Phelps-Brown, H. 1983. *The origins of trade union power.* Oxford: Oxford University Press.

Rati, Ram. 1982. Dependency rates and aggregate savings: A new international cross-section study. *American economic review* 72, no. 3 (June):537–44.

————. 1984. Dependency rates and savings: Reply. *American economic review* 74, no. 1 (March):234–37.

Riedel, J. 1984. Trade as the engine of growth in developing countries revisited. *Economic journal* 94, no. 373 (March):56–73.

Sachs, J. 1979. Wages, profits, and macroeconomic adjustment: A comparative study. *Brookings papers on economic activity* 2:269, 319.

————. 1981. The current account and macroeconomic adjustment in the 1970s. *Brookings papers on economic activity* 1:201–68.

————. 1983. Real wages and unemployment in OECD countries. *Brookings papers on economic activity* 1:255–89.

Sargent, T. J., and N. Wallace. 1981. Some unpleasant monetarist arthmetic. *Federal Reserve Bank of Minneapolis quarterly review* 5, no. 3 (Fall):1–17.

Scott, M. Fg., and R. A. Laslett. 1978. *Can we get back to full employment?* London: Macmillan.

Soskice, David. 1978. Strike waves and wage explosions, 1968–70: An economic interpretation. In C. Crouch and A. Pizzoruo, eds. *The resurgence of class conflict in Western Europe since 1968.* Vol. 2. New York: Holmes and Meier.

Summers, Lawrence H. 1983. The non-adjustment of nominal interest rates: A study of the

Fisher effect. In J. Tobin, ed. *Macroeconomics, prices, and quantities.* Washington, D.C.: Brookings Institution.

Svensson, L., and A. Razin. 1983. The terms of trade, spending, and the current account: The Harberger-Laursen-Metzler effect. *Journal of political economy* 91, no. 1 (February):97–125.

Thompson, L. H. 1983. The social security reform debate. *Journal of economic literature* 21, no. 4 (December):1425–67.

Tobin, J. 1965. Money and economic growth. *Econometrica* 33, no. 4 (October):671–84.

———, ed. 1983. *Macroeconomics, prices, and quantities.* Washington, D.C.: Brookings Institution.

U.S. Department of Commerce. 1975. *The national income and product accounts of the United States, 1929–1974.* Washington, D.C.: U.S. Department of Commerce.

van Wijnbergen, S. 1984. The Dutch disease: A disease after all? *Economic journal* 94, no. 373 (March):41–55.

Wilcox, J. A. 1983. Why real interest rates were so low in the 1970s. *American economic review* 73, no. 1 (March):44–53.

Chapter 8

Debt, Deficits, and Distortions

Deepak Lal and Martin Wolf

AFTER THE LONGEST and most severe recession in the world economy for fifty years, there are now (in 1984) signs of world economic recovery. Among the developed countries the United States is experiencing the strongest recovery, but prospects for Japan and Europe are also improving. For the developing countries the recovery appears to offer the hope of relief from the economic—and consequently political—pressures that many nations have experienced in the past five years, and there is even the possibility that they will achieve a return to sustained growth.

Does the recovery really offer the prospect of a return to rapid, sustained, and stable growth of a kind not experienced since the late 1960s, when business cycle upswings were strong and long and downswings shallow and short, or is this unlikely? If it is unlikely in view of present policies, can action be taken by both developed and developing countries to make sustained and rapid growth a reality, or is such growth no longer feasible? Finally, if sustained growth in the developed world is not regained, what can developing countries do to minimize the adverse consequences for themselves?

The discussion in the final part of the present chapter is almost entirely concerned with these questions. Although all of them concern the future, they cannot be answered just by peering into the future. The prospects for a future different from the recent past depend on whether the underlying causes of the malfunction in the world economy have been first understood and then removed. This chapter therefore considers the recent recession in the context of the longer-term trends in the global environment. *World Development Reports* have emphasized two major aspects of the global environment that provide links between economic performance in developed and developing countries. The first has been the link through foreign trade. Trade enables developing countries to develop efficiently, in line with their comparative advantage. Because the maintenance of high growth and near full employment in industrial countries provides a fillip to world trade and reduces the inherent pressures for protection from declining industries, the prosperity of developed countries has been considered to be helpful for the efficient growth of the developing world.

The second link comes through the flow of capital from the industrial and oil-exporting countries, which allows higher levels of investment in developing countries than can be financed through their domestic savings alone. In the 1950s and 1960s, official transfers and direct foreign investments were the major form of capital flows to developing countries. As these were considered to depend partly on the economic health of developed countries, the growth prospects of industrial countries have been taken to be an important determinant of the prospects of developing countries. Commercial bank lending began with the development of the Eurocurrency markets in the mid-1960s and accelerated in the 1970s with the emergence of the large financial surpluses of the oil-exporting countries. Such commercial lending has diminished the relative quantitative importance of the more traditional forms of capital flows to the middle-income developing countries. Moreover, by integrating industrial, oil-exporting, and oil-importing developing countries into a worldwide financial network, commercial bank lending has enhanced the financial links between the developed and developing world.

Initially considered to be a benign accompaniment of the recycling of oil surpluses in the Organization of Petroleum Exporting Countries (OPEC), the buildup of commercial debt by many developing countries is currently seen as threatening a global debt crisis. The reduction in commercial lending and the rise in nominal and real interest rates in the last few years have both contributed to the difficulties that a number of developing countries are experiencing in servicing their accumulated stock of commercial debt. To understand the causes, consequences, and possible cures for this current financial crisis in the global economy, it is necessary to grasp the growing importance of the financial links between developed and developing countries. One of the consequences of the global financial integration of the 1970s has been the creation of a global market for savings in which the price at which these savings are available (the real interest rate), for investment in both developed and developing countries, is increasingly determined by the global balance between the demand and supply of savings; see chapter 7 in this book for an analysis of these financial interactions. In view of the relative sizes of industrial, oil-exporting, and oil-importing countries in the world economy, the determinants of the supply and demand for savings in industrial countries are a major determinant of world interest rates. These in turn, through their effects both on the costs of servicing past debt and on the real cost of future investments, will influence the growth prospects of many middle-income developing countries. There is thus now an important second link—the financial one—between the macroeconomic policies and performance of developed and developing countries.

We argue in the first part of this chapter that, to comprehend the causes of the current global crisis and to assess the options and prospects for developing countries, it is necessary to examine the reasons for the persistence of stagflation in the industrial countries since the late 1960s. To the extent that the causes of stagflation have not been addressed, we contend, the prospect of further disruptive cycles exists. Thus the first part of the chapter attempts to delineate the underlying and often deep-seated structural problems in *developed* countries (problems that have been exposed rather than caused by the supply shocks of the 1970s) and their repercussions on the global economy. In this context the causes and nature of the debt crisis will be assessed, as will the performance of developing countries, in terms of the underlying "structural" weaknesses. The next part of this chapter discusses the effects of the recent recession on *developing* countries. The final part assesses the options and opportunities for developing countries in the context of two alternatives: (a) a continuation or (b) a likely resolution of these underlying problems. The final part will also consider the policies required in both developed and developing countries to restore stability and growth in the world economy.

This chapter thus attempts to show that an emerging commonality in the problems of both developed and developing countries is reflected in the symptoms of an unsustainable buildup of public debt, fiscal deficits, and policy-induced distortions in the working of the price mechanism. We shall argue that there are common problems concerning the design and conduct of public policy—in particular fiscal policy—that need to be addressed in nearly *all* countries if the underlying causes of the malfunctioning of the global economy are to be removed.

Underlying Problems of the Global Economy

Figure 8-1 illustrates the experience of the seven major industrial countries since the mid-1960s. As far as GDP growth is concerned, there have been three marked downturns since 1968, and the present appears to be the third strong recovery. Inflation and unemployment have tended to follow GDP growth—in opposite directions—with a lag in each case of about a year. The present is the third marked downturn in the rate of inflation since 1970. Unemployment has, unfortunately, not had any significant downturns but has had three marked upturns since 1969.

The most important point illustrated by figure 8-1 is the deterioration

Figure 8-1. *Growth, Inflation, and Unemployment in Seven Industrial Countries, 1966–83*

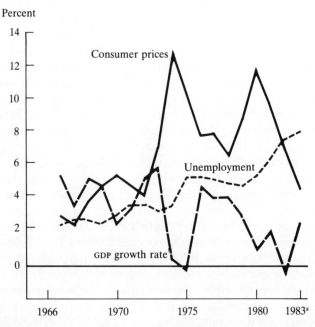

Note: Data are for Canada, France, Germany, Italy, Japan, the United Kingdom, and the United States.

a. Estimated.

Source: World Bank (1984*b*).

in economic performance over successive cycles. Both the unemployment and inflation troughs and the peaks have risen since the late 1960s. The latest unemployment trough was 5 percent (in 1979), the unemployment peak, 12.2 percent (in 1980); the latest inflation peak was 12.2 percent (in 1982), and the inflation trough, 7.1 percent (in 1982).

Following the last recession, inflation at last fell below its previous cyclical trough of 8 percent (in 1976), which might be viewed as a break in the tendency toward progressive deterioration, but the conclusion may be unwarranted. The important difference between the last recession and previous ones is the price in terms of output and unemployment that governments have been prepared to pay in order to lower inflation. The short-term tradeoff between inflation and unemployment itself was far worse in the early 1980s than in the late 1960s or mid-1970s. Thus as inflation was lowered to a level still above the average for the 1960s, unemployment rates rose to three times the level of the 1960s. The illusion that there is a stable tradeoff between inflation and unemployment is just one of the casualties of the last fifteen years.

Why has inflation become embedded in industrial economies, and why has unemployment tended to rise with hardly any interruption? Why has the tradeoff between inflation and unemployment deteriorated? Why have these economies failed to regain the dynamism of the pre-1973 period, with even the recovery of 1976 wilting after 1978? These questions must be considered if prospects for sustained recovery in 1984 and beyond are to be assessed in an informed way.

The main causes of the deterioration in the long-term performance of the industrial countries appear to have been the result of policy choices rather than underlying economic conditions (which is fortunate, because the former can be remedied more easily than the latter). Nevertheless, it may be argued that certain inevitable developments would have tended to create lower growth in industrial countries in any case. These developments included the successful progress of the trade liberalization that began after World War II. By the late 1960s, although boosts to growth similar in scale to those brought about by the earlier reintegration of the industrial economies may not have been expected from continued trade liberalization, the emergence of competitive labor-intensive exports from the newly industralizing countries suggests that, if the degree of liberalization had been maintained, there could have been a boost to growth in the developed countries through shifts in their allocation of investment away from low productivity, relatively labor-intensive industries. Furthermore, the opportunities for catching up with the technology of the United States had been largely exploited by both Japan and Western Europe. In this respect too an earlier opportunity for exceptional growth had become of declining significance.

Finally, signs were emerging in some industrial countries—at least in manufacturing—of rising capital-output ratios and declining rates of profit. (See appendix 1 and chapter 7 in this book.) Among the countries thus affected were the Federal Republic of Germany, the United Kingdom, and the United States. This development suggests that capital was being accumulated more rapidly than technical advance and the growth of the labor force would warrant. This rapid accumulation of capital, however, in turn was induced by the relative underpricing of capital and overpricing of labor, which were policy induced, as we shall see. For all these reasons, some decline in potential growth rates in industrial countries could be expected. The decline in the growth rate, however, need not have been accompanied by steadily rising unemployment, inflation, and destructive stop-go cycles. These are better explained by policy-induced malfunctioning of economies rather than by such underlying changes in the potential rate of growth.

By the mid-1960s there seemed to be a general consensus regarding the role of public policy, namely that high and stable growth could easily be maintained; that the benefits of that growth should be shared through increasingly generous public welfare provisions and regulations to enhance job security; that unemployment could be controlled through the manipulation of aggregate demand alone; that there was a stable and favorable tradeoff between unemployment and inflation; and that budget deficits should be defined in relation to a presumed full employment position.

The 1970s have seen an erosion of this consensus, partly because of the effects of the policies pursued in the earlier period. The major effects were the increasing rigidity of the labor market and the strong upward pressure on real wages, plus the growth of public sector expenditures, taxation, and deficits. The interaction between these two underlying forces is now increasingly seen by many observers to be at the root of the problems of inflation, unemployment, low growth, and stop-go cycles. The oil shocks severely aggravated these difficulties because they required adjustments that the industrial economies were unable to make in an efficient manner. In this sense the oil shocks may be said to be the proximate cause of a decade of low growth, but they were not the underlying reason.

In the late 1960s real wages in many industrial countries were rising at a rate faster than warranted by underlying productivity growth (see table 7-2 in this book). Although there exist forms of labor-using technical progress that could justify such a development, the tendency toward rising unemployment shown in figure 8-1 suggests that such progress was not occurring. In Western Europe, in particular, the tendency to excessive rises in real wages continued for much of the 1970s, although it was of much shorter duration in the more competitive labor market conditions of the United States, where a much lower proportion of the labor force is unionized than in Europe.

In the short run, labor market pressures of this kind could be dealt with in three ways: by allowing unemployment to rise; by allowing inflation to rise if wages are not indexed to prices either formally or de facto; or by direct intervention in the labor market in order to achieve the nominal wage consistent with stable prices and full employment. Until the first oil shock, governments generally attempted a combination of all three. The early 1970s, in particular, witnessed a major and ultimately unsuccessful attempt by the governments of the United States and the United Kingdom to achieve the required economic stability by fiat in the labor market through some form of incomes policy combined with fiscal and monetary expansion.

The second major structural change in the industrial countries has been the growth of public sector expenditures in relation to GDP. For the industrial countries as a whole, the rise was from about 29 percent in 1961 to nearly 40 percent in 1981 (see table A1-2 in this book).

More important, perhaps, than the overall rise was the changing structure. Among the seven major industrial countries, the share of government expenditure on public goods—defense, general administration, and economic services—fell from 16.4 percent to 10.9 percent of GNP between 1954 and 1980 and rose from 10.5 percent to 23.4 percent of GNP. In essence, the entire purpose of government was changing (see appendix 1 and chapter 7 in this book).

The rising share of expenditures on social goods and income maintenance in GNP reflects two basic forces: demographic change and political pressures. Important demographic changes include the lower share of children and the higher share of the old and the very old in the population. Political pressure reveals itself in improvements in coverage and benefit levels, of which the latter have been the more important. Between 1960 and 1975, eligibility change and demographic change each contributed about 20 percent of the growth of expenditures on social goods and income maintenance, whereas benefit improvement contributed 60 percent. Between 1975 and 1981, changes in eligibility had ceased to be a factor. Demographic change then contributed 17 percent of the growth, and improved benefits 78 percent (see appendix 1). To a large extent, therefore, the problem of control over public expenditures is one of resisting pressures for improved welfare benefits. These pressures come from large and politically significant groups in the population that are increasingly dependent on income transfers.

Rising shares of public expenditures in national income have one almost inevitable consequence and one likely consequence. The inevitable consequence is a tendency toward rising shares of tax receipts in GNP. For all industrial countries together, the rise was from 28.7 percent of GDP in 1961 to 37.5 percent in 1981. The increase was, however, smaller than the rise in both current disbursements and total outlays of government as a share of GDP: the share of revenues grew by 8.8 percent of GDP, whereas that of expenditure grew by more than 11 percent of GDP (see appendix 1 in this book). Rising public sector deficits as a share of GDP, then, were the likely consequence.

In conjunction with labor market pressures, rising shares of taxation in

GDP contributed to two problems. In the first place the higher taxes had to be paid by someone, but real wage resistance tended to shift them onto profits. This shift had disturbing implications for long-term investment, employment, and growth. Furthermore, as profit rates tended to decline, governments tried to shift the tax burden back from capital onto labor. The result was growing taxation of employment, especially of unskilled labor, which is most adversely affected by rising payroll taxes (see Bacon and Eltis 1978). In the second place, where governments wanted to mitigate the pressures on profits and employment, rising inflation became difficult to avoid. As a result, returns on equity were maintained at the cost of impoverishing people who held bonds, and some relatively well-organized workers benefited at the expense of individuals who were not (including the unemployed).

The significance of the general rise in public sector deficits is a hotly debated issue, in part because of the difficulty of separating the effects of business cycles and inflation from the effects of structural trends in these deficits and in part because of opposing views on the economic signifi-cance of deficits. It does not appear that there has been—at least until recently—any general tendency toward structural deficits in industrial countries if the commonly made cyclical adjustments are accepted, but deficits—and their financing—have been an important cause of difficulty in certain countries at critical junctures. This statement is particularly true of the deficit of the United States in the late 1960s and again today and has also been true of Belgium, Denmark, Italy, the United Kingdom, and several other countries from time to time in the 1970s and 1980s.

In the industrial countries gross savings as a percentage of GDP peaked at 25.2 percent of GDP in 1973 and has since tended to decline, reaching its lowest point of the last twenty years in 1982 at 19.7 percent, as the list below shows. Meanwhile, the less well known, much more speculative net savings rate fell from 14.8 percent in 1973 to its nadir of 8.9 percent in 1981.

Year	Gross savings (percentage of GDP)	Year	Gross savings (percentage of GDP)
1962	21.7	1977	21.9
1967	22.3	1978	22.9
1972	23.5	1979	22.8
1973	25.2	1980	21.8
1974	23.7	1981	21.5
1975	21.2	1982	19.7
1976	21.6		

What explains the decline in savings rates in industrial countries? Household savings rates held up very well in the 1970s, whereas corporate and government savings rates were strongly procyclical (see table A1-28 in this book). Profit shares fall in recessions, and governments run larger deficits. The principal reason for the decline in gross and net savings rates, therefore, is simply slow and unstable growth. It is as yet unclear whether there has also been a fundamental underlying trend toward lower rates of gross savings, although it is true that virtually all industrial countries had worse savings performance after 1973 than before.

In interpreting the figures on savings, two points should be mentioned. The first concerns the effects of inflation. Savings might best be defined as the change in the real value of assets in a given period. In the 1970s, however, the household sector—which is a creditor of the corporate and government sectors—experienced a large decline in the real value of its initial claims on the other sectors because of unanticipated inflation, but large capital gains on real estate partially compensated for this decline. Thus, just as public savings were higher than appears by virtue of the proceeds of the inflation tax, so must household savings have been correspondingly smaller in real terms. The question is whether households fully internalized the increased wealth or declining real indebtedness of the other two sectors. In other words, was it the actual real rate of saving by households or their observed nominal rate of saving that was the target? If the former, household nominal savings rates will fall as inflation falls, and the overall national savings rates will also fall, unless governments, in particular, take measures to replace the inflation tax with some other source of revenue that does not itself bear heavily on savings.

The other question relates to the *net* savings rate (that is, gross savings less depreciation as a percentage of natural income), which is now at a historically low level (see table A1-28 in this book). Changes in the net savings rate appear to be largely explained by reductions in gross savings rates. Because depreciation depends on the size of the capital stock and on existing accounting conventions, a given decline in the gross savings rate causes a more than proportionate decline in the net savings rate. Nevertheless, net savings rates have fallen absolutely by more than the gross savings rates because depreciation has risen as a proportion of GDP in the industrial countries, from 9.3 percent in 1962 to 10.4 percent in 1973 and 12.6 percent in 1981. Moreover, it should be noted that, because the capital stock is not generally adjusted for inflation, these estimates of depreciation could seriously underestimate the true rate of depreciation in terms of replacement cost.

The difficulties in interpreting the rise in rates of depreciation are two: first, much depreciation is the result of arbitrary accounting conventions that may have little economic meaning; second, even the part of gross savings that is offset by depreciation will increase output, because new machinery is more productive than old. Nevertheless, inasmuch as capital output ratios appear to have risen since 1973 in most industrial countries and real depreciation rates are probably underestimated (because of the absence of inflation accounting), it is quite likely that the observed rise in depreciation rates is economically significant. If so, even constant rates of gross savings may imply a reduction in the potential rate of growth for a given level of technology.

Pressures in the labor market and on public finance and the decline in domestic savings can be related to three key features of the economic performance of industrial countries since the late 1960s: inflation, unemployment, and a broadly defined protectionism. Perhaps the most obvious consequence of the underlying changes was the rising trend in inflation that emerged by the late 1960s. Inflation may be seen as having resulted from accommodation of labor market pressures or from deficit financing or from both.

Many of the most important economic effects of inflation result from its interaction with accounting conventions, tax systems, and financial markets that assume price stability (Feldstein 1983). Thus accounts—corporate, public, and national—are rendered misleading; tax systems become extremely distorting (for example, via taxation of illusory profits and nominal capital gains); there is intertemporal discoordination of production stemming from the fact that investors do not know what is the right "real interest rate," at which their investments break even; and finally, willingness to hold financial assets declines, maturity of financial assets shortens, and implicit real front loading of financial contracts rises.

As the financial system changed with unanticipated inflation, the banks rose in importance. In an economy in which most of the available liquidity is created by credit expansion, the deposit-taking institutions receive much of the immediate benefit of the inflation tax on money. In a competitive system, however, the transfer from those who hold low-interest-bearing deposits will be bid away in favor of the borrowers. Nevertheless, because of this transfer, which rises with the extent of unanticipated inflation, banking institutions will tend to be the most profitable form of market intermediary, because all their overhead and other fixed costs can be covered by the return on lending against their low-cost deposits. This advantage is temporary, because deposits will be withdrawn or will become increasingly expensive as expectations adjust. In the interim, however, banks will thrive on low spreads at the margin as other forms of financial intermediation contract. These phenomena are important in understanding the reasons for the explosion of commercial bank lending to developing countries in the 1970s, as we shall see in a later section.

Inflation has important effects on the distribution of income, especially in periods when it has been incorrectly anticipated. During the 1970s, all debtors enjoyed large windfalls, not least governments. Unanticipated inflation can impose large taxes and in certain cases was an important mechanism for covering budget deficits while also allowing reductions in real public indebtedness. The real return on government debt—even before taxes—was zero or negative for the United States, Japan, France, the United Kingdom, and Canada for almost all years between 1972 and 1980 (see table A1-20 in this book). Furthermore, in all these cases other than Japan—most strikingly in that of the United Kingdom—the ratio of debt to GDP fell during most of the 1970s, despite large, cyclically unadjusted deficits, because of the effects of unanticipated inflation. It was to be expected that the resulting deterioration in the ability of individuals to plan for their own security would place pressure on governments to provide more generous social security benefits, for government is the only organization in society that can provide a credible guarantee against the effects of inflation.

One of the most important consequences of inflation is its effect in raising the degree of uncertainty about the future. This uncertainty manifests itself in various ways, for example in the high inflation premiums demanded in long-term interest rates. Looking back at the late 1960s and early 1970s, we can observe another way and perhaps one that is still more important—exchange rate instability. Inflation was the principal cause of the breakdown in the Bretton Woods system of fixed but adjustable exchange rates. Although considerable concern has since been expressed about exchange rate instability and consequent uncertainty, we cannot blame the messenger for the message. The monetary disorders that made floating exchange rates inevitable also ensured that they would be volatile (see chapter 2 in this book). Perhaps the most important aspect of uncertainty, however, is created by the inflationary stop-go cycle itself. Experience that expansion breeds first inflation and then policy-induced contraction is itself an important constraint on long-term investment. In this way the bottlenecks in the economy that lead to inflation are to some degree self-generating.

Inflation is one important characteristic of the malaise. Unemployment is another. The rise in unemployment is most closely related to real wage pressures exacerbated by the productivity slowdown of the 1970s. The entry of the baby boom generation into the labor force also increased the supply of labor. Although the fact of the productivity slowdown is clear, the extent to which it is an autonomous event or a reaction to the oil shock is not. It is certain, however, that the effect was to lower the rate of rise of the real wage that was compatible with full employment. In the United States and Japan, real wages appear to have adjusted rapidly to the new trend—in the United States real wages hardly rose at all after 1973 (see table 7-1 in this book). In Western Europe, however, the same was not true. The result was not only a more consistently adverse trend in unemployment in Western Europe but a much poorer record of employment creation. In the 1970s employment grew by about 20 million in the United States as against only about 2 million in the European Community as a whole.

With real wage rigidities and rising unemployment, governments were under great pressure to protect specific industries just because management of aggregate demand was increasingly ineffective. Often protection is viewed in terms of border measures alone and its costs are seen in terms of the prevention of other countries' exports. Protection can also be viewed, however, as the attempt to prevent or slow change by preserving outmoded forms of economic activity. The costs are then largely borne by the protecting society, and such protection can take many forms, including subsidies.

Because it has taken covert and obscure forms, the evidence on the growth of protection is poor. In the present context, however, it is relevant that the share of public expenditures on subsidies to economic activity was rising—principally in Western Europe—by the late 1960s (Blackhurst and Tumlir 1977). This rise in subsidization is partly to be explained by the fact that it is the main mechanism for industrial assistance for European countries, which are prevented from employing border measures against one another. Thus in the case of broadly defined protectionism, as in that of unemployment, inflation, and the tradeoff between them, adverse trends were already clearly visible by the late 1960s or early 1970s.

The oil "shock" of October 1973 exposed the underlying weaknesses in industrial economies but not because of the scale of the shock itself, which amounted to an annual transfer of about 2 percent of GDP from the industrial countries, or roughly half a year's growth. Much of this transfer could at least initially be borrowed back, and in addition, as the surplus available for borrowing fell between 1975 and 1979, so did the real price of oil. A transfer of this size and the associated required changes in relative factor prices could not in themselves explain subsequent problems of low growth, unemployment, and inflation except in the context of already inflexible economies.

One effect of rigidities on the response to the oil shock was in the labor market. The rise in the price of energy lowered the real wage that was compatible with full employment. It also led to an ex ante incentive to shift away from energy and, therefore, away from capital-intensive modes of production toward more labor-intensive modes of production. This substitution explains a part of the observed slowdown in labor productivity growth, which was to that extent desirable. The slowdown was particularly marked in the United States and Japan just because labor markets in those countries adjusted most completely. Where the requisite reductions in real wages and real wage growth did not occur—as in Western Europe—the productivity slowdown was smaller, but the oil price rise gave a permanent upward boost to unemployment (Bruno, 1984; Sachs 1983). This upward boost was not successfully offset by expansionary fiscal and monetary policy where that strategy was tried, and indeed it could not have been.

The changing price of energy also brought about accelerated obsolescence of significant parts of the capital stock, especially in industries like steel, shipbuilding, chemicals (including petrochemicals), and motor vehicles. The political response was increased attempts to prop up such industries with protection and subsidization.

Despite the failure of real wages to adjust, investment demand and thence economic activity were partially sustained for nearly a decade by abnormally low levels of real rates of interest, which were actually negative for long periods and thus maintained returns to risk capital. There is even evidence from the United States that without the transfer of income from lenders to equity owners, which is consequent on low rates of interest, much of the corporate investments that took place could not have been undertaken (Fellner 1984). It is not yet clear why the decline in real rates of interest occurred. Although lenders might not have distinguished between nominal and real returns and might have continued to lend, other factors would include the increase in ex ante global saving in the form of OPEC's surplus and the decline in the demand for capital following a large rise in the relative price of complementary inputs, especially energy (see chapter 7 in this book). The economic situation in the 1970s and the "debt crisis" that subsequently emerged can be understood only in relation to the peculiar relationship between real wages and real rates of interest that lasted for nearly a decade.

Negative real rates of interest were a spur to a rapid expansion of borrowing. Furthermore, although in the 1950s and 1960s the pattern of international lending was evolving in a stable manner (the roles and shares of different continents and groups of countries in it were changing only gradually), in the 1970s a suddenly rising share of the increased international lending began to flow to the non-oil developing countries. The great increase in lending was largely the result of the OPEC surplus, but it must be asked why the industrial countries were not large net borrowers themselves. The proximate cause was the sluggish growth of investment in industrial countries after 1973, in spite of the apparent need for an expansion of investment, in order to bring about the adjustments necessitated by changes in the world economy. This sluggish growth in turn was symptomatic of the declining adjustment capacity of the advanced industrial economies. Increased investment would have implied a more rapid structural transformation, which the advanced industrial economies refused, through the political process, to tolerate.

In the absence of an acceptance of change in the industrial countries at the core of the world economy and an acceptance of the need for efficient adjustment to change, there was no way of safely investing the additional savings that OPEC was generating in the world economy. In fact, as the flow of international lending expanded, underlying trade opportunities were probably not growing at an equivalent rate, a state of affairs that reflected the sluggishness of the industrial market-oriented economies, itself aggravated by the growth of trade restrictions and subsidies. Inasmuch as international lending is ultimately deferred trade, these two processes could not run in tandem for very long.

Although negative real rates of interest may have helped to reduce the effects of labor market distortions on economic activity, they also added new distortions through their effect on investment patterns. The main source of waste tended to be an excessive bias toward labor-saving investment, especially in Western Europe, where real wages did not adjust (Scott and Laslett 1978). At the same time there is some evidence that uncertainty about the future course of inflation, partly through its effect in drying up the bond market, discouraged long-term investments in favor of those having shorter payback periods (which are less efficient for restructuring the economy, as they are essentially defensive investments) offering greater liquidity (Giersch and Wolter 1983).

In brief, the oil price rises revealed the extent of the underlying problems of industrial countries, but the concomitant inflation veiled its severity. By the end of the 1970s, a correction was overdue if the inflationary spiral was not to get out of hand, but it was also likely to reveal, unfortunately, the unviable disposition of a part of the world's stock of financial and real assets.

Recession in Retrospect

The recession of 1974–75 was sharp and deep in the industrial countries but had relatively little effect on the rates of growth of GDP in many developing countries. Growth rates in industrial economies declined from 6.1 percent in 1973 to 0.8 percent in 1974 and −0.4 percent in 1975. Developing country growth rates declined less, from 7.4 percent in 1973 to 5.9 percent in 1974 and 4 percent in 1975. Low-income Africa was hard hit, however (the growth rate declined to 2.5 percent in 1975 from 8.3 percent in 1973). Even in this region the 1974–75 recession was short, with the growth rate recovering in 1976. The recent recession, which was more prolonged, has severely affected the growth rates of developing countries. Although they showed some resilience at the start, their growth rates eventually declined along with those in the rest of the world (figure 8-2 and table 8-1). The decline was particularly marked for Latin America and the Caribbean, where growth rates were negative for 1981–

Figure 8-2. *Growth Rates of GDP for Developing and Industrial Countries, 1961–83*

a. Estimated.
Source: World Bank (1984*b*).

Table 8-1. Population, GDP, GDP per Capita, and Growth Rates, 1960–83

Country group	1980 GDP (billions of dollars)	1980 population (millions)	1980 GDP per capita (dollars)	GDP growth rates (average annual percentage change)					
				1960–73	1973–79	1980	1981	1982	1983[a]
Developing countries[b]	2,118	3,280	650	6.3	5.2	2.5	2.4	1.9	1.0
Low income	549	2,175	250	5.6	4.8	5.9	4.8	5.2	4.7
Asia	497	1,971	250	5.9	5.2	6.3	5.2	5.6	5.1
China	284	980	290	8.5	5.7	6.1	4.8	7.3	5.1
India	162	675	240	3.6	4.3	6.9	5.7	2.9	5.4
Africa	52	204	250	3.5	2.1	1.3	1.2	0.5	-0.1
Middle-income oil importers	915	611	1,500	6.3	5.6	4.3	0.9	0.7	0.3
East Asia and Pacific	204	183	1,110	8.2	8.6	3.6	6.7	4.2	6.4
Middle East and North Africa	28	35	800	5.2	3.0	4.2	-2.4	5.5	2.0
Sub-Saharan Africa[c]	37	60	610	5.6	3.7	5.5	3.9	1.1	0.3
Southern Europe	201	91	2,210	6.7	5.0	1.5	2.3	0.7	-0.9
Latin America and Caribbean	445	241	1,840	5.6	5.0	5.8	-2.3	-0.4	-2.2
Middle-income oil exporters[d]	654	494	1,320	6.9	4.9	-2.4	2.4	0.9	-1.7
High-income oil exporters	228	16	14,250	10.7	7.7	7.4	0.0	n.a.	n.a.
Industrial market economies	7,463	715	10,440	4.9	2.8	1.3	1.3	-0.5	2.3

n.a. = not available.

a. Estimated.

b. Data for 1982 and 1983 are based on a sample of ninety developing countries.

c. Does not include South Africa.

d. The estimated 1983 data exclude Angola, the Islamic Republic of Iran, and Iraq.

Source: World Bank (1984b:11).

83. Thus although growth in developing countries has not been immediately and mechanically determined by that of the industrial world, stagnation in the latter eventually took its toll. Developing countries fared better in the mid-1970s not only because the recession was much shorter but because for a time their heavy borrowing allowed them to grow. In the course of the longer recession that started in 1979, however, the availability of foreign capital (particularly of private medium- and long-term loans) abruptly declined after 1981, and this change imposed very substantial adjustments on countries that had come to rely on foreign capital as a principal instrument for "riding out" the recession. The question to be considered is whether this negative impact on developing countries was just a temporary matter of adjustment to an unexpectedly severe recession, combined with higher costs of borrowing than expected, or is more permanent.

The proximate causes of the recession were two: the rise in oil prices in 1979, due to supply disruptions in Iran, and the strong emphasis on disinflation of the monetary authorities in most major industrial countries (see chapter 2 in this book). It is impossible to reduce inflation of the magnitude experienced in the 1970s without experiencing transitional losses of output and increases in unemployment. The extent of these losses does, however, depend on the flexibility of prices and thus of production patterns, in the face of reduced demand—that is, on the extent to which there exists effective competition in goods and factor markets (Sachs 1979, 1983)—which in turn depends on the degree to which the government's commitment to reduce inflation is credible to the agents involved (Fellner 1976, 1979, 1980). If people do not believe that the authorities will do what they announce, they can be convinced only by experience, and the more deeply rooted is their disbelief, the more painful and protracted must be their experience.

There is considerable evidence that in the industrial countries both real and nominal prices have over time come to respond more slowly to declines in demand during recessions (Sachs 1979). This is not in any way a recent phenomenon but by the 1920s had already begun to concern economists in the United Kingdom (Eichengreen 1981; Phelps-Brown 1983). The problem has become worse, however, and more general over time. In addition, inflation has been an increasingly significant feature of the environment in industrial countries since the mid-1960s, and governments have repeatedly announced their intention of doing something about it. These announcements have had no obvious effect, so it is not surprising that by the late 1970s the markets needed a great deal of convincing about the seriousness of government's intentions.

Disinflation has effects that are not at all dissimilar to those of deflation. There is an unanticipated tightening of the monetary environment, and there tend to be high real interest rates during the period of adjustment. As the monetary tightness of the late 1970s was not anticipated, the disinflation of the early 1980s had consequences—not least for financial markets—that were similar in kind to those of the 1930s (Friedman and Schwartz 1963) although less severe to the extent that the change in the monetary environment was less dramatic. The result was the worst recession since the 1930s (see chapter 1 in this book). The difference between the two periods is also worth noting: the deflation of the 1930s was in substantial part the result of an unplanned collapse in the money supply, whereas the disinflation of the 1980s was the result of a deliberate intention to restore some stability to the value of money.

Although disinflation was an important reason for the rise in real interest rates—especially short-term interest rates—it was probably not the only one. With growing budget deficits in several industrial countries, including the United States, and the decline in the surplus of oil-exporting developing countries after 1980, the supply of real savings also declined (see chapter 7 in this book). The decline itself was likely to lead to a rise in real interest rates.

There are two reasons why the disinflation created particularly severe problems for the internationl financial system. The first reason related to the mix of fiscal and monetary policies pursued by the United States. With a growing budget deficit financed by borrowing in a country with a relatively low savings rate, a substantial capital inflow developed. This inflow generated a large real appreciation in the exchange rate, which allowed the required current account deficit (the counterpart of the capital inflow) to emerge. In a world where a very large part of international indebtedness is denominated in dollars, the appreciation of the dollar exchange rate greatly increased the cost of debt service (Cline 1983).

The second reason for difficulty was more deep-seated. For reasons to be considered further below, the real interest rate averaged only about 0.5 percent in the Eurocurrency markets between 1973 and 1980 and at various points was negative. In such an environment it is almost impossible to owe too much, and in consequence, the tendency toward increased indebtedness was a pervasive feature of the world economy and in no way unique to developing countries. Both corporations and governments in industrial countries tended with few exceptions to go increasingly into debt, as did the governments of a number of developing countries. Where there was no increase in real indebtedness at the end of the day, the reason was largely that unanticipated inflation eroded the value of past indebtedness faster than borrowers managed to contract new indebtedness. It was partly because of the resulting financial vulnerability that the jump in real interest rates to about 7 percent in 1981 and 1982 created so much difficulty (Fellner 1984).

For developing countries the rise in interest rates was accompanied by a reduction in new medium- and long-term loans by commercial banks in the second half of 1982. The net capital transfers to all developing countries (disbursements less debt service), which had fallen from $30.4 billion ("billion" means "thousand million") in 1981 to $6.6 billion in 1982, fell a further $17 billion, leading to an unprecedented net *outflow* of $11 billion in capital from developing countries in 1983. The situation was even worse for the thirteen major borrowers, who had a net *outflow* of $6.6 billion in 1982 and $21 billion in 1983 (World Bank 1984*a*).

In the industrial countries GDP grew by 1.3 percent between 1979 and 1980 and between 1980 and 1981, fell by 0.5 percent between 1981 and 1982, and is expected to have risen by about 2.3 percent between 1982 and 1983. Meanwhile the average rate of unemployment in industrial countries doubled from 5.1 percent in 1979 to more than 10 percent in 1982—the highest rate since the 1930s (OECD 1983). Furthermore, world trade grew by 1.5 percent between 1979 and 1980, stagnated between 1980 and 1981, and then fell by 2 percent between 1981 and 1982. In the case of trade, the principal reason for stagnation was the sharp fall in the volume of trade in fuels. World exports of manufactures grew more rapidly than other categories but performed far worse than in the past, rising 5 percent between 1979 and 1980 and 3.5 percent between 1980 and 1981 before falling by 1.5 percent between 1981 and 1982 (GATT 1982–83). Viewed against the background of the past three decades, this was a period of dismal economic performance both in the industrial world and in world trade, but it still was never as bad as in the Great Depression of the 1930s (see chapter 1 in this book).

The recession did at least bring about a marked fall in inflation. Among major industrial countries the reduction in the rate of rise of the consumer price index was particularly sharp in the United Kingdom (from 18 percent between 1979 and 1980 to 8.6 percent between 1981 and 1982); the United States (from 13.5 percent between 1979 and 1980 to 6.1 percent between 1981 and 1982); and Japan (from 8 percent between 1979 and 1980 to 2.7 percent between 1981 and 1982). With few exceptions, however, even in the trough of the cycle, rates of inflation remained above the average for the 1960s (OECD 1984).

The international economic environment impinges on any economy via prices and terms of access to markets for—and supplies of—traded goods, services, and factors of production, including the supply of capital. In 1974–75 a deterioration of opportunities to trade in goods and services was offset for many developing countries by an improvement in the expanded opportunities for the migration of labor to the Middle East and for the import of capital based on the recycling of the large financial surpluses of the oil producers. Between 1979 and 1983, by way of contrast, most developing countries initially—and virtually all ultimately—faced an unanticipated deterioration in the environment in all significant respects.

Weak demand in the industrial countries during 1980–83 was the main cause of the declines in the prices of the exports of developing countries (table 8-2). Prices for industrial raw materials fell for the additional reason that high interest rates discouraged storage, whereas food prices dropped because of bumper world harvests. Overall, the prices of primary goods reached a record low for the postwar period relative to prices of manufactures in 1982. By 1983, however, the recession had begun to give way to recovery, and supply was limited by both unfavorable weather and government policies; consequently, the prices of primary goods started to rise again. Nevertheless, prices remained low relative to their levels in better times, and almost all developing countries faced worse terms of trade in 1983 than they had in 1980 (table 8-2).

As for quantities exported by developing countries (table 8-3), volumes of raw materials and fuels fell absolutely during the recession,

Table 8-2. *Change in Export Prices and in Terms of Trade, 1965–83*
(average annual percentage change)

Country group	1965–73	1973–80	1981	1982	1983[a]
	Change in export prices				
Developing countries					
Food	6.6	7.8	−16.1	−14.1	5.2
Nonfood	3.7	10.1	−14.6	−9.4	10.3
Metals and minerals	1.6	5.6	−12.0	−8.0	−2.2
Fuels	6.7	24.7	10.5	−2.6	−14.5
Industrial countries					
Manufactures	4.7	10.9	−4.2	−1.8	−3.2
	Change in terms of trade				
Low-income Asia	−0.5	−1.4	−0.1	−1.6	−0.6
Low-income Africa	−0.1	−1.5	−9.9	−0.9	4.6
Middle-income oil importers	−0.6	−2.2	−5.5	−1.9	3.0
Middle-income oil exporters	1.1	8.1	9.0	−0.4	−7.0
Developing countries	0.4	1.6	−0.5	−1.2	−0.6

Note: Calculations are based on a sample of ninety developing countries.
a. Estimated.
Source: World Bank (1984b:24).

Table 8-3. *Exports from Developing Countries, 1965–83*

Commodity and developing country group	Change in export volumes (average annual percentage change)					Value of exports (billions of current dollars)	
	1965–73	1973–80	1981	1982	1983[a]	1965	1981
Commodity							
Manufactures	14.9	10.6	16.3	-1.6	6.0	7.1	134.6
Food	1.3	6.0	19.7	5.0	0.9	13.3	74.8
Nonfood	3.7	1.5	2.5	-6.1	1.7	5.4	24.5
Metals and minerals	6.3	5.9	2.6	-2.1	-1.9	4.5	26.9
Fuels	6.4	-1.3	-21.9	5.1	6.1	7.3	165.1
Developing-country group							
Low-income Asia	2.9	7.6	17.2	-3.8	4.6	5.2	36.0
Low-income Africa	4.0	-1.3	-2.6	10.6	0.2	1.9	6.6
Middle-income oil importers	8.1	7.6	12.5	-0.5	3.2	18.5	219.0
Middle-income oil exporters	5.7	-0.8	-17.0	5.2	5.7	12.0	150.5
All developing countries	6.3	3.1	0.4	1.1	4.1	37.5	412.1

Note: Data for 1982 and 1983 are based on a sample of ninety developing countries.
a. Estimated.
Source: World Bank (1984b:28).

whereas exports of food—always relatively insensitive to income—continued to grow. Perhaps most dramatic was the decline in the growth rate of developing countries' exports of manufactures, from 10.6 percent a year between 1973 and 1980 to only 6.9 percent between 1980 and 1983. Given that the rates of GDP growth in industrial countries were very low, however, it is clear that penetration of their markets for manufactures by developing countries must have continued despite the recession.

Although the situation is extremely difficult to disentangle, low growth of income in the industrial countries rather than increased protection appears to have been the main immediate cause of deteriorating opportunities for trade. It is nevertheless possible that the costs of protection, subsidization, and other forms of resistance to change, as well as uncertainty about future policies, figured importantly among the causes of slow growth in industrial countries and that the last recession was more protracted because of existing protection and associated rigidities in the industrial countries' economic structure. Pressures for further protection were strong, but governments were for the most part able to resist them. New protectionist actions and agreements largely concerned trade among industrial countries, especially imports into Europe and North America from Japan. There were, moreover, several other developments that adversely affected developing countries, including a more restrictive renegotiation of the multifiber arrangement in 1981 and subsequent restrictions on textiles and clothing (especially in the United States); the further evolution of comprehensive restrictions on imports of steel into the United States and the European Community; and increased resort to less-than-fair value provisions of United States trade law.

As two-thirds of developing country indebtedness was in the form of dollar-denominated debt, the sharp rise in real interest rates represented a fundamental change in the environment faced by developing countries. It greatly increased the costs of borrowing and thereby postponing domestic adjustment by comparison with the opportunities available during the 1974–75 recession. Indeed, such a policy of postponing adjustment of real expenditure levels and real exchange rates, in the context of a sharp deterioration in the terms of trade for so many countries, could have been justified only if the high cost of borrowing and the recession itself had turned out to be of brief duration. Unfortunately, they did not.

Because of the failure to anticipate the significance of the change in the environment, the impact of the recession on developing countries came in two distinct phases. The first—a period during which adjustment was postponed by many developing countries—ended in the middle of 1982. The second—a period of rapid, dramatic, and extremely painful adjustment for some developing countries—has continued since that time but may now be ending. Oil-importing countries had hoped that the shock would prove to be of relatively brief duration, whereas oil-exporting countries had not expected an adverse shock at all. By 1982 it was evident that both groups had been wrong.

Oil-importing developing countries as a group were forced to make some adjustments to the real level of their imports from the beginning of the recession. Nevertheless, the adjustment was very far from complete. The combined current account deficits of oil-importing developing countries appear to have grown from nearly $29 billion in 1978 to $70 billion in 1980 and nearly $82 billion at their peak in 1981 (see table 8-4).

Despite growing current account deficits, there was still a squeeze on imports in oil-importing developing countries until 1982 because of the huge increase in interest payments. In 1982, for example, interest due from all developing countries, including that on short-term debt, was $66 billion ($48 billion on medium- and long-term debt), and this interest accounted for approximately one-half of the total developing country current account deficit (see tables 8-4 and 8-5). Nevertheless, in the aggregate, interest was being capitalized for oil-importing developing countries, and in addition, there was sufficient lending to cover a substantial real resource gap—that is, deficit on goods and nonfactor services—as well.

For oil-exporting developing countries, the experience in the early part of the recession was markedly different from that of oil-importing developing countries, although the dénouement turned out to be similar. In 1979 and 1980 the oil exporters had both current account surpluses and increased levels of real imports. The rise in the real price of oil was not sustained, however, and the volume of oil exports fell. In consequence, in 1981 the oil exporters too slipped into deficit—a deficit of $26 billion followed by one of $32 billion in 1982 (see table 8-4). In both years the oil-exporting countries drew down reserves, and the oil-importing countries did so as well (see chapter 5 in this book for the causes of the current economic crisis in many oil-exporting countries).

Thus by 1982, starting from very different points of origin, both oil-importing and oil-exporting developing countries had reached a similar impasse. To understand the subsequent events, we must consider the circumstances under which lenders will be prepared to capitalize interest payments and to provide additional lending as well. "Credit" derives from a Latin word meaning "to believe." We are therefore asking what determines the lenders' faith in the ability or willingness of debtors to service debt from their own income (rather than from additional borrowing) if it is necessary to do so.

The question was considered more extensively in the first part of this

Table 8-4. *Current Account Balance and Its Financing, 1970–83*
(billions of current dollars)

Country group and item	1970	1980	1981	1982	1983[a]
Developing countries					
Net exports of goods and nonfactor services	−9.8	−55.2	−80.5	−57.1	−10.9
Net factor income	−3.6	−16.4	−30.0	−43.2	−48.3
Interest payments and medium- and long-term loans	−2.7	−32.7	−41.2	−48.4	−49.0
Current account (excludes official transfers)[b]	−12.7	−69.6	−107.8	−97.6	−56.2
Financing					
Official transfers	2.4	11.6	11.7	10.8	11.1
Medium- and long-term loans					
Official	3.7	21.5	21.2	21.4	17.6
Private	4.6	35.7	49.6	33.5	39.9
Oil importers					
Net exports of goods and nonfactor services	−8.9	−69.3	−70.5	−46.9	−26.0
Net factor income	−1.5	−4.3	−14.4	−21.8	−23.0
Interest payments on medium- and long-term loans	−2.0	−21.3	−26.7	−31.7	−32.3
Current account (excludes official transfers)	−9.8	−70.3	−81.8	−65.6	−46.1
Financing					
Official transfers	1.8	9.6	9.4	9.0	8.9
Medium- and long-term loans					
Official	2.9	16.9	16.5	15.9	13.9
Private	3.7	24.6	30.8	22.0	11.1
Oil exporters					
Net exports of goods and nonfactor services	−0.9	14.2	−10.0	−10.1	15.1
Net factor income	−2.1	−12.1	−15.6	−21.4	−25.3
Interest payments on medium- and long-term loans	−0.7	−11.5	−14.5	−16.7	−16.7
Current account (excludes official transfers)	−2.9	1.7	−26.1	−32.1	−10.0
Financing					
Official transfers	0.6	2.2	2.3	1.8	2.2
Medium- and long-term loans					
Official	0.8	4.6	4.7	5.5	3.6
Private	0.9	11.1	18.8	11.6	28.9

Note: Calculations are based on a sample of ninety developing countries.

a. Estimated.

b. Current account does not equal net exports plus net factor income due to omission of private transfers. Financing does not equal current account because of omission of direct foreign investment, other capital, and changes in reserves.

Source: World Bank (1984b:30).

Table 8-5. *Debt Indicators for Developing Countries, 1970–83*
(percent)

Indicators	1970	1974	1975	1976	1977	1978	1979	1980	1981	1982	1983[a]
Ratio of debt to GNP	13.3	14.0	15.4	16.6	18.1	19.3	19.5	19.2	21.9	24.9	26.7
Ratio of debt to exports	99.4	63.7	76.4	79.6	84.7	92.9	83.7	76.1	90.8	108.7	121.4
Debt service ratio[b]	13.5	9.5	11.1	10.9	12.1	15.4	15.0	13.6	16.6	19.9	20.7
Ratio of interest service to GNP	0.5	0.7	0.8	0.8	0.9	1.0	1.3	1.5	1.9	2.2	2.2
Total debt outstanding and disbursed (billions of dollars)	68.4	141.0	168.6	203.8	249.8	311.7	368.8	424.8	482.6	538.0	595.8
Official	33.5	61.2	71.6	83.5	99.8	120.1	136.0	157.5	172.3	190.9	208.5
Private	34.9	79.8	96.9	120.3	150.0	191.6	232.8	267.3	310.3	347.1	387.3

Note: Calculations are based on a sample of ninety developing countries.
a. Estimated
b. Ratio of interest payments plus amortization to exports.
Source: World Bank (1984b:31).

chapter. Concern about creditworthiness is related both to the *likelihood* that service of debt from income will become necessary and to the *cost* of debt service. That cost depends on the ratio of debt to wealth (in the case of a country the present value of future national income), on the real rate of interest, on the ease with which the necessary adjustments to expenditures in relation to output can be made, and—in the case of external debt—on the cost of making external transfers. The situation was deteriorating in almost all these respects in the case of many developing countries. Table 8-5 shows, between 1979 and 1982, that ratios of debt to GNP had risen from 19.5 percent to 24.9 percent, that ratios of debt to exports had risen from 84 percent to 109 percent, and that ratios of debt service to exports had risen from 15 percent to 20 percent. In effect, without some adjustment, debt was on an explosive path, and sooner or later lenders were bound to want to see the growth contained.

If any single event can be isolated as the turning point in the attitude of the lenders, it probably occurred in August 1982 when Mexico found itself unable to service its debt. Because the debt structure was characterized by short maturities, high nominal interest rates, and a high nominal rate of required refinance and still higher real rate, Mexico's difficulties quickly spread elsewhere (see chapter 6 in this book). Because of the number of lenders involved, the immediate resolution of these difficulties also involved intense activity by the monetary authorities of the industrial countries and a degree of involuntary lending, the latter representing a far from stable solution.

There is, inevitably, widespread disagreement about the source of the resulting difficulties over international indebtedness, about the appropriate methods for resolving them, and about the implications of failure both for developing countries and for the international financial system. It is impossible to resolve these disagreements in the present discussion. In this section, however, we shall say something about how the problem emerged; our final part will focus on measures needed to resolve the debt crisis.

In considering how the problem emerged, we may ask whether developing countries have contracted too much debt. It should be remembered that even the larger debtors have ratios of debt to GNP and to exports that are significantly lower than those of many countries during the pre-1914 era (Lal 1983). If those debt ratios were perfectly acceptable then, there is no reason why they should be intrinsically unacceptable now.

One possibility is that debt is excessive in view of the policies pursued by the debtors. It is true that the overall efficiency with which the borrowed resources were used is at least questionable in some important cases. There are two related issues, both of which are suggested by the behavior of governments: the policy environment within which private and public investments were made and also the extent to which the borrowing served to cover public budget deficits, which were themselves not incurred to finance efficient public investment. In a number of countries, sizable public sector deficits were financed by borrowing from abroad, which in turn sustained overvalued real rates of exchange and was associated with substantial microeconomic distortions. In particular, the overvaluation of real rates of exchange was associated with trade policies that were biased toward import substitution via import quotas and extremely high tariffs. Such policies significantly impaired microeconomic efficiency. One particular problem led simultaneously to budgetary difficulties and microeconomic inefficiencies, namely the poor performance, in a number of countries, of public sector enterprises. In Brazil, Mexico, and Turkey, for example, such enterprises were a significant component of overall budgetary and debt problems. In Mexico, indeed, public enterprise deficits in 1982 were on the order of 10 percent of GNP (see chapter 6 in this book).

Too much should not be made of these policy problems. In many debtor countries, rates of growth were quite high, certainly well above real rates of interest. The long-run solvency criterion that the marginal return on investment exceeds the real interest rate was probably satisfied—at least until recently. This long-run solvency criterion is, however, neither a necessary nor a sufficient condition for creditworthiness. It is not necessary as long as there is domestic saving, the returns on which can be transferred abroad. It is not sufficient if the debtor himself cannot extract the income needed to service the debt. In the latter respect it may be reasonable to say that too much debt was contracted, because essentially *short-term* changes in the global allocation of financial claims and liabilities became internalized in many of the borrowing countries as *long-term* expectations. Moreover, these expectations were internalized in the form of political commitments to increased consumption and investment that, in the first case, could not easily be reversed and, in the second case, did not generate income directly for the government that could be used to service the debt.

Furthermore, the level of debt that is appropriate if real interest rates are zero or negative will obviously be excessive if real interest rates rise to 7 percent. There is another sense, however, in which debt may have been excessive, namely in the context of the particular nature of the debtors, the creditors, and the forms of indebtedness. The problem created by the nature of the debtors is that they were for the most part sovereigns. Sovereign lending is lending in the absence of legal enforcement of property rights. It is secure if there are lenders who will cover the service obligations. The willingness of sovereign debtors themselves to pay debt service, if required, may always be questioned. For that reason even if they are, in fact, willing, lenders may easily take fright and may thus create an immediate liquidity crisis.

There is also a problem associated with the fact that, in the postwar period, banks were the principal lenders. In contrast, in the nineteenth and early twentieth centuries, when most sovereign lending was in the form of bonds, banks were intermediaries between sovereign borrowers and the lending public at large. Banks are guaranteed in various ways because of their role in creating money. A major reason for the concern about the present situation is fear about the monetary consequences of bank insolvencies. Moreover, because banks are very highly leveraged, it is possible for small proportionate reductions in the value of their asset portfolio to render them technically insolvent. For this reason the obvious step of creating a market in the debt instruments is seen by many observers as an exercise fraught with hazards.

Finally, we must also take into account the fragility of the present financial structure and the consequent liquidity problems. In an inflationary period a large portion of the supposed interest burden does, in fact, represent real repayment. In addition, the maturity of much of the present debt is quite short (especially in relation to its use in long-term investment). Consequently, the rate at which debt must be repaid in real terms is very high, as much as a quarter every year for some borrowers. It is obvious that debtors who are investing in long-term assets neither will (nor can nor should) repay at this rate. The stability of the financial arrangements depends, therefore, on an equally high rate of refinance. If such refinance is not made available, a rescheduling crisis is inevitable. In effect, any such crisis is, therefore, largely one of mutual confidence. In the short term, credit hangs by its own bootstraps. It can come as little surprise that a sudden and unexpected change in the economic environment—disinflation, recession, and high real rates of interest—has triggered both a loss of confidence and, in the context of a fragile financial structure, a series of rescheduling crises.

In sum, there are senses in which debt was excessive, but the most important causes of the problem are a largely unexpected concatenation of circumstances as well as unsustainable domestic expenditure policies in many developing countries (as mentioned earlier). Few observers could have foreseen that developing countries would be competing with the treasuries of the United States, France, and other industrial countries for a limited supply of savings in the context of a severe recession and appreciated dollar exchange rate. It is possible that this situation resulted from serious errors or from the moral hazards of the insurance provided to banks but more likely that it was produced by the arrival of events judged to be of low probability (chapter 3 in this book).

Equally, however, in many of the crisis countries—Argentina, Mexico, and Turkey, for example—domestic expenditure policies were unsustainable. They would have required retrenchment even if the external environment had not deteriorated. In contrast, other borrowers, such as Indonesia, the Republic of Korea, and Peru, followed domestic policies that were less bad and either did not or would not have become crisis debtors if the unlikely deterioration in the world economy had not occurred.

It is customary to focus on the external adjustment, because it is evident that adjustment to deteriorating terms of trade, high real rates of interest, and a decline in opportunities to borrow must involve a reduction in the external resource gap in real terms. If this reduction is to be achieved, however, there must first be an internal adjustment—that is, a reduction in real expenditures in relation to real output.

In the case of most developing countries, these internal adjustments had to start with the public sector. When countries were attempting to maintain real expenditures in the face of a decline in the real value of national income, they obviously had to borrow. The principal borrower was the public sector. (Even where it was not the only borrower, the importance of government as the third party in any contract, but especially one involving a commitment to make service payments in foreign exchange, led lenders to seek government guarantees.) The internal counterpart of external borrowing and the accumulation of external debt was a rise in public sector deficits. By 1982 in a number of developing countries public sector deficits had reached 10 percent, or in certain cases even as much as 15 percent, of GNP. Moreover, in the context of undeveloped domestic capital markets, such deficits could be financed even in the short term only by inflation or by borrowing abroad (see Sjaastad 1983 and chapter 6 in this book).

The foreign indebtedness of concern is largely that of the public sector. It may exceed that of the country as a whole if the private sector holds foreign assets. There is evidence that some developing countries experienced private capital flight. This conclusion can be inferred from the fact that their stock of international debt outstanding exceeds the sum of measured current account deficits. In this case there has probably been an unmeasured capital outflow. The government is, however, unable to use these private resources to meet its own liabilities, and indeed, not only the import and exchange controls but also the increased taxation frequently employed to deal with the balance of payments make it less likely that the private outflow will be reversed.

In 1982 the decline in lending to developing countries was very marked: total private loans fell from about $56 billion in 1981 to about $29 billion in 1982, with most of the drop occurring in the second half of the year. In the first quarter of 1983, private lending was only $3.3 billion and consisted mostly of involuntary lending under the auspices of the International Monetary Fund (IMF) rescheduling agreements. Thus the increase in medium- and long-term private lending shown in table 8-5 for 1983 or 1982 is almost entirely due to the rescheduling of existing short-term debt.

The required internal adjustments to this sharp decline in lending have taken two forms: an overt attempt to reduce the size of the public sector deficit and a de facto increase in taxation through a rise in the inflation tax (see chapter 6 in this book). Indeed, the acceleration in inflation that has occurred in a number of the principal debtor countries is not an accident. It is one important way of financing existing public sector deficits in the context of the decline in foreign lending. Closing the deficits by increased taxation (whether overt or covert) has often led to a marked squeeze on the private sector, with serious consequences for long-term investment and growth. The same adverse effects on long-term growth must occur when public sector investment is cut, and the public sector generally finds it easier to cut investment than consumption.

Given a large enough reduction in real expenditures, the current account of the balance of payments is bound to improve. Experience shows that there are, however, more and less wasteful ways of achieving this result (see chapter 4 in this book). The present situation is one in which—for instance, in the southern cone countries of Latin America—the more wasteful ways are frequently being employed. The problem is that adjustment requires a reduction of expenditures in relation to output, whereas reductions in output themselves provide no contribution to adjustment and represent pure waste. Unfortunately, however, a rapid compression of expenditures is bound to bring about large reductions in output, and as a result, the attempt to reduce expenditures in relation to output also creates a wasteful recession.

A less costly adjustment involves switching output from the domestic market toward international markets and toward import substitution while switching consumption in the opposite direction. This adjustment usually requires a real exchange rate depreciation. The process of switching will be less costly if it does not occur too swiftly, if a large proportion of domestic output is easily tradable—that is, if domestic and international prices are reasonably closely aligned—and if it is easy to expand exports rather than necessary to compress imports. Unfortunately, many of the principal indebted countries found themselves in difficulties just because these conditions did not exist: exchange rates had become seriously overvalued; economies were highly protected, often by import controls whose effect was to make the protected goods effectively non-tradable; and export sectors were relatively undeveloped and in addition faced growing external restraints. These very conditions and the implied economic waste, combined with the large current account deficits, had made lenders nervous in the first place.

A large number of developing countries have made sharp reductions in real expenditures since 1982. There have also been substantial improvements in external accounts. For oil-importing developing countries, the current account deficit (excluding official transfers) fell from $82 billion in 1981 to $66 billion in 1982, with expected levels of $46 billion in 1983 and $49 billion in 1984 (table 8-4). For oil-exporting developing countries, the deficit fell from $32 billion in 1982 to expected levels of $10 billion in 1983 and 1984. Indeed, the combined deficit in 1983 was only a little larger than the interest due in that year.

These improvements in the current account appear to have been largely the result of the compression of imports in relation to output and the recession-induced reductions in demand for imports. Export promotion has not been an important part of the immediate adjustment process, which has, therefore, brought about serious domestic recession and associated waste. Thus in the major debt crisis countries, for instance, imports were compressed in real terms by about half in Argentina between 1981–82, by about 40 percent in Mexico between 1981 and 1982, by 30 percent in Venezuela between 1982 and 1983, and progressively by about 33 percent between 1980 and 1983 in Brazil. In contrast the real value of exports declined in Argentina and Venezuela during this period and was stagnant in Brazil. Furthermore, the import restrictions employed in many indebted countries to curb imports threaten to cause a long-term deterioration in the efficiency of trade regimes and so further waste in future. On the other hand, a number of indebted countries—Korea and Turkey, for example—followed more appropriate adjustment policies and succeeded in expanding both their real imports and their exports during the 1980s.

One of the most important consequences of import reductions by developing countries is their recessionary impact on the world economy as a whole. Developing countries are more important markets for the European Community, the United States, or Japan individually than either of the other two. They are also of great importance to one another. The problem is particularly serious in Latin America, where a long history of import substitution and schemes for regional trade integration have led countries to engage in significant trade with one another—especially in manufactures. For Brazil, for example, the reductions in imports by the rest of Latin America and also by other developing countries have seriously impaired export opportunities. In consequence, the required external adjustments are more difficult and the corresponding internal adjustments more painful.

Prospects and Policies for Sustained Recovery

In the light of the poor performance of the industrial countries over a long period and the consequent deterioration in the world economy, from which developing countries have finally been unable to escape, the questions posed at the beginning of this chapter are not academic. The extent to which the underlying problems have been resolved is uncertain. In consequence, so is the durability of the world economic recovery.

The discussion below begins with a consideration of the constraints on recovery, paying particular attention to savings and public finance, protection, and debt. On all but the last topic, the focus is on industrial countries. The problems and opportunities faced by developing countries in a volatile external environment are considered next. Finally, priorities for policy change in developed and developing countries are considered.

The conditions for sustained recovery and high growth in the world economy are three:

- Rapid growth of underlying opportunities for increases in the productivity with which resources may be used
- The availability of finance to exploit the opportunities for long-term growth
- The capacity to exploit the opportunities efficiently, which entails flexible working of economies at the microeconomic level, a tight curb, with possibly even a rolling back of protectionism, and monetary stability.

In all these long-term aspects the prospects are far from encouraging.

In part 1 of this chapter we briefly considered some of the factors suggesting the conclusion that the underlying opportunities for growth have probably deteriorated in the industrial countries, especially Western Europe and Japan, since the 1950s and 1960s. For the completion of the "catch up" phase of growth and of trade liberalization among industrial countries we might add the declining opportunity to transfer labor from less to more productive activities—especially from agriculture to manufacturing. The increasing importance of the service sector, in which measured productivity growth is relatively low, may itself act as a constraint on future rates of growth. On the other hand, some favorable factors should help in enlarging growth opportunities: the increase in the labor force with the maturation of the baby boom generation and the revolution in information technology and other scientific advances associated with the microchip and biotechnology.

Another aspect of underlying opportunities is the availability of natural resources, especially oil. The marginal cost of supplying energy is expected to rise, and it is an open question whether technical ingenuity will continue to offset this trend. Thus far the reduction in the demand for energy—especially oil—per unit of GDP in industrial countries has been remarkable. Concern has been expressed, however, that if energy supply proves to be a problem, the brake will again be applied with violent and disruptive jerks.

One important question relates to the underlying causes of the productivity slowdown in the industrial countries. Does it reflect cyclical factors, changes in relative prices of inputs, remedial defects in economies and policy, or a more fundamental deterioration in the rate of invention and innovation? Unfortunately, the literature on this topic is both vast and inconclusive (Giersch and Wolter 1983; Lindbeck 1983; Matthews 1982). Certainly there appears to be no indication that technical progress itself is declining. In certain areas—telecommunications, computing, electronics, biotechnology—the reverse appears to be the case.

There are offsets to the declining opportunities for growth in industrial countries. Among them is the potential dynamism of the developing countries, which still need to catch up. In consequence, the growth of trade between developed and developing countries—especially within manufactures—is an important opportunity for the world economy. If it were allowed to proceed, this form of international economic integration could perhaps boost growth as much as did the integration of industrial economies—especially in Europe—after World War II. There is also the opportunity to put presently unemployed individuls back to work in the industrial countries, which is not dissimilar to labor's earlier opportunity to shift from agriculture to manufacturing industry.

Although there may be doubts about the potential of the industrial countries, there are none about the potential of the developing countries. Their capacity for growth is revealed by the gap between output per caput in industrial and developing countries (subject to whatever constraint the availability of natural resources may impose). As the frontier of knowledge advances, the gap between the richest and poorest economies increases, and so does the potential growth rate of the latter. Partly for this reason, each successive wave of latecomers to successful development has grown more rapidly than the last.

On balance, there is some reason to believe that industrial countries will encounter significant difficulties in returning to the dynamism of the 1950s and 1960s. At the same time, there is no reason to doubt their ability to achieve a rate of growth considerably higher than that attained in the last decade. There is similarly no doubt that developing countries have the capacity for fast growth in the right environment. Whether the potential of both industrial and developing countries is achieved depends on policy decisions, to which our discussion now turns.

In looking at the future we must distinguish between immediate and long-run prospects. In either case savings will certainly depend on the rate of growth itself. In other respects there are important differences between the two.

In the short term—the next two to three years—prospects for savings are obscure for two important reasons: first, disinflation has had large real wealth effects. Financial claims and equities have become more valuable, whereas certain classic inflation hedges—such as precious metals and real property—have lost value if we compare their worth today with expectations for them a few years ago. Furthermore, real interest rates are generally highly positive. The effects of such changes on spending and saving plans are difficult to predict. The second issue is: what will happen to public sector deficits with recovery? The effect of inflation itself in raising taxation via a progressive tax system has generally been lost because of the indexation of tax thresholds and reduced rates of inflation. Moreover, there are large structural deficits in two important industrial countries, Japan and the United States. Although Japan's deficit can be covered by domestic saving, it will still affect global savings capacity. Because the OPEC surplus has disappeared and the United States is running a large budget deficit, the immediate prospect is that growth will restore global savings rates but probably not to the level of the early 1970s. This is not necessarily a problem, but to the extent that recovery in the context of lower inflation leads to increased demand for money and greater investment, both short- and long-term real rates of interest are likely to remain high in the immediate future.

Turning to the longer term, we can see the savings prospects for the industrial countries in broad perspective as follows: if the dominant reason for saving is to meet the expenses of retirement (whether provided publicly or privately), then growth of income per head and population growth will be the principal determinants of the national savings rate at any point in time. With declining rates of population growth, a growing proportion of the aged in society, and prospects for slower growth in income per head, the savings rate will then tend at best to stagnate and will probably decline (see appendix 1 and chapter 7 in this book). The only offset to this tendency in the long term would be the growing expected duration of retirement, which would tend to raise the savings rate of potential retirees.

More specifically, publicly provided pensions are increasingly important in many industrial countries, and in addition, most such pension schemes are underfunded, that is, they operate on a pay-as-you-go basis. It is theoretically possible for such schemes to have no effect on the household savings rate, the necessary assumption being that each generation regards the welfare of subsequent generations as being of equivalent value to its own. The empirical evidence suggests, however, that the effect of such schemes is to lower household and national savings to some extent (see chapter 7 in this book). It is almost certainly no accident that Japan, with the least developed public provision of pensions, has also had the highest household savings rate among the industrial countries.

Apart from the effect of public transfer programs on private savings, there is also the question of the long-term prospects for public sector deficits in industrial countries. In most countries this amounts to a question about the pressures for expansion of social expenditures, on the one hand, and against paying the taxes to finance it, on the other hand.

Although there do exist serious demographic pressures on expenditures for social goods and income maintenance, they will be at their strongest in the early twenty-first century when the post–World War II baby boom generation retires, leaving the job of paying its pensions to the smaller subsequent cohorts (see appendix 1 in this book). In the next twenty years, the main demographic pressure will be on expenditures for health, because of the rising proportion of the very old (people over seventy-five) in the populations of industrial countries and the high cost of the new technologies being developed to treat them. At the same time demographic pressure on the education system is declining and will continue to do so.

In our consideration of the likelihood of real expenditure increases, the main issue is the political pressure for improvements in benefits, which—as was noted in appendix 1—has been the most important single reason for increased expenditures on social goods and income maintenance. Significant attempts have been made to control this growth in some major industrial countries in the past few years and with a certain degree of success. The proportion of the electorate, however, that directly and immediately benefits from the principal expenditure programs is large enough to exert formidable pressures. Inasmuch as there has also been a reversal in several countries of the earlier trend toward declining shares of defense expenditure in GDP (see appendix 1), the prognosis must be that public expenditures are likely to continue on their long-term trend toward rising shares of GDP.

Meanwhile, there are growing difficulties on the revenue side. Inflation no longer serves the purpose of raising tax rates without legislating the increase. Moreover, in most industrial countries there is now substantial resistance to legislation of higher taxes. At the same time, many tax codes have over time become increasingly replete with legal possibilities for tax avoidance, whereas fiscal authorities are also increasingly concerned with the opportunities for tax evasion that are associated with the "black economy." (Olson 1982 has an interesting discussion of why these loopholes emerge.)

The result is a tendency toward rising deficits that, in the context of capital markets fully awake to inflation, cannot easily be covered by the inflation tax. Governments will find borrowing to finance deficits expensive, and for that reason alone deficits will tend to cumulate as the real interest burden is compounded over time. Although some models suggest that deficits do not matter, and that taxation and borrowing are equivalent in their effects, these are based on assumptions that most observers find highly implausible (see chapter 7 in this book). Under more realistic assumptions, and in the light of long experience as well, growing deficits are ultimately monetized.

Finally, mention should be made of corporate savings in industrial countries. These savings depend largely on the share of profits in GNP. The question is, therefore, whether the share of profits will reverse its historic decline. What will happen will depend on underlying opportunities for substitution between capital and labor, on rates of capital accumulation, and on real wage pressures. Over the long term declines in profit shares are likely to be reversed either as wage pressures ease or as firms shift to more capital-intensive techniques. In the latter case, however, unemployment problems will be exacerbated.

Turning to developing countries we find a tendency toward rising savings rates except in low-income Africa. In some countries the savings performance has been remarkable—in China and India, for example. The Indian savings rate has risen from about 10 percent in 1950 to nearly 20 percent in 1980. Other Asian and Latin American countries, however, have also succeeded in raising their savings rates to this level (see appendix 2 of this book).

There is thus of course the possibility that developing countries will reverse the trends and will catch up with the high savings rates observed in most Latin American and Asian countries. In view of the relative weight of these economies in the world economy, however, the improvement would not be sufficient to offset the decline in industrial countries. Still, the evidence does suggest that, even with high global real interest rates, developing countries should be able to fund substantial investment programs from their own resources. The problem created for developing countries by high real interest rates and tight global credit markets may therefore be largely one of immediate adjustment.

In view of the technical opportunities and adequate incentives for investment and savings, it is crucial that there also be adequate flexibility in economies so that resources can flow in the direction of highest return. In the industrial countries, however, there have been growing pressures toward a broadly defined protectionism, that is, toward an attempt to preserve outmoded forms of economic activity through subsidization, cartelization, and protection at the border.

The rigidities to which these policies have responded antedate the oil shocks. They are not just the consequence of higher unemployment. On the contrary, they made higher unemployment after the oil shocks inevitable. Nevertheless, the tendency toward higher unemployment has increased the drift toward such counterproductive policies. Because of these underlying rigidities and the policy response to them, the political process has replaced the market as a principal determinant of firm survival in one developed country after another.

Probably the most important protectionist policy in practice has been open-ended, firm-specific subsidization. Many of the worst problems of structural overcapacity—in steel, chemicals, motor vehicles, and shipbuilding, for example—have directly resulted from governments' support of investment and their commitments to cover losses (Curzon-Price 1982). It is possible that without government assistance most of the problems of these industries would by now have been solved, since no private firm could have borne the losses.

Although the subsidy problem has not been resolved—it is, for example, a source of continuing difficulty in the European Community and in international trade—there is a natural constraint. As governments find public finance an increasing problem, they are being forced to curb subsidy expenditures. For that reason some of the required adjustments are now being made.

With the tendency to reduce subsidies there is growing pressure to increase protection at the border. In the European Community there is discussion of a "Fortress Europe" strategy that is already increasingly realized in relation to Japan. Exports from Japan to the European Community, or to individual members, of cars, videocassette recorders, color televisions and tubes, numerically controlled machine tools, watches, and several other items, accounting for more than half of Japan's exports to the Community, are under restraint or surveillance.

In the United States, subsidization has not been a significant feature of past policy, and this may be one reason why the return on the rather modest rate of investment in the United States—the lowest among the major industrial countries—has been relatively high. Moreover, the United States generally avoided any increased protection throughout the 1970s. The current problem is largely the effect of the rise in the dollar exchange rate since 1980, combined with the recession. The rise brought about the contraction of traded goods–producing industries and had its greatest effect on industries—such as steel and textiles—that produce goods for which imports are easily substituted and that were already not very profitable. Unfortunately by protecting these industries, countries shift the burden of exchange rate appreciation onto the potentially more competitive industries, on which future prosperity depends.

As far as border measures are concerned, there has been a slow erosion of the General Agreement on Tariffs and Trade (GATT) system via policies of discrimination, especially bilateral export restraints, sometimes called "voluntary." Such policies were adopted in part in order to avoid the alternative of repudiating past agreements to reduce and bind tariffs. In this regard they have been successful, with the paradoxical consequence that, in order to preserve liberalization agreements negotiated under the GATT, the GATT itself has been turned on its head: the tariff—the sole instrument permitted under GATT (with very few exceptions)—is hardly used anymore, and bilateral quantitative restrictions, which violate the fundamental GATT principles of nondiscrimination and transparency of measures, have become prevalent.

The threats created by creeping discriminatory quantitative restrictions are four: first, the market mechanism is impaired by actions that cut the link between domestic and international prices; second, there is an added source of uncertainty in the world economy, with potentially serious effects for long-term, trade-oriented investment and thus for returns on investment in general; third, there is resistance to the accommodation of change, with adverse consequences for the newcomers to world trade—principally the developing countries—and for the ability to exploit the underlying opportunities for greater international competition and specialization; and finally, there is a reduction in the capacity of developing countries to service international debt, because such service depends on trading opportunities. In the 1930s, it may be recalled, protection and deteriorating terms of trade triggered widespread defaults on international lending (see chapter 1).

In many ways resistance to protectionism has been commendable. The latest recession has also seen reduction in subsidization and—equally important—changes in the degree of wage flexibility. The important challenge now is for industrial countries to resist the continuing pressures for protection at the border and to reverse and roll back existing protection.

It should be remembered that, if concern about the future is concentrated on whether the growth momentum of the 1950s and 1960s can be regained, the question is *not* whether protectionism grows but whether liberalization slows. In the earlier period exceptional opportunities were created by the general trade liberalization. Although opportunities for rapid growth of trade still exist—especially between developed and developing countries—the best that may reasonably be expected now is no rapid growth of protection. In that case, trade is unlikely to be the source of exceptional opportunity that it was in the 1950s and 1960s.

As has been remarked in *World Development Reports*, there is an association between developing country economic performance and outward-looking, less inefficient trade regimes. This lesson has been confirmed more recently by experience with the accumulation of debt. Developing countries have an interest, therefore, in improving their own policies while also encouraging other countries, whether developing or industrial, to liberalize their policies. The ability of developing countries—in concert with industrial countries—to turn their strong interest in maintaining an open multilateral trading system into effective policy will prove to be one of the principal determinants of the future performance of the world economy.

The ability to preserve monetary stability—low and predictable inflation—is an important precondition for regained flexibility and enhanced efficiency. Its absence is also directly related to the possibility that the divergent oscillations discussed in part 1 of this chapter will continue in the future.

There is a heated debate about the usefulness of discretionary macroeconomic stabilization policy (see chapter 2 in this book for a summary). The efficacy of increases in nominal demand in bringing about increases in real output undoubtedly declined during the past fifteen years. In the United Kingdom, for example, nominal expenditures rose by 340 percent in the 1970s, but real output by only 20 percent. The fundamental reason is also not in doubt. There has been a decline—and ultimately virtual disappearance—of money illusion, that is, of the failure to distinguish between nominal and real changes during inflation. In consequence, economies much more closely follow the classical paradigm, in which monetary policy affects inflation and real variables determine real performance.

In this context, stop-go cycles tend to be sharper, because as soon as it is widely believed that governments are embarked on an inflationary course, nominal wages rise, and bond prices and exchange rates fall. The result, especially under floating exchange rates, is that inflation rises more quickly than anticipated, and the authorities in turn are forced to choke off the expansion sooner than would have been necessary with less hypersensitive markets.

One precondition of avoiding further stop-go cycles is therefore also to avoid premature monetary expansion. Such an expansion, however, may result from the accumulation of large public deficits. Inflationary expectations are still embedded, and inflation itself is far from dead. In the major developed countries, the "core" rate of inflation, the rate of rise of the GDP deflator, is running between 1 percent a year in Japan and 9 percent a year in France, with that in the United States at about 4.5 percent. Long-term bond rates continue to show large inflation premiums. There is a fear that deficits in public sectors will be monetized, and there is a corresponding skepticism about the willingness of governments to control inflation.

Another precondition for control of inflation is microeconomic flexibility. After major changes in relative prices of inputs, combined with a history of policies to expand the capital stock in sectors facing chronic excess supply, a part of what is considered to be the capital stock is probably unusable. Meanwhile, it is also probable that the industries for which there is likely to be increased future demand have invested inadequately and in some countries will also face serious shortages of skilled labor. In this context there is the possibility that inflationary bottlenecks would soon emerge in the course of expansion. If this possibility is to be avoided, it will be important for every incentive to be given to shifting scarce resources into these industries. The avoidance of protection and subsidization is thus also directly related to the avoidance of inflationary stop-go cycles. Similarly greater real wage flexibility would reduce the incentive to use monetary expansion as a short-run—and ultimately unsuccessful—instrument to lower unemployment.

Whatever the cause of the debt crisis, the issue now is what to do about it. One element of an immediate resolution is to avoid self-fulfilling panics by controlling the free rider problem involved in coordinating many lenders (Sachs 1984; chapter 3 in this book). There are a number of solutions. That chosen has been general burden sharing among all creditors in rescheduling. Although it is workable in the short run, this solution may not be stable in the longer term, because it involves a certain amount of coercion, to the extent that the fundamental situation does not change. Moreover, there remains the problem of resuming *net* financial transfers to developing countries once they have adopted appropriate domestic policies.

How, then, must the fundamental situation change? Briefly, if the debt is to be held willingly, and if there is to be hope of further lending in the not too distant future, the debtors must show that they are at least prepared to pay interest from their own income. They must do so not only to anchor the value of debt in the willingness to service it but also—in the present context of high real interest rates and low growth in indebted countries—to avoid the prospect of explosive growth of capitalized interest in relation to GDP in debtor countries.

The need to service debt creates a conflict, because debtors are unlikely to be happy with a situation in which they have to run trade surpluses for a number of years. In view of the present budgetary situation in industrial countries and the state of confidence, however, trade surpluses for debtors will probably be necessary as long as real interest rates remain high. It is not obvious that *net* borrowing would be economical at real interest rates of 7 percent to 8 percent. Under what circumstances will developing countries be willing to service debt in this way? The answer—that their willingness will depend on the costs of servicing debt—has virtually nothing to do with the notion of solvency, because countries are never insolvent (in the sense of having a present value of GNP less than the value of their external debt). This cost, moreover, will differ, depending upon whether the current situation is expected to continue, or whether real interest rates are expected to fall, and whether through appropriate domestic policies the debt service ratios of the debtor countries are restored.

The servicing problem of the debtor countries can be analyzed, conceptually, in two parts. The debt-carrying entities must produce a surplus in their current operations equal to the amount of debt service (less any new credit obtained). This first stage may be called the domestic currency equivalent of debt service charges. To service foreign debts, however, domestic resources must be translated into foreign exchange for remittance to the creditors. This second stage may be called the transfer problem.

The public sectors of the debtor countries, accounting for up to two-thirds or more of their respective GNPs, are in deficit everywhere. Much emphasis has, therefore, necessarily been placed in stabilization programs on reducing budget deficits. The private sector could possibly produce a surplus that more than offsets the public sector deficit, but very strong pressure on expenditures by the private sector would then be required, and much of this pressure would inevitably fall on investment and, consequently, on future growth.

Theoretically, inasmuch as the debtor countries account for only a small fraction of world trade, and in view of a competitive exchange rate, the closing of internal deficits should be translated smoothly into an improvement in the current account balance, without any loss of employment or, at any rate, with only relatively brief "transitional" unemploy-

ment. A shift of $60 billion in developing country trade balances is
equivalent to only 3 percent of world exports. In that sense the transfer
problem is secondary. As it is, however, a proportion (its size depends on
the country) of the exports of debtor countries faces actual or potential
restrictions and other obstacles in foreign markets, these usually being
concentrated against the exports of industries in which the debtor countries have the greatest comparative advantage, for instance Brazilian
steel. It takes great pressure, and almost certainly implies more unemployment in the exporting countries, to "push out" exports against such
resistance in foreign countries. Equally important, however, the domestic system of incentives is biased against exports in most developing
countries, which makes it more difficult for them to exploit the opportunities for exports that do exist.

Partly because of the difficulty in expanding exports and partly because
of this domestic policy bias against exports, imports are being cut instead.
Many of the imports of developing countries are intermediate or investment goods, however; that is, they are essential inputs into current or
future production. Hence as a result of the need simply to *adjust* expenditures *in relation to* output, there is also a large *loss* of both present and
future output. The loss of output would then make necessary a still
sharper reduction in expenditures than would otherwise have been necessary. Moreover, reducing imports by reducing domestic expenditure by
closing the operating deficits of the indebted countries is different from
cutting imports by direct restrictions. The latter may not produce the
needed external surplus because the resulting rise in protection introduces a further bias against exports. Most of the crisis debtors have
unfortunately followed this second method of reducing imports (see
chapter 6 in this book).

The essential point is that, if the world economy were again to grow
rapidly and in a sustained way, the problems facing the debtor countries
would be substantially eased. First, prices and volumes of export commodities would rise, which would be directly beneficial for both their
national income and their public revenue. Second, if faster growth in the
world economy was accompanied by diminishing protectionism (as it
would probably have to be to maintain the increased rate of growth),
improved access to markets would give their exports a more permanent
boost, greatly increasing the likelihood that the debtor countries would
be able to adjust through expansion of exports. This boost would increase
the confidence of their creditors and would lead to increased commercial
lending.

In sum, in many cases it is necessary to stabilize the present situation by
rescheduling, but this is not a long-term solution. On the debtor side it is

necessary for the public sectors to continue to service the debt. On the creditor side it is essential to accommodate the increased imports that will follow from efficient export expansion by debtor countries. The latter accommodation would be easier in the context of stable growth in the world economy. Trade liberalization is, therefore, a condition for successful resolution of the problem. Also necessary is control over the budget deficits of industrial countries that are making *net* capital outflows from some developing countries both necessary and very expensive at the same time.

Turning from the policy issues to prognosis, we must recognize that there are elements of instability in the present situation. Present financial weaknesses could have two distinct effects. The first, though extremely unlikely, would be a disaster in which repudiation triggers banking collapses and a dramatic shrinkage of both global credit and the supply of money. Alternatively, investors might be unwilling to provide funds for some of the most efficient investments, especially in developing countries. In this way even if there were no financial collapse there could be a persistent drag on long-term economic performance.

The availability of resources and the efficiency with which they are utilized will remain the major determinants of developing country performance. Many developing countries apart from sub-Saharan Africa have succeeded in raising their domestic savings to maintain a sufficient growth momentum. If we assume that potential returns to investment remain high, however, and that the accompanying income increases are necessary to redress the poverty of their populations, inflows of foreign capital are still required to supplement domestic savings. To the extent that the current debt crisis has involved a capital outflow from some of the crisis debtors, it is important that the debt crisis be resolved so that normal flows to the debtors can be resumed. As we emphasized in the last section, more appropriate domestic policies in these debtor countries are necessary for such resolution, and we shall discuss these policies shortly.

The problem of resource availability is particularly acute for low-income Africa, in view of the decline in domestic savings rates *and* in capital inflows there. The restoration of the domestic savings rates once again requires domestic policy reforms in these countries. Even if the savings rates were to recover to their 1970 level, however, Africa's need for capital inflows to supplement domestic savings would still remain and would be greater than for most other areas of the developing world. Moreover, to the extent that one of the essential preconditions for improving the absorptive capacity for investment is the provision of physical and social infrastructure, a large part of investment will have to go into projects that have relatively long gestation lags, whose outputs are not tradable and are often not even marketable (see chapter 7 in this book). Hence commercial private financing of such investments is unrealistic. Much of the infrastructure needs to be provided by the public sector, and its financing poses a serious fiscal problem in most of sub-Saharan Africa. Although more can be done to raise domestic resources through more efficient tax systems in these countries, nevertheless it is unlikely that tax revenues will be sufficient to meet the infrastructural needs of much of sub-Saharan Africa in the near future. In this context the recent decline in capital flows to the region, particularly concessional flows, is very lamentable.

Concessional flows are also required in sub-Saharan Africa on a sustained basis to enable domestic policy reforms that are needed and are to some extent being instituted to have their beneficial effects on the structure of these economies—thus on output, on the budget, and on the balance of payments—over a number of years. Given their limited ability to service commercial debt, which is in part due to their past failure to change their domestic economic and, particularly export, structures, much of the capital flow will have to be on concessional terms. It is vital, therefore, if the dismal prospects of this region are to be reversed, for official flows to expand on a sustained basis rather than diminish in real terms, as they have in the past few years.

In both sub-Saharan Africa and the crisis debtor countries, the major problems as well as opportunities are related to the inefficiences that policy-induced distortions in the working of the price mechanism have caused for the efficient utilization of available resources. The World Bank's report, *Accelerated Development in Sub-Saharan Africa* (1981), characterized the crisis in the region as a production crisis caused by the widespread adoption of structures of prices and incomes that provided inappropriate production incentives. In particular, the inefficient incentives to agricultural production, the creation of costly and inefficient agricultural marketing systems for both inputs and outputs, and the maintenance of overvalued effective exchange rates were identified as major policy-induced distortions in these economies. Domestic policy reform, therefore, has a high payoff for these countries, as it will allow significant increases in production even with the overall constraints that these countries may face in terms of the availability of resources and technology and the existing levels of skill of their peoples.

Although a move toward more efficient pricing policies in agriculture and foreign trade is, as we have seen, essential for Africa, progress in this direction has been insufficient. Despite the need to keep effective exchange rates at internationally competitive levels, which in view of the balance-of-payments problems requires effective depreciation, most

African countries have failed to devalue their effective exchange rates and have sought to close their trade deficits by cuts in imports. This tactic not only worsens the bias against exports indirectly but also leads to a much larger cut in domestic output than would a more efficient adjustment to external shocks (see chapter 5 in this book).

The same conclusion applies to the insufficient changes in pricing policies, particularly those in agriculture. Although nominal producer prices have been increased in many cases, even when they have been larger than the increase in input prices they have been lower in real terms (that is, deflated by the cost of living of the farmers) in 1982 than in 1980 in Kenya, Madagascar, Tanzania, and Togo. In some other countries— Burundi, Ivory Coast, Liberia, Mali, Malawi, Niger, Nigeria, and Upper Volta—although the prices of a few agricultural commodities have been raised, those for many others have fallen in real terms.

The continuing problem of fiscal deficits in sub-Saharan Africa requires efforts to boost domestic revenue, greater efficiency in the allocation of the available budgetary resources, and greater attention to the proper evaluation and programming of public expenditures. Such efforts seem to be being made in some countries—for example, Ivory Coast, Liberia, Madagascar, Senegal, Sudan, and Togo. In others, however, such as Burundi, Guinea, Mali, Malawi, and Sierra Leone—public expenditure has increased despite budgetary constraints.

Similar problems of insufficient adjustments in the crucial relative prices in the economy, which determine the efficiency of the economy's use of resources, are also to be found in many other areas of the developing world. Thus even a country such as Korea, which has followed relatively efficient domestic policies for most of the 1970s and has achieved rapid and uninterrupted growth through most of this period, found that its policy-induced shift toward import-substituting heavy industry was inefficient. GNP declined for the first time in 1980, inflation approached 30 percent, and the real appreciation of the exchange rate dampened export growth, leading to a current account deficit of more than 9 percent of GNP. The recent reversal of these policies suggests that these policy-induced distortions will be reduced in the near future.

The performance of developing countries in the turbulent 1970s therefore suggests that the domestic problem of maintaining efficient incentive structures through appropriate pricing remain of great importance. Moreover, the varied experience of developing countries during the past decade also underlies the importance of flexibility in their economies and public budgets. This flexibility is particularly required to reduce the losses of income and output in the face of adverse shocks. Most important of all, it is essential that unsustainable public expenditure commitments based on temporarily favorable conditions not be made, as these are difficult to reverse, and the ensuing public sector deficits exacerbate the problems of domestic inflation and the maintenance of internationally competitive effective exchange rates.

Prospects for both the future growth of world trade and capital flows from the developed to developing countries thus remain uncertain, and the macroeconomic disturbances in the developed world seem likely to lead to adverse developments in developing countries. It might therefore seem advisable for developing countries to delink from the developed world. A relatively closed economy such as India, which moreover chose not to borrow commercially, might in retrospect seem to have weathered the turbulent 1970s decade better than developing countries that were increasingly integrated into a worldwide trading and financial system. This conclusion would be unwarranted for a number of reasons, however.

First, the case for a particular country's maintaining an open trading and payments system is unaffected by the trade restrictions or worsening financial conditions in the rest of the world. Although the gains to a country from such a system will obviously diminish if there is an increase in foreign trade restrictions or instability in external financing, there will still be greater gains than there would be in a situation of autarky. The well-known reason, which needs reiteration, is that international trade in goods and financial securities *extends* the domestic opportunities for converting domestic resources into goods and services required for either investment or consumption. Although external factors might diminish these opportunities or make them more volatile, as long as there *are* these opportunities, it would be foolish to eschew them. Putting it differently, whatever the external environment, an open trading and payments system provides an opportunity for improving the efficient use of available resources. These effects on the domestic supply side of an open economy in inducing efficiency of resource use are the most important developmental benefits of an open trade and payments system. In contrast, many of the arguments that are used to support the case for delinking by developing countries (see Lewis 1980) from a volatile and increasingly protectionist developed world are more concerned with demand factors. This engine-of-growth view of an open trading system's effects on developing countries' prospects is questionable both historically (in the nineteenth century) and for the postwar period (Kravis 1970; Lal 1983; and Riedel 1984).

Second, stability of domestic incomes achieved by delinking from the world economy can lead to lower average income than there would be if the world economy roller coaster were ridden efficiently. Thus India's growth rate, though relatively stable (its fluctuations being tied much more to the effects of domestic weather on agricultural output than to fluctuations in the external environment), has been low compared with that of other developing countries, such as Brazil, Korea, and Mexico, which have maintained relatively more open economies. If the price of the seemingly greater stability of the Indian economy in the 1970s through its promotion of autarky has been levels of income and employment growth well below those that were feasible as long as it maintained an open trading and payments system, its example cannot be recommended for emulation.

Third, although some of the instability experienced by the developing countries that chose fuller integration into the world economy was unavoidable, in many cases inappropriate domestic policies concerning exchange rates, public expenditures, and domestic pricing policy accentuated the short-run domestic costs of coping with the volatile external environment. As reform of these policies would be required even if these countries were to delink themselves in order to attain the then lower feasible growth rate of output, the policy reforms recommended in the later sections of this part, and in *World Development Reports*, would still remain essential. If these appropriate domestic policies are in place, then, for the other reasons given above, the exploitation of even diminished and fluctuating opportunities in the global economy would yield higher levels of income and output in the long run than autarky.

To sum up, the domestic policy reforms that are considered necessary when the global environment is relatively stable become doubly important in inducing the flexibility in domestic production structures and expenditure levels that is vital if a country is to thrive in a more volatile world economy. Countries that turn their backs on an increasingly turbulent outside world will not secure levels and rates of growth of income and output any higher than are achievable by an efficient economy integrated into the world trading and payments system.

What policies and actions would increase the efficiency of resource use in the developing countries and would improve export prospects? What policies are required to improve the performance of industrial countries? The major themes of the analysis in the two preceding parts of this chapter as they relate to industrial countries can be summarized as follows. First, the real economy in many developed (and some developing) countries has become more inflexible, in substantial part because of inappropriate public policies. Second, there is increasing doubt about the intellectual framework used to justify past macroeconomic policies in developed countries. This framework implicitly assumed that private agents were myopic in forecasting the effects of nominal aggregate demand boosts that fueled inflation on real variables of concern to these agents, such as real wages and real interest rates. It seems likely that this form of money illusion in developed country labor markets disappeared in the late 1960s and in the capital markets in the 1970s (see chapter 7 in this book). It is unlikely, therefore, that either higher employment or lower interest rates can be brought about on any persistent basis by merely increasing nominal aggregate demand. Finally, the financing of public expenditures is likely to become an increasing problem in developed countries, as in many of them taxation has already been raised close to the limits of the system's tolerance. With the increasing sensitivity of the populace to inflation, it is also unlikely that developed countries will be able to use hidden taxes to generate the required revenues to close the incipient and actual public deficits. In particular, the inflation tax will be less effective and bond financing will be expensive, because bonds will have to be sold at higher nominal interest rates to compensate their holders for the danger that the real value of government debt will be reduced in future through inflation, as happened in the 1970s.

For these reasons and despite the continuing controversies about the proper macroeconomic framework within which public policy choices should be assessed, most industrialized countries will probably have no choice but to follow tight monetary *and* fiscal policies in order to avoid a resurgence of inflation. With the reduced credibility of governments and the diminution of the public's myopia about inflation, there appears to be no reasonable inflation target short of zero that macroeconomic policy can credibly aim to achieve in most industrial countries. As monetary policy seems to be relatively tight, the trend increase in public sector deficits in some industrial countries needs to be reversed. In most cases restraints on increases in the real level of social benefits should be sufficient, with even a modest recovery in economy growth, to reverse the trend toward structural public sector deficits (see appendix 1 in this book). There may also be a need to reconsider the appropriate level and form of funding of various age-related social benefits. Current demographic trends in developed countries imply that the increase in the ratio of the aged to the working population after the turn of the century will make pay-as-you-go schemes unviable. As it would be both morally wrong and politically difficult to renege on entitlements to the aged, on which old people have based their irreversible life cycle consumption decisions, the present is the best time to deal with this emerging problem. As the last two chapters have emphasized, many of the current ills of the global economy are the result of inappropriate policies whose costs were large but emerged only in the long run. Shortsightedness has reduced the credibility of governments, and it would be unfortunate if they continue to provide such hostages to fortune.

Other shortsighted public interventions that need to be reversed in developed countries include creeping protectionism and the indiscriminate subsidization of declining industries. Although these policies might succeed in the temporary maintenance of the real incomes of various sectional groups, they are harmful and not only in the long run. They prevent a country from making the adjustments to its emerging and changing comparative advantage that alone can assure continuing growth in the real incomes of sectional and other groups in the economy. In this sense the oft-cited tradeoff between economic growth and economic security is a mirage. It is important to maintain an open trading system as a means of controlling microeconomic distortions. It is also a way of capturing the potential for increased integration between developed and developing countries.

A trade liberalization initiative that concentrates on the newer and proliferating forms of protectionism in the form of various nontariff barriers is required. It is also essential to initiate the liberalization of trade in agriculture. Just as the liberalization of trade in manufactures provided a once and for all but important boost to productivity growth in the late 1950s and early 1960s, the liberalization of trade in agriculture, combined with the reversal of the recent protectionist measures on industrial products, could provide a much-needed productivity boost in the 1980s.

The liberalization of trade, or at the very least the eschewing of further protection in developed countries, is also vital for solving the debt crisis. A country must be able to pay the interest on existing debt in order to avoid writing off past loans as bad debt. Before the developing countries can effect this external transfer, however, without excessive cost, they must expand their exports rather than just reduce imports. Solving the debt crisis, therefore entails maintaining an open trading system.

At least a part of past commercial borrowing by developing countries was unwise because it sought to finance social overhead investments with long gestation periods through short-term commercial loans. It will therefore be necessary to provide alternative sources of long-term capital for these essential investments. For many low-income countries—particularly in sub-Saharan Africa—the only source of such long-term capital is concessional flows, whereas for many others the viability of various poverty-redressing social expenditures and the funding of adequate social overhead investment also depend upon the level of such flows. The increase in concessional capital flows from industrialized countries is essential for the future growth of low-income countries.

Moreover, there is a case for a further enhancement in the intermediation function of multilateral financial institutions. They can borrow competitively in international capital markets, can tailor their loans (maturity and interest rate structure) more closely to the needs of public sector borrowers in developing countries, and—through their information-gathering and policy advisory role—can exercise indirect influence on the economic policies of the borrowers, which commercial banks alone cannot. There is, therefore, a case to be made for financing the growing demand for social overhead investment in developing countries by a combination of domestic taxes and noncommercial foreign capital inflows. Commercial borrowing is probably best reserved for the financing of private sector investment (particularly that tied to the direct generation of foreign exchange) but—in the future—without any publicly provided guarantees.

Although this might be a reasonable strategy for the future evolution of capital flows from developed to developing countries, there is still the danger to the banking system of a default by one or more large developing country borrowers. Limitations of space prevent us from elaborating on the details and often doubtful merits of the various schemes that have been recently propounded to solve the debt crisis. It should be noted, however, that, for the time being, various forms of involuntary lending under the aegis of rescheduling agreements have contained the immediate liquidity crisis. Nevertheless, any worsening of global prospects in terms of increased protectionism and further rises in dollar interest rates will erode the ability and perhaps even the willingness of sovereign borrowers to service their foreign debt. On the other hand, if with the adoption and maintenance of appropriate monetary, fiscal, and trade policies in industrial countries the conditions for noninflationary growth in the world economy can be reestablished, then the debt crisis may dissolve as rapidly as it arrived.

Given the changed expectations of lenders about the future prospects of major developing country borrowers, voluntary net lending is unlikely to increase markedly in the near future as lenders attempt to reduce the relative share of Third World debt in their portfolios. If world savings and growth can be revived, however, over time lending to a number of semiindustrialized countries is bound to seem attractive once again, for their inherent growth prospects, particularly if they pursue appropriate domestic policies in a well-functioning world economy, remain very bright.

Meanwhile one essential element must underlie the solution of the immediate liquidity crisis. Both the desire to extend credit and the investment it finances are based on expectations of future returns. The immediate source of the liquidity crisis is a change in these expectations such that the present value of the income stream that was expected from the financing is lower. In that sense, a capital loss appears to have been incurred on the past debt. Any orderly resolution of the debt crisis will involve the writing down of the assets side of financial balance sheets unless these more pessimistic expectations reverse themselves.

What must developing countries do individually to make the best of a global environment that remains highly uncertain? The most important characteristics that need to be stressed in their economic and policy frameworks are flexibility and efficiency. *World Development Reports* have emphasized the importance of efficiency and the paramount role played by appropriate pricing policies in ensuring that the most efficient use is made of a country's available resources. Efficiency and appropriate pricing are even more important when rapid economic adjustments in a fast-changing and uncertain environment are called for.

In this context it is also important to remove various distortions that limit the tradability of a country's output. An efficient (that is, low-cost) adjustment to any adverse external shock requires switching of consumption away from traded goods and production toward traded goods. The more easily this switching can be done, the lower will be the transitional costs in terms of lost output and employment. The promotion of outward-looking policies recommended in *World Development Reports*, to generate both foreign exchange and an efficient domestic production structure, is therefore of equally great importance in the uncertain times that lie ahead.

Finally, it is imperative that developing countries introduce some flexibility in their budgets. Many of the crises in semi-industrial countries in the past decade have been due to heightened public sector commitments financed either through external borrowing or through natural resource rents that accrue to the public sector. When these sources of finance dry up or diminish, the necessary retrenchment in public expenditures required to balance the budget becomes politically very difficult, and recourse to the inflation tax, through the monetization of the resulting public sector budget deficit, becomes almost inevitable. Budgetary flexibility and compressibility should therefore be an important element of budgetary practice in developing countries.

One feature common to both developed and developing countries may thus be an emerging and growing fiscal problem. Control of the budget deficits in industrial countries is required to facilitate sustained noninflationary growth in the world economy. To the extent that this control has a favorable impact on dollar interest rates, it will also ease the debt service burden of developing countries. Furthermore, to the extent that the pressures for publicly provided economic security that have generated the emerging structural element in these deficits are also reflected in the demands for increased protection, governments in industrial countries face a general problem of resisting sectional pressures in order to serve the common weal.

Similarly, in developing countries there is continuing pressure to increase public expenditure on social overhead investments as well as to increase various forms of subsidies. Whereas an economic case can be made for most of this expenditure, it is imperative that its financing not create a current or future fiscal problem for the country. The reforms of tax systems and pricing policies and the ending of open-ended expenditure commitments advocated in *World Development Reports* must form an intrinsic part of any attempt to control the public sector budgets in developing countries. If fiscal control is not reestablished globally, actions undertaken in the belief that public action provides the solution to various economic and social problems may render such well-intentioned public action the problem.

References

Bacon, R., and W. Eltis. 1978. *Britain's economic problem: Too few producers*. 2nd ed. London: Macmillan.

Blackhurst, R., and J. Tumlir. 1977. *Trade liberalisation, protectionism, and interdependence*. Studies in international trade no. 5. Geneva: General Agreement on Tariffs and Trade (GATT).

Bruno, M. 1984. Raw materials, profits, and the productivity slowdown. *Quarterly journal of economics* 99:1(February):1–32.

Cline, William R. 1983. *International debt and the strategy of the world economy*. Policy analysis in international economics no. 4. Washington, D.C.: Institute for International Economics.

Curzon-Price, V. 1982. Government intervention as a factor in slower growth in advanced industrial nations. In R. C. O. Matthews, ed. *Slower growth in the Western world*. London: Heinemann.

Eichengreen, B. 1981 *Sterling and the tariff, 1929–32*. Studies in international finance no. 48. Princeton: Princeton University Press.

Feldstein, M. 1983. *Inflation, tax rules, and capital formation*. Chicago: National Bureau of Economic Research.

Fellner, W. 1976. *Towards a reconstruction of macroeconomics: Problems of theory and policy*. Washington, D.C.: American Enterprise Institute.

———. 1979. The credibility effect and rational expectations: Implications of the Gramlich study. *Brookings papers on economic activity* 1:167–78.

———. 1980. The valid core of rationality hypotheses in the theory of expectations. *Journal of money, credit, and banking* 12:4, pt. 2(November):763–87.

———. 1984. Monetary and fisal policy in a disinflationary process: Justified and unjustified misgivings about budget deficits. In *Essays in contemporary economic problems: Disinflation*. Washington, D.C.: American Enterprise Institute.

Friedman, M., and A. J. Schwartz. 1963. *A monetary history of the United States*. Princeton: Princeton University Press.

General Agreement on Tariffs and Trade (GATT). 1982–83. *International Trade 1982/83*. Geneva.

Giersch, H., and F. Wolter. 1983. Towards an explanation of the productivity slowdown: An acceleration-deceleration hypothesis. *Economic journal* 93:369(March):35–55.

Kravis, I. B. 1970. Trade as a handmaiden of growth: Similarities between the nineteenth and twentieth centuries. *Economic journal* 80:320(December):850–72.

Lal, D. 1983. *The poverty of "developmental economics."* Hobart paperback 16. London: Institute of Economic Affairs.

Lewis, W. A. 1980. The slowing down of the engine of growth. *American economic review* 70:4(September):555–64.

Lindbeck, A. 1983. The recent slowdown of productivity growth. *Economic journal* 93:369(March):13–34.

Matthews, R. C. O. 1982. *Slower growth in the Western world*. London: Heinemann.

Olson, M. 1982. *The rise and fall of nations: Economic growth, stagflation, and social rigidities*. New Haven: Yale University Press.

Organisation for Economic Co-operation and Development (OECD). 1983. *Economic outlook*. Paris.

———. 1984. *Economic outlook*. Paris.

Phelps-Brown, H. 1983. *The origins of trade union power*. Oxford: Oxford University Press.

Riedel, J. 1984. Trade as the engine of growth in developing countries revisited. *Economic journal* 94:373 (March):56–73.

Sachs, J. 1979. Wages, profits, and macroeconomic adjustment: A comparative study. *Brookings papers on economic activity* 2:269–319.

———. 1983. Real wages and unemployment in OECD countries. *Brookings papers on economic activity* 1:255–89.

———. 1984. *Theoretical issues in international borrowing*. Princeton studies in international finance no. 54. Princeton: Princeton University Press.

Scott, M. Fg., and R. A. Laslett. 1978. *Can we get back to full employment?* London: Macmillan.

Sjaastad, L. 1983. International debt quagmire: To whom do we owe it? *World economy* 6(September):305–24.

World Bank. 1984a. *Debt and the developing world*. Washington, D.C.

———. 1984b. *World Development Report 1984*. New York: Oxford University Press.

Appendix 1

OECD Deficits, Debt, and Savings Structure and Trends, 1965–81: A Survey of the Evidence

Leonardo Hakim and Christine Wallich

THIS APPENDIX surveys the role of the public sector revenues expenditures, budget deficits, and debt in the context of trends in national savings in order to quantify somewhat the likely crowding out of private investment if current trends in deficits and savings continue. We outline, first, revenue trends, second, trends in public expenditures, third, the resulting trends in budget deficits, and fourth, trends in national savings. The final section looks at the relationships of projected deficits to trends in savings.

Trends in Government Revenues

Trends in central government revenues of the Organisation for Economic Co-operation and Development (OECD) show that the share of income taken by the central government has risen substantially in the past period. Figure A1-1 outlines the trends for individual OECD countries since 1960. Dramatic increases have taken place across the board. Overall, for the OECD countries taken together, the government's current revenues as a percentage of GDP were only 28.3 percent in 1960. Since then, however, this share, which includes social security taxes and contributions, has risen from 31.9 percent in 1970 to 37.2 percent in 1982.

This appendix represents a synthesis and summary of work carried out in the OECD Economics and Statistics, Social, and Monetary and Fiscal Policy divisions. The OECD has been instrumental in carrying out work in the area of social expenditures, monetary and fiscal policy coordination, and implications of government debt. The authors here review and consolidate the information found in some thirty separate documents, drawing together the "pieces of the puzzle" for a broadly based view of the role and implications of the public sector's net expenditure policies in OECD countries. The reference list at the end of this appendix includes the OECD papers which have been synthesized in this overview. The conclusions and interpretations of this work are the authors' own, however, and should not be taken as necessarily representing the views of the OECD secretariat.

Figure A1-1. *Ratio of General Government Expenditure and Revenue to GNP in Selected Countries, 1960 and 1980*

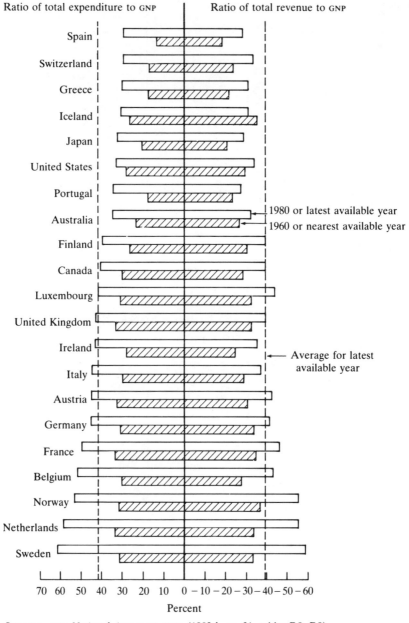

Sources: OECD *National Accounts*; OECD (1982*d*, no. 31, tables R8, R9).

Table A1-1. *The Composition of General Government Revenues as a Percentage of GDP*

Receipts	1965	1970	1971	1972	1973	1974	1975	1976	1977	1978	1979	1980	1981	1982
Direct taxes	11.2	12.1	12.0	12.3	12.5	13.4	12.6	13.0	13.4	13.4	13.6	13.9	14.1	13.8
Indirect taxes	13.0	10.9	10.9	10.7	10.5	10.3	10.1	10.1	10.2	10.0	10.0	10.3	10.6	10.5
Social security contributions	5.6	7.5	7.7	7.9	8.3	8.8	9.3	9.5	9.7	9.7	10.0	10.2	10.5	10.8
Other receipts	1.5	2.5	2.5	2.4	2.5	2.6	2.7	2.8	2.9	3.0	3.0	3.3	3.5	3.8
Current receipts total	29.2	31.9	31.8	32.2	32.7	33.9	33.7	34.5	34.9	34.9	35.7	36.6	37.1	37.2

Note: Totals may not sum because of rounding.
Sources: OECD *National Accounts,* table 9; and Chouraqui and Price (1983).

Table A1-1 outlines the trends in the composition of government current receipts. The role played by direct taxes (personal and corporate income taxes plus social security taxes) increased from 16.8 percent of GDP in 1965 to almost 24.6 percent of GNP in 1982. As a result, the fraction that direct taxes contributed rose from 57 percent of total government current revenues in 1965 to more than 65 percent of government revenues in 1982. Meanwhile the indirect tax burden decreased, from 13.0 percent of GDP in 1965 to 10.5 percent of GDP in 1982. Although the share of government revenues has increased as a portion of GDP, the increase in government revenues has not been sufficient to match the growth in government expenditures. This difficulty, as well as the differential growth rates of the various revenue components away from indirect taxes toward direct taxes, especially personal income taxes and social security charges, has had political repercussions and has made the job of fiscal policy much harder.

The reason for the changing composition was the shrinking buoyancy of indirect taxes, which in many countries grew less rapidly than GDP, and the greater buoyancy of direct taxes. Taxes on households rose faster than other types of direct taxes, implying a decline in direct corporate taxes. Social security taxes grew even more rapidly than other direct taxes. Indirect taxes have shown buoyancy in many countries because of the introduction of energy taxes in the 1970s. Both oil exporters and oil-importing countries have introduced an energy tax or royalties. Energy taxes, for example, are the primary indirect tax in the United Kingdom, contributing 2.1 percent of GDP to the United Kingdom government receipts in 1981. Other countries that have introduced energy taxes include the United States (where their contribution was 1.3 percent of GDP), the Netherlands (3.6 percent), and Norway (4.0 percent; OECD 1983a). It is probably valid to say that, in the absence of these energy taxes, the overall burden of direct taxes would have been higher still.

With the rising tax burden, there is now an increasing reluctance among a number of OECD governments to garner additional revenues through "fiscal drag" (Chouraqui and Price 1983). In some ten of the twenty-one OECD countries, including the United Kingdom, France, and the Netherlands, there is now explicit indexing of the personal income tax. In three others—Belgium, Spain, and Switzerland—indexing exists in a de facto manner, although it is not always applied. In the United States, partial indexing is expected to be introduced in 1985, barring policy changes. This would leave only eight countries (including Japan and Germany) unindexed. These trends suggest that, in general, the prospects for increased responsiveness of tax revenues to GNP are reduced. It has been estimated that the elasticity of revenues to GNP, once

Table A1-2. *Shares of Total General Government Expenditure in GDP/GNP*
(percent)

Country	1960	1965	1970	1971	1972	1973	1974	1975	1976	1977	1978	1979	1980	1981	1982
United States	27.8	28.0	32.2	32.2	31.9	31.2	32.9	35.4	34.4	33.5	33.1	32.8	33.2	33.6	35.5
Japan	18.3	18.6	19.3	20.8	21.8	22.1	24.5	27.3	27.9	29.0	31.1	31.6	32.7	33.6	35.2
Germany	32.0	36.3	37.6	38.9	39.7	40.5	43.4	47.1	46.4	46.5	46.5	46.4	46.9	47.9	48.3
France	34.6	38.4	38.9	38.3	38.3	38.5	39.7	43.5	44.0	44.2	45.2	44.7	46.7	49.4	51.3
United Kingdom	32.6	36.4	39.3	38.4	40.0	41.1	45.2	46.9	46.1	44.1	43.7	43.5	45.4	46.4	46.5
Italy	30.1	34.3	34.2	36.6	38.6	37.8	37.9	43.2	42.2	42.5	46.1	45.5	46.1	51.5	54.0
Canada	28.9	29.1	35.7	36.6	37.2	36.0	37.4	40.8	39.6	40.6	41.0	39.3	40.7	41.7	46.4
Total for major seven countries	28.7	30.0	32.6	33.0	33.1	32.9	34.8	38.0	37.2	36.8	37.3	37.5	37.8	38.9	40.6

Note: Weighted averages calculated from the total GDP and total outlays of general governments for the group of countries, with both aggregates expressed in U.S. dollars at current exchange rates.

Sources: Chouraqui and Price (1983); OECD *National Accounts*; and, for 1981 and 1982, secretariat estimates. The data in this table are measured according to the standard definitions of the OECD–United Nations system of accounts so that they are comparable across countries. "Total general government spending" is defined as current disbursements (including capital consumption) plus gross investment. It is the sum of lines 23, 28, 29, and 30 less line 26 in table 9 of *National Accounts*, vol. 2: *1962–1979*.

full indexation of income taxes takes place, could reduce the tax elasticity to less than one. Coupled with this concern over direct taxes, there is substantial resistance to increasing indirect taxes because of their inflationary impact, especially when inflationary expectations are latent.

In short, there appears to have been a secular change in both the level and composition of government receipts in the 1970s and also in the responsiveness of revenues to GDP growth as a result of indexation provisions on direct taxes and inflationary concerns preventing increases in indirect taxes. As a result, concerns are beginning to be expressed about a possible "tax threshold."[1]

Expenditures and Expenditure Trends

We begin our analysis of trends in general government public expenditure by examining the changes over time in the overall level of public expenditures relative to GNP. We shall then consider the changes that have taken place in the composition of expenditures, disaggregating expenditures into broad categories of public sector outlays. We shall analyze the determinants of each of these expenditure levels and assess the extent to which cyclical factors, such as slow growth and unemployment, have contributed to these levels of expenditure as compared with structural factors, such as the demographic changes (including growth in the nonworking population) and programmatic factors (such as commitments made to growing benefit levels), which have also contributed.

As table A1-2 shows, the level of public expenditures in relation to GDP has risen substantially since the 1960s for most OECD countries, from 28.7 percent of GDP in 1960 to more than 40.6 percent of GDP in 1982. Although this summary statistic obscures the intercountry differences in expenditure *levels*, the *trend* of increase has been common across countries. In Sweden, the share of expenditures has risen from 31 percent of GDP in 1960 to 68 percent in 1980; in Germany the increase has been from 32.0 percent of GDP in 1960 to 48.3 percent of GNP in 1982. In Japan, where the proportion of government expenditure in GDP was lowest, the level has doubled, from 18.3 percent of GDP in 1960 to 35.2 percent in 1982, the same level as in the United States.

In addition to rapid increases in the overall level of public expenditures, the higher level has been accompanied by a change in the composition of expenditures as well. Table A1-3 shows trends in the components of public expenditure since the early 1950s. Defense expenditures have fallen sharply from their high levels of the 1950s and presently compose some 3.3 percent of GDP. Outlays on social goods, here defined as educa-

Table A1-3. *General Government Expenditure*
as a Percentage of GNP
(average, seven major OECD countries)

Expenditure	1954	1973	1980
Total	28.5	32.8	37.7
Defense	9.6	4.0	3.3
General government	4.7	3.5	3.9
Social goods	4.9	9.7	11.1
Education	3.1	5.3	5.4
Health	1.3	3.3	4.3
Housing	0.5	1.1	1.4
Income maintenance	5.6	10.0	12.3
Pensions	2.9	6.2	7.6
Sickness	0.3	0.4	1.1
Family allocations	0.7	0.8	0.6
Unemployment compensation	0.5	0.4	2.6
Other	1.7	2.2	4.0
Economic services	n.a.	6.2	3.7
Capital transactions	n.a.	3.6	1.6
Subsidies	n.a.	1.7	0.9
Other	n.a.	0.9	1.2
Public debt interest	1.6	1.9	2.9

n.a. = not available.

Sources: OECD 1982c; World Bank estimates; 1954 from OECD *National Accounts*, 1950–68, supplemented as follows: 1954 welfare state expenditures for European countries from Dewhurst and Associates (1961), pp. 313 and 336 for education, p. 383 for medical care, pp. 222 and 235 for housing, p. 391 for pensions, p. 393 for sickness and family payments, p. 386 for unemployment benefits, and p. 399 for total transfer payments (including health); Japan 1954 from Emi (1963:173, 179) and Ohkawa and Shinohara (1979:372, 378); United States 1954 from U.S. Department of Commerce (1976:94, 128, 131).

tion, health, and housing, have risen substantially. Expenditures on education rose from 3.1 percent of GDP in 1954 to 5.3 percent and 5.4 percent in 1973 and 1980, respectively. The rapid increase in health expenditures is striking, from 1.3 percent of GDP in 1954 to 3.3 percent in 1973 and to 4.3 percent by 1980. Growth in housing expenditures has also taken place, from 0.5 percent of GDP in 1954 to 1.4 percent in 1980. Total outlays on social goods have risen from 4.9 percent of GDP in 1954 to 9.7 percent in 1973 and 11.1 percent in 1980.

Income maintenance payments, which include pensions, disability benefits, family allowances, and unemployment transfer payments, have also increased. Pension expenditures have tripled and now, at 7.6 percent of GDP, represent the largest expenditure category. Sickness expenditures have also risen. Family allowances, in contrast, have fallen from 0.8

percent of GNP in 1973 to 0.6 percent in 1980. Unemployment expenditures have undergone a striking rise and now amount to 2.6 percent of GNP.

The final expenditure category—public debt interest—has also increased from 1.6 percent of GNP in 1954 to 1.9 percent in 1973 to 2.9 percent in 1980, the latter constituting a 53 percent increase in seven years.

Expenditure elasticities are higher than the revenue elasticities (OECD 1983p); the overall expenditure elasticity is 1.25 for the 1970–80 period. Defense expenditures have grown but only about as rapidly as GNP. (The growth rate may have increased since 1980.) The largest elasticity attaches to "income maintenance programs," and in these, the increase in pension expenditures has been the largest factor. Income maintenance programs have grown almost 40 percent faster than GNP. Next most rapidly growing have been interest expenditures, with an elasticity of 1.37, followed by health expenditures, with an elasticity of 1.3. Education expenditures increased at a faster rate than GNP, some with an elasticity of 1.14.

Government outlays on "social goods" have grown rapidly in almost all OECD countries. Included in this category are expenditures on health, education, sickness, and housing. Table A1-4 shows the proportion of total expenditures in these three areas from 1960 to 1980, for the major OECD countries. In 1960, education outlays absorbed 12.6 percent of total government spending, followed by health (6.3 percent). By 1980, these figures had risen to 15.0 and 13.0, respectively. For each country shown in table A1-4, governments' social goods expenditures also increased as a percentage of GNP in the period 1960–81. For the major countries, the share nearly doubled, from 6.12 percent of GDP in 1960 to 12.1 percent in 1981. Thus one-eighth of all the resources generated in OECD countries are presently being directed toward social goods expenditures. In relation to total public expenditures, outlays on social goods rose from 20.2 percent of total public expenditure in 1960 to just under 30 percent of public expenditure in 1981.

Disaggregating by subperiod, table A1-5 shows the change in overall trends in social goods expenditure since 1960. From 1960 to 1970, public sector social goods expenditure grew at an average rate of 9.9 percent per annum. From 1970 to the present, the rate of growth increased, and it is now about 12.6 percent per annum.

Table A1-6 derived from an OECD study of social expenditures (OECD 1983i), summarizes the changed shares of the subcomponents of transfer and income maintenance expenditure in the years 1960 and 1981 for the seven major OECD countries. If we take the countries together, the

Table A1-4. *Social Goods Expenditure Shares*
in Total Public Outlay
(percentage shares in 1960 and 1981)

Country	Year	Educa-tion	Health	Sick-ness	Total social goods
United States	1960	12.8	4.6	0.8	18.2
	1981	16.4	11.7	0.6	28.7
Japan	1960	23.6	8.0	0.9	32.5
	1981	16.5	15.4	1.1	33.0
Germany	1960	7.8	9.8	3.3	20.9
	1981	10.6	13.9	1.3	25.8
Canada	1960	10.4	8.3	n.a.	18.7
	1981	14.8	14.2	n.a.	29.0
France	1960	n.a.	7.1	3.2	10.3
	1981	n.a.	13.2	2.4	15.6
Italy	1960	12.7	9.4	0.6	22.7
	1981	14.1	13.5	1.9	29.5
United Kingdom	1960	10.5	10.1	1.7	22.3
	1981	13.1	12.0	0.5	25.6
Total	1960	12.6	6.3	7.3	20.2
	1981	15.0	13.0	1.1	29.1

n.a. = not available.
Source: OECD (1983g:6–7).

Table A1-5. *Growth Rates of Social Goods Expenditures*
(percent)

Country	1960–70	1970–80
United States	10.9	13.1
Japan	7.0	19.3
Germany	9.9	11.1
France	12.6	16.9
United Kingdom	10.3	18.6
Italy	13.6	20.7
Canada	13.2	14.7
OECD average[a]	9.9	12.6

a. 1960, 1970, and 1980 weights were used.
Sources: World Bank estimates; OECD *National Accounts*; OECD (1983g).

following picture emerges for transfer expenditure in this period. In 1960, pension expenditure was the largest subcomponent of total expenditure (16.1 percent). Family benefits absorbed 2.1 percent of total expenditure, with unemployment taking the smallest share, 2.0 percent. The ordering

Table A1-6. *Transfer and Income Maintenance Expenditures*
(percentage of total public expenditure)

Country and year	Pension	Unem- ployment	Family	Others	Total
United States					
1960	15.1	2.3	0.8	2.7	20.9
1981	20.5	1.8	1.2	5.9	29.4
Japan					
1960	13.7	1.4	0.0	4.2	19.3
1981	16.5	1.1	5.7	0.6	23.9
Germany					
1960	31.3	1.3	0.7	11.1	44.4
1981	26.4	3.3	2.6	7.9	40.2
Canada					
1960	9.5	5.0	4.6	3.7	22.8
1981	11.1	5.8	1.6	5.3	23.8
France					
1960	17.5	0.4	11.1	0.4	29.4
1981	24.4	3.9	4.4	0.5	33.2
Italy					
1960	16.0	0.6	8.3	12.7	37.6
1981	28.9	1.3	2.6	1.9	34.7
United Kingdom					
1960	12.2	0.8	1.7	4.6	19.3
1981	16.4	3.3	3.3	6.0	29.0
Total					
1960	16.1	2.0	2.1	4.0	44.4
1981	20.7	2.3	2.8	4.4	59.3

Source: OECD (1983g:6–7).

has changed little since then, although the percentage shares of some subcomponents has. The pension share has risen slightly to 20.7 percent of social expenditures, followed by expenditure on family allowances (2.8 percent) and unemployment at 2.3 percent of public expenditure.

If we combine social goods outlays with transfers, the share rose from 44.3 percent (1960) to 60 percent (1981) of total expenditures. These trends are outlined in figure A1-2.

Determinants of Social and Income Maintenance Expenditures

The specific determinants of expenditure levels in each of the subcomponents discussed earlier vary by country. Strategic factors common to all countries, however, together determine expenditure levels. These include demographic factors, levels of eligibility and coverage, demand or

Figure A1-2. *Growth of Public Expenditures in Seven Major OECD Countries, 1960–81*

Percentage of GDP

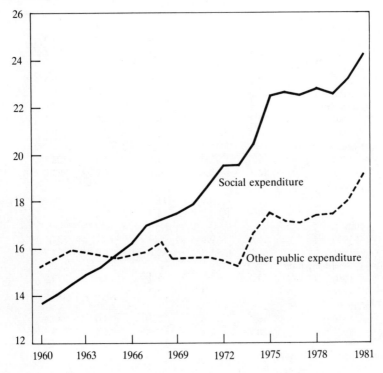

Source: OECD (1983*i*).

takeup of benefits, levels of benefits, and economic conditions. Inflation is an important determinant of expenditures, as are improvements in technology. These elements have been quantified in an OECD study (OECD 1983*g*; see table A1-7). In both periods, the primary contributor to increased social goods expenditures as well as transfers was increased benefit levels. Moreover, real increases in benefit levels were more important than the effects of increases in prices on benefit levels.

In the 1960–75 period, eligibility growth or increases in coverage and demographic change equally contributed just over 40 percent of the increase of total expenditure until 1975 and higher benefit levels contributed 60 percent. In the past six years, 1975–81, demographic factors contributed about 18 percent to increases in social expenditure; eligibility

Table A1-7. *The Determinants of Growth in Social and Transfer Expenditure: Average Annual Growth Rates at Constant Prices*

(four main programs in the seven larger economies)

Program	Percentage of GDP[a]	Total change in real expenditure	Total change in nominal expenditure	Component of real increases				
				Demographic change	Eligibility	Benefit levels	Relative prices	Real increase
			Growth rates, 1960 to 1975					
Social goods								
Education	4.2	6.1	14.7	0.29	1.90	3.83	2.19	1.60
Health	2.7	9.6	17.1	1.03	0.60	7.83	2.19	5.25
Income maintenance								
Pensions	4.5	8.4	14.3	2.23	1.62	4.35	0.00	4.35
Unemployment	0.4	12.0	18.2	5.08	0.00	6.60	0.00	6.60
Other	2.5	7.7	13.5	n.a.	n.a.	n.a.	n.a.	n.a.
Total social and income maintenance expenditure	14.3	8.0	14.6	1.36	1.43	5.03	1.28	3.71

(Table continues on the following page.)

Table A1-7 *(continued)*

Program	Percentage of GDP[a]	Total change in real expenditure	Total change in nominal expenditure	Component of real increases				
				Demographic change	Eligibility	Benefit levels	Relative prices	Real increase
			Growth rates, 1975 to 1981					
Social goods								
Education	5.1	1.8	12.9	−1.74	0.20	3.40	1.28	2.00
Health	5.1	3.1	14.2	0.26	0.00	3.10	1.28	1.80
Income maintenance								
Pensions	7.3	6.6	17.0	1.77	0.78	3.94	0.00	3.94
Unemployment	1.1	6.4	15.7	7.84	−2.30	1.00	0.00	1.00
Other	3.4	3.6	13.6	n.a.	n.a.	n.a.	n.a.	n.a.
Total social and income maintenance expenditure	22.0	4.2	n.a.	0.75	0.22	3.38	0.70	2.65

n.a. = not available.

a. 1960 GDP for the period 1960–75; 1975 GDP for the period 1975–81.

Sources: OECD (1983g:19 and 1983i:35) based on unweighted averages for the seven larger economies: the United States, Japan, Germany, France, the United Kingdom, and Italy. Data come from OECD (1983f) and from the corresponding papers on health, education, old-age pensions, and unemployment insurance. The estimates above should be read as only an approximate breakdown of the main changes in the two periods 1960 to 1975 and 1975 to 1981.

factors only 5 percent and increased average benefit levels about 73 percent.

The relative impact of these factors of course varies according to the program. The following sections seek to analyze the factors contributing to growth in individual expenditure programs. Finally, we offer a prognosis for trends to 1990 in light of past patterns, assumptions about future demographic trends, and finally political and managerial changes that might affect future levels.

Three principal features in the development of overall expenditures for health services have been (a) rapid growth of expenditure by individuals, (b) changes in the way health expenditures have been financed, leading to a substantial increase in the share financed by government, and (c) rapid improvement in technology (OECD 1983*i*).

The rapid growth in expenditures, as table A1-7 illustrated, has related most to increases in "benefit levels," that is, health expenditures per person. In the 1960–75 period, real average benefits grew at more than 5.5 percent per annum, in 1975–81, at 1.8 percent, accounting for 55 percent of the increase in health expenditures. At the same time, the price of health care increased relative to other prices (the increases in health care costs were 50 percent greater than the overall expenditure deflator), so that a fraction of these higher expenditures was compensating for higher costs (or higher quality and standards) of health care. In both periods the importance of demographic factors was very small (less than 10 percent).

Technical change has increasingly been associated with greater hospital use (hospitals now account for more than 50 percent of total health care costs and 40 percent of publicly financed costs) and with specialization of secondary personnel. In many OECD countries, technical change has proceeded in a cost vacuum, with little thought given to the costliness of procedure, and little political thought has been directed to the "screening" of access to health procedures. In this context, it is interesting to note that improved access has been reflected in both greater numbers of hospital admissions and longer stay per admission: this is so in spite of higher incomes and "better health" since 1960 (see table A1-8). The result has been increasing concentration of health services, with an estimated 50 percent of total health expenditure consumed by 3–4 percent of the total population (OECD 1983*i*:16). This unwillingness to decide who shall receive publicly financed care, instead allowing everyone access, has contributed significantly to the uncontrolled expansion of health care costs per individual. Another factor has been the proclivities of the health care profession, which has urged that "best practice" medicine be the standard that patients should demand, without any consideration of

Table A1-8. *Trends in Hospital Utilization, 1960–80*

Item	1960	1975	1980
Admission rates (admissions per 1,000 population)	9.5	13.1	13.5
Average length of stay (days per admission)	15.1	19.6	18.6

Note: Figures are averages for seven major OECD countries.
Source: OECD (1983*d*).

costs. Table A1-9 outlines the components of real expenditure on health since 1960.

Pharmaceutical costs have risen the most rapidly, with large drug costs resulting in part from capitalization of enormous research and development expenditures into drug prices and into the prices of medical machinery, followed by growth of hospital services. Increases in eligibility contributed less to increased expenditure in the 1970s largely because desired coverage had been achieved in most OECD countries by the end of the 1960s, a period in which rapid extension of coverage took place, with the introduction of public programs in a number of countries. By the 1970s, either employment-linked private insurance or universal access health services covered the bulk of the OECD population.

Demographic factors are responsible for about 10 percent of total growth of health care expenditure, however, and the proportion of health care expenditure following on demographic change is expected to rise in

Table A1-9. *The Growth of Real Expenditure on Health Care, 1960–80*

Expenditure	Percentage composition in 1980	Percentage per year 1960–75	Percentage per year 1975–80
Private	24.3	4.1	3.2
Public	75.7	9.6	4.2
Hospital services	37.9	7.2	3.4
Ambulatory care	17.3	7.2	3.4
Pharmaceuticals	7.6	10.1	6.1
Other	12.9	n.a.	n.a.
Total	100.0	7.6	4.0

n.a. = not available.
Note: The figures are averages for six major OECD countries: Canada, France, Germany, Italy, the United Kingdom, and the United States.
Sources: OECD (1983*i*:39, 1983*c*).

the future. Table A1-10 outlines the relative public expenditure on the aged as a percentage of expenditure on the population under sixty-five. As table A1-10 indicates, expenditures on the aged population are some four to eight times greater than expenditure on the population under sixty-four for hospital care, and for ambulatory care they are twice as great, on average. With the aged population growing in OECD countries by about 1–2 percent per annum on average (far less than population growth), the potential for upward pressure on public health expenditure is sizable unless changes in health care delivery are made.

Table A1-10 also shows a striking variance in expenditures across countries. Notably, expenditures on the aged in the United States are some two times higher than the average for the other countries, whether we consider hospital care, ambulatory care, or medicines. Although some of the difference may be due to quality of care, it also involves cost structures and the pricing of health care. The variance suggests that there is scope for containing this category of expenditure without compromising quality.

In virtually all OECD countries, the proportion of the populace of educable age is shrinking. In the past, growth of expenditure on education increased at 6.1 percent per annum, but since 1975, expenditure on education has decelerated substantially, growing at only 1.8 percent per annum. As with health expenditure, education benefit levels—or increases in real expenditure per pupil—were the primary cause of this increase. The difference before and after 1975 was that in the recent period, demographic factors, such as the decline in births and in the school age population, reduced by half the impact of the increases in benefit levels on overall education expenditures.

Table A1-10. *Relative per Capita Public Expenditure on the Aged in OECD Countries, Late 1970s*

Country and year	Hos- pital	Ambulatory care	Medicines
Canada, 1978	7	2	n.a.
Finland, 1976	5	2	n.a.
France, 1978	5	2	4
Japan, 1979	4	n.a.	n.a.
United Kingdom, 1978	4	1	3
United States, 1978	8	9	6

n.a. = not available.

Note: The figures show the ratio of expenditure for people over sixty-five to people under sixty-five.

Sources: OECD (1983*d*) and surveys quoted in OECD (1981*c*).

Expenditure on pensions and social security is both the largest subcomponent of OECD governments' expenditure and the fastest growing. In OECD countries pensions now absorb 19.4 percent of public sector expenditure (8.8 percent of GDP) and have increased at a rate of more than 6 percent in real terms since 1975.

Social security expenditure is largely a function of the number of beneficiaries and the level of pension paid them. The former, in turn, is related to the size of the aged population and the number of the aged who are eligible for this transfer program. In accounting for increased expenditure levels, it is clear from table A1-10 that most of the increased expenditure is due to rapid growth in benefit levels, that is, in the real value of pensions paid, which may be a function of past earnings and labor participation (in semiinsurance systems) or of some publicly determined pension level (in the universal schemes). In either case, pensions are frequently related or tied to previous earnings, the so-called replacement ratio. Table A1-11 shows how replacement ratios have risen since 1965. The increase has averaged 50 percent over the fifteen-year period, or 4 percent in real terms per annum. In a number of countries, this increase was due to advantageous changes in the pension indexation formula or in the earnings base used to calculate previous earnings levels (France, Japan, the United Kingdom, and Italy). In others, it has been the result of the introduction of new schemes (Sweden). Denmark and Japan have seen an erosion of pension level since 1965, as has Germany

Table A1-11. *Replacement Ratios for Social Security Pensions*

Country	1965	1969	1975	1980	Index (1965 = 100)
Canada	21	24	33	34	161
Denmark	35	31	29	29	83
Sweden	31	42	57	68	219
France	49	41	60	66	135
Germany	48	55	51	49	102
Italy	60	62	61	69	115
Japan	n.a.	29	37	54	86[a]
Netherlands	35	43	43	44	126
United Kingdom	23	27	31	31	135
United States	29	30	38	44	152

n.a. = not available.

Note: See the sources for more details of the replacement rate computation. The figures represent percentage of past income for a single person.

a. 1960 = 100.

Sources: OECD (1983e); World Bank estimates.

since 1969. It is interesting to note that social security benefit levels were entirely protected from inflation; on average, changes in relative prices did not adversely affect real benefit levels.

Demographic changes also had an impact on growth in social security expenditure, accounting for just under 30 percent of the increase in social security expenditure. The proportion of overall growth due to demographic factors was slightly greater in the latter period, with substantial variation from country to country. In a number of OECD countries (Australia, New Zealand, and Italy, for example) there is virtually no aging of the population. In future years, after 2000, demographic factors will be the most important factor contributing to overall pension expenditure levels. Increases in eligibility have contributed least to growth in social security expenditures in the latter 1975–81 period; increases in coverage, introduction of new schemes, reduction in pensionable age, and provisions of early retirement had all been introduced by 1975 in most OECD countries.

The implications of this situation for future levels of social security expenditure are outlined at the end of this section. With social security expenditure the largest percentage of public social expenditure, and the fastest growing, the demographic changes overtaking OECD countries suggest that social security expenditure may at some point have to be constrained. This burden will not develop in the near future, as the demographic component of social security expenditure, over the next ten to twenty years, will remain relatively stable. The major growth is expected after the turn of the century. Only in Japan is an aging population already a reality. Table A1-12 shows that the proportion of the population over age sixty-five is expected to rise from 11.3 percent in 1980 to 16.5 percent in 2020.

Attempts to reduce pension expenditure have principally involved two measures. The first is increases in retirement age (that is, reduction of

Table A1-12. *Age Distribution of Total Population*
in Seven Major OECD Countries
(percent)

Age group	1980	2000	2020
0–19	31.6	27.0	26.0
19–64	57.1	58.7	57.5
Over 65	11.3	13.4	16.5

Source: Vu and Zachariah (1983).

eligibility) or adjustments to pensions that provide incentives for later retirement (normally, the trend has been toward a lowering of the retirement age). In the United States the present plan is to raise the retirement age to sixty-six in the year 2000. This type of adjustment will not have a major effect in the short run. Another measure is reduction in the rate of increase of benefits, to be attained typically by a change in the indexation formula. Germany, the United States, and the United Kingdom have made the change; Germany and the United States have corrected for past overindexation.

Determinants of Transfer Payments

Unemployment insurance expenditure accounts for a relatively small but growing share of GNP. In 1960, unemployment expenditure amounted to 0.4 percent of GDP; by 1975, it had almost tripled, to 1.1 percent. In the period to 1975, it was thus the fastest growing subcomponent of social expenditures, growing at 12 percent per annum. From 1975 to 1981, expenditure growth was less rapid, although in the 1982–83 period it has again increased.

Contributing to the rapid growth to 1975 were, almost equally, increased benefit levels and demographic changes. In the recent period, demographic changes—that is, growth in the labor force—have been the primary force behind growth in expenditures. Also strikingly evident in table A1-7 is the negative impact on expenditures of reduced eligibility in the post-1975 period as growing numbers of workers became unemployed for longer periods and benefits ran out.

Controlling Future Growth

The general consensus on the impact of the "welfare state" in reducing poverty and income inequality is clearly that the old and the poor are better off. There is, however, evidence that the increasing expenditure in the 1960s and 1970s has not been accompanied by the equity gains we might expect, as reflected in, for example, lower morbidity rates, lower mortality rates or increased equality in the distribution of income (Beckerman 1979; EEC 1981; OECD 1976, 1983j; and other studies). It appears that the underlying inequities in the distribution of income and wealth are stubborn and that redistributive social programs have limited ability to reduce or change them. In sum, the consensus seems to be that government involvement of a more limited sort, at far less cost could have achieved very nearly the same results.

The point has repeatedly been made that the gross costs of social programs are substantially greater than the net benefits to recipients. Figure A1-3 outlines the gross expenditures and net benefits flowing to different levels of the income distribution. It is clear that social goods expenditures and transfer payments assist not only the very poor, or even just the fairly poor, but those middle classes whose taxes finance the expenditure (OECD 1983*j*:6–7). The same is true of pensions, education, and health and also unemployment benefits. This pattern has been quite firmly established in a variety of OECD countries, including Canada, the United States, and the United Kingdom.

Figure A1-3 shows that, in principle, the same redistribution (net flow) could be achieved with much reduced gross flows. Any shift in redistribution is difficult, however, precisely because, across almost all levels of the income distribution, there is dependency on these social programs, and

Figure A1-3. *Social Expenditure Benefits, Total Personal Taxation, and Net Benefits in Seven Major OECD Countries*

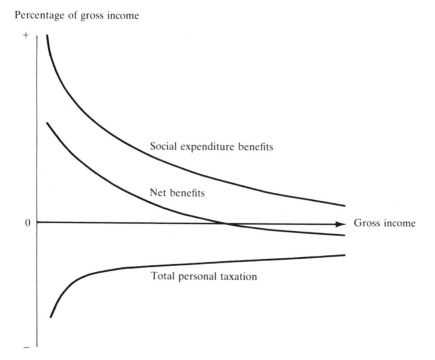

Percentage of gross income

Social expenditure benefits

Net benefits

Gross income

Total personal taxation

Source: OECD (1983*i*:48).

the constituencies are important. As our OECD study notes, income support benefits are often extended to the nonpoor so as to avoid high marginal tax rates and the accompanying disincentives implied by rapid withdrawal of benefits as incomes rise. Stigler (1970) has concluded that this "churning" of resources is necessary if a political consensus in favor of redistribution policy is to evolve. The middle class will not continue paying for social programs if it too is not granted some access. This statement may explain the absence of a "tax revolt" in many European countries where access to public social services is broad based, in contrast with the situation in the United States, where health programs, higher education grants, and medicare are limited to individuals who satisfy fairly strict eligibility criteria.

These inefficiencies have highlighted another concern, the "excess burden" inefficiencies that social programs generate. The behavioral changes on the part of recipients that result from government intervention in turn often produce higher costs. These inefficiencies are most often noted in the case of health care, where service may be overconsumed, as the user's perception of the value of the service is divorced from the cost of providing it, in the case of unemployment insurance, which has been alleged (Feldstein 1974) to induce the unemployed to increase their job search time and their period of unemployment, and in the case of pensions, which have induced a trend to earlier retirement.[2] In each instance the behavioral changes increase the costs and extension of the publicly financed programs.

The growth of social and transfer expenditure in the 1980s and 1990s, and the pressures that this growth will engender, will be a function of policy changes, economic conditions, and demographic changes. The former determine both the economic base that will be available to generate the resources required and the rate at which (indexed) expenditures grow. The latter determine the structural changes that we may expect in the level of demand for committed benefits.

Drawing on OECD studies, this section discusses the outlook to 1990 for the level of social and transfer expenditures in OECD countries, in line with certain assumptions about economic growth and demographic change. The economic outlook is detailed in table A1-13; table A1-14 outlines demographic assumptions. The outcomes are presented in table A1-15.

The OECD (1983g) study assumes that the level of social and transfer expenditure relative to GNP (22.8 percent in major OECD countries in 1982) has reached a threshold level and will not be increased. It also assumes that there will be no increased coverage and that eligibility will not increase, as the extension of most social programs in OECD countries is already large. Demographic changes, however, are incorporated, as are

Table A1-13. *Economic Climate: Weighted Average Growth Rates for Seven Major OECD Countries, 1960–90*
(percent)

Item	1960–75	1975–82	1982–90, pessimistic scenario	1982–90, optimistic scenario
Real GDP	4.25	2.67	2.80	3.70
Employment	0.94	1.03	0.84	1.31
Productivity	3.28	1.63	2.00	2.35
Unemployment rate at end of period	5.30	8.00	8.00	5.60

Source: OECD (1983*l*).

increases in the relative prices of social expenditure (especially health and education), which are assumed to increase 1 percent more rapidly than the general price level.

Because demographic changes and movements in relative prices are adverse, holding the ratio of social and transfer expenditure to GNP constant implies a decline in the rate of increase of real benefits (column 6 in table A1-15) relative to GNP. In the scenario that reflects optimism about growth (the scenario with lower unemployment, higher productivity growth, and GNP growth 1 percent higher than under the pessimistic scenario), the decline in real benefit growth is on the order of 0.2 percent per annum. In other words, real benefit levels grow 3.5 percent per annum, whereas GDP grows 3.7 percent per annum. Historical growth of real average benefit levels in 1960–75 was 3.7 percent and in 1975–81, 2.65 percent per annum. In the pessimistic scenario (unemployment at 1982 levels, GNP growth at 1980–82 rates), the growth of real benefit levels, given a constant share of social expenditure to GNP, and given demographic change, is 0.6 percent less per annum than the growth of

Table A1-14. *Demographic Changes: Industrialized Countries, 1950–2000*

Year	Dependency ratio	Part ≤ 14	Part ≥ 65
1950	35.4	27.8	7.6
1979	44.3	40.5	3.8
2000	34.6	34.2	13.1

Source: United Nations (1980).

Table A1-15. *Social and Transfer Expenditures in 1990:*
Implications of the Economic Scenarios

Program	Per-centage of GDP (1)	Change in rela-tive prices (2)	Total change in real expen-diture (3)	Demo-graphic change (4)	Eligi-bility (5)	Benefit levels (6)
				Component of (3)		
1982 growth rates, optimistic scenario[a]						
Social expenditure						
Education	4.8	1.0	3.4	−0.51	n.a.	3.9
Health	5.2	1.0	4.2	0.25	n.a.	3.9
Income maintenance						
Pensions	8.8	0.0	4.4	1.42	n.a.	2.9
Unemployment	1.2	0.0	−2.7	−5.70	n.a.	2.9
Total social and transfer expenditure	22.8	0.5	3.7	0.22	n.a.	3.5
1982 growth rates, pessimistic scenario[b]						
Social expenditure						
Education	4.8	1.0	2.2	−0.51	n.a.	2.7
Health	5.2	1.0	3.0	0.25	n.a.	2.7
Income maintenance						
Pensions	8.8	0.0	3.1	1.42	n.a.	1.7
Unemployment	1.2	0.0	1.7	0.03	n.a.	1.7
Total social and transfer expenditure	22.8	0.5	2.8	0.56	n.a.	2.2

n.a. = not available.
Note: Figures are averages for the seven major OECD countries.
a. 3.7 percent GDP growth.
b. 2.8 percent GDP growth.
Source: Secretariat estimates, OECD (1983g).

GDP. That is, real benefit levels grow 2.2 percent per annum, whereas GDP
grows at 2.8 percent. Most likely these slower rates of growth would be
achieved by an (under) indexing of benefits to less than real earnings
growth. As the OECD study notes, these figures are broad averages across
all social and transfer programs and across countries. The actual changes
in expenditure levels that take place are likely to vary by country and by

program, in line with each country's priorities and constraints. The conclusion, however, that only a small reduction in the real growth of benefit levels can achieve a stabilization of expenditures relative to GNP is encouraging. Expenditure growth at a rate that implied real benefit growth at the same rate as GNP, on the other hand, would imply a 25 percent share in GDP by 1990. This share would be greater still if governments desired to increase coverage or eligibility.

There are two important caveats to this conclusion. The first is that there may in fact be substantial increases in demand for these social goods from new sectors of the population who have not previously had access or have not previously had adequate access. The analysis has thus assumed that these demands can be contained and that there will be *no* increases in coverage or eligibility. (Alternatively, through better targeting, these demands could be met with no increases in costs.) The second caveat is that the analysis refers to a steady-state scenario. If, for example, there is a sharp supply-side shock to the system, and income falls, expenditure levels will probably remain nearly constant, and their share will rise in consequence.

The previous example assumed that the ratio of social expenditure to GNP would remain constant at its 1982 level. A more stringent set of measures implemented by governments wishing to constrain social expenditures might place the burden of budgetary adjustment on social expenditures. Table A1-16 indicates the cut in social expenditure required to balance overall OECD budgets. If the burden of budgetary adjustment were to be put on social and transfer expenditures, a decline of some 18 percent would be required in the social expenditure category,

Table A1-16. *Balancing the Budget: Social and Transfer Expenditures, 1979–82*

Year	Government deficit[a]	Social and transfer expenditures[a]	Deficit[b]	Social expenditure[a] to balance budget
1982	−4.2	22.8	18.0	18.6
1981	−2.8	22.8[c]	12.0	20.0
1980	−2.5	22.8[c]	11.0	20.3
1979	−1.9	22.8[c]	8.3	20.9

a. As a percentage of GDP.
b. As a percentage of total social expenditure.
c. From World Bank estimates.
Source: Table A1-7.

from 22.8 percent of GDP to 18 percent of GDP. The question, of course, is whether budgetary policy can be made by full adjustment on the expenditure side.

Yet another option is to examine the implication of zero real increase in benefit levels (that is, constant benefit levels). In this instance, benefit levels would be adjusted to any increase in relative prices, and overall expenditure would also rise in line with demographic movements. There would be no real increase, however, in benefit levels. Again, no increases in coverage are assumed. Table A1-17 outlines the implications for social expenditure as a share of GDP.

If no real increase in average benefit levels takes place, social expenditure could be reduced to some 17 percent of GNP by 1990, with the demographic assumptions outlined earlier and given the optimistic GNP growth of 3.7 percent. If average real benefit levels are not permitted to grow, and expenditures rise only to cover demographic changes and relative price increases, but GDP grows at the slower rate of 2.8 percent, the share will fall to 18.5 percent of GDP.

In sum, it appears that there is some slack in social and transfer expenditure programs. If real benefit levels remain constant in *real* terms, the social expenditure burden can be substantially reduced. If the share remains constant, *real* average benefits can grow by 3.5 percent, only 0.2 percent less than the rate of growth of real earnings, implying that recipients do share in the fruits of economic growth. Political will, and the development of policy alternatives, especially better targeting, will be required. All these elements will be necessary, because such a shift will imply a change from past trends in benefit growth and in people's expectations of entitlements. Implied in the optimistic scenario is a growth of real benefit levels of 3.5 percent, as compared with a growth rate in 1960–75 of 3.7 percent. Nonetheless, the optimistic scenario implies faster growth in benefit levels (2.8 percent) than actually took place in 1975–81.

The more restrictive scenarios imply a more radical change from past trends, that is, the zero *real* benefit increase represents quite a departure even from the 2.8 percent growth rate of benefits from 1975 to 1981.

This solution will be feasible, as we noted earlier, only if (a) *new entitlements* are not granted (or targeting compensates for any new entitlements) and (b) no further supply shocks take place. There must be no increases in coverage. If governments find it impossible to observe these constraints, then the future augurs much less well for containing budget deficits through expenditures policy.

The following section completes our examination of OECD expenditure trends with a discussion of trends in interest payments.

Table A1-17. *Alternative Scenarios to 1990: Four Main Programs in the Seven Larger Economies*

			Component of (2)			Nominal component of (5)	
Program	Percentage of GDP (1)	Growth of total real expenditures to 1990 (2)	Demographic change (3)	Eligibility (4)	Benefit levels (5)	Relative prices (6)	Real increase (7)
1990 optimistic scenario[a]							
Social goods							
Education	3.7	0.50	−0.51	—	1.0	1.0	0.0
Health	4.3	1.25	0.25	—	1.0	1.0	0.0
Transfer payments							
Pensions	7.3	1.42	1.42	—	0.0	0.0	0.0
Unemployment	0.6	−5.70	−5.70	—	0.0	0.0	0.0
Total social expenditure	17.1	0.7	0.22	—	0.5	0.5	0.0

(Table continues on the following page.)

Table A1-17 *(continued)*

Program	Percentage of GDP (1)	Growth of total real expenditures to 1990 (2)	Component of (2) Demographic change (3)	Component of (2) Eligibility (4)	Benefit levels (5)	Nominal component of (5) Relative prices (6)	Nominal component of (5) Real increase (7)
			1990 pessimistic scenario[b]				
Social goods							
Education	4.0	0.05	-0.51	—	1.0	1.0	0.0
Health	4.6	1.25	0.25	—	1.0	1.0	0.0
Transfer payments							
Pensions	7.9	1.42	1.42	—	0.0	0.0	0.0
Unemployment	0.7	0.30	0.03	—	0.0	0.0	0.0
Total social expenditure	18.5	1.06	0.56	—	0.5	0.5	0.0

Note: The figures are average annual growth rates at constant prices. Dashes indicate that no change is assumed.
a. 3.7 percent GDP growth.
b. 2.8 percent GDP growth.
Source: World Bank estimates.

Table A1-18 indicates the share of government debt interest payments in total government expenditure. After government expenditure on the very broad category "social goods and transfers," the largest share of public outlays goes to debt interest. The overall OECD average (table A1-19) almost equals outlays on defense expenditure for many countries. This is a tremendous change from the not-too-recent past, when interest on the public debt was generally half its present level. Table A1-20 shows this trend since 1972 (Chouraqui and Price 1983). For major OECD countries, the share of interest in government expenditure rose 56 percent, from 4.9 percent to 8.8 percent of expenditure. For some countries, such as Japan, the United Kingdom, and Australia, the figure was about half again as high, and in a few countries (Canada, Belgium, and Italy), it approached 18 percent in 1982.

This rapid growth was a function of three factors: rapid growth of government deficits financed by borrowing, increases in nominal interest rates during the period (see table A1-21), and declining inflation, which has resulted in higher real interest rates. The discussion below draws on OECD studies of this area (Chouraqui and Price 1983; OECD 1981*a*, 1983*p*).

The first factor is perhaps the most important. OECD debt and deficits are discussed in greater detail in "The Deficits" section below. Briefly, however, the growth of outstanding debt has been rapid in recent years. Table A1-22 shows the ratios of central government debt to GDP, from 1960 to 1980, and total government debt for the years 1975 and 1981. These ratios decreased from 1960 to 1970, largely because of the erosion of real debt levels due to inflation, and then increased between 1975 and 1980. (See also table A1-24.)

Most countries in our sample experienced an increase in their central-government-debt-to-GNP ratios between 1975 and 1981. Total-government-debt-to-GNP ratios have also risen in the past five years. Likely future growth in this ratio is a function of future growth in government deficits (and the manner in which governments chose to finance them) and of future inflation. The alternatives and likely trends are discussed further in "The Deficits" below.

As a result of the higher nominal interest rates prevalent in OECD in the recent past, the interest burden component of government expenditure rose substantially. Table A1-21 shows trends in the long-term bond rate of major OECD countries. With the exception of countries such as Germany and Japan, these rates have doubled or tripled between 1965 and 1982.

The higher real interest rates that the government has needed recently to raise debt are due to a variety of factors. Because inflationary expectations are still high, despite the restrictive monetary environment, bond-

Table A1-18. *Share of General Government Debt Interest Payments in Total Government Spending*
(percent)

Country	1970	1971	1972	1973	1974	1975	1976	1977	1978	1979	1980	1981	1982
United States	3.8	3.6	3.3	3.8	3.5	3.5	3.9	3.8	4.0	3.8	4.2	5.3	5.8
Japan	4.9	4.5	5.0	5.8	5.3	5.8	7.2	8.7	9.8	11.1	12.6	13.6	14.8
Germany	3.0	2.9	2.9	3.1	3.2	3.2	3.6	4.0	3.9	4.1	4.5	5.2	6.1
France	3.3	3.0	2.6	2.4	2.6	3.3	3.1	3.3	3.4	3.7	3.8	4.7	4.5
United Kingdom	12.3	11.4	10.8	11.2	11.5	10.1	11.0	11.5	11.4	12.0	12.3	12.3	12.2
Italy	5.4	5.6	5.9	6.7	7.9	10.4	11.7	12.7	14.0	14.1	15.0	15.5	17.2
Canada	11.6	11.7	11.7	11.9	10.9	10.7	11.7	11.9	12.9	14.1	14.1	15.6	16.6
Total	4.9	4.7	4.6	5.0	4.9	5.0	5.7	6.1	6.4	6.7	7.3	8.2	8.8

Source: Chouraqui and Price (1983).

320

Table A1-19. *Debt-to-GNP Ratios, OECD*

Country	Central government debt					Total public debt	
	1960	1965	1970	1975	1980	1975	1980
Australia	59.8	49.7	39.6	24.7	n.a.	n.a.	n.a.
Austria	—	—	9.1	10.5	19.1	24.1	33.4
Belgium	70.2	58.5	48.9	40.7	57.9	50.4	71.8
Canada	44.6	36.7	29.2	22.6	28.4	n.a.	n.a.
Denmark	23.3	12.6	7.2	n.a.	n.a.	15.6	44.1
Finland	8.9	11.4	8.4	3.0	9.2	n.a.	n.a.
France	28.4	17.4	12.6	8.9	10.1	15.0	14.0
Germany	7.4	7.2	7.0	10.5	15.6	24.8	31.4
Ireland	61.0	72.6	67.1	71.4	n.a.	72.7	89.5
Italy	37.0	32.3	35.9	53.7	60.8	58.4	49.5
Japan	6.0	4.3	6.8	10.4	24.6	17.8	41.9
Netherlands	44.0	31.9	28.6	22.3	31.5	40.7	48.9
Norway	28.4	22.8	23.7	27.9	n.a.	35.7	48.6
Spain	n.a.	n.a.	11.4	7.8	7.7	n.a.	n.a.
Sweden	31.5	19.2	21.2	24.4	34.1	35.4	53.2
Switzerland	15.5	7.9	5.7	7.3	8.0	28.3	26.6
United Kingdom	n.a.	n.a.	52.9	42.9	40.1	68.3	57.2
United States	46.6	37.6	29.3	28.1	28.0	49.1	47.4
Mean	34.2	28.1	24.7	24.5	26.8	37.1	45.1

n.a. = not available.

Sources: OECD (1983p:58); IMF, *International Financial Statistics*; and Bundesministerium der Finanzen (1982).

holders require higher real yields for the risk they take on. This insistence on higher *real* yields is reinforced by the fact of growing government debt, which carries with it fears that the debt will be monetized, causing higher inflation. In sum, new debt is issued, and refinanced debt is rolled over, at higher real rates, and pressure is now beginning to be felt by even low-inflation countries such as Japan, Germany, and Austria. Moreover, as real interest rates rise and the interest burden is financed, it is capitalized into outstanding debt, and the effect rapidly becomes cumulative.

OECD has carried out a study estimating the contribution to the growth of the debt made by these factors (OECD 1981a). The components are outlined in table A1-20, which shows the contribution of inflation, interest payments, and borrowing requirements to increased indebtedness for six OECD countries. Statistics are not comparable with those in table A1-19, which refers exclusively to *central* government debt. In column 1, table A1-20 shows the proportion of government debt to GNP. The second column outlines the total change in the share. Column 3 begins the

Table A1-20. *Central Government Debt in Six Major OECD Countries: Changes, 1972–79*

Financial years[a]	Share of GDP	Change in share[b]	*Factor causing change[c]*			
			Inflation	Interest payments	Borrowing requirement	Average real return (percent)
United States						
1972–73	20.3	−1.7	−1.0	1.1	−0.6	0.5
1973–74	18.9	−1.4	−1.4	1.1	−0.7	−1.0
1974–75	20.2	1.3	−1.5	1.2	1.3	−2.0
1975–76	22.5	2.3	−1.3	1.2	3.1	−0.5
1976–77	21.9	−0.6	−1.5	1.7	0.4	0.5
1977–78	20.4	−1.5	−1.4	1.4	−0.4	0.0
1978–79	19.1	−1.3	−1.5	1.2	−0.1	−1.5
1979–80	20.1	−1.0	−1.5	1.3	1.2	−1.0
Japan						
1972–73	11.8	2.1	−0.6	0.4	3.7	−1.5
1973–74	11.2	−0.6	−1.5	0.5	1.1	−9.0
1974–75	11.6	0.4	−2.0	0.5	1.6	−12.5
1975–76	14.4	2.8	−1.1	0.6	3.2	−4.5
1976–77	17.9	3.5	−1.2	0.8	4.4	−3.0
1977–78	23.8	5.9	−1.2	1.2	6.8	0.0
1978–79	29.4	5.6	−0.9	1.4	6.7	2.0
1979–80	33.9	4.5	−1.4	1.7	5.0	1.0
Germany						
1972	6.7	−0.1	−0.4	0.4	−0.1	0.0
1973	6.7	0.0	−0.4	0.4	0.3	0.0
1974	7.3	0.6	−0.4	0.4	0.7	0.0
1975	10.5	3.2	−0.4	0.5	3.0	0.1
1976	11.4	0.9	−0.5	0.6	1.2	1.0
1977	12.5	1.1	−0.4	0.7	1.2	2.0
1978	13.8	1.3	−0.3	0.8	1.4	3.5
1979	14.4	0.6	−0.6	0.8	1.1	2.0
1980	15.3	0.8	−0.8	0.8	1.0	0.5
France						
1972	8.0	−2.1	−0.6	0.4	−1.5	−1.5
1973	7.0	−1.0	−0.6	0.4	−0.5	−2.0
1974	6.9	−0.1	−0.8	0.4	0.4	−6.5
1975	8.5	1.6	−0.7	0.6	1.7	−1.5
1976	8.0	−0.5	−0.7	0.6	0.0	−1.5
1977	8.0	0.0	−0.7	0.7	0.2	−0.5
1978	8.8	0.8	−0.7	0.7	1.1	0.0
1979	9.1	0.3	−0.8	0.8	0.7	−1.0
1980			−1.1			
United Kingdom						
1972–73	46.7	−5.5	−3.3	1.9	−1.6	−2.5
1973–74	44.4	−2.3	−4.2	1.6	0.8	−5.5

(Table continues on the following page.)

Table A1-20 *(continued)*

Financial years[a]	Share of GDP	Change in share[b]	Factor causing change[c]			Average real return (percent)
			Inflation	Interest payments	Borrowing require-ment	
United Kingdom (cont.)						
1974–75	42.8	−1.6	−7.2	1.5	4.2	−13.0
1975–76	42.6	−0.2	−8.1	1.4	7.1	−15.5
1976–77	44.0	1.4	−5.4	2.2	5.2	−7.5
1977–78	43.6	−0.4	−5.3	2.5	3.3	−6.5
1978–79	44.9	1.3	−3.4	2.9	3.8	−1.0
1979–80	41.9	−3.0	−5.7	3.1	0.8	−6.0
Canada						
1972–73	38.9	−1.8	−2.1	2.1	1.0	0.0
1973–74	35.0	−3.9	−3.0	2.0	0.1	−2.5
1974–75	33.4	−1.6	−3.4	1.9	1.9	−4.3
1975–76	33.7	0.3	−3.0	2.1	2.2	−2.5
1976–77	33.5	−0.2	−2.4	2.3	1.8	0.0
1977–78	36.3	2.8	−2.5	2.4	3.3	0.0
1978–79	37.5	1.2	−3.0	2.6	2.1	−1.0
1979–80	35.5	−2.0	−3.2	3.0	−0.5	−0.5

Note: United States: federal government debt held by the public, less foreign and state holdings; United Kingdom: total central government liabilities to the domestic sector; Canada: total federal liability, excluding foreign holders; Japan and Germany: total central government debt outstanding; France: "dette intérieure."

a. United States: July–June until 1975–76; October–September from 1976–77; Japan, United Kingdom, and Canada: April–March; Germany and France: calendar years.

b. Figures are percentages of GDP/GNP at market prices.

c. Component changes do not sum to total change because the effect of relative price changes and real GDP growth is excluded. Figures are percentages of GDP/GNP at market prices.

Source: OECD (1981a).

disaggregating, showing the estimates of the effect of inflation on (reducing) the real value of the debt-GDP ratio. In all cases, the impact of inflation has been to erode the real value of the debt, sometimes quite substantially, as in the United Kingdom and Canada.

In column 4 of table A1-20, the estimated effects of debt interest payments are shown. As noted earlier, higher *real* interest rates have been required to compensate bondholders for the potentially higher risk of taking a capital loss on their bonds. In the past ten years, in most countries, the effect of real interest rates on debt-to-GDP ratios has been larger than that of increased borrowing requirements. Exceptions are Germany and Japan, whose debt and GDP ratios rose most. The increased

Table A1-21. *Nominal Long-Term Interest Rates, 1965–82*

Year	Canada	France	Germany	Italy	Japan	United Kingdom	United States
1965	5.21	5.270	7.100	6.940	n.a.	6.560	4.270
1966	5.69	5.400	8.100	6.540	6.860	6.940	4.770
1967	5.94	5.660	7.000	6.610	6.910	6.800	5.010
1968	6.75	5.860	6.500	6.700	7.030	7.550	5.460
1969	7.58	7.640	6.800	6.850	7.090	9.040	6.330
1970	7.91	8.060	8.300	9.010	7.190	9.220	6.860
1971	6.95	7.740	8.000	8.340	7.280	8.900	6.120
1972	7.23	7.350	7.900	7.470	6.700	8.910	6.010
1973	7.56	8.250	9.300	7.420	7.260	10.720	7.120
1974	8.90	10.490	10.400	9.870	9.260	14.770	8.060
1975	9.04	9.490	8.500	11.540	9.200	14.390	8.190
1976	9.18	9.160	7.800	13.080	8.720	14.430	7.870
1977	8.70	9.610	6.200	14.620	7.330	12.730	7.670
1978	9.30	8.960	5.800	13.700	6.090	12.470	8.490
1979	10.26	9.480	7.400	14.050	7.690	12.990	9.330
1980	12.49	12.990	8.500	16.110	9.220	13.790	11.390
1981	15.22	15.663	10.383	20.578	8.660	14.742	13.718
1982	14.76	15.561	8.950	20.895	8.055	12.880	12.917

n.a. = not available.
Source: International Monetary Fund, *International Financial Statistics*, long-term bond yields.

public sector deficits have been a contributor to overall growth of debt as well. The role of the higher borrowing requirement, *net* of interest payments, is shown in column 5.

Finally, the last column shows real rates of return on central government debt. In most countries (Germany excepted), the real rate of return on government debt has been negative for almost a decade. There is some evidence that it is becoming less so, however. Tentative figures for 1982 and 1983 (not shown) suggest that real rates are becoming highly positive and, as a result, are contributing substantially to growth in government debt.

Summary

Social expenditures and debt interest have been the largest factors accounting for the growth in budget deficits. Our survey suggests that both of these factors have structural elements but that there is some room for containing increases, especially in social expenditures. Interest expenditures, of course, have a dynamic of their own. Having summarized trends in the important components of government expenditure since

Table A1-22. *General Government Financial Balances: Surplus or Deficit as a Percentage of Nominal GNP/GDP at Market Price*

Country	1971	1972	1973	1974	1975	1976	1977	1978	1979	1980	1981	1982
United States[a]	-1.7	-0.3	0.5	-0.2	-4.2	-2.1	-0.9	0.0	0.6	-1.3	-1.0	-3.8
Japan[a]	1.4	0.4	0.5	0.4	-2.6	-3.8	-3.8	-5.5	-4.8	-4.5	-4.0	-4.1
Germany	-0.1	-0.5	1.2	-1.4	-5.7	-3.4	-2.4	-2.5	-2.7	-3.2	-4.0	-3.9
France	0.7	0.8	0.9	0.6	-2.2	-0.5	-0.8	-1.9	-0.7	0.3	-1.9	-2.6
United Kingdom	1.5	-1.2	-2.7	-3.8	-4.6	-4.9	-3.2	-4.2	-3.2	-3.3	-2.5	-2.0
Italy	-7.1	-9.2	-8.5	-8.1	-11.7	-9.0	-8.0	-9.7	-9.5	-8.0	-11.7	-12.0
Canada	0.1	0.1	1.0	1.9	-2.4	-1.7	-2.6	-3.1	-1.9	-2.1	-1.4	-5.5
Subtotal[b]	-0.5	-0.4	0.1	-0.5	-3.8	-2.7	-2.1	-2.3	-1.9	-2.5	-2.8	-4.2
Australia	-0.8	-0.7	-0.1	-0.8	-4.3	-3.0	-2.2	-2.4	-1.8	-2.5	-2.6	-4.1
Austria	2.4	2.2	0.6	2.0	-1.8	-2.0	0.0	-1.9	-1.5	-1.0	-0.1	0.4
Belgium	1.5	2.0	1.3	1.3	-2.5	-3.7	-2.4	-2.8	-2.5	-2.0	-1.8	-2.5
Denmark	-3.0	-4.0	-3.5	-2.6	-4.7	-5.4	-5.5	-5.9	-6.9	-9.3	-13.1	-12.2
Netherlands	3.7	4.6	5.8	1.5	-1.2	-0.2	-0.5	-0.2	-1.6	-3.2	-7.1	-9.1
Norway	-0.5	0.0	1.1	-0.1	-2.6	-2.2	-1.8	-2.7	-3.7	-3.9	-4.9	-5.6
Spain	4.3	4.5	5.7	4.6	3.8	3.1	1.6	0.6	1.9	5.7	4.8	4.4
Sweden	-0.6	0.3	1.1	0.2	0.0	-0.3	-0.6	-1.8	-1.7	-2.1	-3.3	5.9
Subtotal[b]	5.2	4.4	4.1	2.0	2.8	4.5	1.7	-0.5	-3.0	-4.0	-5.3	-6.9
Total[b]	1.1	1.2	1.5	1.0	-0.9	-0.9	-0.9	-2.1	-2.6	-2.8	-3.9	-4.9

Note: On a system of national accounts basis except for the United States, the United Kingdom, and Italy, which are on a national income account basis. "Financial balances" are equivalent to "net lending"; a negative sign indicates net government borrowing. The general government borrowing requirement is equal to the financial balance *plus* financial transactions and accruals adjustments.

a. As a percentage of GNP.

b. 1981 GDP weighted. The first subtotal is for the preceding seven countries; the second subtotal is for the preceding eight countries.

Sources: OECD *National Accounts*, national sources (see Note above), and OECD secretariat estimates.

1970, we shall now discuss the trends in government deficits and their implications.

The Deficits

There is widespread concern among many OECD countries that the present level of budget deficits is unsustainable, and many of them have taken steps to correct it. A number of OECD studies have analyzed the sustainability of budget deficits (Chouraqui and Price 1983; OECD 1981a, 1983i). In general the aim in all OECD countries has been to bring budget deficits down to historically normal levels. These aims have been more difficult to achieve in practice, however, than in principle. The United States, for example, has gone from a target policy of "budget balance in 1984" to a target deficit of no more than 2 percent of GDP in 1988. Table A1-22 and figure A1-4 show actual government deficits since 1971 for seven OECD countries and the total for the OECD as a whole. The evolution since the 1970s, over the first and second oil shocks, has been quite striking. Before 1970 deficits were on the order of − 0.5 percent of GDP to 0.5 percent—that is, of GDP, more or less balanced—but the trend has changed dramatically. In 1975, the average deficit of the major seven OECD countries was − 4.3 percent of GDP. As the OECD notes, after the first oil shock, deficits generally increased, as governments took the adjustment burden on themselves rather than forcing it onto the private sector.

Subsequently, however, the inflationary consequences of increasing deficits led to unacceptable weaknesses in currencies and trade balances and a consequent need to reverse the policies. In the more recent years, however, the very slow recovery has led to an increase in public sector deficits to 1983. This increase partly results from the nonaccommodative monetary policies that have been followed in some larger OECD countries, with the consequent growth in the interest burden. Another factor has been the interaction of monetary and fiscal policies in prolonging slow recovery.

The slow growth has also meant, however, that income and employment-related revenues have been reduced, whereas expenditure patterns have exhibited rigidities. Although almost all OECD governments have adopted balanced budget targets for 1984 or 1985, the persistence of the deficits in OECD countries has stymied many governments. There is a fear that spending and revenue patterns may be structural in nature and that the policy prescription of the past can no longer be used. There is a question as to whether new prescriptions may be called for and above all as to whether the deficits will disappear when the recovery gathers steam.

Figure A1-4. *Budget Deficits in Seven Major OECD Countries, 1960–82*

Percentage of GDP

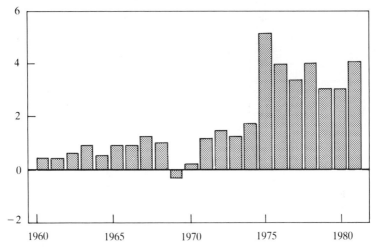

Source: OECD (1983*l*:46).

Another feature of government deficits in recent years, representing a major change from previous trends, is the component of deficit that is financing government consumption expenditures. Deficits that finance government capital expenditures are nothing new, although typically government *current* savings also contributed to capital formation. Nonetheless, in the 1970s government *current* savings have not contributed greatly to financing the deficit in all major OECD countries (OECD 1981*a*). On average, the contribution of government current savings to the overall financial deficits was 65 percent. In the 1980s, government *current* savings to the overall financial deficits was 65 percent. In the 1980s, government current dissaving has been the rule, as table A1-22 indicates, so that, in the 1980s, deficits were at least in part due to higher government *consumption*, with any global expenditure reductions typically directed at government *capital* expenditures, that is, at investment and not at government consumption.

The implication of the consumption-based deficits for future growth and capital formation are worrisome, because deficits will not then be financed out of future growth. As the OECD notes, where economic growth is less than the real interest rate, deficits will imply borrowing to finance interest payments on the public debt (OECD 1983*n*).

Table A1-23 provides corroborating evidence, showing the shrinking

Table A1-23. *Government Expenditures and Financial Balances, OECD*

Item	1970	1971	1972	1973	1974	1975	1976	1977	1978	1979	1980	1981	1982
Current expenditures, total	29.0	29.6	30.0	29.8	31.6	34.4	34.2	34.2	34.4	34.4	35.9	37.2	39.0
Saving[a]	2.9	2.3	2.3	2.8	2.2	-1.0	0.0	0.6	0.3	0.9	0.2	-0.2	-1.7
Gross investment[a]	4.2	4.3	4.2	4.2	4.1	4.2	3.9	3.8	3.8	3.9	3.8	3.7	3.5
Net capital transfers received[a]	-0.3	-0.4	-0.3	-0.4	-0.4	-0.5	-0.5	-0.5	-0.5	-0.5	-0.5	-0.5	-0.6
Financial balance	0.2	-0.5	-0.4	0.1	-0.5	-3.9	-2.7	-2.2	-2.3	-1.9	-2.5	-2.8	-4.2
Gross investment as percentage of total expenditures	12.6	12.6	12.2	12.3	11.4	10.8	10.2	10.0	9.9	10.1	9.5	9.0	8.1

Note: Aggregate for the major seven countries plus Australia, Austria, Belgium, Denmark, the Netherlands, Norway, Spain, and Sweden: 1981 GDP/GNP weights.

a. Weighted average excluding the United States; the components will therefore not add to the totals.

Source: See table A-1.

proportion of government investment as a share of GDP relative to total government expenditure. From 12.6 percent of total government expenditure in 1970, government investment expenditure fell to 8.1 percent in 1982. And in fiscal year 1982, for the major OECD countries, 40 percent of the deficit was due to *current dissavings*. If this is a purely cyclical phenomenon that will reverse itself with a return to economic health, the present level of actual deficits is of less concern, as it represents counter-cyclical macroeconomic policy.

In general, public sector reliance on external financing was greater at the end of the decade than at the outset. As table A1-24 shows, between 1971 and 1981, the proportion of OECD central government debt held overseas rose nearly 30 percent from 11.0 percent of the total to 13.5 percent. In the case of the United States, the increase is especially striking—between one-third and one-quarter of all government debt is

Table A1-24. *Central Government Debt Held by Domestic and Foreign Sectors*

| | Year-end value as percentage of GDP | | | | Percentage of total government debt held by foreign sector | |
| | Debt held by domestic sector | | Debt held by foreign sector | | | |
Country	*1971*	*1981*	*1971*	*1981*	*1971*	*1981*
United States	16.6	15.1	3.1	4.7	15.7	23.8
Japan	9.6	27.3	0.2	0.3	0.2	0.3
Germany	7.0	14.6	0.2	2.9	2.8	16.6
France	9.3	10.7	0.9	0.5	10.2	4.0
United Kingdom	52.9	42.5	13.0	5.2	20.0	10.9
Italy[a]	40.1	51.3	0.7	1.2	1.7	2.2
Canada	41.5	37.8	0.3	1.5	0.7	3.8
Australia[a]	24.2	15.6	4.6	3.6	15.9	18.7
Seven-country average	20.0	20.6	2.5	2.97	11.0	13.5

Note: United States: fiscal year ending June until 1976, ending September from 1977 on; Japan: fiscal year ending March; Germany and France: calendar year; United Kingdom: fiscal year ending March; Italy: calendar year; Canada: fiscal year ending March; Australia: fiscal year ending June; Austria and Beglium: calendar year; Denmark: fiscal year until 1977, calendar year from 1978; Finland: calendar year; Ireland: fiscal year ending March until 1974, calendar year from 1975; Netherlands: calendar year; New Zealand: fiscal year ending March; Norway, Portugal, Spain, Switzerland, and Turkey: calendar year.

a. Total public sector debt.

Source: Chouraqui and Price (1983), weighted by GDP.

presently held abroad. As a share of OECD gross domestic product, the proportion of foreign debt grew from 2.5 percent to almost 3 percent of GDP, an increase of 20 percent. In sum, the OECD has increasingly drawn on capital inflows from the foreign section for the financing of government deficits; in many countries this has been an important factor in helping to keep domestic interest rates down.

A recent OECD study (OECD 1983b) has attempted to separate the effects of the structural components of these government deficits from those that have been cyclically induced by the recession and by the economies' slow recovery. The questions examined include the extent to which OECD countries face structural problems with respect to deficits and whether or not the levels of structural deficit are compatible with governments, other economic objectives, such as price stability, employment, and output growth. The study attempted to measure the nature and size of structural budget deficits. Overall, in brief, its conclusion was that the deterioration in budget deficits is primarily due to the impact of inflation, slow growth, and unemployment. These three factors, in the past, would probably have been classified as purely cyclical. Recent thinking, however, suggests that they have structural components and contribute to structural deficits.

Figure A1-5 presents the structural budget deficit for major OECD countries combined. The structural deficit is defined as the deficit that would result at "potential output"; that is, these are "full employment" deficits. The trends differ by countries. Taken together, however, from 1970 to 1983, OECD countries' deficits, when adjusted for cyclical factors were negative throughout the period except in 1970, ranging from -0.1

Figure A1-5. *Structural Budget Deficits in Seven Major OECD Countries, 1973–80*

Percentage of nominal GNP

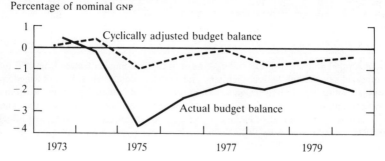

Source: OECD (1981a).

percent of GDP to − 2.0 percent of GDP (1976). In the last few years, since 1980, the structural deficit overall for the OECD has been smaller than in the past. In 1983, the structural deficit is estimated to be − 0.6 percent of OECD potential GNP, or very near being in balance. Structural surpluses exist in a number of countries, including the United Kingdom and France, and throughout the past decade (until 1983), the United States was in structural surplus.

If we disaggregate revenue and expenditures from 1970 to 1975, structural public expenditures increased from 31 percent of potential output to just under 35 percent (see table A1-25). In the second half of the decade, expenditures rose again, approaching 36 percent by 1980. Contributing to this increase was a steady growth in social security payments (column 4), from 9 percent to 12 percent of potential GDP, and an increase in the interest bill, from 1.9 percent to 4.8 percent of potential GNP (column 6). On the revenue side, full employment revenues did increase throughout the decade, from 31.7 percent of potential GDP to 35.6 percent of GDP in 1983. At almost every point in the decade, full employment expenditures exceeded full employment revenues, some-times by a margin of as much as two percentage points. The contribution of expenditure rigidities may perhaps be a factor in determining the long-run gap between revenues and expenditures (in the United States, tax reductions have also been responsible).

The need to reduce structural deficits has been given a great deal of weight. In general, measures taken by the OECD countries to reduce structural deficits have been partially successful. At full employment, since 1981 the structural OECD deficit has, in fact, been quite small. As we noted earlier, the 1983 estimate represents the failure of the United States to contain its deficit, which is now structurally estimated at 0.8 percent, as well as that of Japan, which has an estimated structural deficit of 1.8 percent of potential GDP. In other OECD countries, the estimated structural deficit was close to zero (Germany and Canada) or in surplus (the United Kingdom and France).

Despite the reduction in structural deficits as measured, actual deficits have continued to grow, reaching 4.5 percent of GDP in 1983. In this measure, a large cyclical component is responsible for the actual deficits. In 1983, less than 15 percent of the actual deficit was due, in the estimate of OECD (OECD 1983*b*), to structural factors. Nonetheless, there is reason to fear future growth in these actual deficits, even ignoring, for the moment, any impact they may have on financial markets. The *actual* deficit can feed back into the structural deficit in two ways, first, by its impact on higher debt and interest charges, and second, by the impact that prolonged recessions and high interest rates may have on capital formation and future growth. Thus the actual, cyclical deficit may possibly be converted into a structural deficit, as potential growth is affected by the deflationary policies that are followed to reduce the actual deficits. This conversion results from the alleged effects of the *level* of actual deficits on capital formation and the effects of the *structure* of revenues and expenditure on efficiency of resource allocation.

The concern that large actual deficits may have structural implications arises because of concern about the private sector responses, including savings propensities, to these deficits. In the United States the prospect of prolonged high borrowing requirements of the government has already had an impact manifested in the level of long-term interest rates, which results from expectations. Large deficits, which rapidly add to the stock of government debt, cannot be accommodated in investor portfolio preferences and balances except at substantially higher interest rates. The potential crowding out is discussed in "Trends in Savings" and "Uses of Savings" below.

Summary

The structural balance figures shown in table A1-25 corroborate the discussion of revenue and expenditures elasticities and suggest that the deficit problems *cannot* be solved simply by increasing taxes (see figure A1-6). If expenditures increase structurally at a rate faster than GNP because of entitlement programs and the cumulative impact of debt interest, then raising taxes cannot close the deficits. If expenditure growth can be maintained at constant levels (that is, if it can grow at the same rate as GNP or less), then taxes *can* do the job. The analysis in "Controlling Future Growth" suggested that public expenditures—especially on entitlement programs, subsidies and health—have been growing rapidly but that reductions in these expenditures, especially pricing changes, are feasible. If the changes can be made to bring expenditures in line with revenues in a structural sense, future structural deficits can be contained.

Trends in Savings

Examination of the savings rate in the 1960–82 period suggests that the apparent downward trend in savings ratios since 1975 represents the more relevant trend for analysis and projections. Fluctuations in savings rates have been procyclical, and a decline in savings ratios is expected and normal during periods of recession, as is an increase during the recovery

Table A1-25. *Potential Output Budget Balances for the Major Seven Countries as a Percentage of GDP, 1970–83*

| Year | Actual budget balance | Component of cyclically adjusted balance | | | | 1981 GDP/GNP weights and exchange rates | |
		Reve- nues	Expen- ditures	Social security	Balance	In- terest bill	Inflation adjust- ment
1970	n.a.	31.7	31.1	8.9	0.5	1.9	n.a.
1971	−0.8	31.3	31.4	9.3	−0.1	1.8	1.8
1972	−0.7	31.8	32.2	9.7	−0.4	1.8	1.6
1973	−0.1	32.3	32.9	10.2	−0.6	2.0	2.6
1974	−0.8	33.4	33.6	10.4	−0.2	2.1	4.4
1975	−4.3	32.5	34.5	11.1	−2.0	2.2	3.9
1976	−3.0	33.3	34.6	11.4	−1.3	2.4	2.9
1977	−2.2	33.7	34.6	11.5	−0.9	2.5	3.1
1978	−2.4	33.6	35.2	11.8	−1.6	2.7	2.7
1979	−1.7	34.2	35.3	11.9	−1.1	3.0	3.8
1980	−2.4	35.0	35.9	12.0	−1.0	3.3	5.0
1981	−2.6	35.9	36.3	12.1	−0.4	3.8	4.0
1982[a]	−3.7	35.9	36.1	12.1	−0.2	4.4	2.8
1983[a]	−4.5	35.6	36.2	12.0	−0.6	4.8	2.6

n.a. = not available.

a. OECD estimates and forecasts.

Sources: OECD (1983*b*); 1981 GDP/GNP weights and exchange rates.

periods. Still, the analysis of the trends would support the notion of a structural shift in savings ratios.[3]

In table A1-26 (also see figure A1-7) the savings rate in OECD appears to have fluctuated with changes in income over the cycle and around a declining savings trend. The OECD average savings rate dropped from 13.11 percent of GDP in the 1960–74 period to 10.1 percent of GDP in the 1975–81 period. This figure is below the savings rate of 12.2 percent of GDP for the entire 1961–81 period. There is also evidence that the savings rate at the bottom of the recent recession was lower (8.9 percent of GDP) than in the previous recession (9.8 percent) and that, at cyclical highs, savings were also lower (10.9 percent of GDP in 1979 as compared with 12.3 percent in 1968). This shift in the trend of savings for the whole of the OECD requires an examination of the savings rates in the different countries and an analysis of the components of savings in each country.[4]

Table A1-27 shows trends in the net national savings rate in twenty-three OECD countries for two periods. In the first column, trends in the 1960–73 period are shown. Column 2 shows savings trends over the

Figure A1-6. *Public Expenditure and Total Tax Revenue in Seven Major OECD Countries, 1960–81*

Percentage of GDP

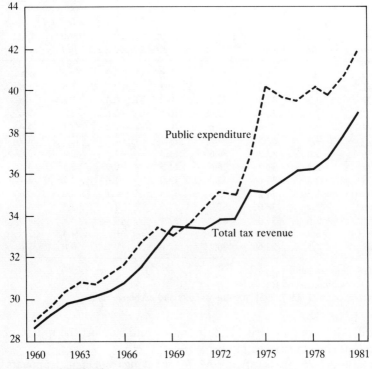

Source: OECD (1983b:46).

longer period, 1960–79. Column 3 indicates the direction of the change in trend, if any, from the 1960–73 period to the 1973–79 period.

A negative change in the trend, shown in column 3, is reflected in a movement from a positive trend to no trend, a reduction in a positive trend value, or a falling trend that becomes more pronounced. During the 1973–79 period there were no rising trends in OECD net savings. Conditions appear to have worsened in the 1980–83 period.

Although the periods here are broken into pre- and post-1973, the fall in the savings rate became more acute after 1975. Although in some countries the saving rate has recovered from the very low 1975 value, in the majority the savings rates have remained low or have decreased even further.

Table A1-26. *Net Savings Rates in the OECD*
(percentage of GDP)

Year	S/GDP	Year	S/GDP
1960	12.49	1971	12.0
1961	12.11	1972	12.2
1962	12.37	1973	14.1
1963	12.28	1974	11.9
1964	10.8	1975	8.9[b]
1965	13.0	1976	9.6
1966	12.6	1977	10.4
1967	11.9	1978	11.4[a]
1968	12.3[a]	1979	10.9
1969	12.9	1980	9.5
1970	12.3	1981	8.5[b]

Note: Growth rates of net savings: 1960–81 = 12.18 percent per annum. 1960–74 = 13.11 percent per annum. 1975–81 = 10.17 percent per annum.
a. Peak of cycle.
b. Bottom of cycle.
Source: OECD *National Accounts*; World Bank estimates.

Figure A1-7. *Saving Rates in OECD Countries, 1964–81*

Percentage of GDP

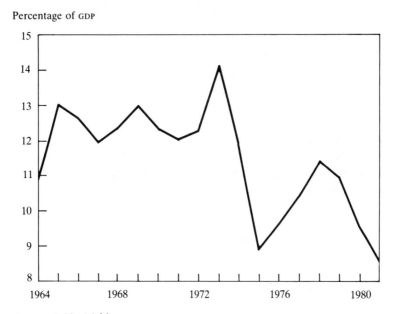

Source: Table A1-26.

Table A1-27. *Savings: Trends and Changes*

Country	Trends in net savings ratios		Changes in savings trend, 1973–79
	1960–73	*1960–79*	
Japan	0.35	No trend	—
Germany	−0.24	−0.46	—
France	0.19	−0.18	—
Italy	−0.27	−0.30	—
United Kingdom	0.18	−0.18	—
United States	No trend	−0.23	—
Canada	0.35	No trend	—
Switzerland	0.16	No trend	—
Netherlands	No trend	−0.33	—
Austria	0.42	No trend	—
Greece	0.84	0.38	—
Australia	0.35	No trend	—
New Zealand	No trend[a]		—
Spain	0.43	No trend	—
Denmark	0.49	−0.43	—
Belgium	0.51	No trend	—
Norway	No trend	−0.32	—
Iceland	No trend	No trend	No trend
Sweden	No trend	−0.39	—
Finland	No trend	No trend	No trend
Ireland	0.39	0.28	—
Turkey	No trend[b]		No trend

Note: Dashes indicate negative trend.
a. 1971–79.
b. 1966–76.
Source: OECD (1981*b*).

The national savings ratio comprises the savings rates in the three principal subsectors in the economy—households, business, and the general government. These are weighted—with their weights determined by the sectoral shares in national income—to provide the overall total. A comprehensive analysis of the savings ratio and the shift in the trend requires an analysis of the sectoral savings ratio and of sectoral shares.

Sectoral savings in OECD can be regarded as the surplus on "current transactions accounts" available for financing real capital formation, lending abroad, or lending to other domestic sectors, where this surplus is used to finance investment or current expenditures.

The primary sources of funds for investment are private and corporate savings, budgetary surpluses arising from government accounts, and borrowings from the rest of the world. Table A1-28 and figure A1-8 indicate the sectoral shares of savings as a percentage of total GDP.[5]

Table A1-28. *Composition of Net Savings
for Seven OECD Countries*
(percentage of GDP)

Year	Total	Corporate	Government	Household
1964	10.8	3.4	2.0	5.4
1965	13.0	3.7	2.5	6.6
1966	12.6	3.5	2.3	6.4
1967	11.9	3.2	1.4	6.9
1968	12.3	3.0	2.2	6.4
1969	12.9	2.4	3.6	6.3
1970	12.3	2.5	2.3	7.4
1971	12.0	2.6	1.9	7.6
1972	12.2	2.9	1.9	7.5
1973	14.1	2.7	2.8	8.7
1974	11.9	0.7	2.1	9.2
1975	8.9	0.7	− 1.3	9.6
1976	9.6	1.4	− 0.2	8.5
1977	10.4	1.9	0.4	8.2
1978	11.4	2.4	0.4	8.6
1979	10.9	2.1	0.9	8.0
1980	9.5	1.2	0.3	8.1
1981	8.5	0.6	− 0.2	8.2

Note: The OECD national accounts include in the household sector both the households themselves and "nonprofit institutions serving households" in the total of "household savings."
Source: OECD *National Accounts*; World Bank estimates.

Table A1-28 suggests that the drop in the net savings of the OECD *corresponds* to increasing *dissavings* in the *government sector* that have not been compensated by corresponding increases in household or corporate savings. Household savings ratios increased in 1974 and 1975, whereas the corporate sector, which showed a deterioration of its financial position in 1974, improved balance sheets in 1975 by contracting investment and inventory expenditures.

After 1975, the household-savings-to-GDP ratio in the major OECD countries had been declining, and corporate sectors' own generation of savings has declined and is substantially below the levels of the mid-1960s or 1970s.

During the 1975–81 period, net government current (dis)savings as a percentage of GDP in the seven major OECD countries was negative in four of six years. When government investments are included, government's overall dissavings was greater still (Chouraqui and Price 1983).

As table A1-27 indicates, household savings have fallen since 1975 because of a complex interaction of microeconomic and macroeconomic factors—which ex ante we may assume to have affected savings behavior.

Figure A1-8. *Sectoral Shares of Net Saving in Seven Major OECD Countries, 1964–81*

Percentage of GDP

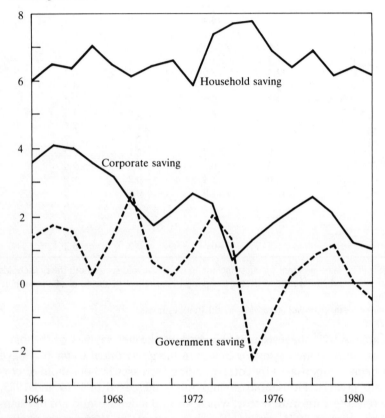

Source: Table A1-28.

These factors include inflation, unemployment, the level of real and nominal interest rates, demographic changes, and income growth.

Table A1-29 outlines the results of a selection of empirical studies of the interest elasticity of the savings rate. In general the results suggest that the relationship is positive though small, that is, that higher interest rates stimulate higher savings. Results, however, are sensitive to specifications. A related factor is the availability of credit, which generally appears, especially in the United States, to be negatively related to savings. The results would therefore support the view that savings will return to a (higher) structural level once households adjust to the no-tion—and remain convinced—that positive returns can be earned on their savings.

The relationship between savings and inflation has also been difficult to quantify. In a period of inflation, savings could be expected to decrease, because there is incentive to accelerate purchases of goods and to switch from money, which is losing its purchasing value, to commodities. Money illusion about inflationary increases in income may also stimulate con-sumption. If interest rates do not adjust during periods of inflation, this is yet another damper on savings incentives. On the other hand, if real interest rates *are* maintained or increased, then the incentive is to shift toward financial instruments instead of commodities. Positive effects on savings derive from the fact that inflation also generates uncertainty. If households expect antiinflationary policies to be put into effect, house-holds will expect increased unemployment and a fall in income growth. This uncertainty will make it rational to increase savings. Finally, there may be attempts to reestablish levels of real wealth, a "target" savings phenomenon that might act to increase savings. This phenomenon appears to have taken place in the United Kingdom (*Bank of England Quarterly Review* 1983). The results outlined in tables A1-30 and A1-31 are sensitive to the period measured. In the studies that include the period to 1980, the effect of inflation on savings is either negative or inconclusive, suggesting that the observed decline in the savings rate from 1978 to the present is due less to structural factors than to microeconomic responses.

The role of budget deficits in the overall savings picture comes into play in part through the effects the deficits might have on inflation and through inflationary expectations, which arise as the result of fears that the deficits will be monetized. Tables A1-30 and A1-31 present the results of a number of studies using the expected inflation variable. The results are not entirely conclusive, but there is evidence that there is a negative relationship also between expected inflation and savings.

A third factor affecting saving is the demographic structure of the population. The life cycle hypothesis of savings is based on a number of demographic factors. They include increases in *life expectancy*, which would cause the household savings ratio of a growing population to rise, because each individual requires higher wealth accumulation to finance a constant consumption stream over the extended retirement period. The *retirement age*, when it is reduced, will increase household savings ratios, because each individual will need a larger stock of wealth to finance consumption. The savings ratio will depend on the distribution of house-holds of certain ages in the total number of households. An increase in

Table A1-29. *Empirical Estimates of the Interest Elasticity*
of Household Savings in the United States

Item	Wright (1967, 1969)	Houth-akker and Taylor (1970)	Taylor (1971)	Helen (1972)	Juster and Watchel (1972)	Juster and Taylor (1975)	Weber (1970)
1 Interest elasticity of saving[a]	0.2	NEG	0.8	1.76	0.28	POS	NEG
2 Dependent variable[b]	CON	SAV	SAV	CON	SAV	SAV	CON
3 Interest rate[c]	NOM	NOM	NOM	NOM	NUM	NOM	NOM
4 Estimation method[d]	OLS	OLS	OLS	NONL	OLS	OLS	NON/NL
5 Periodicity of data[f]	ANN	QRT	QRT	ANN	QRT	QRT	ANN
6 Sample period	1905–49 1929–59	1953–66	1953–69	1948–65	1954–72	1953–73	1930–65 1930–70

a. POS = positive. NEG = negative. (No numerical estimates can be obtained.) NS = not statistically significant.

b. CON = consumption function. SAV = saving function.

c. NOM = nominal. REAL = real.

d. OLS = ordinary least squares. INST = instrumental variables. NONL = nonlinear. ML = maximum likelihood.

the ratio of the working age group (eighteen to sixty-four) as a percentage of the total population would increase savings, and the shift from old (dissavers) to young (savers) would increase savings. Empirically, the OECD has experienced an aging of the population, with further aging expected. Table A1-32 outlines changes in OECD population that might be expected to influence savings rates. The table shows a substantial projected increase in the proportion of the aged population (dissavers) relative to the working population. The proportion of the aged increases from 3.8 percent of total industrialized country working population in 1979 to 13.1 percent by the year 2000. This factor must be considered.

Family size will affect savings, as a larger family affects the overall time profile of consumption and savings (see Leff 1969). The average age of entry into the job market and the period of formal education of young people also affect the dependency period of the young and the aggregate saving ratio. The increases in female participation increase the number of households with two earners. Whether this demographic change has

Item	Blinder (1975)	Springer (1975, 1977)	Mishkin (1976)	Boskin (1978)	Howard (1978)	Howrey and Hymans (1978)	Gly-fason (1981)
1 Interest elasticity of saving[a]	0.03	NEG/POS	NS	0.4	NS	NS	0.3
2 Dependent variable[b]	CON	CON	CON	CON	SAV	SAV	CON
3 Interest rate[c]	REAL	NOM	NOM	REAL	NOM	NOM	NOM
4 Estimation method[d]	OLS[e]	OLS[e]	OLS/INST[e]	OLS/INST[e]	OLS[e]	OLS	OLS[e]
5 Periodicity of data[f]	ANN	QRT	QRT	ANN	QRT	ANN	QRT
6 Sample period	1947–72	1955–71	1952–74	1929–69	1965–76	1951–74	1952–78

e. With Cochrane-Orcutt autocorrelation correction where necessary.

f. ANN = annual. QRT = quarterly.

Source: OECD (1981*b*), but this document does not give complete references for all of the studies cited here and in tables A1-30, A1-31, A1-33, and A1-34.

positive or negative effects on savings depends on the access to consumer credit, the need for precautionary assets, and the substitution of home-produced goods and services by commercial output. A tendency toward a lowering of the savings ratio has been noted as a result of higher female participation in the labor force.

One of the most studied factors among savings determinants is the impact of pension schemes and social security. The theoretical relationship suggests that, if life cycle savings motivations predominate, working generations have little motivation to save for retirement, for which pensions provide. Clearly there is no one-for-one substitution between pensions and private savings, as the characteristics (for example, liquidity) of each are different, and no such one-for-one reduction should be expected. Moreover, since pensions do not typically fully replace past income, there remains some motivation for savings. Empirically, the results presented in tables A1-33 and A1-34 are mixed. In some countries there is evidence of reduced household savings; in others the relationship is difficult to confirm. The reduction of private savings translates into lower national savings because public pension schemes are typically

Table A1-30. *Inflation and Savings: Results of Empirical Studies for OECD Countries*

Item	Deaton (1977)	Howard (1978)	David-son and others (1978)	Shiba (1979)	Koskela and Viren (1980)	Hendry and von Urgern Sternberg (1980)
1 Effect of inflation on savings	POS	POS[a]	POS	POS	POS	POS[b]
2 Estimating equation[a]	SAV	SAV	CON	SAV	SAV	CON
3 Inflation rate	ACT	ACT/EXP	ACT	ACT	ACT	—[b]
4 Estimation method	OLS	OLS	OLS	OLS	OLS	OLS
5 Country	United Kingdom	Canada, Japan, Germany, United Kingdom	United Kingdom	Japan	Finland	United Kingdom
6 Periodicity	QRT	QRT	QRT	ANN	QRT/ANN	QRT
7 Sample period	1955–74	INC	1958–70	1966–75	1959–76	1964–76

Note: POS = positive. NEG = negative. INC = inconclusive. CON = consumption function. SAV = saving function. ACT = actual. EXP = expected. OLS = ordinary least squares. INST = instrumental variables. NONL = nonlinear. ML = maximum likelihood. ANN = annual. QRT = quarterly.

a. These effects are attributed by the authors primarily to uncertainty.

b. No inflation variable is explicitly included in the regression equation, but the income measure used as explanatory variable is adjusted for inflation-induced changes in financial wealth.

Source: OECD (1981*b*).

unfunded. To summarize, these determinants suggest mixed effects, and no clear picture emerges for future savings.

During the 1964–81 period, the corporate sector has generated a declining share of total net savings. The results for the major seven countries for the period are presented in table A1-35. OECD corporate savings made up, on average, 28 percent of total savings in 1964, 19.3 percent in 1970, and 13.6 percent in 1981.

The decrease in the share of corporate savings in the total net savings is not yet explained, although there are a number of hypotheses. One factor may be the (still sparse) evidence on declining trends in profitability in the OECD corporate sector. Higher rates of inflation during the 1974–81 period are another possible explanation (Lintner 1975). Higher inflation, through its effects on profit rates, reduces the portion of retained earn-

Table A1-31. *Inflation and Saving: Results of Empirical Studies for the United States*

Item	Branson and Klevorick (1969)	Houthakker and Taylor (1970)	Juster and Watchel (1972)	Juster and Taylor (1975)	Springer (1975, 1977)	Deaton (1977)	Wachel (1977)	Boskin (1978)	Howard (1978)	Howrey and Hymans (1978)	St. Louis Fed. (1979)	Glyfason (1981)
1 Effect of inflation on savings	NEG	POS	NEG/POS[a]	POS[a]	POS/NEG	POS	POS[a]	POS[a]	POS[a]	NEG	INC	NEG
2 Estimating equation[a]	CON	SAV	SAV	SAV	CON	SAV	SAV	CON	SAV	SAV	SAV	CON
3 Inflation rate	ACT	ACT	ACT/EXP	ACT/EXP	EXP	ACT	ACT/REAL	EXP	ACT/EXP	EXP	ACT/EXP	ACT/EXP
4 Estimation method	OLS/INST	OLS	OLS	OLS	OLS[b]	OLS	OLS	OLS/INST[b]	OLS[b]	OLS	OLS	OLS[b]
5 Periodicity of data	QRT	QRT	QRT	QRT	QRT	QRT	QRT	ANN	QRT	ANN	QRT	QRT
6 Sample period	1955–65	1953–66	1953–71	1953–73	1955–71	1954–74	1955–74	1929–69	1965–76	1951–74	1955–78	1952–78

Note: POS = positive. NEG = negative. INC = inconclusive. CON = consumption function. SAV = saving function. ACT = actual. EXP = expected. OLS = ordinary least squares. INST = instrumental variables. ANN = annual. QRT = quarterly.

a. These effects are attributed primarily to uncertainty by the authors.

b. With Cochrane-Orcutt autocorrelation correction where necessary.

Source: OECD (1981b).

Table A1-32. *Demographic Changes in Industrialized Countries,*
1950–2000

Year	Percentage of working population	
	≤ 14 years of age	≥ 65 years of age
1950	27.8	7.6
1979	40.5	3.8
2000	34.2	13.1

Source: United Nations (1980).

ings used for internal financing. During the 1973–81 period the realized
rate of return in the six major countries (the United States, Japan,
Germany, France, the United Kingdom, and Canada) fell from 20 percent to 13 percent, whereas the share of gross operating surplus fell from
32 percent to 28 percent. These developments have been affected by both
cyclical and secular factors. The secular decline in profitability coincides
with the slowdown in the growth of productivity in most of the OECD
nations. Inflation would also affect profitability, because nonindexed tax
systems lead to a taxation of real capital and wealth.

Uses of Savings

A comparison of gross fixed capital formation as a percentage of GDP in
the larger OECD countries since 1960 and gross savings as a percentage of
GDP (table A1-36) provides the starting point for our examination of the
uses of savings in the OECD. Table A1-37 shows growth rates of GNP,
capital formation, and savings, at current and constant prices. It shows
that, in real terms corrected by a common deflator at 1975 prices and
dollar exchange rates, the weakness in OECD output growth correlates
with a slowdown in fixed capital formation and in savings, here shown as
gross savings. The downward trends that were apparent in net savings are
paralleled in the trend for the variables shown for the period 1974–81.
During the 1960–81 period, the growth rate in capital formation in the
OECD averaged 4.2 per annum. In the 1960–74 period the average was 6.2
percent. The average rate for the 1974–81 period has been 0.8 percent,
less than 1 percent, for fixed capital formation. These outcomes result in
part from the large drop in investment and savings in 1974 and 1975. Both
gross savings and investment have grown at parallel rates in real terms
over the latter period. It is therefore difficult to demonstrate that lower

Table A1-33. *Time Series Estimates of the Effects of Mandatory Public Pension Schemes on Personal Savings (Consumption) in the United States*

Item	Feldstein (1974)		Munnell (1974)[a]		Barro (1974)[a]		Darby (1979)[a]		Leimer and Lesnoy (1980)
1 Dependent variable	CON	CON	SAV	SAV	CON	CON	CON	CON	CON
2 Regression coefficient on gross social security wealth variable	0.021	0.029	−0.030	−0.058	0.014	0.014	0.017	0.011	−0.002
t statistic	3.4	0.83	2.60	1.40	1.40	0.39	1.31	0.59	0.26
3 Estimated depressing effect on personal savings (as a percentage of actual savings, approximate average value)	50% or higher		Much weaker (and statistically insignificant) effect than Feldstein (1974) results						No effect
4 Sample period	1929–71	1947–71	1929–69[b]	1946–69	1929–74[b]	1947–74	1929–74[b]	1947–74	1930–74[b]

Note: CON = consumption function. SAV = saving function.

a. Representative results have been chosen according to Esposito (1978).

b. Excludes the period 1941–46.

Source: OECD (1981b).

Table A1-34. *Time Series Estimates of the Effects of Mandatory Public Pension Schemes on Household Savings (Consumption) in OECD Countries*

Item	Perelman and Pestieau (1981)	Wrage (1980)	Boyle and Murray (1979)	Pfaff and others (1978)	Markowski and Palmer (1979)
1 Country	Belgium	Canada	Canada	Germany	Sweden
2 Dependent variable	CON	SAV	SAV[a]	SAV[a]	SAV
3 Regression coefficient on social security variable					
Social security wealth (*t* statistic)	0.028 (1.9)	−0.008[b] (−0.85)	POS/NEG[d]	n.a.	n.a.
Social security benefits (*t* statistic)	n.a.	−0.031[c] (1.79)	n.a.	−0.199 (−1.33)	−111.65 (2.5)[e]
Social security contributions	n.a.	n.a.	n.a.	n.a.	n.a.
4 Implied depressing effect on savings (as percentage of actual saving, approximate)	40%	—[f]	INC	15%	30%[g]
5 Sample period	1954–77	1953–75	1954–75	1960–77	1952–75

n.a. = not available.

Note: The results included in the table are representative. CON = consumption function. SAV = saving function. INC = inconclusive.

a. Serious misspecification reduces usefulness of results (important explanatory variables are missing from regression equation).

b. Canadian pension plan wealth.

c. Old age security wealth.

d. Both positive and negative coefficients (all statistically insignificant at the 95 percent level) were obtained for different combinations of additional explanatory variables.

e. The benefit variable used is an estimate of the contribution of expected future pensions to permanent income; see Markowski and Palmer (1979) for a detailed description of the variable.

f. Information given insufficient to calculate this figure.

g. According to the study quoted, asset formation of the social security fund more than compensated for the depressing effect on personal savings, so that the net effect on *national* savings was positive.

Source: OECD 1981*b*).

Table A1-35. *Net Corporate Savings as a Percentage of Total Net Savings*

Country	1964	1965	1966	1967	1968	1969	1970	1971	1972	1973	1974	1975	1976	1977	1978	1979	1980	1981
Canada	45.4	42.5	35.7	37.9	41.0	35.3	34.2	38.2	39.5	43.6	42.5	48.6	46.0	51.7	55.0	60.8	57.5	40.0
France	14.3	14.1	16.8	17.5	20.1	22.2	16.7	16.4	17.2	16.4	3.4	-1.5	-8.3	2.9	7.7	9.7	0.02	-16.6
Germany	27.8	28.5	27.6	30.7	29.1	18.4	19.2	15.9	12.8	8.9	5.8	0.8	9.8	5.1	16.3	14.4	3.0	-7.6
Italy	2.4	10.3	14.9	11.9	16.7	16.4	6.9	2.9	4.0	5.6	2.0	-20.6	-7.2	-7.4	-6.1	6.0	8.9	-5.8
Japan	n.a.	n.a.	n.a.	n.a.	n.a.	n.a.	31.6	23.1	24.4	16.6	-2.1	-2.9	4.8	5.7	13.5	12.0	9.3	2.9
United Kingdom	49.6	41.0	28.7	26.3	27.4	21.0	10.5	21.5	33.4	38.4	2.1	-10.1	23.9	50.9	48.4	29.0	-0.3	-8.3
United States	36.3	37.6	38.6	38.6	33.6	24.9	27.9	26.0	31.6	22.3	9.2	31.8	35.2	38.7	34.4	27.6	24.7	22.9
OECD (seven countries)	28.0	35.5	36.0	35.4	30.8	22.8	19.3	24.2	22.7	20.3	6.8	18.5	23.4	25.4	25.0	21.8	15.6	13.6

n.a. = not available.
Source: OECD *National Accounts*, table 7, lines 1.1 and 1.

Table A1-36. *OECD: Gross Capital Formation and Savings*

Year	Gross fixed capital formation[a]	Gross savings[a]	Surplus or deficit with the rest of the world[a]	Net savings[a]
1960	19.5	21.6	n.a.	12.49
1961	19.8	21.2	n.a.	12.11
1962	20.0	21.4	n.a.	12.37
1963	20.2	21.5	n.a.	12.28
1964	20.7	22.2	n.a.	13.23
1965	20.9	22.9	n.a.	13.74
1966	20.8	22.5	n.a.	13.38
1967	20.5	22.0	n.a.	12.76
1968	20.7	22.4	n.a.	13.18
1969	21.1	23.2	n.a.	13.87
1970	21.3	22.9	n.a.	13.55
1971	21.6	22.5	n.a.	13.05
1972	22.1	23.1	n.a.	14.75
1973	23.0	24.9	0.3	14.75
1974	22.4	23.3	−0.	12.78
1975	21.1	20.8	0.4	9.81
1976	20.9	21.5	−0.4	10.31
1977	21.3	22.1	−0.5	10.46
1978	22.0	23.2	0.2	11.04
1979	22.2	23.2	−0.1	11.05
1980	21.8	21.9	−1.0	9.65
1981	21.2	21.4	−0.7	8.90

n.a. = not available.
a. As a percentage of GDP.
Source: OECD *National Accounts*, table 1.

investment derives from lower savings, and overall economic conditions may have been important.

Table A1-38 shows the sectoral composition of capital formation. The sectoral shares have exhibited broad stability over the period, and there is little evidence of a shift in the share of investment, between corporations, government, and households. The corporate share of investment has remained stable at 55 percent of total investment, with government investment at 11–12 percent and households at 30–33 percent of the total. Any decline in corporate investment should therefore perhaps be attributed to overall economic conditions and not to absorption of available shares or financing by governments or households.

Table A1-39 outlines the *net* savings position, or sectoral balance, of each sector. It is derived by subtracting from each sector's gross savings

Table A1-37. *Annual Growth in Output (GDP), Investment, and Gross Savings, OECD, 1960–81*

Year	GDP[a]	Invest-ment[a,b]	Gross savings[a]	1979 exchange rates GDP[c]	INV[c]	Gross savings[c]
1961	9.0	6.8	5.0	4.7	7.1	3.1
1962	9.6	8.5	9.1	5.3	6.7	6.0
1963	8.8	7.7	7.3	4.8	6.2	5.1
1964	12.2	9.3	13.7	6.3	9.4	10.8
1965	9.5	8.8	11.1	5.2	6.7	7.7
1966	9.1	9.3	7.6	5.3	5.8	4.8
1967	5.0	6.9	4.9	3.8	2.8	2.7
1968	10.1	9.7	11.6	5.4	7.0	8.4
1969	12.3	10.4	14.0	5.3	6.8	8.8
1970	11.2	9.4	9.7	3.3	4.2	2.4
1971	11.1	10.0	7.9	3.7	4.8	1.4
1972	12.1	11.3	12.4	5.4	6.6	7.3
1973	16.6	14.2	20.8	6.0	7.5	11.2
1974	10.5	12.6	6.2	0.8	−4.7	−8.1
1975	4.7	10.7	−1.2	−0.2	−5.5	−10.7
1976	11.9	13.3	15.4	4.8	3.8	6.9
1977	13.0	12.2	12.9	3.8	4.6	8.6
1978	13.6	12.5	15.8	3.9	5.4	3.4
1979	14.3	13.0	13.8	3.1	3.8	3.3
1980	11.1	13.3	7.3	1.2	−0.9	−4.2
1981	9.5	12.4	8.5	1.5	−0.2	−1.2

Growth rates	Nom-inal GDP	Fixed capital formation	Gross savings	Real GDP	Real fixed capital formation	Real gross savings
1960–81	11.25	10.5	9.8	3.97	4.2	1.5
1960–74	9.76	9.6	10.0	4.96	6.2	5.1
1974–81	11.07	12.4	9.2	2.36	0.8	0.8

a. Current prices.
b. Fixed capital formation.
c. Constant 1975 prices.
Source: OECD *National Accounts*, table 1.

the "capital formation" of that sector to arrive at the sector's net savings or dissavings position. Net borrowing from outside OECD has averaged about 4.2 percent of savings and about 2 percent of the gross fixed capital formation. The recent trend since 1974 reflects a systematic decline in OECD net lending and a reversal from the position of net lender to that of net borrower (table A1-40).

Table A1-38. *Seven Major Countries: Percentage of Total Capital Formation by Sector*

Year	Corporate	Government	Household
1964	49.9	14.9	34.6
1965	51.6	14.3	33.2
1966	53.7	14.7	30.7
1967	54.0	15.4	29.6
1968	54.0	14.8	30.2
1969	56.5	13.5	29.0
1970	55.4	14.0	30.4
1971	52.4	14.0	33.0
1972	52.7	12.2	35.0
1973	54.7	11.9	33.3
1974	58.7	12.9	28.3
1975	53.9	14.8	31.2
1976	57.0	12.1	30.7
1977	54.8	11.2	33.9
1978	53.8	12.1	34.0
1979	55.9	11.5	32.5
1980	55.4	12.7	31.8
1981	55.9	11.3	32.6

Source: OECD *National Accounts*, vol. 2, table 7.

Deficits and Savings

Table A1-41 (from OECD 1983*b*) examines national savings in relation to government absorption of savings (also see Chouraqui and Price 1983). The table shows, for 1970–83, the claims of government borrowings on the private savings available. Shown are: (a) actual budget deficits as a fraction of *gross* savings; (b) actual budget deficits as a fraction of *net* savings; and (c) actual deficits as a fraction of gross savings at full employment GDP, or "potential savings." For the seven major OECD countries taken together, the government deficit absorbs 51.7 percent of net savings and 21.2 percent of gross savings in 1983. This range varies widely among countries, with the U.S. deficit absorbing some 60.2 percent of private net savings in 1982 and a low of 20.9 percent of net savings taken by the government sector in Japan. The largest fraction occurs in Italy, where the government accounts for almost 75 percent of net savings. The extent of government absorption of saving represents a striking change from past trends—in 1970, OECD government deficits absorbed *less than 1 percent* of gross savings. By 1975 this figure had risen to 44.8 percent and by 1983 to 51.7 percent.

(Text continues on p. 356)

Table A1-39. *Sectoral Financial Balances in the Seven Major OECD Countries, Surplus or Deficit, 1973–82* (percentage of nominal GDP)

Country	1973	1974	1975	1976	1977	1978	1979	1980	1981	1982
United States[a]										
General government sector	0.6	-0.3	-4.2	-2.1	-0.9	0	0.6	-1.3	-1.0	-3.8
Federal government	-0.4	-0.8	-4.5	-3.1	-2.4	-1.4	-0.7	-2.3	-2.0	4.8
Household sector	2.8	4.0	4.7	2.7	1.2	1.2	1.4	2.4	3.1	3.9
Corporate sector[b]	-2.9	-3.3	0.7	-0.2	-1.0	-1.9	-2.0	-0.9	-2.0	-0.2
Foreign sector	-0.5	-0.3	-1.2	-0.3	0.7	0.7	0.1	-0.3	-0.1	0.2
Japan[c]										
General government sector	0.7	0.4	-2.8	-3.8	-3.8	-5.9	-4.4	-3.9	-4.0	-4.0
Central government	0.0	-1.8	-4.2	-4.5	-5.5	-6.2	-5.6	-5.5	-5.6	..
Household sector	8.0	9.9	9.6	10.7	9.9	9.7	8.5	7.9	11.6	11.9
Corporate sector[b]	-8.7	-11.2	-6.9	-6.2	-4.6	-2.0	-5.0	-5.0	-7.2	-7.1
Foreign sector	0	1.0	0.1	-0.7	-1.5	-1.7	0.9	1.1	-0.4	-0.6
Germany										
General government sector	1.2	-1.4	-5.7	-3.4	-2.4	-2.5	-2.7	-3.2	-4.0	-3.9
Central government	0.0	-0.5	-3.0	-2.3	-1.5	-1.6	-1.5	-1.7	-2.4	-2.1
Household sector	7.9	8.6	9.4	7.8	7.0	6.7	7.0	7.3	7.9	7.9
Corporate sector[b]	-7.8	-4.7	-2.7	-3.6	-3.9	2.8	-5.2	-6.3	-5.1	-3.4
Foreign sector	-1.3	-2.6	-1.0	-0.8	-0.7	-1.3	0.9	2.1	1.2	-0.4
France										
General government sector	0.9	0.6	-2.2	-0.5	-0.8	-1.9	-0.7	0.3	-1.9	-2.6
Central government	1.2	0.9	-1.9	-0.1	-0.7	-1.3	-0.8	-0.2	-1.1	-1.9
Household sector	3.5	3.7	5.7	3.8	4.3	5.2	3.6	2.8	3.7	3.7
Corporate sector[b]	-4.6	-6.8	-3.6	-5.0	-4.2	-2.8	-3.0	-4.6	-3.6	-2.9
Foreign sector	0.2	2.4	0.1	1.6	0.8	-0.5	0.1	1.4	1.5	2.1
United Kingdom[a]										
General government sector	-2.7	-3.8	-4.6	-4.9	-3.2	-4.2	-3.2	-3.3	-2.5	-2.0

(Table continues on the following page.)

Table A1-39 *(continued)*

Country	1973	1974	1975	1976	1977	1978	1979	1980	1981	1982
United Kingdom[a] *(cont.)*										
Central government	0.1	-0.4	-2.3	-3.4	-2.0	-3.2	-2.1	-2.1	-2.4	-2.4
Household sector	4.0	5.1	5.4	4.8	3.8	5.6	6.7	8.2	6.6	4.5
Corporate sector[b]	-2.7	-5.3	-2.3	-0.6	-0.8	-0.7	-4.0	-3.6	-1.7	-1.0
Foreign sector	1.4	4.0	1.4	0.7	0.2	-0.6	0.4	-1.3	-2.4	-1.5
Italy										
General government sector	-7.0	-7.0	-11.7	-9.0	-8.0	-9.7	-9.5	-8.0	-11.7	-12.0
Central government	-5.3	-4.0	-7.4	-4.6	-4.9	-11.0	-9.1	-7.4	-9.8	-10.5
Household sector	11.9	12.1	17.5	13.7	14.2	15.2	13.3	9.6	10.6	11.3
Corporate sector[b]	-6.7	-9.8	-6.1	-6.2	-5.1	-3.1	-2.1	-4.0	-1.2	-0.9
Foreign sector	1.8	4.7	0.3	1.5	-1.1	-2.4	-1.7	2.4	2.3	1.6
Canada										
General government sector	1.0	1.9	-2.4	-1.7	-2.6	-3.1	-1.9	-2.1	-1.5	-5.5
Federal government	0.3	0.8	-2.3	-1.8	-3.5	-4.6	-3.5	-3.5	-2.4	-6.0
Household sector	3.9	5.0	5.1	3.9	4.2	5.3	5.1	6.1	6.5	8.0
Corporate sector[b]	-4.8	-7.9	-5.5	-4.2	-3.7	-4.3	-5.1	-4.3	-6.6	-1.7
Foreign sector	-0.1	1.0	2.9	2.0	2.1	-2.1	1.9	0.4	1.6	-0.8
Seven-country average										
General government	0.1	-0.4	-4.3	-3.0	-2.3	-2.5	-2.0	-2.4	-2.8	-4.1
Household sector	4.7	5.8	6.8	+5.6	4.8	5.2	4.8	5.0	+6.1	+6.4
Corporate sector	-4.9	-6.2	-2.3	-2.9	-2.8	-2.3	-3.0	-3.0	-3.5	-2.2
Foreign sector	+0.1	+0.8	-0.2	+0.3	+0.2	-0.4	+0.2	+0.4	+0.2	+0.1

Note: Foreign sector: (−) = capital outflows; (+) = inflow.

a. On an SNA basis except for the United States and the United Kingdom, which are on a national income account basis. For explanations concerning methodology, see annex ("Sources and Methods"), *OECD Economic Outlook* no. 32. The sum of the three domestic sectors may not equal the foreign sector because of rounding.   b. Including public corporations and financial institutions.   c. Percentage of nominal GNP.

Sources: OECD *National Accounts,* and OECD secretariat estimates, net lending to the rest of the world, table 67.

352

Table A1-40. *OECD Net Lending to the Rest of the World*
as a Percentage of Savings and as a Percentage of OECD GDP

Item	1973	1974	1975	1976	1977	1978	1979	1980	1981
Net lending as percentage of savings	2.2	−5.72	0.4	−4.3	−5.02	0.2	−4.2	−10.5	−8.8
Net lending as percentage of GDP	0.32	−0.7	0.04	−0.4	−0.5	0.02	−0.05	−1.02	−0.7
OPEC surplus as a percentage of OECD GDP[a]	1.4	1.0	0.6	0.6	0.4	0.1	0.5	1.00	0.8

a. Surplus of capital surplus oil-exporting countries.
Sources: OECD *National Accounts*, table 7; World Bank estimates.

Table A1-41. *General Government Financial Deficits*
(percentage of private savings)

Country	1970	1971	1972	1973	1974	1975	1976	1977	1978	1979	1980	1981	1982[a]	1983[a]
United States														
Actual gross	5.9	10.3	2.0	-2.8	1.1	22.9	12.4	5.4	-0.2	-3.6	7.6	5.6	20.6	24.2
Actual net	13.3	22.2	4.6	-5.7	2.7	52.4	30.6	13.5	-0.5	-9.6	22.9	16.2	55.5	60.2
Potential gross	-0.9	2.8	-0.7	0.2	-5.2	5.0	-2.2	-3.4	-4.5	-7.3	-3.6	-8.2	-5.9	5.0
Japan														
Actual gross	-5.7	-4.4	-1.2	-1.6	-1.2	9.5	12.1	13.1	18.2	16.6	15.0	14.4	13.3	9.5
Actual net	-9.3	-7.7	-2.0	-2.7	-2.1	17.1	20.6	23.0	31.0	29.8	27.5	28.0	28.1	20.9
Potential gross	-5.3	-5.0	-1.2	-0.2	-1.7	7.1	10.0	11.3	17.2	16.7	15.3	13.8	11.4	7.4
Germany														
Actual gross	-0.9	0.8	2.5	-6.0	6.3	26.5	16.6	12.5	12.2	13.1	15.4	19.8	21.1	21.4
Actual net	-1.6	1.4	4.6	-11.9	12.6	55.9	35.5	28.9	26.2	28.1	36.3	48.9	55.2	61.8
Potential gross	0.9	0.8	2.4	-4.2	4.5	18.2	12.7	8.6	9.9	12.9	13.9	12.7	6.0	0.3
France														
Actual gross	-4.4	-3.5	-3.7	-4.4	-3.1	10.7	2.5	4.2	8.8	3.3	-1.8	8.8	15.3	16.1
Actual net	-7.9	-6.1	-6.3	-7.5	-5.9	20.2	5.8	8.5	16.7	6.5	-4.2	21.8	34.5	36.7
Potential gross	-8.0	-5.9	-3.7	-3.2	-5.2	-0.7	-9.3	-9.9	-5.1	-11.3	-22.2	-20.7	-16.1	-18.0
United Kingdom														
Actual gross	-21.3	-10.8	7.2	14.0	23.4	28.4	27.9	16.5	19.8	15.5	16.9	13.6	13.4	13.5
Actual net	-48.1	-25.9	14.0	24.8	54.7	70.0	61.5	34.0	38.2	31.8	39.1	36.1	43.9	57.6
Potential gross	-21.3	-12.3	3.2	18.6	21.6	17.7	19.2	11.0	23.1	19.0	10.0	-4.7	-9.8	-10.4

Italy

Actual gross	20.9	28.9	32.6	31.7	43.5	33.4	29.9	35.1	33.3	32.6	44.8	45.1	45.4
Actual net	31.2	42.4	47.2	48.7	69.4	52.4	47.9	54.2	50.5	51.4	70.9	71.7	74.4
Potential gross	21.5	27.5	32.4	31.7	38.8	30.0	25.5	30.0	29.4	29.6	40.5	36.2	34.3

Canada

Actual gross	−5.5	−0.8	−5.3	−9.8	12.5	8.5	13.6	15.5	9.3	9.7	6.2	30.5	30.6
Actual net	−13.6	−2.0	−10.5	−19.1	24.1	16.1	27.4	29.5	17.2	18.0	11.9	55.4	54.2
Potential gross	−8.8	−0.8	1.3	−4.8	12.2	10.1	11.6	13.4	6.6	2.1	−2.7	2.1	1.3

Total[b]

Actual gross	0.5	3.1	0.1	3.8	21.0	14.1	10.0	9.3	6.4	11.0	11.7	20.1	21.2
Actual net	0.9	5.5	−0.9	7.7	44.8	30.1	20.4	16.6	10.4	25.3	26.5	48.8	51.7
Potential gross	−2.8	1.6	2.6	0.5	9.4	4.8	3.2	5.6	3.3	3.0	−0.1	−0.2	3.1

Note: Gross private savings = households + business savings net of stock appreciation, where data are available (for the United States, United Kingdom, and Canada) but before allowance for capital consumption. Net private savings = gross savings after deducting capital consumption. Actual gross = ratio of actual general government net lending to actual gross private savings; actual net = ratio of actual general government net lending to actual net private savings; potential gross = ratio of general government net lending at potential output to OECD estimate of private gross savings at potential output.

a. OECD estimates and forecasts.

b. 1981 GNP/GDP weights and exchange rates.

Source: OECD (1983b).

Figure A1-9 depicts these trends in government deficits and in national saving graphically. There has been a substantial narrowing of the gap between the domestic savings available and the deficits that must be financed. The gap has, to some extent, been bridged by foreign savings.

Figure A1-9. *Saving Rates and Budget Deficits in OECD Countries, 1970–81*

Percentage of GDP

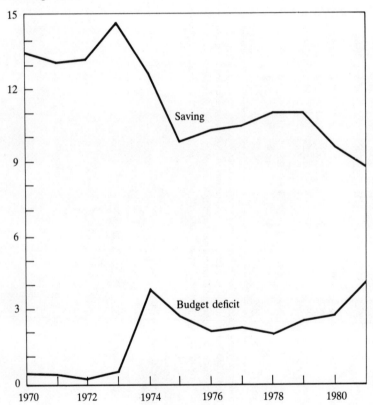

Source: OECD National Accounts, vol. 1, tables 1, 7.

Notes

1. State and local taxes have not been included in the discussion. The conclusion becomes stronger if they are.

2. OECD (1983*d*) offers the example of sending children to the hospital because taking them to a doctor would interfere with the parents' work time.

3. In this section trends in *net* savings are examined. In discussing savings behavior and behavioral determinants, net savings is the relevant concept. Net savings is defined as gross savings less capital consumption allowances. Gross savings thus includes net savings and capital consumption. Because capital consumption allowances are not a behavioral variable but are determined by legal and tax structures in the country concerned, the gross savings concept is less interesting in analyzing changes in savings trends. Gross saving across countries is relatively constant and shows virtually no trend over time. Capital consumption allowances, or depreciation, are relatively more important in countries with lower savings than in countries with higher savings. During the 1970s, capital consumption exceeded net savings by large margins in the United States and the United Kingdom. In countries with very fast rates of capital formation, capital consumption was smaller than net savings and also less important relative to national disposable income.

4. This section examines only the standard national accounts savings data, which, as we shall see, do not take into account country institutional differences. Savings rates need to be adjusted, among other things, for indirect taxes, pensions, consumer durables purchases, and so forth. There have, however, been attempts to explain the variations in the savings ratio in different OECD countries to take into account the importance of institutional factors that the accounting rules in the system of national accounts do not incorporate in detail. Blades (1983) examines household savings ratios and incorporates various changes in the accounting rules of the United Nations System of National Accounts (SNA). The SNA gross savings ratio is 36 percent. The coefficient is reduced to 26 percent when corporate net savings are included or when households and all enterprises are incorporated in the sector. The coefficient of variation rises to 50 percent if the adjustment is made to exclude unincorporated enterprises from the household sector, and the coefficient of variation is reduced to 19 percent when expenditures on consumer durables are included in the savings component. The increased stability of the savings ratio, which includes consumer durables as capital, results in a marked reduction in the difference in savings rates between countries. Nevertheless, despite the adjustments, the data on savings still show a trend toward a reduction in national savings ratios since 1975.

5. The data are based on the classification in the OECD *National Accounts*, table 7, for each OECD country for 1960–81. Estimates for 1982 and 1983 have been made.

References

Bank of England quarterly review. 1983. Vol. 23.

Barro, Robert J. 1974. Are government bonds net wealth? *Journal of political economy* 82 (November/December):1095–1117.

Beckerman, W. 1979. *Income maintenance programs and their impact on poverty*. Geneva: International Labor Organization (ILO).

Blades, Derek. 1983. Alternative measures of saving. *Economic Outlook.* Occasional studies. Paris: OECD. June.

Blinder, Alan S. 1975. Distribution effects and the aggregate consumption function. *Journal of political economy* 83(June):447–75.

Boskin, Michael J. 1978. Taxation, saving, and the rate of interest. *Journal of political economy* 86(February):53–527.

Boyle, P., and J. Murray. 1979. Social security wealth and private saving in Canada. *Canadian journal of economics* 12(August):456–68.

Branson, W. H., and A. K. Klevorick. 1969. Money illusions and the aggregate consumption function. *American economic review* 59(December):832–50.

Bundesministerium der Finanzen. 1982. *Finanzbericht.* Bonn: Bundesministerium.

Chouraqui, Jean-Claude, and Robert Price. 1983. *Medium-term financial strategy: The coordination of fiscal and monetary policies.* Working paper 9. Organisation for Economic Co-operation and Development (OECD), Monetary and Fiscal Policy Division.

Darby, Michael R. 1979. *Effects of social security on income and the capital stock.* Washington, D.C.: American Enterprise Institute.

Davidson, J. E., David F. Hendry, Frank Srba, and Stephen Yeo. 1978. Econometric modelling of the aggregate time-series relationship between consumers' expenditure and income in the United Kingdom. *Economic journal* 88(December):661–92.

Deaton, Angus. 1977. Involuntary saving through unanticipated inflation. *American economic review* 67(December):899–910.

Dewhurst, J.F., and Associates. 1961. *Europe's needs and resources.* New York: Twentieth Century Fund.

Emi, I. 1954. *Government fiscal activity and economic growth in Japan, 1868–1960.* Tokyo: Kinokuniya.

Esposito, Louis. 1978. Effect of social security on saving: Review of studies using U.S. time series data. *Social security bulletin* 41(May):9–18.

European Economic Community (EEC). 1981 *Poverty report.* Brussels: EEC.

Federal Reserve Board (FRB). 1983. *Public policy and capital formation.* Washington, D.C.: FRB.

Feldstein, Martin S. 1974. Social security, induced retirement, and aggregate capital accumulation. *Journal of political economy* 82(September/October):905–26.

Glyfason, Thorvaldor. 1981. Interest rates, inflation, and the aggregate consumption function. *Review of economics and statistics* 63(May):233–45.

Howrey, Philip E., and Saul H. Hymans. 1978. The measurement and determination of loanable-funds saving. *Bookings papers on economic activity,* no. 3:655–705.

International Monetary Fund (IMF). 1983–84. *International financial statistics.* Washington, D.C.: IMF.

Juster, F. Thomas, and Lester D. Taylor. 1975. Towards a theory of saving behavior. *American economic review: Papers and proceedings* 65(May):203–09.

Juster, F. Thomas, and Paul Wachtel. 1972. Inflation and the consumer. *Brookings papers on economic activity,* no. 1:71–121.

Leff, N. 1969. Dependency rates and saving rates. *American economic review* 59(December):886–96.

Leimer, Dean, and Selig Lesnoy. 1980. *Social security and private saving: A re-examination of the time series evidence using alternative social security wealth variables.* Washington, D.C.: U.S. Social Security Administration, Office of Research and Statistics.

Lintner, John. 1975. Inflation and security returns. *Journal of finance* 30(May):259–80.

Markowski, A., and E. Palmer. 1979. Social insurance and saving in Sweden. In George von Furstenberg, ed. *Social Security versus private saving.* Cambridge, Mass.: Ballinger.

Munnell, Alicia H. 1974. *Effects of social security on private savings.* Cambridge, Mass.: Ballinger.

Ohkawa, I., and M. Shinohara. 1979. *Patterns of Japanese development.* New Haven: Yale University Press.

Organisation for Economic Co-operation and Development (OECD). 1954–83. *National accounts.*

———. 1976. *Public expenditure on income maintenance programs.* OECD.

———. 1981*a*. Public sector deficits: Problems and policy issues. CPE/WP1(81)1. OECD.

———. 1981*b*. International differences and trend changes in savings ratios. CPE/WP1(81)9. OECD.

———. 1981*c*. Document for the ad hoc experts group on health policy and health systems. SME/SAIR/HI/81.03. OECD.

———. 1982*a*. Profit rates in OECD countries. DES/NI/82.6. OECD.

———. 1982*b*. The role of the public sector: Issues for discussion. CPE/WP1(82)5. OECD.

———. 1982*c*. CPE/WP1(82)1. OECD.

———. 1982*d*. *Economic outlook,* nos. 31, 32.

———. 1983*a*. Structural budget deficits and fiscal policy responses to the recession. CPE/WP1(83)1. OECD.

———. 1983*b*. Structural budget deficits and fiscal policy responses to the recession. CPE/WP1(83)2. OECD.

———. 1983*c*. Expenditure on health under economic constraints. Pt. 2: Estimates of expenditure: Costs and selected indicators. MAS(83)4. OECD.

———. 1983*d*. Expenditure on health services. SME/SAIR/SE/83.04. OECD.

———. 1983*e*. Old-age pensions. SME/SAIR/SE/83.06. OECD.

———. 1983*f*. Unemployment compensation. SME/SAIR/SE/83.07. OECD.

———. 1983*g*. The growth of social expenditure: Recent trends and implications for the 1980s. SME/SAIR/SE/83.01. OECD.

———. 1983*h*. Expenditure on education. SME/SAIR/SE/83.05. OECD.

———. 1983*i*. The growth of social expenditure: Overview and main issues. SME/SAIR/SE/ 83.09. OECD.

———. 1983*j*. The control of social expenditure: Policies and problems. SME/SAIR/SE/83.03. OECD.

———. 1983*k*. The present unemployment problem. CPE/WP1(83)6. OECD.

———. 1983*l*. Statistical and technical annex. SME/SAIR/SE/83.02. OECD.

———. 1983*m*. Perspectives on macroeconomic performance in the 1970's. *Economic Outlook.* Occasional studies. OECD.

———. 1983*n*. Public sector deficits: Problems and policy implications. *Economic Outlook.* Occasional studies. OECD.

———. 1983*o*. Consequences of public sector size and growth: Summary and issues for discussion. CPE/WP1(83)8. OECD.

———. 1983*p*. The role of the public sector. CPW/WP1(82)4. OECD.

———. 1983*q*. *Economic outlook,* no. 33.

Perelman, S., and P. Pestieau. 1981. The effect of social security on savings: The case of Belgium. Paper presented for the ISPE conference on taxation of capital and savings. Paris, June 22–24.

Pfaff, Martin, Peter Hurler, and Rudolf Dennerlein. 1978. Old-age security and saving in the Federal Republic of Germany. In George von Furstenberg, ed. *Social security versus private saving.* Cambridge, Mass.: Ballinger.

Shiba, J. The personal savings function of urban worker households in Japan. *Review of economics and statistics* 161(May):206–13.

Stigler, G. J. 1970. Director's law of public income redistribution. *Journal of law and economics* 13(April):1–10.

Taylor, Lester. 1971. Saving out of different types of income. *Brookings papers on economic activity*, no. 2.

United Nations. 1980. ESA/P/WP6.J. New York.

U.S. Department of Commerce. 1976. *The national income and product accounts of the United States, 1929–1974.* Washington, D.C.: U.S. Department of Commerce.

Vu, My T., with K. C. Zachariah. 1983. *Short-term population projection, 1980–2020, and long-term projection, 2000 to stationary stage by age and sex for all countries of the world.* Washington, D.C.: World Bank.

Weber, W.E. 1970. The effect of interest rates on consumption. *American economic review* 60(April).

Appendix 2

ICORS, Savings Rates, and the Determinants of Public Expenditure in Developing Countries

Constantino Lluch

THIS APPENDIX summarizes trends and cycles in investment rates, domestic savings rates, and foreign capital inflows for a number of countries. The first three sections describe these trends for the three major developing country regions. Within regions, countries are ordered by increasing per capita income. The usual periodicity in the reporting of economic data—a year, a quarter, a month—covers cycles in investment rates with different phase and amplitude. Yearly averages over periods other than a cycle phase are not particularly useful to uncover trend regularities.[1] For this reason, and because yearly output growth rates vary for so many other circumstances besides capital accumulation, the basic comparison reported in this appendix is for peak incremental capital-output ratios (ICORS): ratios of the rate of investment at the peak of the cycle to the yearly rate of output growth over the upswing phase.

The distinction between peak and trough ICORS is a useful one. The trough ICOR is the ratio of the trough investment rate to the yearly rate of output growth over the downswing. Trough ICORS vary across countries and cycles much more than peak ICORS do. The fourth section summarizes the results of statistical studies on the socioeconomic determinants of public expenditures.

ICORS and Savings Rates in Africa

Rates of investment, output growth, and inflation in eleven African countries appear in table A2-1. The choice of time periods obeys the following rule: linear interpolation can be used to approximate investment rates in the intervening years not included in the table.[2]

Smoothing the changes in investment rates in this fashion does not

The author is indebted to D. Lal for comments and suggestions and to C. Jen and V. Kozel for assistance.

Table A2-1. *Investment Rate, ICORs, and Inflation in Eleven African Countries*

Country and year	Invest- ment rate	Output growth[a]	Inflation rate	ICOR[b]
Chad				
1961	9.3	n.a.	n.a.	n.a.
1963	11.4	n.a.	n.a.	n.a.
1967	8.2	n.a.	n.a.	n.a.
1975	17.2	n.a.	n.a.	n.a.
Ethiopia				
1961	11.7	n.a.	n.a.	n.a.
1967	14.2	5.2	1.4	2.7
1978	7.5	2.8	3.7	2.7
1982	11.0	4.2	2.4	2.6
Zaire				
1962	6.6	n.a.	n.a.	n.a.
1963	29.2	4.3	91.5	6.8
1964	13.8	4.9	−3.8	2.8
1965	27.8	3.9	34.2	7.1
1966	13.6	3.4	0.0	4.0
1972	32.1	5.2	18.8	6.2
1976	22.9	0.1	25.3	229.0
1977	34.7	0.8	37.3	43.4
1979	13.7	−2.6	71.1	−5.3
1981	19.8	2.4	43.1	8.3
Uganda				
1957	13.2	n.a.	n.a.	n.a.
1963	11.4	n.a.	n.a.	n.a.
1967	20.4	5.3	3.3	3.9
1978	2.9	1.1	22.0	2.6
Tanzania				
1964	11.2	n.a.	n.a.	n.a.
1971	24.2	5.6	1.5	4.3
1977	17.5	5.4	13.9	3.2
1981	21.4	0.4	9.8	53.5
Sudan				
1964	14.3	n.a.	n.a.	n.a.
1966	14.6	2.6	−0.4	5.6
1967	13.0	−3.1	11.1	−4.2
1972	9.2	2.4	5.7	3.8
1976	23.1	4.5	16.8	5.1
1981	12.5	2.1	16.7	6.0
Ghana				
1956	15.9	n.a.	n.a.	n.a.
1958	14.1	n.a.	n.a.	n.a.
1961	20.5	n.a.	n.a.	n.a.

(*Table continues on the following page.*)

Table A2-1 *(continued)*

Country and year	Invest-ment rate	Output growth[a]	Inflation rate	ICOR[b]
Ghana *(cont.)*				
1962	16.8	4.1	2.0	4.1
1965	18.1	2.7	11.2	6.7
1969	9.8	1.2	6.8	8.2
1971	12.4	6.1	5.4	2.0
1973	7.7	1.4	16.6	5.5
1974	11.9	6.9	24.6	1.7
1981	3.4	−3.7	49.0	−0.9
Kenya				
1963	9.9	n.a.	n.a.	n.a.
1972	22.9	8.1	1.3	2.8
1976	20.0	3.2	14.2	6.3
1978	25.0	8.4	9.8	3.0
1982	20.1	3.4	8.3	5.9
Zambia				
1955	26.7	n.a.	n.a.	n.a.
1957	36.8	−12.1	8.4	−3.0
1964	15.2	5.4	1.5	2.8
1968	27.1	12.9	6.8	2.1
1969	21.1	18.7	4.3	1.1
1971	33.3	−5.9	0.7	−5.6
1974	26.5	5.1	11.3	5.2
1975	38.0	−2.4	−14.3	−15.8
1979	17.3	−2.0	15.4	−8.7
1981	24.2	0.6	6.7	40.0
Nigeria				
1950	5.9	n.a.	n.a.	n.a.
1965	18.3	n.a.	n.a.	n.a.
1969	14.3	0.7	2.7	20.4
1977	29.4	9.9	18.8	3.0
1979	24.0	0.0	11.7	—
1981	29.8	−2.4	7.0	−12.4
Zimbabwe				
1966	11.5	n.a.	n.a.	n.a.
1975	23.3	6.6	4.9	3.5
1979	13.7	−3.0	11.8	−4.6
1981	15.6	9.0	17.1	1.7

n.a. = not available.
Note: ICOR = incremental capital-output ratio.
a. Average yearly rates over the preceding years.
b. Ratio of columns 1 and 2.
Source: International Monetary Fund, *International Financial Statistics.*

result in any pattern across countries in the association between investment and growth. There are countries (Zaire, Zambia, and Nigeria) where the investment ratio is quite high by international standards, varies drastically from year to year, and seems quite unrelated to output growth. Other countries (Tanzania, Kenya, and Zimbabwe) have "medium" investment ratios (from 15 percent to 20 percent) and a better growth performance. The remaining countries in the group (Chad, Ethiopia, Uganda, Sudan, and Ghana) have relatively low investment ratios and low output growth.

Besides these broad associations, the major characteristic in the evolution of ICORS in sub-Saharan Africa is the collapse of the investment rate at the end of the 1970s in Uganda, Sudan, and Ghana and the collapse of output growth in the same countries and also in Zaire, Tanzania, Kenya, Zambia, and Nigeria. The investment rate would have collapsed in more countries had there not been a compensating increase in foreign capital inflows (or decrease in outflows), in view of the observed drops in domestic saving rates. The capital importers since 1960 were Chad, Ethiopia, Tanzania, Sudan, and Kenya. The capital exporters were Zaire, Uganda, Nigeria, and Zambia. Ghana alternately imported and exported capital.[3] Domestic saving rates in Chad, Kenya, and Zaire had roughly no trend after 1960.[4] In Ethiopia, Tanzania, Sudan, Uganda, and Zambia, the rates dropped in the late 1970s. The fall of both investment and domestic saving rates has been drastic in Ghana.

Figures A2-1–10 compare rates of investment and domestic saving in graph form. Five countries show some upward trend in investment rates (Chad, Tanzania, Sudan, Kenya, and Nigeria). In the last two countries, the increase is large: from 6 percent to 29 percent in Nigeria, between 1950 and 1981, and from 9 percent to 23 percent in Kenya, between 1963 and 1981. Yet the growth performance in both countries does not reflect this fact, at least since 1978. Foreign capital inflows dominate the upward trend in Kenya, whereas domestic savings (influenced in turn by oil prices) do so in Nigeria.

In summary, the experience of eleven African countries during the last twenty-five years shows many possible combinations of investment rates, output growth, and rates of domestic saving, with no apparent trends and very large yearly fluctuations in the prices of primary commodities.

ICORS and Savings Rates in Asia

In this section I shall consider the evolution of ICORS and saving rates in eleven Asian countries divided into three groups. In the first group

(Text continues on p. 370)

Figure A2-1. *Investment and Domestic Saving Rates, Chad, 1961–76*

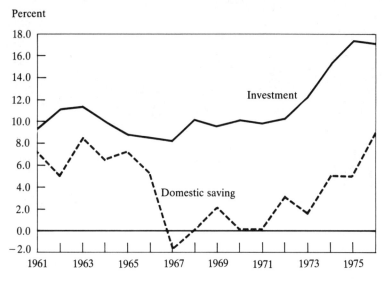

Source: International Monetary Fund, *International Financial Statistics*.

Figure A2-2. *Investment and Domestic Saving Rates, Ethiopia, 1961–82*

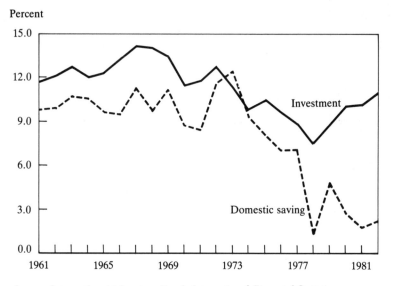

Source: International Monetary Fund, *International Financial Statistics*.

Figure A2-3. *Investment and Domestic Saving Rates, Zaire, 1962–81*

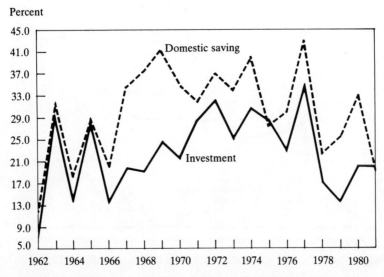

Source: International Monetary Fund, *International Financial Statistics*.

Figure A2-4. *Investment and Domestic Saving Rates, Uganda, 1957–78*

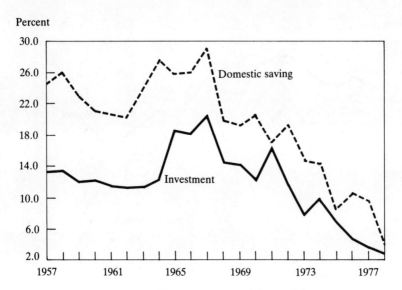

Source: International Monetary Fund, *International Financial Statistics*.

Figure A2-5. *Investment and Domestic Saving Rates, Tanzania, 1964–81*

Percent

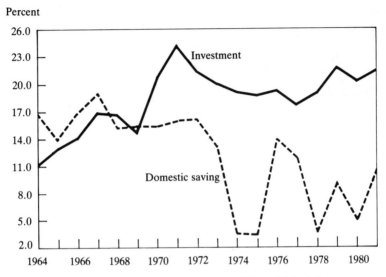

Source: International Monetary Fund, *International Financial Statistics*.

Figure A2-6. *Investment and Domestic Saving Rates, Sudan, 1956–78*

Percent

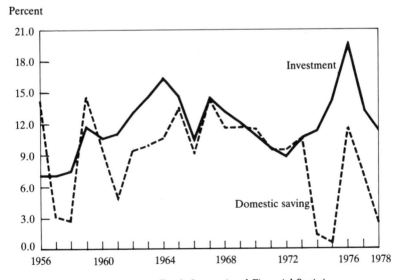

Source: International Monetary Fund, *International Financial Statistics*.

Figure A2-7. *Investment and Domestic Saving Rates, Ghana, 1955–81*

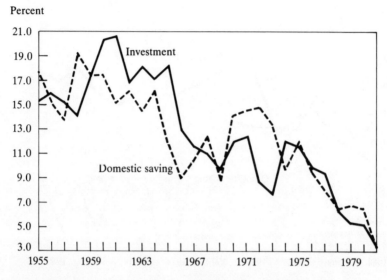

Source: International Monetary Fund, *International Financial Statistics*.

Figure A2-8. *Investment and Domestic Saving Rates, Kenya, 1963–82*

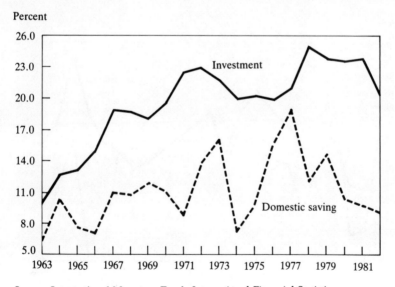

Source: International Monetary Fund, *International Financial Statistics*.

Figure A2-9. *Investment and Domestic Saving Rates, Nigeria, 1950–81*

Percent

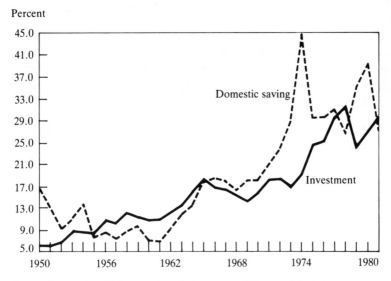

Source: International Monetary Fund, *International Financial Statistics*.

Figure A2-10. *Investment and Domestic Saving Rates, Zambia, 1954–81*

Percent

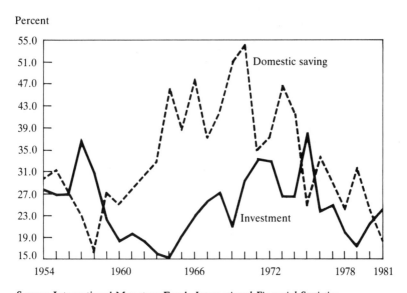

Source: International Monetary Fund, *International Financial Statistics*.

(India, Sri Lanka, Indonesia, and the Philippines), upward trends in the investment rate can be approximated by linear interpolation in between years of trend change (see table A2-2 and figures A2-11 to A2-14).[5] For a second group of countries (Burma, Pakistan, and Thailand), the investment ratios fluctuate in cyclical fashion, and there is no noticeable trend in the peak investment rates; see table A2-3. Furthermore, there is no indication of cyclical behavior in output growth or inflation. A third group of countries (Korea, Malaysia, Hong Kong, and Singapore) shows clear cyclical behavior in the rates of investment, output growth, and inflation; see table A2-4. With the exception of Hong Kong, which had high investment rates throughout, there is also a clear upward trend in the peak investment rates. It is useful to consider separately the experience in these groups of countries.

Table A2-2. *Investment Trends in India, Sri Lanka, Indonesia, and the Philippines*

Country and year	Investment rate	Output growth[a]	Inflation rate	ICOR[b]
India				
1953	8.5	n.a.	n.a.	n.a.
1963	16.0	3.7	2.3	4.3
1974	15.7	2.9	9.0	5.4
1981	19.8	4.7	6.3	4.2
Sri Lanka				
1950	8.6	n.a.	n.a.	n.a.
1956	15.1	1.2	1.1	12.6
1976	15.2	5.1	3.7	3.0
1982	31.7	5.7	16.4	5.6
Indonesia				
1967	8.0			
1974	20.1	8.9	32.3	2.3
1982	22.6	6.8	16.0	3.3
Philippines				
1948	20.6	n.a.	n.a.	n.a.
1952	11.6	8.4	− 1.4	1.4
1964	17.9	5.7	2.1	3.1
1973	15.4	5.5	8.4	2.8
1975	24.3	6.1	19.1	4.0
1982	25.5	5.3	10.9	4.8

n.a. = not available.
a. Average yearly rates over the preceding years.
b. Ratio of columns 1 and 2.
Source: International Monetary Fund, *International Financial Statistics*.

Figure A2-11. *Investment and Domestic Saving Rates, India, 1950–81*

Percent

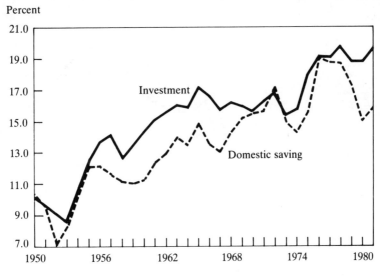

Source: International Monetary Fund, *International Financial Statistics*.

Figure A2-12. *Investment and Domestic Saving Rates, Sri Lanka, 1950–82*

Percent

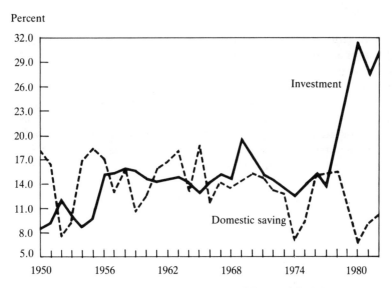

Source: International Monetary Fund, *International Financial Statistics*.

Figure A2-13. *Investment and Domestic Saving Rates, Indonesia, 1967–82*

Percent

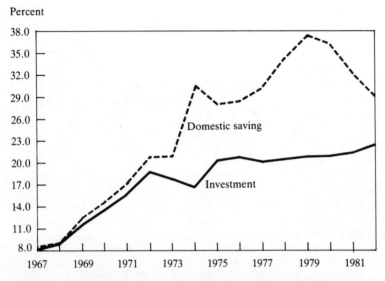

Source: International Monetary Fund, *International Financial Statistics*.

Growth without Cycles

The investment rate experience in India, Sri Lanka, Indonesia, and the Philippines is summarized in table A2-2. In the first three cases there is a substantial jump upward in the rate of investment. In India it went from 8 percent to 15 percent between 1953 and 1963; it stayed at that level until 1974; and it increased to 20 percent in 1981. In Sri Lanka, the initial doubling of the investment rate took place in a six-year period, from 1950 to 1956; the rate then stayed constant at that level for twenty years before doubling again in another six-year period, from 1976 to 1982. In Indonesia, the rate of investment went from 8 percent in 1967 to 20 percent in 1974 and then increased slightly, to 23 percent, in 1982. The jump in the investment rate in the Philippines is also substantial, if the period 1948–52 is ignored (as perhaps too close to the aftermath of World War II).

In India, Sri Lanka, and the Philippines, the large increases in investment rates since the 1950s are not associated with a corresponding increase in the rate of output growth. Thus ICORS tended to increase. One possible explanation is that increases in the rate of investment are due to increases in the relative price of investment goods rather than to an increase in the proportion of investment to consumption goods. This explanation has been examined in the case of India, and the orders of magnitude are such that changes in relative prices can account for only a small fraction of the increase in investment rates.[6]

India and the Philippines have been capital importers since the 1950s. In both countries, capital imports have played a relatively more important role in the accumulation of capital since 1975. The capital imports into India compensated for a drop in domestic saving rates. In the Philippines, capital imports allowed for an increase in the investment rate well beyond the ascending trend in the rate of domestic savings. Indonesia has been a capital exporter since 1967, and increasingly so because of oil revenues. Sri Lanka's trade was balanced, on the average, from 1950 to 1976. Thereafter Sri Lanka imported substantial amounts of capital that made it possible to double the rate of investment despite a declining trend in the rate of domestic saving since 1965. Comparisons between investment rates and the rate of domestic saving for the four countries appear, in graph form, in figures A2-11–14.

Figure A2-14. *Investment and Domestic Saving Rates, the Philippines, 1948–82*

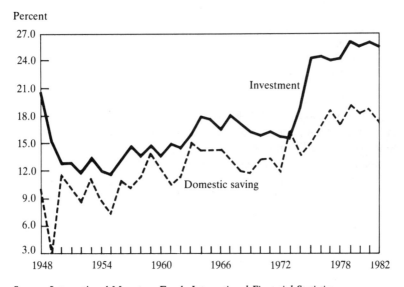

Source: International Monetary Fund, *International Financial Statistics*.

Table A2-3. *Investment Cycles in Burma, 1951–81, Pakistan, 1960–82, and Thailand, 1961–82*

Country and year	Upswing			Downswing		
	Peak invest-ment rate	Output growth[a]	Infla-tion[a]	Trough invest-ment rate	Output growth[b]	Infla-tion[b]
Burma						
1951–62 (1956)	21.2	5.2	0.6	8.7	5.3	−1.8
1962–75 (1967)	12.1	1.0	1.6	7.2	3.9	9.8
1975– (1981)	22.4	6.4	4.0	n.a.	n.a.	n.a.
Average	18.6	4.2	2.1	8.0	4.6	4.0
Pakistan						
1960–73 (1965)	16.9	6.2	2.1	11.4	2.7	1.2
1973–82 (1977)	17.8	4.3	17.3	15.0	6.8	9.5
Average	17.4	5.3	9.7	13.2	4.8	5.4
Thailand						
1961–73 (1970)	24.1	8.2	1.4	20.4	6.3	9.9
1973–82 (1980)	25.9	7.2	10.0	21.9	5.2	6.4
Average	25.0	7.7	5.7	21.2	5.8	8.2

n.a. = not available.

Note: For Burma, peak average ICOR = 4.4; trough average ICOR = 1.7. For Pakistan, peak average ICOR = 3.3; trough average ICOR = 2.8. For Thailand, peak average ICOR = 3.3; trough average ICOR = 3.7. Peak years appear in parentheses.

a. Percentage per year between first trough and peak.

b. Percentage per year between peak and second trough.

Source: International Monetary Fund, *International Financial Statistics.*

Cycles in Investment Rates Only

Cycles in the investment rate of varied amplitude and duration can be observed in a second group of Asian countries. Yet the industrial sector is not important enough for these cycles to be apparent also in the rates of output growth and inflation. The countries in this group are Burma, Pakistan, and Thailand. This last country is a borderline case: the rates of yearly output growth in the upswing phase of the investment cycle are higher than in the downswing, and therefore it could equally well be classified with the next group of countries.

Investment cycles for these three countries are summarized in table A2-3. Each line in the table represents a cycle. In Burma, for example, the first cycle lasted from 1951 to 1962, the peak investment rate occurred in 1956 (21.2 percent), and the (second) trough rate of that cycle was 8.7 percent. The definition of the investment rate cycles is very rough and simple: straight lines between trough and peak years are reasonable approximations of investment rates in any year in between for both the upswing and the downswing phase. This definition provides a convenient summary measure of incremental capital-output ratios. A peak ICOR is the ratio of the peak investment rate to the yearly rate of output growth over the upswing phase. A trough ICOR is the ratio of the trough investment rate to the yearly rate of output growth over the downswing phase. Despite the considerable smoothing implicit in these measures, much variability remains in both peak and trough ICORS across cycles. The

Table A2-4. *Investment Cycles in Korea, 1953–82, Malaysia, 1955–82, Hong Kong, 1961–82, and Singapore, 1958–81*

Country and year	Upswing			Downswing		
	Peak invest-ment rate	Output growth[a]	Infla-tion[a]	Trough invest-ment rate	Output growth[b]	Infla-tion[b]
Korea						
1953–72 (1969)	26.1	6.3	19.3	20.5	8.3	14.3
1972–82 (1979)	32.2	10.5	20.1	28.4	2.8	16.0
Average	29.2	8.4	19.7	24.5	5.6	15.2
Malaysia						
1955–69 (1962)	16.7	n.a.	n.a.	14.6	6.4	0.4
1969–76 (1974)	28.9	8.2	5.7	22.6	6.0	4.5
1976– (1982)	35.0	7.1	6.1	n.a.	n.a.	n.a.
Average	32.0	7.7	5.9	18.6	6.2	n.a.
Hong Kong						
1961–68 (1964)	29.8	10.2	3.3	14.6	9.1	1.8
1968–75 (1971)	21.8	7.6	8.7	19.3	6.5	9.5
1975– (1982)	27.7	12.0	9.1	n.a.	n.a.	n.a.
Average	26.4	9.9	7.0	17.0	7.8	5.7
Singapore						
1958–59 (1958)	13.6	n.a.	n.a.	7.6	n.a.	n.a.
1959–79 (1971)	36.2	9.5	1.4	34.5	8.6	5.4
1979– (1981)	40.9	10.1	5.9	n.a.	n.a.	n.a.
Average	38.6	9.8	3.7	n.a.	n.a.	n.a.

n.a. = not available.

Note: For Korea, peak average ICOR = 3.5; trough average ICOR = 4.4. For Malaysia, peak average ICOR = 4.2; trough average ICOR = 3.0. For Hong Kong, peak average ICOR = 2.7; trough average ICOR = 1.2. For Singapore, peak average ICOR = 3.9. Peak years appear in parentheses.

a. Percentage per year over the period between the first trough and peak.

b. Percentage per year between peak and second trough.

Source: International Monetary Fund, *International Financial Statistics.*

second cycle in Burma, for example, from 1962 to 1975, peaked in 1967, and the peak ICOR was 12. Such extreme values are not uncommon, and they focus attention on the circumstances that affect growth, over and above capital accumulation. In this instance, part of the fall in the growth rate to 1 percent per year over the upswing years 1962–67, relative to the previous upswing growth (5.2 percent from 1951 to 1956), can be linked to the dramatic fall in investment rate between 1956 and 1962, from 21 percent to 9 percent. This drop can account for only a small part, however. Policy or circumstance must have played a large role in the poor growth performance in Burma during 1962–67. Both can probably be identified much more easily for that "medium-run" period than for each year in isolation. Yearly ICORS, or arbitrary averages of yearly ICORS, have little value as a summary measure when we search for an explanation. The peak average ICOR is the arithmetic mean of all peak ICORS in each country. These means are very similar for the three countries in table A2-3: between 3 and 4. This similarity may be useful in providing benchmarks for "normal" or "long-run" ICORS.

Figures A2-15–17 compare rates of investment and domestic saving in the three countries. The facts that differentiate the three countries and

Figure A2-15. *Investment and Domestic Saving Rates, Burma, 1948–81*

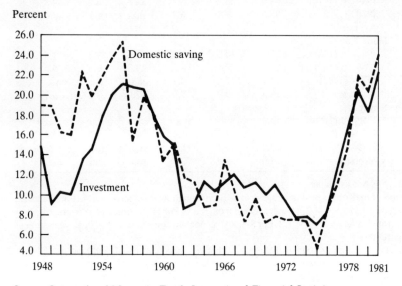

Source: International Monetary Fund, *International Financial Statistics*.

Figure A2-16. *Investment and Domestic Saving Rates, Pakistan, 1960–82*

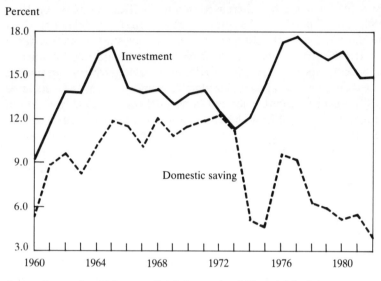

Source: International Monetary Fund, *International Financial Statistics*.

Figure A2-17. *Investment and Domestic Saving Rates, Thailand, 1950–82*

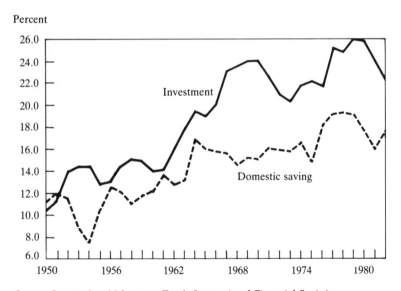

Source: International Monetary Fund, *International Financial Statistics*.

require explanation are the following: (a) the rate of domestic saving declined steadily in Burma between 1957 and 1975, from 25 percent to 5 percent; (b) the same rate increased steadily in Thailand between 1954 and 1982, from 7 percent to 18 percent; (c) foreign saving did not play any role in Burma, so that the dramatic increase in investment rates between 1975 and 1982 (from 7 percent to 22 percent) was entirely "financed" through a corresponding increase in domestic saving; (d) foreign savings did play a key role in Pakistan: although the domestic saving rate declined from 12 percent to about 3 percent between 1973 and 1982, the rate of investment increased during the same period; (e) foreign saving did play an increasingly important role in Thailand, so that the rate of investment increased faster than the rate of domestic saving.[7] Therefore, in only one country, Thailand, is there by now a clear upward trend in the rate of investment.

Cycles in the Rates of Investment and Output Growth

The ICORS and domestic saving rates in Korea, Malaysia, Hong Kong, and Singapore are given in table A2-4 and figures A2-18–A2-21. These are all cases of successful growth performance, with high growth rates

Figure A2-18. *Investment and Domestic Saving Rates, Korea, 1953–82*

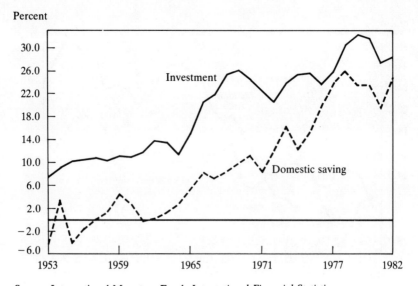

Source: International Monetary Fund, *International Financial Statistics*.

Figure A2-19. *Investment and Domestic Saving Rates, Malaysia, 1955–82*

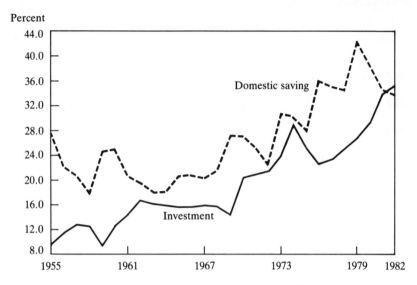

Source: International Monetary Fund, *International Financial Statistics*.

and vast increases over time in the rate of investment. In the last twenty-five years the rate of investment went from 6–8 percent to about 30 percent in Korea, Malaysia, and Singapore. This trend dominates any cyclical pattern apparent in figures A2-18, A2-19, and A2-21, but cycles do exist. Causality between investment and growth is impossible to ascertain from the figures discussed above. Some working hypothesis, however, can be put forward. In the Republic of Korea, for example, the first cycle lasted for about twenty years. During the upswing phase, 1953–69, the investment rate went from 7 percent to 26 percent, and the associated rate of yearly output growth was about 6 percent. It is reasonable to postulate that accumulation preceded ("caused") growth, inasmuch as the downswing was short enough (from 1969 to 1972) and weak enough (the investment rate declined to 21 percent) to be unable to stop the acceleration of output growth, to about 8 percent per year between 1969 and 1972. In the second upswing, which lasted from 1972 to 1979, the rate of investment increased to 32 percent and output growth accelerated even further, to 10.5 percent yearly. In 1979, however, it is likely that the direction of causality reversed itself. Factors affecting growth, besides capital accumulation, must have taken a predominant role in that year and until 1982: the rate of growth went down to 3 percent, despite

Figure A2-20. *Investment and Domestic Saving Rates, Hong Kong, 1961–82*

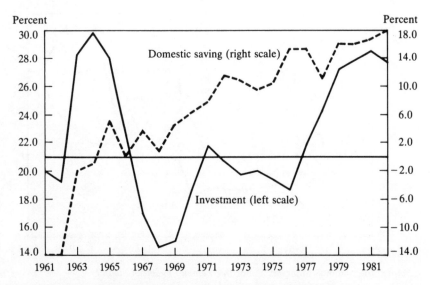

Source: International Monetary Fund, *International Financial Statistics*.

the fact that the rate of investment declined only by four percentage points, to 28 percent. In the last recession, the Korean ICOR thus became 10. Note that in both Korea and Malaysia the rate of domestic saving increased over a twenty-five-year period even more than the rate of investment, with Korea being always a capital importer and Malaysia being always a capital exporter. The rate of domestic saving also increased dramatically in Hong Kong, from minus 10 percent to about 18 percent between 1961 and 1981. The rate of investment in Hong Kong, however, has always been far above the rate of domestic saving. The situation is even more extreme in Singapore, where the rate of domestic saving has been negative since 1958, with no trend and at about minus 8 percent on the average, despite a large increase in the rate of investment, from 7 percent to 40 percent.

ICORS and Savings Rates in Latin America

The peak investment rates and rates of output growth and inflation for seven Latin American countries (Brazil, Mexico, Argentina, Chile, Peru,

Colombia, and Venezuela) during the last thirty years appear in table A2-5. Figures A2-22–28 compare rates of investment and domestic saving in graph form. Cycles in investment rates are quite noticeable in Latin America. In Brazil, Mexico, Argentina, and Colombia, trends in the investment rate dominate the cycle. In Mexico, the investment rate rose from 12 percent to 26 percent between 1950 and 1981. In Brazil, Argentina, and Colombia, the increase has been on the order of 15 percent to 22 percent during the same period. In Chile, the investment rate since 1955 fluctuated at about 14 percent, with no trend. In Peru, there is a downward trend, from 20 percent during the 1950s to about 16 percent during the 1970s.[8] In Venezuela, there has been no trend in investment rates in the last thirty years except for the huge increase, from about 20 percent to 40 percent, after the first oil price boom in 1974.

The record on growth and inflation associated with the accumulation of capital is quite varied across cycles and countries. The outliers, average peak ICOR values are those of Argentina and Venezuela, about twice the usual peak value of about 3.[9] The most "regular" economy is Mexico. The following regularities are apparent. First, there is a clear upward trend in peak and trough investment rates. Second, there is a noticeable fall in

Figure A2-21. *Investment and Domestic Saving Rates, Singapore, 1958–81*

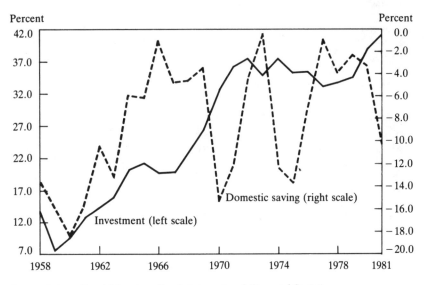

Source: International Monetary Fund, *International Financial Statistics*.

Table A2-5. *Investment Cycles in Brazil, 1955–81,*
Mexico, 1950–81, Argentina, 1951, Chile, 1956–82,
Peru, 1950–81, Colombia, 1951–81, and Venezuela, 1951–81

	Upswing			Downswing		
Country and year	Peak invest- ment rate	Output growth[a]	Infla- tion[a]	Trough invest- ment rate	Output growth[b]	Infla- tion[b]
Brazil						
1950–55 (1951)	18.6	7.0	12.0	13.5	7.0	16.6
1955–64 (1959)	18.5	6.1	19.0	14.0	5.9	54.2
1964– (1975)	25.0	8.5	29.0			
Average	20.7	7.2	20.0	15.6	6.0	44.7
Mexico						
1950–62 (1956)	16.7	6.2	9.3	13.8	5.6	4.3
1962–65 (1964)	18.5	9.8	1.0	17.2	6.5	9.1
1965–71 (1970)	20.0	6.9	4.0	18.0	4.2	5.9
1971–77 (1975)	21.4	7.2	14.2	19.6	3.8	24.9
1977– (1981)	25.7	8.4	23.1			
Average	20.5	7.7	10.3	17.2	5.0	11.5
Argentina						
1951–59 (1956)	20.0	1.1	−6.2	14.3	1.5	59.0
1959–64 (1961)	23.3	7.2	9.6	16.3	−2.4	33.7
1964–73 (1970)	21.6	5.5	16.3	18.0	2.9	54.8
1973–81 (1977)	27.3	2.7	169.3	22.7	−0.4	126.9
Average	23.1	4.1	47.3	17.8	0.4	68.6
Chile						
1956–76 (1963)	17.5	4.9	16.2	8.7	1.4	109.8
1976– (1981)	18.6	8.0	42.9	(13.8)[c]	(−14.3)[c]	(11.9)[c]
Average	18.1	6.5	30.0	11.3	−12.9	60.9
Peru						
1950–54 (1953)	23.1	6.0	6.5	16.9	4.1	12.0
1954–60 (1957)	24.7	3.4	6.9	17.1	5.7	9.3
1960–73 (1962)	20.6	9.5	5.9	12.1	5.1	7.9
1973–78 (1975)	17.4	5.1	18.4	14.0	0.0	44.3
1978– (1981)	19.4	3.5	66.2			
Average	21.0	5.5	20.6	15.2	3.9	18.4
Colombia						
1951–57 (1955)	18.0	5.8	4.3	14.8	3.1	12.4
1957–65 (1961)	18.3	4.7	9.1	15.6	4.6	13.7
1965–73 (1971)	20.8	5.8	10.1	17.5	7.4	17.6
1973–75 (1974)	17.8	6.0	27.6	18.2	3.8	22.2
1974– (1981)	27.7	5.0	23.9			
Average	20.5	5.5	15.0	16.5	4.7	16.5

(Table continues on the following page.)

Table A2-5 *(continued)*

	Upswing			Downswing		
Country and year	*Peak invest- ment rate*	*Output growth*[a]	*Infla- tion*[a]	*Trough invest- ment rate*	*Output growth*[b]	*Infla- tion*[b]
Venezuela						
1950–62 (1954)	30.5	8.7	−0.2	15.7	6.2	1.3
1962–74 (1972)	25.6	5.3	2.2	18.6	6.1	27.2
1974–81 (1977)	41.6	7.0	22.2	24.1	0.6	16.1
Average	32.6	7.0	8.1	19.5	4.3	14.9

Note: For Brazil, peak average ICOR = 2.9; trough average ICOR = 2.6. For Mexico, peak average ICOR = 2.7; trough average ICOR = 3.4. For Argentina, peak average ICOR = 5.6; trough average ICOR = 44.5. For Chile, peak average ICOR = 2.8; trough average ICOR = −0.9. For Peru, peak average ICOR = 3.8; trough average ICOR = 4.2. For Colombia, peak average ICOR = 3.7; trough average ICOR = 3.5. For Venezuela, peak average ICOR = 4.7; trough average ICOR = 4.5. Peak years appear in parentheses.

a. Percentage per year between first peak and trough.

b. Percentage per year between peak and second trough.

c. As of 1982 the downswing was incomplete in Chile. The figures in parentheses represent the one-year change between the peak in 1981 and the first year of the downswing in 1982.

Source: International Monetary Fund, *International Financial Statistics.*

yearly output growth rates during the downswing phase. Third, the rate of inflation accelerated during the downswing and fell in the next upswing in almost all cycles (except for the dominant upward trend during the 1970s).[10] Fourth, the investment rate cycles in Mexico are very close to the cycles in the United States.

Anomalies in the pattern of accumulation are also apparent in Latin America. The obvious one is an extreme version of the downswing ICOR increase that was noticed in Korea. Because the ICOR is undefined at zero output growth, and it has a very large absolute value around zero output growth, the downswing ICORs in Latin America fluctuate wildly. The investment rates fluctuate much less, and it is reasonable to postulate, as for Korea, that the short-run declines in output growth rates during the downswings are "caused" by factors other than the deceleration in the rate at which physical capital is accumulated. In Argentina, for example, output actually fell in the downswing of two cycles, and so it did in the last recession in Chile, since 1982, despite relatively small declines in the rate of (gross) investment. The question of why ICORs differ, and, in particular, why they differ in the downswing, is, as a result, important for policy analysis.

Figure A2-22. *Investment and Domestic Saving Rates, Brazil, 1948–81*

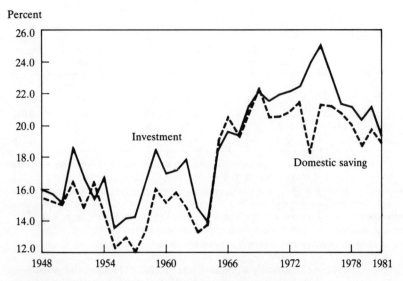

Source: International Monetary Fund, *International Financial Statistics*.

Figure A2-23. *Investment and Domestic Saving Rates, Mexico, 1950–81*

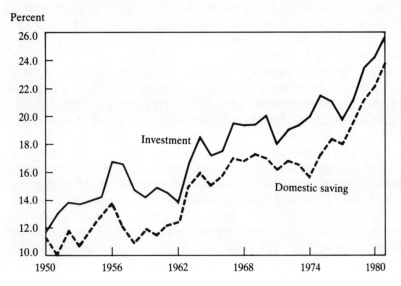

Source: International Monetary Fund, *International Financial Statistics*.

Figure A2-24. *Investment and Domestic Saving Rates, Argentina,*
1953–81

Percent

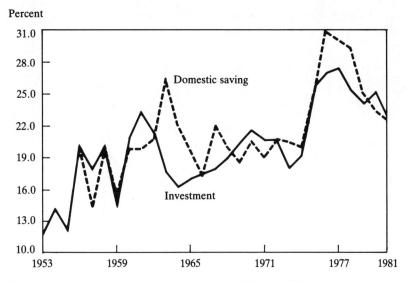

Source: International Monetary Fund, *International Financial Statistics*.

Figure A2-25. *Investment and Domestic Saving Rates, Chile, 1955–82*

Percent

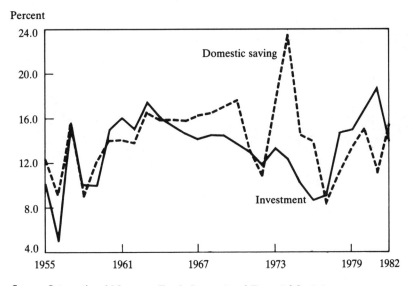

Source: International Monetary Fund, *International Financial Statistics*.

Figure A2-26. *Investment and Domestic Saving Rates, Peru, 1950–81*

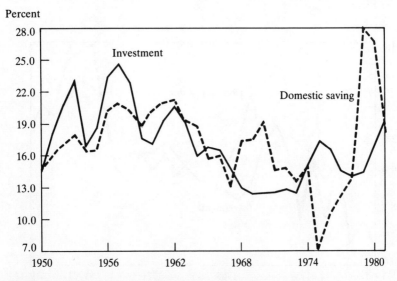

Source: International Monetary Fund, *International Financial Statistics*.

Figure A2-27. *Investment and Domestic Saving Rates, Colombia, 1950–81*

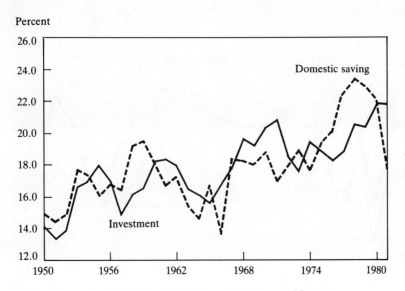

Source: International Monetary Fund, *International Financial Statistics*.

Figure A2-28. *Investment and Domestic Saving Rates, Venezuela, 1950–82*

Percent

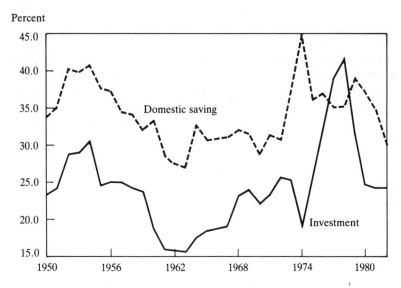

Source: International Monetary Fund, *International Financial Statistics*.

The role of foreign savings in the process of capital accumulation in these seven Latin American countries is depicted in the figures A2-22–28. Again, Mexico is the most "regular" case. It has been importing capital since 1950, but the rate of domestic saving increased with roughly the trend of the investment rate. Brazil has also been a capital importer since 1950, but capital inflows became much more important during the 1970s in relative terms. In particular, there was a decline in the rate of domestic saving in 1974, at a time when the accumulation of capital was accelerating. In Argentina, Chile, and Peru, the rate of domestic saving fluctuates very much, probably because of fluctuation in export prices. The three countries have repeatedly changed the direction of capital flows. The same change in direction is apparent in Colombia, but there again the upward trend in the rate of domestic saving, at least since the mid-1960s, is the dominant factor behind the increase in the investment rate. Venezuela has of course been exporting capital since 1950 except for a brief period during the 1970s. Changes in the rate of investment closely followed the changes in the rate of domestic savings until 1970. Since that time, both rates have often moved in different directions (see figure A2-28). For purposes of comparison, figures A2-29 to A2-33 plot investment and domestic savings rates for Germany, Japan, France, the United

Kingdom, and the United States. Figure A2-34 shows investment and inflation rates in the United States.

Public Expenditure and Its Composition

I shall briefly summarize the main results from cross-section studies. The most recent and comprehensive study on the composition of public expenditure has been conducted by Tait and Heller (1982). They present regression results in which the dependent variables are the functional expenditure categories as a proportion of GDP; the independent variables are income per capita (with differential effect for high- and low-income countries) and other indicators of the level of development (such as urbanization, the structure of output, and the age structure of the population); and the unit of observation is a country in 1977, up to a maximum of ninety-three countries. The study does *not* address whether the public expenditure pattern is affected by increases in expenditure unmatched by taxation. Instead it focuses on how the pattern of expenditure changes as the share of total government expenditure in GDP, and the indicators of levels of development, vary across countries.

Figure A2-29. *Investment and Domestic Saving Rates, Germany, 1950–82*

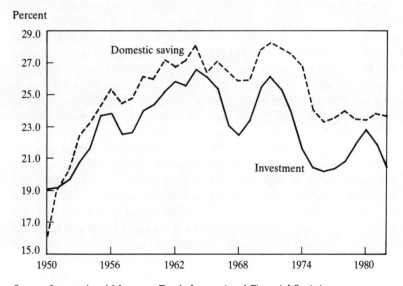

Source: International Monetary Fund, *International Financial Statistics*.

Figure A2-30. *Investment and Domestic Saving Rates, Japan, 1952–81*

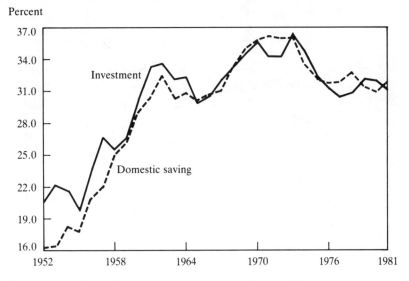

Source: International Monetary Fund, *International Financial Statistics*.

Figure A2-31. *Investment and Domestic Saving Rates, France, 1950–82*

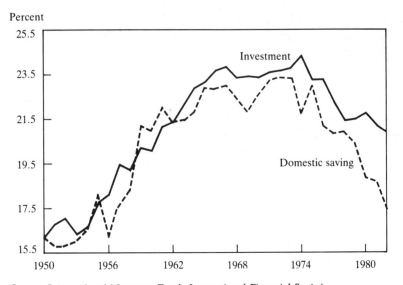

Source: International Monetary Fund, *International Financial Statistics*.

Figure A2-32. *Investment and Domestic Saving Rates, United Kingdom, 1948–82*

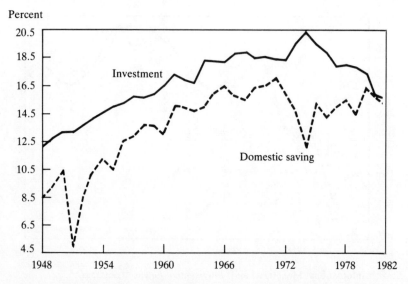

Source: International Monetary Fund, *International Financial Statistics*.

The pattern of public expenditure is broken down into nine expenditure categories. For present purposes, four are of particular interest: defense; education; health, social security, and welfare; and housing. The regression equations account for 15 percent, 28 percent, 84 percent, and 21 percent, respectively, of the variation in the corresponding expenditure shares across countries, so that, if we use this criterion, only the results for the third category should be examined. On the other hand, significant regression coefficients may also be useful. A summary of these is contained in table A2-6 for a subset of all regressors used in the study by Tait and Heller (1982).

The strongest result in table A2-6 is the association across countries between the share of health, social security, and welfare in GDP and the proportion of old people: it has the most significant regression coefficient. An increase of one percentage point in the proportion of old people is associated, in this sample, with an increase of 1.02 percentage points in the share of health, social security, and welfare expenditures in GDP. This result is obtained after controlling for the GDP share of total government expenditure, so that the question of how much this total share varies with the proportion of old people is not posed.

Figure A2-33. *Investment and Domestic Saving Rates, United States, 1948–82*

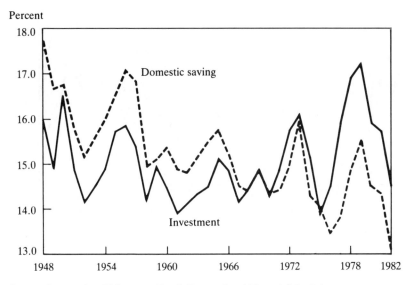

Percent

Source: International Monetary Fund, *International Financial Statistics*.

Because older populations are also richer (when the country is the unit of observation), the associations between the share of total government expenditure and the level of income, and the level of income with the proportion of the old, could be used to obtain an order of magnitude for variation in the total expenditure share with the aging of the populations. None of these associations has been established with much degree of confidence as yet.

The link over time between the share and composition of government expenditures and the level of income in individual countries is a well-researched topic in public finance.[11] The general outcome is a confirmation of Wagner's Law: an elasticity of expenditure with respect to income larger than one. How much larger, however, remains in doubt. Furthermore, Wagner's Law does not appear with any clarity in the cross-section evidence, with countries as the unit of observation (see Lall 1969).

A relevant piece of evidence about the relationship between the overall government expenditure share, demographic variables, and indicators of development has been provided by Mitra (1978). He works with a sample of fifty countries for each of two years (1960 and 1970).[12] To this sample, he fits a simultaneous equation model with two dependent variables: the

Figure A2-34. *Investment and Inflation Rates, United States, 1948–82*

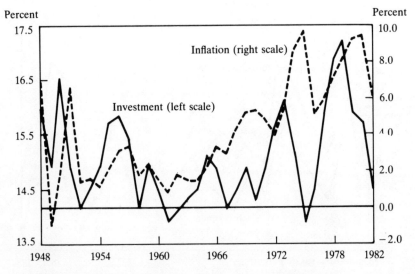

Source: International Monetary Fund, *International Financial Statistics*.

Table A2-6. *Cross-Section Results on Government Expenditure Patterns*

Independent variable	Defense	Education	Health, social security, and welfare	Housing and community amenities
Income per capital (PCI)			0.41 (2.60)	
PCI < $1,750		2.11 (2.92)		0.82 (2.67)
PCI > $1,750		0.20 (2.65)		−0.01 (2.68)
Percentage of population aged 14 and under	0.16 (2.71)			
Percentage of population over age 65			1.02 (8.01)	
Infant mortality rate			0.06 (1.37)	
Share of labor force in industry			0.14 (2.87)	
Share of population in urban areas	0.05 (2.25)	−0.03 (2.28)		

Note: Parenthetical numbers are regression coefficients.
Source: Tait and Heller (1982, table 3, pp. 10, 11).

Table A2-7. *Joint Determinants of the Share of Government Expenditure and Urbanization*

Item	Share of government expenditure	Level of urbanization
Share of government expenditure		.96 (1.66)
Level of urbanization	.12 (1.70)	
Per capita income		.71 (2.03)
Proportion of population aged 65 + to population aged 15–64	.59 (3.70)	
Schooling ratio		.23 (3.83)
Time dummy	2.03 (1.32)	

Note: t ratios appear in parentheses.
Source: Mitra (1978:29–80).

share of government expenditure and the level of urbanization. A summary of the main results appears in table A2-7. Per capita income is associated with the level of urbanization but not with the expenditure share. Both urbanization and the expenditure share are affected by each other. The schooling ratio is associated with urbanization, whereas the proportion of the old to the working age population is associated with the overall expenditure share. This last point reinforces the composition effect present in table A2-2. An increase of one percentage point in the proportion of the old will be associated with an increase in the overall share *and* a switch toward health, social security, and welfare expenditure.

Therefore, the evidence in tables A2-1 and A2-2 could be translated into projections of public expenditure patterns associated with development and the aging of the populations. At the very least, it does suggest that aging does have a significant effect upon public expenditure and its composition.

Notes

1. See World Bank (1983:43) for comparisons of ICORS using yearly averages chosen arbitrarily.
2. Obviously this rule could not be applied in Zaire for the period 1962–66, so that each of those years is included in table A2-3. It could be applied in Ethiopia for 1967 to 1978, however, when the (gross) investment rate fell steadily from 14 percent to 7 percent before increasing to 11 percent by 1982.
3. Figures for Zimbabwe are not available. The foreign saving rate is defined as imports minus exports as a proportion of GDP. Specifically, it is line 71 minus line 70 divided by line 99b in the International Monetary Fund's *International Financial Statistics*. Thus nonfactor services are excluded from the definition of foreign saving.
4. The domestic saving rate is defined as the difference between the rates of investment and foreign saving.
5. Only in one country (the Philippines) and in one time period (1948–52) is there a noticeable decline in the investment rate.
6. See the report of the Working Group on Savings (1982:141–42).
7. In this context, note that the summary measures for Thailand in table A2-5 do not show the investment rate in 1961 of about 14 percent. Thus the trend in investment rates is not apparent in that table.
8. The data for the years before 1960 come from Thorbecke and Condos (1966).
9. See Diaz Alejandro (1970, chap. 6) for a discussion of Argentina's anomalous ICORS until 1964 as a result of policy-induced increase in the relative price of capital goods.
10. The regularity is also apparent in the cycles of many other countries, including the United States.
11. For an early treatment, see Musgrave (1969:92–98). The evidence is for the United States, the United Kingdom, and Germany over the period 1890–1960. See also Gupta (1967), for the same countries plus Canada and Sweden.
12. He also presents estimation results with more countries included in the second year only. These results are not considered here.

References

Diaz Alejandro, Carlos F. 1970. *Essays on the economic history of the Argentine Republic*. New Haven, Conn.: Yale University Press.

Gupta, S. P. 1967. Public expenditure and economic growth: A time series analysis. *Public finance* 22(4):423–53.

Lall, S. 1969. A note on government expenditures in developing countries. *Economic journal* 79(June):413–17.

Mitra, Amit Kumar. 1978. An intertemporal cross-country analysis of the impact of economic and demographic factors on government expenditure share. Ph.D. dissertation, Duke University.

Musgrave, R. A. 1969. *Fiscal systems*. New Haven, Conn.: Yale University Press.

Tait, A. A., and P. S. Heller. 1982. International comparisons of government expenditure. Occasional Paper 10. Washington, D.C.: International Monetary Fund.

Thorbecke, E., and A. Condos. 1966. Macroeconomic growth and development models of the Peruvian economy. In I. Adelman and E. Thorbecke, eds. *The theory and design of economic development*. Baltimore, Md.: Johns Hopkins University Press.

Working Group on Savings. 1982. *Capital formation and saving in India, 1950–51 to 1979–80*. Reserve Bank of India.

World Bank. 1983. *World Development Report 1983*. New York: Oxford University Press.

Index

Africa, 281–82, 283; inflation in, 361; savings in, 361–64. *See also individual countries*

Agricultural Adjustment Administration (United States), 53

Agriculture, 270, 287

Algeria, 118, 125

Amortization of Latin American debt, 155–65

Argentina, 25, 30, 32, 267, 269; debt crisis and, 135, 136–39, 149, 151, 155, 163–64, 166–69

Asia: capital flow in, 373; savings in, 364–80. *See also individual countries*

Austerity programs of IMF, 60

Australia, 123

Baily, Martin N., 73

Balance of payments, 25, 37, 104, 105, 109–10, 179

Bank lending, 240, 248–49, 257, 266, 288

Bank of International Settlements, 166

Banks, 194; debt crisis and, 98–99; financial innovation and, 99–102; Latin American debt and, 149, 151, 153, 166, 177; risk and, 92–97

Belgium, 246

Bond financing, 286; interest rates and, 191–93

Borrowing. *See* Debt *entries*

Boschan, Charlotte, 63

Brazil, 21, 27, 30, 32, 100, 265, 269–70; debt crisis and, 135, 136, 139, 149, 151, 153, 155, 156–62, 169–70

Bretton Woods regime, 53, 75

Bry, Gerhard, 63

Buiter, W. H., 192

Business cycles, 50, 242, 246, 277–78; stagflation and, 3–4

Cagan, Phillip, 65

Capital flow, 240; in Asia, 373; Great Depression and, 25–29; inflow rules and, 223–26; in Latin America, 387

Capital formation, 344–49

Capital markets: interest rates and, 193–200; normalization of, 12; oil windfall and, 125

Carter administration, 52

Chile, 21, 22, 29, 30, 32–33; debt crisis and, 133, 134, 135, 136, 139–44, 149, 153, 165, 170–74

China, 19, 21, 25, 27, 29, 274

Colombia, 21, 30, 36

Competition (perfect), 62

Conservative economic theory, 62–70

Corporations, savings, and, 342, 348

Costa Rica, 131

Credit, 39; savings and, 338

Creditworthiness, 264

Cross-country analysis, 15

Cross-section studies of public expenditures, 388–93

Crowding out of private expenditure: data for model of global, 226–35; financing of social expenditure and, 190–93; model of global, 206–15

Cuba, 22

Darby, M., 196, 197

Data: external shock analysis, 105–06, 112–13; Great Depression analysis, 15–16, 39–43

Debt: amortization in Latin America, 155–65; causes of global, 223; economic growth and, 319–24; global economy and, 247, 260, 264–67, 278–81, 288; global shocks and, 95; infrastructure investment and, 200–06; interest on public, 299, 319–24, 327; recycling of oil surpluses and, 24; World War I and, 18

Debt crisis, 182, 183; amortization of Latin American debt and, 155–65;

396